American Graphic

American Graphic

Disgust and Data in Contemporary Literature

Rebecca B. Clark

Stanford University Press
Stanford, California

Stanford University Press
Stanford, California

©2023 by Rebecca B. Clark. All rights reserved.

No part of this book may be reproduced or transmitted in any form or by any means, electronic or mechanical, including photocopying and recording, or in any information storage or retrieval system without the prior written permission of Stanford University Press.

Printed in the United States of America on acid-free, archival-quality paper

Library of Congress Cataloging-in-Publication Data

Names: Clark, Rebecca (Rebecca Bennett), author.
Title: American graphic / Rebecca Clark.
Other titles: Post 45.
Description: Stanford, California : Stanford University Press, 2022. | Series: Post*45 | Includes bibliographical references and index.
Identifiers: LCCN 2022011836 (print) | LCCN 2022011837 (ebook) | ISBN 9781503630970 (cloth) | ISBN 9781503634237 (paperback) | ISBN 9781503634244 (ebook)
Subjects: LCSH: American fiction—History and criticism. | Grotesque in literature. | Affect (Psychology) in literature. | Aesthetics, American.
Classification: LCC PS374.G78 C55 2022 (print) | LCC PS374.G78 (ebook) | DDC 813.009/15—dc23/eng/20220425
LC record available at https://lccn.loc.gov/2022011836
LC ebook record available at https://lccn.loc.gov/2022011837

Cover photographs: Shutterstock
Cover design: David Drummond
Typeset by Elliott Beard in Minion Pro 10/15

Contents

Acknowledgments

I OWE THE MOST THANKS to Namwali Serpell, my advisor at UC Berkeley, who, as this project unfolded, joined me on (or saved me from) all manner of questionable pun-laden tangents, inspired me with her scholarly and creative work, and pushed me to grow as a thinker and a writer. Thanks to Mark Goble for being a thoughtful reader of drafts and ever-delightful font of media miscellany. And Donna Jones, you had me at *Zardoz*.

These people made grad school, and me, better: Jane Hu, Lise Gaston, Ariel Baker-Gibbs, Diana "small round things" Wise, Katie Bondy, Evan Wilson, Jeehyun Choi, Brandon Callender, Mary Wilson, Hannah Ehrlinspiel, and Jason Treviño. Special tam-tips to my comrades in regalia, Jen Lorden and Erin Greer. Once a grad student, now a sailor, thank you Kristen "Skipper" Johannes. Thanks, too, to the orthopedic trauma surgeon and anonymous bone chip donor without whom I would not be the ambulatory zombie/cyborg writing this acknowledgments section today.

Dartmouth Society of Fellows gave me time and space to take a break from and then return to this book. Hanover is cold place, but some dogs and people made it warmer: the incomparable Naga, Lakshmi Padmanabhan, Aaron Kovalchik, Summer Kim Lee, Golnar Nikpour, Yumi Lee, Emily Raymundo, Mingwei Huang, Yui Hashimoto, Yana Stainova, Laura McTighe, Derek Woods, and Whitney Barlow Robles. I'm also grateful for the equally incomparable Dolly, Anna Childs, who knows more vocationally about the graphic than I ever will, Madi Gamble, and Brandon Smith.

Thank you to Post*45 series editors Kate Marshall and Loren Glass and to Erica Wetter and Caroline McKusick at Stanford University Press for being so refreshingly efficient, enthusiastic, and fun to work with. I am also exceedingly grateful to the manuscript's anonymous reviewers, who were fast, thorough, generous, and kind enough to say they laughed at some of my jokes. Thanks, too, to Jennifer Gordon, copyeditor extraordinaire.

Finally, most importantly, thank you to my parents, Laurie Bennett and Rachel Clark, and to my Aunt Susan. I also acknowledge Sam Clark, my brother dearest.

American Graphic

INTRODUCTION
The Graphic and the Graph-ick

graphic, *adj.*
1. a. of or relating to the pictorial arts
   c. of or relating to the art of printing
2. formed by writing, drawing, or engraving
3. a. vividly or plainly shown or described // a *graphic* sex scene
   b. using offensive or obscene words: including swear words
   c. marked by clear lifelike or vividly realistic description
4. of, relating to, or represented by a graph

graphic, *n.*
2. a. a graphic representation (such as a picture, map, or graph) used especially for illustration
   b. a pictorial image displayed on a computer screen
   c. **graphics** *plural in form but singular or plural in construction*: the art or science of drawing a representation of an object on a two-dimensional surface according to mathematical rules of projection
4. a printed message superimposed on a television picture[1]

WE LIVE IN A GRAPHIC WORLD. Heedless of warning labels on discs, pics, and screens, we increasingly see, read, feel, and render ourselves and each other through, in, and as the "graphic." Recombinant iterations of this promiscuous word seem to pop up everywhere in post-45 art, literature, and life: graphic design, infographics, graphic novels, graphic user interfaces, graphic sex, graphic violence, in graphic detail. As contemporary culture becomes a warren of the graphic, how can we make sense of its contradictory and rapidly accumulating meanings?

Branching upward and outward from the Greek *graphikos*, the graphic family tree is a vivid, knotted, obscenely organic body; it is also a flatly inorganic diagram, helping us visualize probability structures, mathematical sets, programming codes, and syntactical schema. At the end of each of its limbs, skin is pulled taut across or peeled painstakingly away from the tasty and/ or tortured bodies of strange fruit; but at the same time, these are apples of a different stripe, pixelated icons, flesh not fermenting into rot but abstracted into near immateriality.

This book presents a theory of this increasingly ubiquitous, yet critically underexamined word. "Graphic" can be both an aesthetic and an affective description. It can be a noun or an adjective—a thing or a set of sensations, feelings, or formal attributes that modify it. It can be a suffix, a linguistic appendage that refers back to a body of knowledge production. It can signal an uncensored account of things done with and to appendages of flesh and blood bodies. While the graphic has its roots, etymologically, in form (a product of drawing or writing), it yields its ripest contemporary colloquial harvest in feeling (productive of disgust, recoil, arousal). Except when it doesn't.

The graphic is about both epistemology and display. But it is also a term that is, itself, splayed—drawn (if you will, and quartered, if you must) in seemingly contradictory directions. "Graphic" as a word is tellingly at odds with itself. On one hand, it seems to evoke the grotesque. It warns us away from the upsetting excesses of texts and images that inadequately temper their taboo-violating content. It guards content creators against liability from the easily offended and litigiously inclined. This graphic is about innards, in all of their three-dimensionality. It is gross, sticky, shocking. On the other hand, "graphic" seems to revoke all of that. Instead of oversharing, this graphic is about paring. It promises the geometrically streamlined—graphs, diagrams, computer screens, user interfaces. This graphic is about two-dimensional surfaces. It is calculated, detached, clinical. It is the look and feel of data, abstraction, and management: the way in which we make sense of information-age overload.

American Graphic explores moments in twentieth-century American literature when these two senses of the graphic—what I call the grotesque and the geometric graphics—come into contact: when affectively and aesthetically disparate branches of the graphic tree are grafted onto each other. What happens when the same moment in a piece of media—be it literary, visual, or performance art—is somehow graphic in both ways at once? When it vibrates with both excess and exactitude? When the pulsatingly gross meets the diagrammatically abstract? When flesh meets data? These literary, visual, and performance works are at once viscerally gross and coolly clinical. In them, readers are forced into the affective bind of a mode of engagement that is simultaneously empathic and classificatory, demanding identification and, at the same time, denying it. I posit that we see a marked turn in contemporary American literature away from the well-theorized gross aesthetic of the grotesque towards the ambivalent feeling of this "double graphic"—simultaneously disgusting and disinterested. I argue that this graphic turn indexes a newly prominent way of approaching the desire to know other people. It reveals the unseemliness of a lust, in our contemporary culture of information, for cool epistemological mastery over the bodies, and feelings, of others.

Toggling between emotional saturation and affective evacuation, the double graphic creates a crisis within the politics of affect and identification. As the sentimental tradition weeps and keens and flays its way into the era of database aesthetics and information overload, the double graphic reworks how sympathy operates in texts that do upsetting things with bodies. It forces us to face how closely and discomfitingly yoked together disgust and data—identification *with* and identification *of* the other—have become in our increasingly graph-ick world.

Graphic Affect

"Affect" has been a tasty term du jour in literary studies for more than a few days now. There are now not only theories of affect, but theories of theories of affect. Affect, emotion, feeling, and sensation, as they swap or share places, have now been defined in a panoply of ways, with more or less precision, often wafting ever atmospherically higher on gusts of increasingly mixed metaphor, by esteemed thinkers across multiple fields.

One of the contributions to the field of affect studies that is the most useful for this book is Sianne Ngai's expansion, begun in her germinal work *Ugly Feelings*, of the category of "aesthetic emotions . . . or feelings unique to our encounters with artworks."[2] Anchoring affect in artworks, too, Eugenie Brinkema argues in *The Forms of the Affects* that

> *it is only because one must read for it that affect has any force at all.* The intensity of that force derives from the textual specificity and particularity made available uniquely through reading, the vitality of all that is not known in

advance of close reading, the surprising enchantments of the new that are not uncovered by interpretation but produced and brought into being as its activity.[3]

The feelings associated with and complicated by the double graphic are summoned by the specifics of the texts I closely read in the chapters that follow. While one of the most generative and frustrating aspects of the double graphic is the way in which it forces the question of how it is we (can) read (for) affect at all, I follow Ngai and Brinkema in averring that actively read for it must be.

In literary studies, the turn to affect is generally considered an effort to recenter the corporeal in discussions of literary texts and their effects, while at the same time decentering the private individual as the privileged site of feeling and emotion. The affective turn has often dismissed the word "emotion" itself as inadequate for reorienting discussions of feeling away from some mythic self-contained subject out of whom feelings exclusively spring and in whom they proprietarily reside.[4]

Central, then, to theories of affect (and theories about those theories) is the question of the relationship between affect, the body, and particular *individuated* bodies. For many, affect is of and about the body, but it neither lives within nor emerges sui generis from it. Affect is about "impersonal intensities,"[5] potentiality, and what bodies can or might do—"a body's capacity to affect and to be affected."[6] For a rarer few, affect not only fully sheds the subject but completely dissociates from the body or bodies altogether. Brinkema regards "any individual affect as a self-folding exteriority that manifests in, as, and with textual form."[7] I don't quite go as far as her on that count. It is to the question of the body and bodies, rather than debates about the separation between affect and emotion,[8] that my concept of the double graphic might have the most to contribute. In many ways, the crux of the affective discomfort of doubly graphic moments is that they explicitly and invasively display vulnerable characters as both the abstracted body—often through the figures of the silhouette, the sex doll, and the data point—and as intimately particular fleshy bodies at the same time.

This book enters into this conversation with the affect theorists Eve Sedgwick, Sara Ahmed, and Eugenie Brinkema. That these scholars aren't always in direct agreement or dialogue with one another is a source of productive friction. Where Sedgwick, Ahmed, and Brinkema's theories of affect vibrate most temptingly with and against one another is in their respective emphases on texture. Each, in her own way, insists that affect exists in and as texture, and must be closely read for it.

Texture is a touchstone in Sedgwick's *Touching Feeling*. To read for affect, Sedgwick asserts, is to read for texture and all the questions—narrative, temporal, and agentive—that it begs:

> To perceive texture is never only to ask or know: What is it like? nor even just How does it impinge on me? Textural perception always explores two other questions as well: How did it get that way? and What could I do with it?[9]

Texture is "intrinsically interactive" and even encourages an approach to perception that Sedgwick evocatively avers is resonant with "the postwar moment of cybernetics and systems theory."[10] Going even farther, Sedgwick cites Renu Bora's distinction[11] between two types of texture, "texture" and "texxture":

> Texxture is the kind of texture that is dense with offered information about how, substantively, historically, materially, it came into being. A brick or a metalwork pot that still bears the scars and uneven sheen of its making would exemplify texxture in this sense. But there is also the texture—one x this time—that defiantly or even invisibly blocks or refuses such information; there is texture, usually glossy if not positively tacky, that insists instead on the polarity between substance and surface, texture that signifies the willed erasure of its history.[12]

If feeling is about touching, then, it is about relationality, surface, pattern, and material particularity, even as the word "affect" has been made to waft stratospherically away from the individual.

Ahmed also uses the figure of texture, particularly the opposition between the sticky and the smooth, to theorize emotion as a networked, relational thing. Emphasizing that "emotions are not simply located in the individual, but move between bodies,"[13] Ahmed eschews "affect," which she says is often used "to explain how emotions move beyond subjects,"[14] in part because "when the affective turn becomes a turn to affect, feminist and queer work are no longer positioned as part of that turn. Even if they are acknowledged as precursors, a shift *to* affect signals a shift *from* this body of work."[15] Ahmed argues that this work has already shown that emotions "involve bodily processes of affecting and being affected."[16] Emotions circulate. Not of their own amorphous accord, however, but rather via their attachment to, or association with, particular objects—"it is the objects of emotion that circulate, rather than emotion as such."[17] Not all objects are equally texturally prone to emotional glomming, however. "Feelings may stick to some objects, and slide over others."[18] As they stick (texxturally) and slide (texturally) onto and over them, "emotions shape the very surfaces of bodies."[19] In other words, emotions tex(x)ture. Bodies thus emotionally accoutered become particular sorts of objects. "The circulation of objects of emotion involves the transformation of others into objects of feeling."[20] For both Sedgwick and Ahmed, then, affect/emotion is relational in an emphatically tactile way. Feeling is about contact, touch, and texture. Surface matters, not because of its promises of depths to be plumbed, but because of its potential to contact and be contacted with.

The double graphic arises at moments of the emphatic "transformation of others into objects of feeling," to borrow Ahmed's phrase.[21] But, in the graphic moment, the feelings, perplexingly, seem at once to stick to and slide off of these human objects. The bodies that are identified by and with ethnographic, pornographic, or infographic attention become, in Ahmed's words "sticky, or saturated with affect, as sites of personal and social tension,"[22] but they are also presented perplexingly in ways that formally shrug off, even zero out emotional attachment. They are disgusting, sympathetic, appalling emotional voids. Stickily smooth. Smoothly sticky. Geometrically grotesque. Doubly graphic. The second "x" of Sedgwick's texxture winks, à la Schrödinger's cat, in and out of existence before our eyes (maybe even under our fingers).

Both Sedgwick and Ahmed briefly ponder what it means for an object of feeling to be ostensibly texture-less. In doing so, they each make gestures towards the relationship between texture and history. In Sedgwick's interpretation of Bora, texxture displays its material history, while texture denies history itself (though the very adamancy of the denial makes it counterproductive: "[H]owever high the gloss, there is no such thing as textural lack."[23]) Ahmed seems to argue nearly the opposite, that "once an affective quality has come to reside in something, it is often assumed as without history."[24] Once feeling stickily adheres to an object (be it inanimate or human), the processes by which it stuck there in the first place seem to drop away. Or, to return to Brinkema's provocation about affect and form, those processes need to actively be read for, lest they be considered innate and divorced from history. Particular histories saturate certain bodies qua objects unequally with emotion.

It is far from a coincidence that the most powerfully sticky objects of feeling are also often those with the least amount of power otherwise: racialized and/or feminized people. These are the figures throughout American literature, particularly American literary genres of feeling, that have oscillated most violently between being saturated with and evacuated of emotion. Calling this unequal distribution a key operation of biopower, Kyla Schuller argues that "racialization and sex difference do the work of unevenly assigning affective capacity throughout a population."[25] An increasing number of thinkers have pushed back against the proliferation of theories that define affect as disembodied potentiality, shimmering "passional suspension"[26] freed from the subject, an unmediated and unmotivated motive force. Scholars like Clare Hemmings, Claudia Garcia-Rojas, and Tyrone S. Palmer critique the whiteness, both conceptually and demographically, of affect theory, which they argue results in privileging the quirky and particular at the exclusion of, rather than in conversation with, discussions of systems of power and histories that actively inflect and constrict the ostensible freedom from the constraints of the subject that affect promises.[27] In short, as they see affect theory pushed as a "panacea," oversold as the only way to "break free of our paranoid attachment to unfreedom and turn towards the possibilities offered by feeling,"[28] Hemmings and others advocate for the study of affect "*in context.*"[29]

Others, from Lauren Berlant to, most recently, Xine Yao, call attention to the ways in which unfeeling and disaffection have come to be associated with—or mobilized as a form of resistance by—particular sorts of racialized subjects.[30] Yao argues that in nineteenth-century American literature in particular, "sympathy is the fundamental mode of apprehending affects, feelings, and emotions—and deeming them legitimate."[31] And sympathy has been anything but equally distributed by its white arbiters.

> One must be recognized *as* sympathetic to be deserving of sympathy from those with the agency to sympathize. Thus, the marginalized do not have the luxury of being unsympathetic without forfeiting the provisional acceptance

of their capacity for affective expressions and, therefore, the conditional acceptance of their humanity.[32]

In American letters and culture, fellow feeling—the bedrock of affective apprehension—has historically been unevenly and conditionally allocated, perpetually precarious for some and inviolable for others. Belying its prefix, then, sympathy has always in practice smacked of parasitism.

Citing Denise Ferreira da Silva,[33] Yao explains how, in global modernity shaped by Western Enlightenment notions of universality, "affectability defines raciality: the 'transparent I' has the agency to know and affect, while the 'affectable I' is the susceptible, the 'scientific construction of non-European minds.'"[34] (The susceptible opacity of this "affectable I," as exemplified by the figure of the silhouette, will be the focus of Chapter 2 on *the ethnographic*). Without attempting any pat reparative readings, Yao examines what happens when racialized people in nineteenth-century American texts, who "are legible only through their affectability," opt out of feeling altogether.[35] Continuing in the vein of what Berlant identifies as "countersentimental texts," which "withdraw from the contract that presumes consent with the conventionally desired outcomes of identification and compassion" to explore the "democratic pleasures of anonymity and alterity, let alone sovereign individuality,"[36] Yao draws attention to authors who abjure "the coloniality of sympathy."[37] Drawing on and expanding from Berlant's recessive "underperformativity,"[38] Yao groups a range of affective modes together under the umbrella of "unfeeling":

> withholding, disregard, growing a thick skin, refusing to care, opacity, numbness, dissociation, inscrutability, frigidity, insensibility, obduracy, flatness, insensitivity, disinterest, coldness, heartlessness, fatigue, desensitization, and emotional unavailability.[39]

She aligns them with minoritized subjects, engaged in the nineteenth century in the potentially "dangerous gambit" of refusing to be the affectable I, of withdrawing from their slotted place within the culture of sentiment.[40]

This book shares Berlant and Yao's concern with what affective absence does when it occurs in scenarios that seem generically sentimentally scripted for emotional excess instead. The double graphic traces these stymied scripts of sympathy forward into our data-saturated information age. It gives us moments impossibly both redolent with and utterly absent of feeling. It cleaves the concept of identification irreconcilably in two, while at the same time homophonically turning back on itself and cleaving identification right back together again. The double graphic is less about the portrayal of unfeeling subjects than the display of affectively saturated scenarios as if they were "merely interesting" interludes, diagrammatic exhibits, abstracted addenda.[41] The objects of emotion are not necessarily themselves unfeeling or disaffected. We (their consumers, viewers, and readers) are, at the same time that we—maybe also—are not.

Flesh and Data

The crux of the affective bind of the double graphic is the arresting interpenetration of flesh and data—and the ostensibly oppositional modes of identification we expect to get from (and give to) each. The double graphic makes us realize that what we call identification (as in empathy) is often—possibly always—also identification (as in classification). And that this is more and more explicitly a preoccupation of post-45 American literature, especially in depictions of minoritized bodies.

The post-45 periodization can have its limitations, but it does help to mark approximately what is generally agreed to be the blossoming of a new sort of "information age." While many scholars have argued that there have been many ages of information,[42] it is irrefutable that the quantity of readily accessible information has increased at an exponential rate of late. More specifically, "more data has been created and stored since the turn of millennium than in the entire history of humanity."[43] And with this unprecedented creation and storage of information has come a rapid proliferation and pervasion of new ways of organizing, manipulating, and visualizing it.

Maurice S. Lee marks the nineteenth century as when "the word *information* took on modern connotations, referring not only to edification and news (something one comes across in everyday life) but also to objective, reconfigurable data (something that functions within rule-bound systems)."[44] This new colloquial understanding of information coincided with what Joseph Entin calls "the discourse of scrutiny," a mode of realist representation that emerged in the latter half of the nineteenth century in the United States and "insisted that the personal and cultural identities of the poor and disempowered were imprinted on their bodies, which were exposed to the reader's or viewer's eye for close, unobstructed inspection."[45] Legibility, reconfigurability, objectivity, and impersonality become the watchwords of the domain Lee calls "the informational" and the literary texts into which its conventions soon began to seep.[46]

Informational reconfigurability and calculation reach their apotheosis with the computer age, which also sees the establishment of information theory as its own academic and industrial subfield.[47] Lev Manovich has called the database the symbolic form of the computer age.[48] Digital artist and scholar Victoria Vesna goes a step farther by declaring that in this age "we are increasingly aware of ourselves as databases."[49] Databases are bodies of raw material that is not yet properly "knowledge," but that has been made prone and accessible for use and extraction. Database, Manovich argues, is also anathema to narrative:

> As a cultural form, database represents the world as a list of items which it refuses to order. In contrast, a narrative creates a cause-and-effect trajectory of seemingly unordered items (events). Therefore, database and narrative are natural "enemies."[50]

In its ostensible incompatibility with narrative, the database—with its parceled and assembled packets of data, ostensibly scrubbed of either context or emotional content—has a strange structural resonance with what might seem to be its opposite: the affectively saturated object of emotion, which Ahmed describes as having, as a fetish, effectively effaced any historical narratives of how it came to be so charged with emotions.[51]

In the computerized age of information, bodies are dematerialized,[52] abstracted, and, as subjects/objects of information, made more than ever into "objective, reconfigurable data" (to return to Lee's phrase). While our information age's symbolic form may be the database, what sets this age apart from previous ones is how reading publics interact with such information and/as each other: via graphics. In a world awash in undifferentiated data, "graphics of all kinds have become the predominant mode of constructing and presenting information and experience."[53] The graphical user interface (GUI) revolutionized how people see and think about and with information on screens. Johanna Drucker boldly argues that "no single innovation has transformed communication as radically in the last half century as the GUI."[54] It is through graphics that we read our world, and ourselves, as both become increasingly databased.

Graphics (n.), in other words, is increasingly the prevailing contemporary form, aesthetic, and conduit of information. Graphics, according to Jacques Bertin, encompasses maps, networks, and diagrams and is "one of the major 'languages' applicable to information processing."[55] The language of graphics lets us easily, even instantaneously, compare data, placing disparate figures extracted from the physical world commensurably beside one another on a flat plane. The object of graphics, "which operates in areas linked to the tri-dimensionality of spatial perception," is to enable us to connect predefined signs to "propositions in a sequence," which can then become "'undebatable,' that is, 'logical.'" Bertin explains how, in this way, graphics, like mathematics, "construct the 'rational moment.'"[56]

In her account of how we got here, Drucker emphasizes that there is nothing particularly self-evident about this now-commonplace mode of displaying and interpreting data gathered from the world. "*Data are capta*," she reminds us. They are "taken not given, constructed as an interpretation of the phenomenal world, not inherent in it."[57] Unprocessed data becomes information by being "ordered, formed, and otherwise manipulated so as to communicate meaning and enact intentions."[58] The vaunted objective self-evidence of information has always been a bit of a ruse, but a stubbornly sticky one. "The very idea of graphic-ness, attention to the surface of a visual plane on which compositional elements interacted—not merely as representations of other things, but as elements in themselves—required a conceptual leap."[59]

Data visualizations, in other words, are fundamentally interpretive, abstractions of abstractions. Indeed, Lev Manovich claims data visualization as "a new abstraction," one that approaches mind- and body-dwarfing cataracts of information not with the awe-filled surrender of the Romantic sublime but, quite the opposite, by calmly, unfeelingly, staring down the torrential outflows of "infowhelm" before setting about taming and mastering it.[60] By mapping phenomena and effects erstwhile considered unrepresentable, data visualization is thus the aesthetic realm of the "anti-sublime."[61]

The management via abstraction of this new anti-sublime requires a certain measure of discrimination. In 1996, Hal Foster asked "is our media world one of a cyberspace that renders bodies immaterial, or one in which bodies, not transcended at all, are marked, often violently, according to racial, sexual, and social differences?"[62] The ostensibly objective action of cataloguing and abstracting data and information is never divorced from the operation of power. The postwar notion of information overload—and the tools and systems, like the computer and information theory, that rallied to meet, regulate, and tame it—"could be said to emerge at the complex intersection of military, corporate, and educational interests."[63] The interests Stephens lists as converging upon information are of course more than passingly interested themselves in bodies and their management.

The feeling that racially and sexually marked bodies are violently left behind by the promise of abstracted, informational, utopic immateriality is not new to the most recent information age. Lee argues that "in nineteenth-century literature, romantic and racialized characters stand outside informational modernity."[64] In the chapters that follow, I look at examples of the double graphic in which, instead, these "romantic and racialized" figures become the very stuff of informational modernity, mined for the raw data of identification, broadly construed. The aesthetic emotions of graphics qua data visualization give us a framework for thinking about the diagrammatic side of the double graphic: capturing, containing, processing, and abstracting all manner of incomprehensible excess; making it reasonable, reconfigurable, comparable, manageable. When bodies in grotesque states of distress and overexposure are seen, written, and read through the aesthetic and epistemological logics of data visualization, we get the double graphic.

Disgust

Now, with some understanding of what I mean by affect and the information age, in order to begin describing how, who, or what the double graphic feels—what complexities, congestions, and forms of affective force it either loosens up or constipates—we first need to get a little gross. We need to define disgust.

Disgust is an affect of violent reaction, an "urgent and specific" mix of attraction and repulsion.[65] Where the grotesque body "crosses borders, ignores boundaries, and overspills margins," disgust works viscerally and aggressively to reinscribe them.[66] Different in ilk from other "ugly feelings" Ngai catalogues—like paranoia and animatedness, in which "the obscuring of the subjective-objective boundary becomes internal to the nature of [the] feelings"—disgust instead "strengthens and polices this boundary."[67] It is through this policing function, both on an interpersonal and societal level, that "disgust for all its visceralness turns out to be one of our more aggressive culture-creating passions."[68] There is a coercive sociality to the affect. It calls for us to stand apart together from the object of disgust and "expects concurrence."[69] It creates culture by codifying social mores and penalizing their violations, by distinguishing—and then violently expelling—the abhorrent other from the body politic and/or the sovereign self. The sovereignty of the state and self must first be threatened, uncertain, or in need of assertion, however, in order for the affect to erupt at all. Disgust can only be in the business of creating culture and policing boundaries as a reaction against their violation. Its quintessential action is exemplified by vomiting, an instant and involuntary creation of distance that is activated by an untoward proximity. As Ahmed writes in her analysis of the emotion, "Borders need to be threatened in order to be maintained, or even to appear as borders."[70]

The grotesque body, which refuses to be smoothly impenetrable, "transgresses its own confines, ceases to be itself," wreaks havoc on borders (and often reeks, as such).[71] It provokes disgust because it threatens the integrity of the surfaces and selves of those who come into contact with it. "Something is disgusting when it pops our phantasm of an orderly object world and with it our narcissism; the smooth skin of the world bursts and the inside, whose existence we suspected all along but repressed all the more vehemently, gushes forth."[72] Identity—in its definitional play between singularity and sameness[73]—is always, therefore, implicated in disgust reactions: "The limits between the body and the world are erased, leading to the fusion of the one with the other and with surrounding objects."[74] The grotesque body disgusts because it threatens to make contact, to stick to us and, in sticking, to besmirch or even usurp us. Ahmed, drawing on Sartre, identifies stickiness as a key aspect of the disgust affect. In many ways, disgust is the exemplary emotion for Ahmed's model of the sort of affective flypaper-ification that happens to bodies when they are made into circulating objects of emotion. "When the body of another becomes an object of disgust, then the body *becomes* sticky."[75] The exact mechanism of this "becoming" sticky is itself obscure and confuses the agency of disgusting and the disgusted: "[T]here is not a distinction between passive or active, even though the stickiness of one object might come before the stickiness of the other, such that the other seems to cling to it."[76] Disgust adheres, transfers, and transforms.

For Julia Kristeva, disgust is yoked to abjection. "What is *abject* . . . the jettisoned object, is radically excluded and draws me toward the place where meaning collapses."[77] Collapse of meaning, particularly the subject/object distinction, defines Kristevan abjection. "It is thus not lack of cleanliness or health that causes abjection but what disturbs identity, system, order. What does not respect borders, positions, rules. The in-between, the ambiguous, the composite."[78] Not only do subject and object lose their distinction, but "in abjection, it is the border that is transformed into an object."[79] The abject parts of us are often our borders, "those aspects of oneself that one cannot be rid of, that seem, but are not quite, alienable—for example, blood, urine, feces, nails, and the corpse."[80] Abjection horrifyingly fixates on the dividing lines that we would prefer to never have to look at, that we would like to think of in clean two-dimensional abstractions, if at all, but are forced to touch, to palpate, to stick with (and to) when immersed in the world of the grotesque.

The in-betweenness of abjection resonates with the ongoing "becoming" of both grotesque bodies and the disgust they elicit. Inorganic stasis, many critics have argued, is rarely disgusting:

> Indeed, [Aurel] Kolnai's insistence that the non-organic is not itself ever disgusting (nor is fresh meat or the cold hard skeleton) suggests that it is movement as such—dissolution, transition, the process of putrefaction—that offends in rot, which is never just rot, but always in the expanded time of the gerund as rotting.[81]

For Brinkema, disgust resides not in any particular object or class of objects, but rather in its gerundive nature,

> the promise of worsening, this possibility of something more disgusting than the disgusting. Giving disgust its contents, then, filling in its gut with objectal specificities, avows that the excluded can be known, perceived, bounded, and therefore limited.[82]

Sympathy and disgust are both about breaking down and/or through the boundaries between people. Whether they see that interpenetration as a promise or a threat reveals in large part to what extent and in which direction they are protesting too much about how permeable they really want such boundaries to be. Sympathy protests too much that such a crossing is both possible, desirable, and Good. Disgust, its mirror and handmaid, frantically reinscribes boundaries that it seems to know are too flimsy to ever truly hold. Though asserting the essential knowability and commensurability of the other, sympathy is often really in the business of cementing power differentials.

Grid Your Loins

Disgust invokes the borders that it reifies even as it exceeds them. This boundlessness of a response that is also about establishing boundaries lends the affect a unique, perhaps impossible spatiality, which Brinkema expands upon using geometric figures of mapping:

> The mapping of disgust involves two distinctly different models: a three-dimensional plot of relative positions in space in disgust's affinity to notions of nearness or its threat of proximity (linked to what [Winfried] Menninghaus calls its "hyperreality" and to the aesthetician's argument that it fails to leave adequate room for contemplative distance and reflection) *and* a series of points on a line, beyond which one must not pass, the model of disgust whereby it derives from excess. These two spatial models are contradictory—or, rather, they cannot be mapped on the same set of axes, for the one involves a coming-too-close, while the other involves a going-too-far: figured onto a singular site, the pull-me-push-you tension might rip a body apart.[83]

Brinkema means "mapping of disgust" two ways at once, with disgust as both subject and object. For just as she is offering us a critical map of the form, she is also defining disgust as a thing that maps, that is "a spatial operator, delimiting zones of proximity that are discomforting versus acceptable, drawing lines in the thick mud."[84] Her description of the dual, contradictory spatiality of disgust—"a three-dimensional plot" and "a series of points on a line"—is an apt way to visualize a similarly constitutive tension of the double graphic: the incongruous dimensionality of its gross/grotesque and geometric/diagrammatic poles. This leads us to a figure of mapping that seems to delineate both the modes of rationalism against which the grotesque has been defined and the complex dimensionality Brinkema ascribes to disgust: the grid.

Scholars of the grid tie its prevalence in the twentieth and twenty-first centuries to the new technologies and modes of knowledge production and management that have become ever present and that favor abstraction, standardization, and scopic informational mastery. The grid undergirds our information age. Lex Morgan Lancaster suggests that "the grid is particularly resonant as a dominant matrix for modernity, for instance, because it was central to industrialism and colonialism and because it offers a visualization of the assertive rationalism that structures actual and virtual spaces, from urban landscapes to power grids."[85] Hannah Higgins goes so far as to call the grid "the dominant mythological form of modern life."[86] Grids flatten space, make ungainly three-dimensional bodies into fungible figures, and enforce a computational, visual commensurability among disparate data points that can be both creative and destructive. Nico Israel calls grids "modes of control, of rendering legible and hence, at least in part, captive."[87]

Grids provide the spatial grounding for a specific form of graphic inscription: the diagram. Jakub Zdebik, in a study that synthesizes Gilles Deleuze's thinking about the diagram across his long career, describes it as "a drawing conveying information about something incorporeal. From the Greek *diagramma*, it means to mark out by lines, to draw—where *dia* is through, across, apart and *graphein* is to write."[88] While grids abjure mimeticism, diagrams are a more hybrid form, neither fully representational nor abstract. They are "visual forms of description that make few concessions to imitation, meaning by 'imitation' a staging of content as if belonging to a world both contiguous with and similar to our own."[89] The diagram's utility as a "flexible tool of research" depends on its capacity to simplify.[90] It does not aim to resemble what it represents, but rather to "display abstract functions that make up a system,"[91] streamlining material realities while embodying "incorporeal data" so it may be analyzed.[92]

Bruno Latour argues that the proliferation of "two-dimensional inscriptions" like grids and diagrams, which he also calls "graphisms," has been central to both scientific advancement and colonial expansion in modernity. Defined by being "*mobile* but also *immutable, presentable, readable* and *combinable* with one another," graphisms are modernity's tools for scientific discovery, territorial expansion, and rhetorical persuasion:[93] "Scientists start seeing something once they stop looking at nature and look exclusively and obsessively at prints and flat inscriptions."[94] Flatness is key to the power that these inscriptions hold, their ability to facilitate "mastery."[95] And this mastery through flatness is violent in a way that the clean, antiseptic lines of such inscriptions' gridded surfaces belie. Latour notes:

> [T]he extraordinary obsession of scientists with papers, prints, diagrams, archives, abstracts and curves on graph paper. No matter what they talk about, they start talking with some degree of confidence and being believed by colleagues, only once they point at simple geometrized two-dimensional shapes. The "objects" are discarded or often absent from laboratories. Bleeding and screaming rats are quickly dispatched. What is extracted from them is a tiny set of figures.[96]

The manipulation of grids of various ilk gives objects that were once three-dimensional and ungainly what Latour calls "optical consistency"[97]—enabling disparate and distant figures to be manipulated and made commensurable upon the same coordinate plane while jettisoning the "bleeding and screaming" bodies from which they were extracted. Double graphic moments in literary texts, as we'll see, bring the three-dimensional "bleeding and screaming" bodies uncomfortably back into intimate contact with the grid lines through and by which they were once "quickly dispatched."

Graphic Axes: Ethno-, Porno-, Info-

Graphic moments in American literature complicate the release theorists have argued is afforded by the disgust of the grotesque, leaving us caught instead with a discomfiting ambivalence, whose crux is the promise (and perversity) of identification. Where the grotesque side of the graphic dissolves and distorts boundaries that disgust retchingly reaffirms, the cool side of the graphic inscribes lines—maps, grids, diagrams—and sharply cleaves to categories. The (grotesque/gross) graphic makes boundary lines into bodies; the (geometric/cool) graphic makes bodies into lines—maps, grids, diagrams. The double graphic arises in moments of bodily exposure that are both sorts of graphic at once.

This book is organized not unlike a grid. Like Sianne Ngai, I follow Barbara Johnson in laying out the objects within my categories via a "method of disjunctive alignment . . . intended to allow the texts to become 'readable in new ways' and thus generate fresh examinations of historically tenacious problems."[98] I analyze the graphic along three specific axes: the *ethnographic*, the *pornographic*, and the *infographic*. Whether dealing primarily with race, sex, or data, each manifestation is marked by the discomfiting affective ambivalence of coercive identification. We both empathize with and clinically document other people in moments of taboo overexposure. In each chapter, my explication of the double graphic hinges on pairing a canonical text read against the grain with a noncanonical work that engages in the same dynamics of clinical viscerality. Gridding canonical and noncanonical works with one another other in this way, I put texts that have neither been thought about together nor in these theoretical terms side by side on the same horizontal plane. The pairings (and triplings) of texts I consider in this book reveal how different authors put to drastically different use the way that the double graphic arrests and congests the pleasures of identification—or the catharsis of the classical grotesque—and, with it, the longer sentimental tradition with which it is deeply imbricated.

I argue that each axis of the double graphic can be best understood through a corresponding figure (what is a grid without figures?). I use the term "figure"[99] advisedly, as it connotes both bodies and calculations. The figures that I abstract from my three categories in order to then re-concretize them (very diagrammatic of me) are the *ethnographic* silhouette, the *pornographic* sex doll, and the *infographic* data point. In the graphic moment, I argue, people shift unsettlingly into and back out of things—be they flat black silhouettes, hollow dolls, or sets of dimensionless data points—and we don't quite know how we are meant to feel about it. This ambivalence reveals the disturbing coupling of disgust and data in our increasingly graph-ick world.

Before I reach those categories and their attendant figures, however, in Chapter 1, "The American Grotesque: A Graphic Digest," I provide a topographic rereading of the aesthetic category of the grotesque through three key American modernist texts usually placed firmly within its canon: William Faulkner's *As I Lay Dying*, Nathanael West's *Miss Lonelyhearts*, and Flannery O'Connor's *Wise Blood*. The chapter illuminates how some of their most gruesome moments, particularly surrounded by descriptions of faces, are also the most clinically and diagrammatically plotted. The geometric faces of these texts coolly freeze the grotesque and, in doing so, become graphic.

These examples reveal that the crux of the distinction between the two is *dimensionality* and the havoc that mistranslations between or misapplications of two- and three-dimensionality wreak on the affective legibility of bodies. Faulkner, West, and O'Connor uneasily flatten the bulbous excrescences of the three-dimensional grotesque body into planar, impenetrable diagrams, both visual and verbal. These bodies, these others, are at once too round and too flat for comfort. The feelings that stick to and circulate through them expose the uncomfortable and paradoxical intimacy of poses towards the bodies of others—cool evaluation and sticky attraction/revulsion—that we assume to be diametrically opposite.

"The Ethnographic" begins with *The Narrative of Arthur Gordon Pym of Nantucket* by Edgar Allan Poe, Toni Morrison's primary example of "American Africanism" in U.S. literature. The chapter demonstrates how forms of vaunted "scientific" calculation—charts, diagrams, logbooks, but particularly the silhouette—collide with and enable violence: disfigurement, cannibalism, sexual violation. Poe's "Africanist" characters are not just stereotypes or caricatures, but silhouettes—flat, matte, black—at once constitutively opaque and seemingly readily legible to the nineteenth-century gentleman-scholar's "scientific" eye. These two-dimensional figures are made available for both classification and laceration, produced by cutting and perhaps inclined, too, to cut back. I argue that Kara Walker's silhouette tableaux take Poe's ethnographic forms, in all of their violent flatness and affective ambivalence, into the twentieth and twenty-first centuries. Her visual compositions seem to lift the Tsalalians and their ilk from the pages of *Pym*, project them at larger-than-life scale, and set them dancing in unseemly shadow puppet theatrics through the landscapes of a phantasmagoric American South—demonstrating both Ngai's aesthetic category of "the interesting" and her "ugly feeling" of "racial animatedness."[100] The chapter concludes with an exploration of Mat Johnson's revision of Poe in his 2011 novel *Pym*, which refleshes the ethnographic silhouette and renders overidentification with figures that were once flat its own form of discomfort.

"The Pornographic" considers the graphic's relationship to gender and sex through Vladimir Nabokov's *Lolita*, one of the twentieth-century's signal cases of graphic literary sexual content; Fran Ross's *Oreo*, a polyglot multi-ethnic satiric romp, punctuated by mathematic-ish equations and diagrams;

and the obscene burlesque performances of the contemporary "avant-porn" mixed-race artist Narcissister, who never removes her plastic Barbie-esque mask. These texts beg uneasy questions about sexual objectification and the affective dynamics of visual and literary voyeurism. The figure of the sex doll emerges in all three as the pornographic object par excellence. It materializes, and makes tactile, the lust for "the 'knowledge-pleasure' of sexuality" that Linda Williams locates at the core of the pornographic: the desire to make the sexual object fully, ecstatically, calculably, manufacturably knowable.[101] The sex doll points to how such a drive uneasily—unethically, uncannily, and often quite humorously—elides people with things and messily merges empathic and documentary identification. Along the way, Narcissister and Ross pose answers to the question of what happens when the sex doll learns to masturbate.

In my fourth chapter, "The Infographic," I use Thomas Pynchon's *The Crying of Lot 49* and Teju Cole's *Open City* to explore how the graphic appears in postmodern novels structured by incidental revelations of, or casual contact with, trauma. Both novels unfold via the rapid proliferation of tangential information, usually sparked by physical contact between the protagonists and other, often fleetingly minor, characters. I argue that each moment of contact is followed by either paranoid or parasitic incorporation of those others' stories into the protagonists' own. This rendering of violence and viscera into data—a Wikipedic mastery of information that translates public and personal atrocities into dimensionless factoids—characterizes the chill of a particular type of information-age graphic in these novels. This chapter analyzes the work of narrative and geometric "tangents" in both texts, their analogous ways of disposing of diegetically useful others, and the ethical and affective import of their protagonists' modes of informatics-inflected narrative parasitism.

The conclusion of *American Graphic* probes the medium specificity of the double graphic with a brief look at the fraught dynamics of identification in comics and graphic narratives that depict and elicit its poles of disgust and detachment. Robert Crumb exemplifies the grotesque, Chris Ware, the diagrammatic extremes of the graphic. Phoebe Gloeckner's work, at once convulsive and clinical, marks their ambivalent convergence. I end with thinking about other possible axes of the double graphic.

The American graphic, as I map it across the ethnographic, pornographic, and infographic, is about bodies read into and against binaries—racial, sexual, computational—and how emotions stick to or slide off of them in those readings. A sex doll masturbates. Sentimental black silhouettes start cannibalizing and fellating each other. We walk (or swipe) our way through the world viewing one another as data points: peripatetic, fungible Wikipedia entries cataloguing illicit desires and disfiguring traumas. The double graphic that comes of age in mid-twentieth-century information culture coerces identification—in the sense of both empathy with and documentation of others—in moments of overexposure. In doing so, it warps, buckles, and plays a strange tune upon old but persistent saws about how identification functions in literary and cultural works that do upsetting things with bodies. It enforces a discomfiting politics that divorces affect from identification, at the moments when we most want them to be wed.

1. The American Grotesque
A Graphic Digest

CHARTING THE AESTHETIC AND AFFECTIVE topographies of the double graphic requires an initial, sustained engagement with the category of the grotesque—aesthetically, affectively, and historically. A term with its own long and storied genealogy, "the grotesque" maps onto the gross side of the graphic. Or, put another way, the graphic both encompasses and, in important ways, exceeds this more established aesthetic category. In what follows, I offer a digest of the grotesque, a brief history of this aesthetic category. I then turn to moments from three modernist texts in the canon of the American grotesque: William Faulkner's *As I Lay Dying*, Nathanael West's *Miss Lonelyhearts*, and Flannery O'Connor's *Wise Blood*. I argue that the work of these denizens of the American grotesque reads in exciting new ways when seen as more properly exemplary of the double graphic. A topographic reading of faces in these three texts—attending to their surfaces and contours, reading the detailed lines that describe them for texture and texxture both—lays the groundwork for the crises of reading (for and as) identification that emerge in the following chapters. But first, that "slipperiest of aesthetic categories,"[1] the grotesque.

A Genealogy of Grottoes

While the forms of the grotesque have changed remarkably over the centuries, the emotional complex denoted by the word has remained fairly constant. . . . For an object to be grotesque, it must arouse three responses. Laughter and astonishment are two; either disgust or horror is the third.

—GEOFFREY HARPHAM, "The Grotesque: First Principles"

The grotesque was born in grottoes. Derived from the Italian *la grottesca* and *il grottesco*, the word was first invented to describe the decorations found in the fifteenth century on the walls of grotto caves excavated in Pompeii and Herculaneum. The caves were covered with depictions of plant, animal, and human forms intricately intertwined into hybrid creations that "violate not only the laws of statics and gravity, but common sense and plain observation as well."[2] Grotesque, in this context, was pitted against a classical visual style, with its vaunted, serious, and ostensibly mimetic representation. These designs, instead, were playful, imaginative, and flamboyantly decorative.

James Goodwin asks that we not forget the reparative promise of the term's birth in grottoes: "For all the associations of the grotesque in later centuries with repulsiveness, depravity, and terror, we do well to remember the grotto's original significance as an accommodating, hospitable, restorative place."[3] The political, ethical, and moral import of grotesquerie is one crux not only of its critical history, but of my own argument about its relation to the double graphic. I am less concerned here with nailing down a definition of the aesthetic category than with highlighting some salient throughlines—major arteries, if you will—that have animated critical discussions of it, in order to provide a characterization of its attendant affects and point to where and how the graphic picks up and peels away from it.

Before the word "grotesque" was coined or used to name an aesthetic category, Aristotle defined the sort of affective release by which many of its later theorists would describe it. According to Aristotle, art can evoke certain negative, even dangerous feelings in order to safely release and thus regulate them. "Through pity and fear it achieves the purgation (catharsis) of such emotions."[4] Catharsis, a medical metaphor, comes from *kathairein*, meaning to purify or purge (originally in the sense of menstrual fluid or other reproductive material).[5] For the Greek philosopher, however, this purgation was the purview only of high tragedy. Comedy trades in a less noble form of tempered relief, an instantiation of distasteful things that is harmless but not necessarily cathartic:

> The ludicrous is a species of ugliness: it is a sort of flaw and ugliness which is not painful or injurious. An obvious example is the comic mask, ugly and twisted but not painful to look at.[6]

The distinction here between tragedy and comedy is akin to, but not entirely parallel to, Aristotle's ethical distinction between noble and ugly things. In

Nicomachean Ethics, he distinguishes "the admirable," "fine," or "noble" (*kalon*) from the "shameful" or "ugly" (*aischron*), implying that ethical virtue consists in actively choosing the former while eschewing the latter.[7] Theorists of the grotesque take up the possibility that decidedly ugly, ludicrous, unpleasant things—hybrid mixes of the fearful and the comic—might produce the sort of cathartic release that Aristotle confines to the noble realm of tragedy.

After Michel de Montaigne's first application of the term to a literary work (as a formal description his own essays) in 1580,[8] the rise of Romanticism in the eighteenth century saw "grotesque" develop its modern (though still frequently contested) usage in English. John Ruskin was one of the first to attempt a rigorous definition of the grotesque, which he said is "composed of two elements, one ludicrous, the other fearful."[9] For Ruskin, such a combination of fancy and fear can allow the grotesque, in the right hands, to convey otherwise inaccessible truths. This transcendent, "noble" grotesque is the sphere of the true artist, who is set apart from the mere "workman" by his depth of feeling and ability to empathize.[10]

> The master of the noble grotesque knows the depth of all at which he seems to mock, and would feel it at another time, or feels it in a certain undercurrent of thought even while he jests with it; but the workman of the ignoble grotesque can feel and understand nothing, and mocks at all things with the laughter of the idiot and the cretin.[11]

If approached by a master, the noble grotesque exposes and "*plays* with *terror*,"[12] giving it a "symbolical" outlet that, through turning the inward outward in imaginative, even untoward ways, makes it ennobling.

Though it was first named for the grottoes of Rome, the literary grotesque is properly housed in the grottoes of the body. Few theorists have gone spelunking through those caves with greater zest than Mikhail Bakhtin, in his cornerstone work *Rabelais and His World*, written in 1940 but first published in 1965. Bakhtin identifies the grotesque as a form of realism and the modern instantiation of the medieval carnival, in which bodies are no longer clearly delimited from the world around them, and hierarchies are flamboyantly inverted through laughter and excess.

Bakhtin's bodies are radically positive. The grotesque body abjures smoothness, fixity, and stasis: "The artistic logic of the grotesque image ignores the closed, smooth, and impenetrable surface of the body and retains only its excrescences (sprouts, buds) and orifices, only that which leads beyond the body's limited space or into the body's depths."[13] This body, in a constant state of "becoming," favors animated three-dimensionality and rejects fixed two-dimensionality:

> The grotesque body has no façade, no impenetrable surface, neither has it any expressive features. It represents either the fertile depths or the convexities of procreation and conception. It swallows and generates, gives and takes.[14]

Bakhtin opposes this carnivalesque, grotesque body to what he calls "the new bodily canon" of modernity, in which individuals are strictly separated from one another, orifices are closed, and "the basis of the image is the individual, strictly limited mass, the impenetrable façade."[15] Wolfgang Kayser's 1957 *The Grotesque in Art and Literature* defines the grotesque not according to its practitioners' intentions, but by the holistic effect it produces in its viewers: "The grotesque is the estranged world."[16] Its motifs are monsters, vermin, bats, tangled jungles, horrific puppets, and encounters with madness.[17] It shows us "the fusion of realms which we know to be separated, the abolition of the law of statics, the loss of identity, the distortion of 'natural' size and shape, the suspension of the category of objects, the destruction of personality, and the fragmentation of the historical order."[18] In short, "the grotesque is a play with the absurd."[19]

This play, not unlike Ruskin's characterization of the effects of the "symbolical grotesque," is, for Kayser, "an attempt to invoke and subdue the demonic aspects of the world."[20] While not grounded in or dependent on the noble spirit of its master creator, Kayser's conception of the grotesque shares with Ruskin's a notion of catharsis via the dredging up and display of hidden depths. Where Kayser differs from Ruskin is in his historical situating of the grotesque. He sees its "secret liberation" as being from not just "the dark forces which lurk in and behind our world and have power to estrange it," but also from a specifically modern sense of rationalism, akin to Bakhtin's characterization of "the new bodily canon": "The various forms of the grotesque are the most obvious and pronounced contradictions of any kind of rationalism and any systematic use of thought."[21] The grotesque can be a violent, comic, even terrifying rejection of rationalism and systematism. The double graphic ambivalently combines many of Kayser's motifs with the scientific pose against which he claims the grotesque aesthetic has traditionally been a violent reaction.

A number of recent monographs have brought the theories of Ruskin, Bakhtin, Kayser, and others to bear on more focused historical periods and modes of political or social utility.[22] Asserting that "every culture has its grotesque"—its liminal figure against which it defines itself, and through which it safely expels untoward feelings—Leonard Cassuto looks to early America and the racialized other:

> For the American Puritans, the Indians were grotesque. For nineteenth-century Americans, the objectified African slave and his descendants came to occupy a similar shifting space in the system of meaning and value.[23]

These avatars of the national grotesques—conjured out of recoil, guilt, and paranoia—became the objects of sympathetic control on which the sentimental literary tradition in America fixates. They are created by the policing of boundaries between human and inhuman and are the result of the fact that "human objectification never fully succeeds; that is, a person never actually becomes a thing."[24] Cassuto's work begins to point to the uncomfortable slide between disgust at and sympathy towards "racial grotesque" in white American literature. Meanwhile, Mary Russo, in her study of the "female grotesque," characterizes grotesquerie as a return of the repressed, "those hidden cultural contents which by their abjection had consolidated the cultural identity of the bourgeoisie."[25] The grotesque female, in particular, "intends to baffle, intimidate, and shock the viewer or reader and to stimulate his own (critical) thought process."[26]

Despite their differences in emphasis, for all of these theorists the grotesque remains a mode of cathartic release—one that recalls and refleshes the Greek term's roots (*kathairein*) in bodily purging. It discharges, disgorges, divulges violently at its viewer/reader and demands a reciprocal sort of explosively embodied affective response—laughter, shuddering, vomiting, even weeping. Philip Thomson, in his 1972 study of the term, avers that the function of the grotesque is to "bring the horrifying and disgusting aspects of existence to the surface, there to be rendered less harmful by the introduction of a comic perspective."[27] That surfacing is, nearly all theorists agree, a convulsive process. The release that the grotesque offers is hardly unequivocal—or univocal—but, in Anthony Di Renzo's words, "its ultimate purpose is therapeutic: it is a comic shock treatment. Even at its most menacing, it seeks to liberate."[28]

But what happens when the shock treatment fails? When the promised disgorging is the wrong kind of gag—not a comedic or even erotic release but a stifling? A getting stuck in the collective craw? And what's modernism got to do with it?

American Grotesque Topographics

It is a remarkable coincidence that Flannery O'Connor, William Faulkner, and Nathanael West, all authors given pride of place in studies of the grotesque in the American context, were all also initially visual artists. Faulkner drew uncharacteristically lithe and winsome jazz-age ladies and gents, and while in college, both West and O'Connor aspired to be cartoonists. Faulkner's drawings are well documented in at least one monograph.[29] Though archival evidence is sparse, biographies attest to West's college-years cartooning, and he certainly used the language of the medium liberally in describing his own formal experiments in his novels.[30] O'Connor's visual juvenilia has been both published and archived.[31]

This commonality between these famed American practitioners of the grotesque serves as an opening to think through the myriad graphic qualities of their written work. Doing so clarifies not just my definition of the differences between the grotesque and the graphic but also demonstrates why this difference matters. What is at stake is the relationship between flesh and data, and the status of literary modes of identification in a new sort of information age. I juxtapose the diagrammatic versions of the graphic with these authors' more well-examined grotesquerie, particularly in the faces we read and, after a fashion, see in their novels. None of the three affords its readers the release or the revelry of fully fleshed disgust. Rather, these graphic moments confound previously theorized affective responses to the grotesque, instantiating a lineage of the double graphic texts that I pursue in the later chapters of this book.

Faulkner's novel combines all the ooze and stench of the grotesque with the geometric praxis of the carpenter's auger and box-maker's bevel, succinctly epitomized in the holes that bore through both wooden and flesh (sur)faces of Addie Bundren. West sketches, in a book he first envisioned as a comic strip, characters that have been called caricatures, whose grotesquerie is likewise clinically and geometrically two-dimensional. And O'Connor's first novel coolly warps the dimensionality of the human face in a way that deeply troubles our capacity for identification and empathy. In each text, we see and feel what happens when disgust, in response to excrescences of the grotesque, coexists with affective reactions that seem to be anathema to it: when sticky recoil is uncomfortably simultaneous with a smooth, schematic level—and leveling—gaze; when fleshy bodies are flattened onto and *into* evaluative grids, diagrammatically parsed out in a way that both freezes and friezes the boundless "becoming" of Bakhtinian grotesque bodies, while not quite negating their grossness.

As I Lay Dying: "The Body Turns a Cartwheel"

Before William Faulkner rose to prominence as a behemoth of southern modernism, he drew whimsical Art Deco pen-and-ink illustrations for the University of Mississippi's student newspaper, *The Daily Mississippian*. Lothar Hönnighausen has noted the obvious influence of the English illustrator Aubrey Beardsley (who is mentioned by name in *Absalom, Absalom!*) on the stylization of young Faulkner's visual art.[32] With none of the textural grotesqueness for which his novels came to be known, Faulkner's drawings instead are decorative planes on which showily serpentine curves play smoothly beside geometrically uniform motifs—parallel lines and checkered grids (Figure 1.1). The grids don't establish the illusion of realistic space by, say, creating Cartesian single-point perspective. They are flat overlays (or are they underlays?) of geometric patterning, often seemingly at odds with, or willfully oblivious to, the ostensible three-dimensionality of the human figures (themselves barely invested with a mimetic sort of fleshing out).

Though Rosalind Krauss's famous "Grids" essay is focused specifically on the post-45 work of artists like Piet Mondrian and Agnes Martin, her statement on the planar spatiality of grids, and their antagonist relationship to mimetics is helpful for thinking about Faulkner's early visual grids and, more importantly, how their phantom presence carries through a grotesque work like *As I Lay Dying*: Krauss defines the grid as autonomous, "antimimetic," imperiously aesthetic, and "antinatural." It is "the means of crowding out

FIGURE 1.1. Early William Faulkner drawings from the 1920s, originally published in Ole Miss's student paper *The Daily Mississippian*.

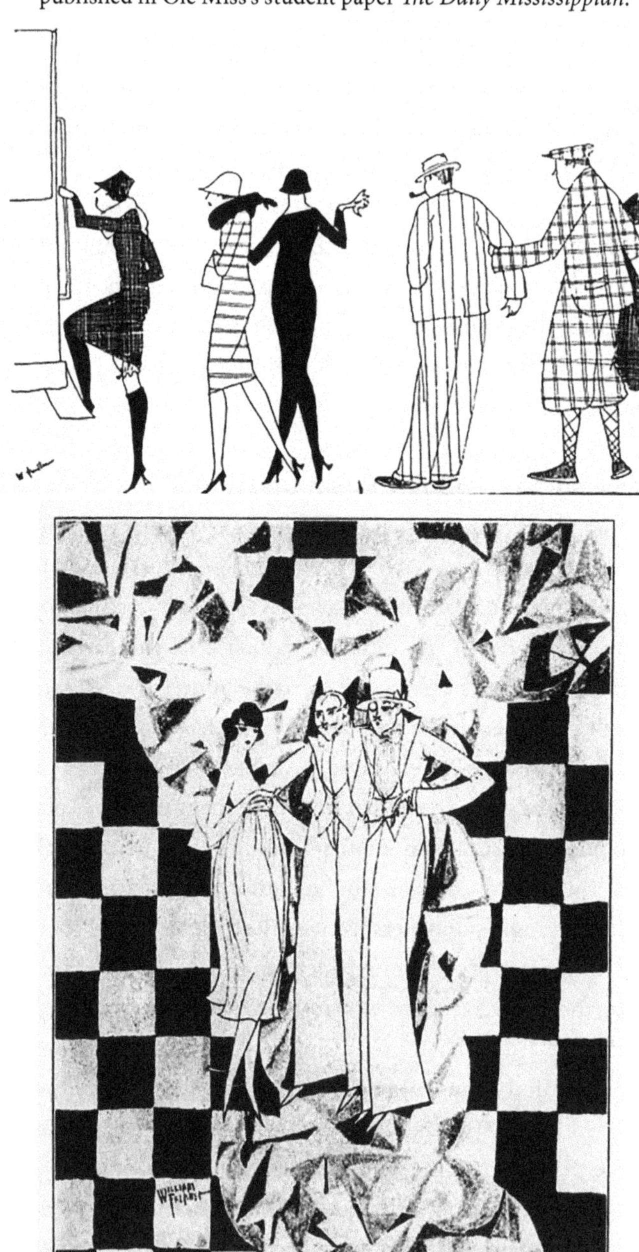

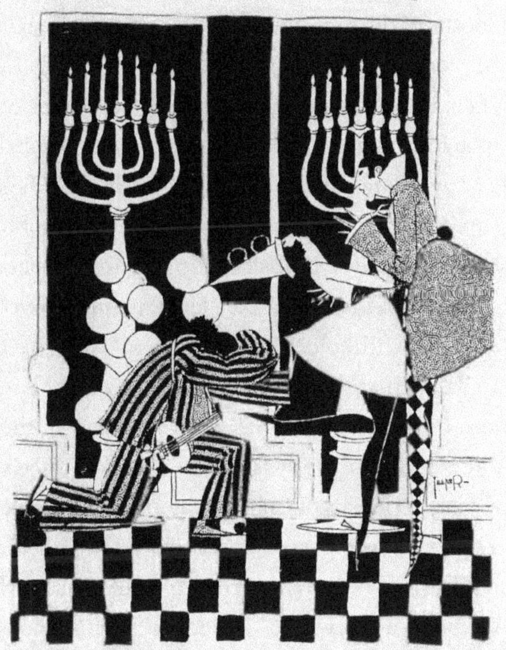

OLE MISS
SOCIAL ACTIVITIES

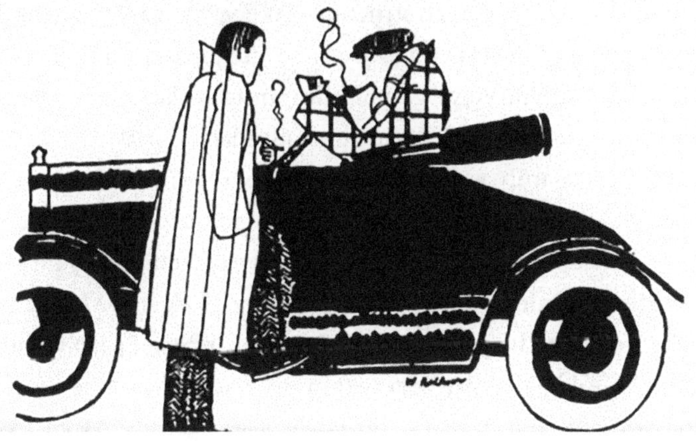

the dimensions of the real and replacing them with the lateral spread of a single surface."[33] This aggressive lateral spread that Krauss attributes to the grid is generative for understanding how moments in *As I Lay Dying* produce a discomfort that cannot quite be accounted for by the myriad theories of the grotesque that have been applied to it. At moments in the novel, a planar geometry "crowds out" all other dimensions, while still ostensibly displaying the modes and motifs of the grotesque. In these moments, readers lose the sort of space necessary for the recoil of disgust or the release of a Kayserian "secret liberation."[34] When the book's grotesquerie repeatedly turns coldly geometric, its flat, lateral, planar and geometric "aesthetic decree" unbalances not only the action of *As I Lay Dying* but also its affect."[35] Just as Addie's wrong-way up corpse ends up upending the family's wagon as they attempt to ford the swollen river, the novel is affectively unbalanced. This ambivalence emerges most forcefully in the modes of identification—faces, names, icons—that the book seems both to offer and withhold.

According to Bakhtin, the fundamental logic of the grotesque is "the body turns a cartwheel."[36] The plot of *As I Lay Dying* rides, in multiple ways, on cartwheels.[37] Addie Bundren's body is rotated head over heels into her coffin and then carried precariously off-balance atop a mule-pulled wagon; Darl even figures Addie as a wheel part: "[T]he red road lies like a spoke of which Addie Bundren is the rim."[38] The novel seems to make this maxim of grotesque theory, "the body turns a cartwheel," at once too literal and too figurative— Addie is turned bodily head over heels, propels the wheels of a cart forward, and becomes a rotating wooden structure.[39] When it uneasily flattens the bulbous excrescences of the carnivalesque body into planar, impenetrable visual and verbal diagrams, the novel graphically translates classically grotesque elements into a dimensionality that feels uneasily inappropriate.[40]

Faulkner awkwardly wedges a pictogram of a coffin within two lines of text in the middle of Vernon Tull's account of Addie's funeral, as he describes the family's attempt to maintain the flared shape of Addie's wedding-turned-funerary dress by laying her the wrong way in the clock-shaped box that Cash made (Figure 1.2).[41] The graphic symbol rests as uncomfortably within the typesetting as Addie's corpse does within the object it describes. Just as Addie's body is "laid in it reversed," the image itself is on the wrong axis to fit easily into the verbal/visual simile that ostensibly explains its introduction into the text. If it were really to be "clock-shape, like this," the image of the coffin would have to be on a vertical axis, like the grandfather clock to which it is compared. A grandfather clock arrayed "like this"—horizontally, as we see it in the text—would, of course, be a defunct one—prostrate, incapacitated, its pendulum inert, no longer a functional timekeeper. A "clock-shape, like this," gives us time-telling at a standstill. Well, a lie-still. An as-I-lay-dying-still. And so, the not-quite-right mixed media simile is in some way a thing of economical perfection. It is a slant analogy that says more about the just-off-balance-ness of the book and its characters' myriad attempts to compare and combine unlike elements than any straight verbal metaphor could. The clean lines of the diagram suggest a clarity and simple self-evidence that its awkward placement—both typographically and within its beveled/bedeviled analogy—then undercuts.

The care taken to maintain the aesthetic integrity of Addie's wedding dress is at darkly comic odds with the holey/unholy violations already visited on her face, and the readymade "mosquito bar" veil that attempts to hide them—as though laid upon her violated surface in cruel parody of the patternings of Faulkner's early Beardsley-inspired illustrations. This belated, stubborn mechanical fastidiousness is evinced as well in Cash's insistence on repairing the holes in the lid with painstakingly whittled wooden plugs,[42] reminiscent themselves of Jewel's eyes,[43] in lieu of easier and more effective aluminum squares. The juxtaposition of this mechanical meticulousness and the impul-

FIGURE 1.2. Coffin pictogram in *As I Lay Dying*.

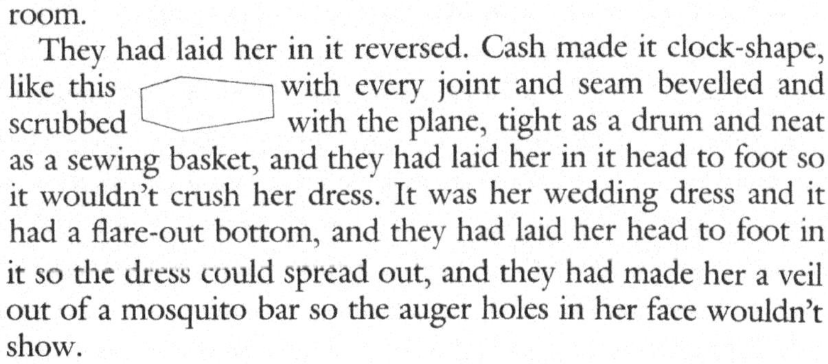

room.

They had laid her in it reversed. Cash made it clock-shape, like this ⬡ with every joint and seam bevelled and scrubbed with the plane, tight as a drum and neat as a sewing basket, and they had laid her in it head to foot so it wouldn't crush her dress. It was her wedding dress and it had a flare-out bottom, and they had laid her head to foot in it so the dress could spread out, and they had made her a veil out of a mosquito bar so the auger holes in her face wouldn't show.

Source: Faulkner, *As I Lay Dying*, 88.

sive, gruesome bodily violation it covers is the crux of both the novel's humor and horror.

An "auger," the instrument that makes the holes in Addie's body, of course verbally puns with "augur" in much the same slanted way that the misused coffin is akin to a toppled grandfather clock. In the auger/augur pun, a precision tool that missed its mark finds its (un)easy homonym in a word for the reading of portentous signs. Where an auger plots out points, an augur points to plots. In the coffin-shape/clock-shape slant analogy, the outlines of two sorts of timekeepers, both of which imply veneration, are put to improper use, with opportunistic, short-sighted axial shifts making a mockery of both craftsmanship and functionality. Neither a coffin with a corpse laid in reverse nor a weight-driven pendulum clock laid impotent on its side will, in Cash's oft-repeated word, "balance."[44] In each of the puns (visual and verbal) that this passage introduces, we can read the double graphic—clinical and corporeal, abstract and embodied, measured and mangled. As it oscillates back and forth quickly in a condensed space, this double graphic wreaks havoc on tone and makes for the novel's elusive dark comedy, its aggressive affective ambivalence, its identificatory impotence. Violated bodies are like broken clocks, carpentry is barely distinguishable from prophesy, and profane and sacred cease to be strictly opposed.

Faulkner's pictogram is also a diagram, an "inscription" or "graphism" of the sort Latour theorizes. It is an abstracted rendering of information, but one that, unlike a grid, cannot wholly crowd out a sort of descriptive representation: "A diagrammatic drawing is not wholly representational (some details are omitted so as not to overburden the design) but cannot be absolutely abstract (or the viewer would be unable to receive actual information)."[45] The diagram, straddling representation and abstraction, is defined by its two-dimensionality. It delivers information by flattening it. This flattening can be both destructive and generative. "The diagrammatic process could be imagined as a physical state or system being atomized into incorporeal abstract traits and then reconfigured into another state or system."[46] The trials and tribulations of the Bundren family, toting their diagrammatic totem, feels, as it progresses, increasingly like a sadistic obstacle course, human rats run through a maze by an unseen technician—which is indeed more or less how Faulkner described his attitude towards writing this, his most "deliberate" book.[47]

Critics have noted the mechanistic quality of the novel in a variety of ways.[48] John Tucker describes the coffin as "a type of primitive machine, which can be set in motion all too easily."[49] Its pictogram's effect, he argues, is "to undercut the inertial realism of narrative and to insist on the geometric abstraction of Faulkner's vision."[50] These descriptions of the function of Addie's coffin evoke one of Deleuze's many characterizations of the diagram: "a machine that is blind and mute but makes others see and speak."[51] In both form and content, then, the pictogram of the coffin makes Addie Bundren oddly, coldly, diagrammatically machine-like, even as she also is (or ought to be) at her most grotesque: as a decomposing corpse.

Through the coffin pictogram, Faulkner diagrams and defaces Addie—or perhaps re-faces her (clocks are hardly faceless). As Tucker notes, the diagramming of Addie's coffin seems to be a sort of catalyst for the transformations and reconfigurations its contents undergo in the rest of the text: "It is the reducing of Addie to the status of totem that prepares her for change. The coffin is threatened by metamorphic pressures from within as well as from without."[52] A diagram is a "flexible tool of research," which privileges one mode of identification (classification, definition, taxonomy) over another (empathy, emotional association).[53]

Jewel—one of the most discomfiting characters in the novel—is a walking, vertical version of Addie's coffin, down to the wooden plugs covering up the auger holes: "Jewel's eyes look like pale wood in his high-blooded face."[54] Jewel's face is the most oft-described in the novel and the one that most denies any ethics of recognition that would privilege the face as a portal of interpersonal connection.[55] It is an inorganic, fixed mosaic, seemingly capable of neither acknowledgment nor repudiation. It is hard to know how to read or react to it. The faces of *As I Lay Dying* are neither exemplars of a sort of Levinasian ethics nor of the radically open, phallic-nosed, gaping-mouthed grotesques of the Bakhtinian carnivalesque. They are flat, closed, stubbornly illegible. Jewel's face unnerves in part because we've seen it before—in the form of the flat board nailed onto the box that contains his mother's rotting corpse.

His body, like his face, is a thing of planar, wooden construction:

> [H]e is coming up the road behind us, wooden-backed, wooden-faced, moving only from his hips down. He comes up without a word, with his pale rigid eyes in his high sullen face, and gets into the wagon.[56]

In *As I Lay Dying,* coffin diagrams are not so much shaped like bodies as humans are all coffin diagrams. Jewel even comes to participate, in an off-kilter way, in the augur/auger pun. Armstid, a one-off narrator at whose farm the Bundrens spend a night during their journey, describes Jewel's face "shaking like he had a aguer."[57] "Auger" invokes "augur" invokes "aguer"—the letters turning their own subdued cartwheels within the word. Tool, portent, fever. Jewel is like a wooden box, and the box shudders with the paroxysms of ailments its putrefying inhabitant can no longer contract.

Roughly halfway through the novel, the diagram speaks. Addie's monologue chapter contains a white space—a hole—that seems to be her answer to the coffin pictogram in which she is earlier inscribed (and perhaps the holes posthumously augered into her face).[58] The visual compliment to the coffin pictogram is the blank absence that stands in for the "shape," "vessel," "jar" that is Anse, whose name the dead Addie Bundren narrates herself forgetting (Figure 1.3). She describes Anse becoming a word, a vessel, and then an absence as a process of violent three- to two-dimensional transformation and back again. Anse is a man liquefied into a cold molasses to fit into a flat word, which Addie then spins out into a rounded jar. None of these translations are described as easy or painless, though they are all, in the end, coolly impersonal (cf. the molasses).

Impersonality, for Sharon Cameron, occurs "when persons are represented in relation to a force that effaces what individuates them."[59] While Cameron posits definite and positive creative potential in impersonality, she also argues that "surrender to that power . . . is directly linked to violence."[60] Anse, who "did not know that he was dead, then," seems to go through the

FIGURE 1.3. Blank space in *As I Lay Dying,* as Addie tries to recall Anse's name.

the name of the jar. I would think: The shape of my body where I used to be a virgin is in the shape of a   and I couldn't think *Anse,* couldn't remember *Anse.* It was not that I could think of myself as no longer unvirgin, because I was three now. And when I would think *Cash* and *Darl* that way until their names would die and solidify into a shape and then fade away, I would say, All right. It doesn't matter. It doesn't matter what they call them.

Source: Faulkner, *As I Lay Dying,* 173.

process of bodily putrefaction from which Addie herself narrates, as she describes herself watching him grossly "liquify and flow" into the "motionless" graphic vessel that his name has become. Though for Cameron, the impersonal has a potentially liberatory "disintegrative" force,[61] Addie's alchemy of "im-personing" Anse is an act of graphic assessment and dimensional transmutation that feels, for all its liquidity, calcifying in the end—perhaps its own sort of retributive justice on her part.

Erin Edwards asserts that

> Addie's absent body functions as an epistemological aporia, a blind spot that undoes the certainty of medical diagnosis and knowledge about the body. . . . [T]he novel erodes such certainty, showing that which escapes inscription— the body's dimensionality, its densities and volumes, the "terrific hiatus[es]," to use Darl's phrase, that comprise bodily existence.[62]

I disagree. Three-dimensionality, density, and volumes are precisely what the coffin diagram abstracts out of the picture. None of the bodies in *As I Lay Dying* are classically smooth and balanced, but neither are they are allowed the boundless overflow of the Bakhtinian grotesque. Nor are readers fully able to access the "secret liberation" of staging a revolting revolt against rationalism and systematism by facing down the horrifyingly absurdity of an estranged world à la Kayser.[63] Addie remains in her wooden box. By the end of the novel, she is replaced by another Mrs. Bundren who carries her own—in the form, evocatively, of a graphophone:[64] an early technology of mass mechanical impersonality pours people into and out of resonant wooden boxes.[65]

Miss Lonelyhearts: "A Novel in the Form of a Comic Strip"

Three years after *As I Lay Dying* came Nathanael West's *Miss Lonelyhearts* (1933), a very different novel, now equally consecrated within the canon of the American grotesque. In his introduction to a recent edition of the book, Jonathan Lethem calls it a "nihilistic, hysterical, grotesque-poetic frieze" and "a mercilessly unsympathetic novel on the theme of sympathy."[66] According to West, he originally planned to subtitle the book "A novel in the form of a comic strip":

> The chapters to be squares in which many things happen through one action.
> The speeches contained in the conventional balloons. I abandoned this idea,

> but retained some of the comic strip technique: Each chapter instead of going forward in time, also goes backward, forward, up and down in space like a picture. Violent images are used to illustrate commonplace events. Violent acts are left almost bald.[67]

Elsewhere, he notes that "in America violence is idiomatic."[68] In *Miss Lonelyhearts*, we might say, West structurally weds one American idiom (violence) to another (the comic strip), while choosing as his subject matter a third (the personal advice column). The omnidirectionality of the comic strip, which he hoped to retain in the novel, begs a closer examination here not just for the ways in which *Miss Lonelyhearts* functions spatially "like a picture," but more specifically for the grid that is the backbone of the comics page.

A year after the publication of *Miss Lonelyhearts*, John Dewey described the function of the grid like this: "[N]ew patterns are almost automatically constructed. The squares run now vertically, now horizontally, now in one diagonal, now in another."[69] Yet while the grid allows for multidirectional temporal interactions, its spatial fixity is implicated in the violence with which West fills it. The unyielding, flat boundedness of "squares in which many things happen through one action" requires that "violent acts are left almost bald." There is no room for the explanatory strands that would lend them cover, texture, or warmth. Critics remarked on this unnerving baldness of West's violence when the first installments of the stories that would become the novel were published in the journal *Contact*. In *The Criterion*, edited by T. S. Eliot, reviewer Hugh Sykes Davies dismissed the work's "attitude of impersonal observation, of scientific and photographic reproduction."[70] West's attitude, featuring descriptive details stripped of narrative cushion, means that the reader's horrified reaction is not "anticipated and catered for in a proper way."[71] Or, as Goodwin rephrases Davies's complaint, *Miss Lonelyhearts* suffers from a "hypertrophy in description and a corresponding atrophy of narrative."[72]

Scott McCloud argues that a certain sort of baldness actually facilitates identification in comics themselves. Cartooning, he posits, is "a form of amplification through simplification" that allows readers to put themselves in the place of the simple line-drawn characters they see. "When you enter the world of the cartoon—you see yourself."[73] For McCloud, the comics form implicates the vaunted objectivity of more "scientific" grids as well. When we see a sequence of images in bounded boxes, we pull them together into a narrative through what McCloud calls "closure": "the phenomenon of seeing the parts but perceiving the whole."[74] Comics work through and across gaps, and we as readers fill them in from our own reserves of imagination. Closure "allows us to connect" the medium's "jagged, staccato rhythm of unconnected moments" and, in doing so "mentally construct a continuous, unified reality."[75] The engine of closure is "the agent of change, time, and motion."[76]

These affordances in turn make us "willing and conscious *collaborator*[s]."[77] "Every act committed to paper by the comics artist is aided and abetted by a silent accomplice, and equal partner in crime known as the reader."[78] Narrative and affective closure are both tasks that West moves almost entirely into the reader's column in *Miss Lonelyhearts*. As Justus Nieland notes, "West regularly refuses to provide the affective codes that might give his reader a clue about how to feel."[79] Nieland assesses this problem of affective closure as one of distance:

> [I]n *Miss Lonelyhearts,* our laughter, like our sympathetic identification with either the subject or the object of the violence, is foreclosed—stalled by the scene's suspended presentation as neither fully proximate, inviting sympathy and pity, nor sufficiently distant, allowing a consoling disidentification. This is the tyranny of materiality in Lonelyhearts's world: things are once too near and too far, never fully appearing, but never really disappearing either.[80]

The parade of misfortunes that Miss Lonelyhearts receives as letters are destined for translation into the gridded space of the newspaper page and the pat uplift formulae of the advice column. West envisioned the plotting of his book as a series of square modules, meant to be equally legible in any direction. Within the novel, Miss Lonelyhearts, too, is in the business of geometrically plotting the "square modules" of the individual cases of desperation and deformity he receives in the form of letters onto the coordinate plane of the newspaper page.

This movement from life to grid illuminates some of the grid's key attributes, according to Hannah Higgins: its visualization of the fraught relationship between part and whole, individualization and universalism; and the dilemma of settling on the correct spectatorial distance from which to take in and evaluate both at once.

> Grids would be said to state the opposition between the detail and the totality, the chaotic and the ordered, and the individual and society geometrically, as a relationship between the square module (or what it contains) and the grid. This opposition is resolved by the homogenizing power of the gridded field.[81]

The letter-writers' stories are both painfully specific and, once slotted into Miss Lonelyhearts's/*Miss Lonelyhearts*'s grid, made to be homogenously typical, known only by their signatory epithets like "Desperate" and "Broad Shoulders":

> The letters' ontological ambiguity (are they material manifestations of singular ills or codified abstractions of universal suffering?) means that, much like vaudeville comedy and the New Humor, they oscillate between social embeddedness and disembeddedness—pulled, like Lonelyhearts himself, between negotiating affective particularity and embracing putative universals.[82]

Where Nieland, above, ties the oscillation to the dynamics of vaudeville comedy and the New Humor, though, I would argue that the doubly graphic structure of the novel's gridwork undergirds its unnerving affect and makes it sit awkwardly within the canon of the American grotesque. This affective ambivalence of the novel comes less from the various "Desperate" and "Broad Shoulders" being made the butts of jokes than from them being gridded as entries into the abstracted structure of a coolly geometric sort of knowledge, tied inextricably to the mass media "typing" of newspaper and comic strip alike.

Miss Lonelyhearts is a novel full of cruel, often convulsive mistranslations between two- and three-dimensionality. Characters' faces are unnaturally flat, while things that ought to remain safely planar become grotesquely animate. Against a gray sky that "looked as if it had been rubbed with a soiled eraser," Miss Lonelyhearts watches a newspaper fly through the air "like a kite with a broken spine."[83] This unsettling anthropomorphic shape returns as an image for a woman, a solace seeker lifted from the pages of the Lonelyhearts column, who contacts Lonelyhearts and arranges to meet him in person:

> He thought of Mrs. Doyle as a tent, hair-covered and veined, and of himself as the skeleton in a water closet, the skull and cross-bones on a scholar's bookplate. When he made the skeleton enter the flesh tent, it flowered at every joint.[84]

Meanwhile the sky remains a flat, failed surface for graphic inscription: "Still thinking of tents, he examined the sky and saw that it was canvas-colored and ill-stretched."[85]

When women aren't flesh tents, they're stylizing machines or geometric pieces of architecture: "She [Shrike's wife] was wearing a tight, shiny dress that was like glass-covered steel and there was something cleanly mechanical in her pantomime."[86] Jonathan Greenberg argues of West's later novel, *The Day of the Locust*, that "a grotesque image of the human body—meaty, pockmarked, excessive—serves to reaffirm, through the revulsion it elicits, Tod's human, even sympathetic, relation to Faye."[87] But in *Lonelyhearts*'s vision of Mrs. Doyle's body as a "flesh tent," West flattens, stretches, and mounts it upon an inflexible frame. This is not a reaffirmingly revulsive image of the human body, and neither is the later figuration of Mrs. Shrike as modern skyscraper qua automaton. Their planar violence crowds out the three-dimensional space that seems necessary for grotesque disgust to resolve—or revolve—itself into release.

The novel's most aggressively two-dimensional character is Shrike, Miss Lonelyhearts's editor and nemesis, who speaks only in deadpan and turns all of Lonelyhearts's aspirations for sympathetic connection into ammunition for his rapid-fire jokes. Critics who have argued that Shrike "functions as grotesquery's spokesman"[88] in the novel miss the significance of his defining physical characteristic: fixity. His face and affect are both pure planar geometry:

> Although his gestures were elaborate, his face was blank. He practiced a trick used much by moving-picture comedians—the dead pan. No matter how fantastic or excited his speech, he never changed his expression. Under the shining white globe of his brow, his features huddled together in a dead, gray triangle.[89]

West at once personifies the parts and dehumanizes the whole of Shrike's face. His features become either actors on a stage or suspects in an interrogation room, crammed together "under the shining white globe of his brow." All together, they shape a flat geometrical figure: "a dead, gray triangle." West's description of Shrike's face again participates in grid logic: a "dead, gray triangle" that is also a crowd of features is both particular and universal. Shrike weaponizes his cinematic deadpan against Miss Lonelyhearts's ostensibly sincere, if fraught, quest for sympathetic identification with his reader- (and writer-) ship.[90] His "dead, gray triangle" "visualize[s] the communicative estrangement [that] lies frozen at the icy heart of the novella."[91]

Virus-like, Shrike's deadpan seems to replicate its not-quite-living self throughout the novel. When Lonelyhearts comes across a group of young male friends swapping increasingly explicit rape jokes at a speakeasy, West notes that,

> like Shrike, the man they imitated, they were machines for making jokes. A button machine makes buttons, no matter what the power used, foot, steam or electricity. They, no matter what the motivating force, death, love or God, made jokes.[92]

The machining of people is central to the novel, both thematically and structurally. Nieland argues that Shrike's deadpan, in its "shrewd mockery of Lonelyhearts's instrumentalization of feeling" is the book's richest critical gesture, "stalling while staging the violence of an Enlightenment ideology of affect that would secure community through sympathy or the logic of identity that subtends identification."[93] The double graphic at large disrupts affect by surfacing the violence inherent in certain modes of condescending sympathetic identification.

The face with which Lonelyhearts briefly believes he has secured "community through sympathy" is described as hardly a face at all. Peter Doyle, the disabled husband of the woman described as a flesh tent, finds Miss Lonelyhearts in the speakeasy after the advice columnist's liaison with Mrs. Doyle:

> The cripple had a very strange face. His eyes failed to balance; his mouth was not under his nose; his forehead was square and bony; and his round chin was like a forehead in miniature. He looked like one of those composite photographs used by screen magazines in guessing contests.[94]

The imbalance of Doyle's face recalls Addie's coffin in *As I Lay Dying*. Through these diagrammatic figures, West and Faulkner both play on the tantalizing resonance, the temptation of drawing an etymological connection between imbalance and ambivalence. The failure of faces—be they of coffins or humans—to "balance" seems to cause affective response to teeter and oscillate as well. Doyle's face presents Lonelyhearts—and the novel's readers—with a puzzle of identification. Analogized to a guessing game in which contestants must dissect and reclassify a collage of the sliced up facial features of larger-than-life public figures, his face is somehow not even the sum of its parts. It indexes mass media and publicity, not his own individuality. It's as if the adamant protuberances of the first half of the description are flattened, pressed between the cheap pages of a magazine, in the second.

The description also evokes Lonelyhearts's earlier figure for his own hysteria: "a snake whose scales are tiny mirrors in which the dead world takes on a semblance of life."[95] Lonelyhearts can only, it seems, feel sympathetic connection with Mr. Doyle once he rewrites the cripple's face as a reflection of his own, beaming back from the fractured surface of his own hysteria. To look into Doyle's face only to see a composite of other faces, potentially a fractured version of Lonelyhearts's own, suggests again the novel's—and, with it, the double graphic's— sympathy-stymying affective bind of both dimension and distance.[96]

Wise Blood: Linocut to the Quick

Flannery O'Connor, a self-proclaimed prophetic "realist of distances," who read and recommended Faulkner and West, was both a theorist and a practitioner of the American grotesque.[97] In her 1960 lecture on "Some Aspects of the Grotesque in Southern Fiction," O'Connor maps a vision of the grotesque as a mode of realism:

> I think the writer of grotesque fiction does [things] in the way that takes the least [doing], because in his work distances are so great. He's looking for one image that will connect or combine or embody two points; one is a point in the concrete, and the other is a point not visible to the naked eye, but believed in by him firmly, just as real to him, really, as the one that everybody sees. It's not necessary to point out that the look of this fiction is going to be wild, that it is almost of necessity going to be violent and comic, because of the discrepancies that it seeks to combine.[98]

O'Connor's surprisingly geometric definition of the grotesque, as it bridges beliefs and bodies, also gestures toward the previously overlooked graphic dimensions of key works in the American grotesque canon. I use "dimensions" advisedly here. O'Connor's cartography of the grotesque is grounded in a diagrammatic spatiality that is both representational (realism, regionalism) and abstract (prophecy, the realm of belief) and purposefully combines discrepant modes of dimensionality. This sort of spatiality has implications for affect, too.

Though O'Connor avers that the bridging of distances in grotesque fiction will be "violent and comic," her diagrammatic model has no room for sentiment, nor does it promise readerly satisfaction. She voices particular disdain for "compassion." Instead, "when the grotesque is used in a legitimate way, the intellectual and moral judgments implicit in it will have the ascendency over feeling."[99] The grotesque, in O'Connor's theorization of it, precludes saccharine compassion by insistently and without warning expanding, contracting, and collapsing a reader's sense of distance:

> In the novelist's case, prophecy is a matter of seeing near things with their extensions of meaning and thus of seeing far things close up. The prophet is a realist of distances, and it is this kind of realism that you find in the best modern instances of the grotesque.[100]

O'Connor's tone in her stories often evinces a combative flatness in line with this markedly geometric theory of the southern grotesque.

It is unsurprising, then, that her first aspiration was to be a cartoonist. She collected clippings from *The New Yorker*, filled store-bought scrapbooks with the carefully alphabetized work of her favorite artists, and even created her own homemade cartooning encyclopedia from loose-leaf lined paper bound together by brass fasteners.[101] She often sketched cartoons in pencil or pen and ink, but her favored medium was printmaking, particularly linoleum block printing. Linoleum block, or linocut, is a relief printing technique in which a design is cut into a sheet of linoleum with a sharp knife, chisel, or gouge. The uncarved surfaces, which remain raised, are inked using a brayer and then applied to paper either by hand or with a press. Unlike wood, on which the same carving and printing techniques can be used, linoleum blocks have no directional grain. The uncarved, inked surfaces thus create flat, matte planes of color.

In any printmaking medium, save offset lithography, the final print on paper is the mirror image of what the artist carves into the plate. In relief printing, as opposed to intaglio (in which the incised lines or sunken surfaces hold the ink after it is wiped away from the raised surfaces), the print is also the tonal negative of the carving. The lines an artist "draws" with a burin or knife into the surface of the linoleum—or wood, metal, rubber, or potato—will become, or remain, negative spaces of blank paper in the final print. Describing the linocut process in his introduction to a collected volume of O'Connor's cartoons, Barry Moser sums it up: "Whatever is cut away receives no ink, and thus those areas print as white lines or shapes. Nothing could be more direct or fundamental."[102] This isn't exactly right. Relief printing is a rather *in*direct way of image-making—multi-step, subtractive rather than additive, initially counterintuitive to anyone accustomed to drawing as a form of mark-making with ink. White surface has to be calculatingly carved out in order to be created. Jakub Zdebik writes that

> the feature shared by the text and image is the black line on a white surface. We can see how the simple, sober line is instrumental to classifying knowl-edge according to Michel Foucault: it filters out excessive elements from real-ity and translates the essential elements to the flat surface of the page.[103]

O'Connor's linocuts invert this "black line on a white surface" paradigm. In essence, she is "drawing" with whiteness. Moreover, the cutting actions that create the white lines and shapes in her prints distinguish her cartoons from the pedagogical/didactic mode they at first visually suggest: chalk on a black-board. This learning process is both more permanent and more violent than that.

O'Connor's prints embrace the zero-sum nature of the medium; she rarely attempts to feign halftones through drafting techniques like stippling or hatching. Where she adds patterning to the images, it is often via a skew gesture at perspective that ends up baffling our sense of space even further. Bodies and the surfaces on which they ostensibly rest are often disorientingly tessellated in O'Connor's cartoons. Our point of view seems to be both aerial and ground level at once (Figure 1.4). Planes, building façades, human faces that should be at right angles with one another in three-dimensional space are flatly splayed out for maximum visibility. Noses and fingers and penny loafer toes aggressively mirror and mimic one another as they protrude in white silhouette against black background (Figure 1.5).

In 1952, O'Connor published her first novel, *Wise Blood*, and one can see a relationship between her cartoons' visual logic and the text's descriptive

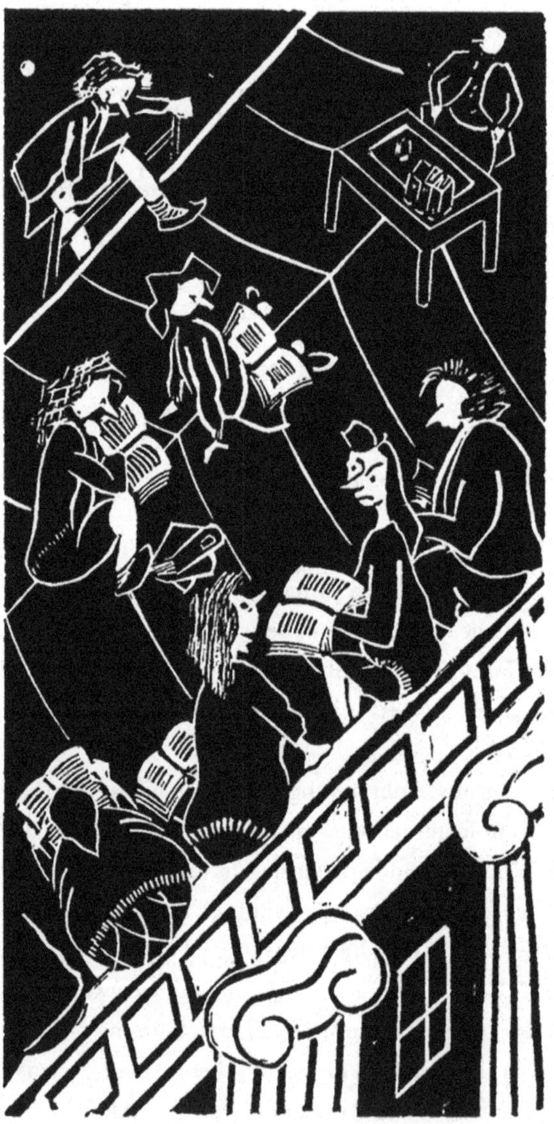

Source: O'Connor, *Flannery O'Connor: The Cartoons*, 46.

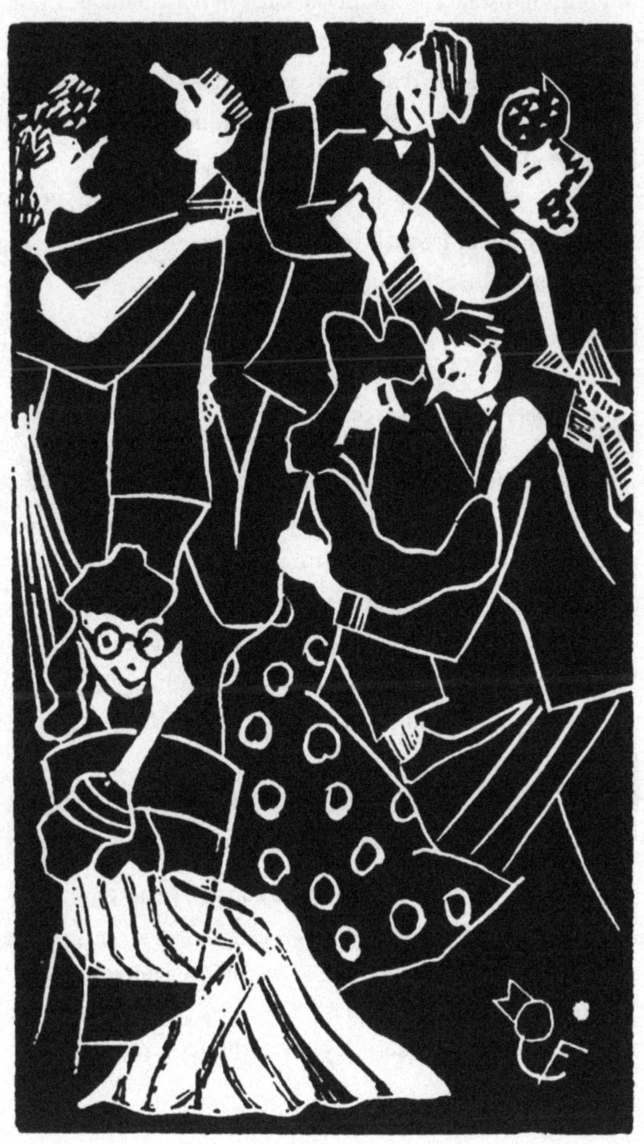

Source: O'Connor, *Flannery O'Connor: The Cartoons*, 34.

tendencies. Gary Ciuba calls *Wise Blood* a "portrait gallery of a novel," filled with faces that "lack both depth and completeness."[104] Kelly Gerald asserts that these "minimalist faces" "recall the faces in her cartoons, in their small, seed-like or ice-pick eyes, or in their exaggerated proportions."[105] The material process of O'Connor's favored mode of cartooning—a process of carving, cutting, and pressing—helps us revise our understanding of how she "flattens a three-dimensional world into two" in her writing.[106]

Hazel (Haze) Motes's face is among the novel's flattest. It is "placed-looking," "wooden," and frequently captured as seen through or against flat transparent or semitransparent planes:

> His face behind the windshield was sour and frog-like; it looked as if it had a shout closed up in it; it looked like one of those closet doors in gangster pictures where someone is tied to a chair behind it with a towel in his mouth."[107]

"His face was so close to the glass that it looked like a paper face pasted there."[108] Motes's expressions seem printed on his countenance not so much by the mechanics of internal, three-dimensional feeling pushing outward from within, but rather according to the cutting and compressing logic of the linocut: "Hazel Motes's face might have been cut out of the side of a rock."[109] Hardly the generative protuberances of the Bakhtinian visage, Motes's features are negatively produced: They are the result of hard-edged excavation and mechanical (im)printing.

Anthony Di Renzo calls *Wise Blood* a "flawed" work because "it is too reductive."[110] He elaborates with his own comparison to printmaking:

> At its best it resembles Goya's *Caprichos*—a funny, frightening, black-and-white world with clever caricatures etched in acid. It is a miniature masterpiece; but it lacks color, subtlety, complexity, and humanity. O'Connor's use of the grotesque in *Wise Blood* does not have the range and depth of her later work. It is solely at the service of satire, not of characterization.[111]

Di Renzo compares *Wise Blood* to Goya's etchings (Figures 1.6 and 1.7), but this comparison is inapt: It's the wrong mode of printmaking. O'Connor never etched anything in acid. She dug into surfaces manually, using hand-held tools, not chemical baths. Moreover, Goya's famous etchings were in fact aquatints—lacking in color, to be sure, but capable of emulating the tonal variety and nuances of watercolor painting. Where an engraving uses a needle to make lines that will print in sold hues, aquatints use a powdered, acid-resistant rosin to achieve tonal variations.

Goya renders phantasmal horrors more horrible by setting them within a comprehensible three-dimensional space (even when fantastical demons are flying away with their hapless victims over a distant countryside). O'Connor's cartoons and her novel, by contrast, produce a planar opacity: An aggressive two-dimensionality paradoxically coincides with a process of three-dimensional, material laceration. Indeed, when Motes does finally etch himself, it's via a chemical inversion of Goya's printmaking process; he blinds himself not with acid, but with a corrosive alkaline, lye.

The face to which Motes's is most often compared in criticism is that of the "blind" preacher Asa Hawks—his nemesis, obsession, and dark double throughout the novel. I'm most interested, however, in the face of the figure that haunts Motes's pseudo-sidekick, Enoch Emory: the shrunken man. Emory first shows Motes the shrunken man in its museum display case. Motes's flat, wooden, "placed-looking" face uncannily overlays that of the desiccated corpse qua artifact:

> All [Enoch] could tell was that Hazel Motes's eyes were on the shrunken man.
> He was bent forward so that his face was reflected on the glass top of the case.
> The reflection was pale and the eyes were like two clean bullet holes.[112]

The meaning and distance of the preposition "on" in "Hazel Motes's eyes were on the shrunken man" shifts uneasily over the course of those three sentences: Hazel Motes gazes upon the object. Hazel Motes gazes upon his own reflection. Hazel Motes isn't even the subject of the sentence. His eyes are. They jump away from his corpus within the syntactical body of the sentence. His eyes are transposed upon, then into, the body of the shrunken man by the flat double exposure of the reflective-transparent glass case, even as the descriptive diction of "like two clean bullet holes" evokes Addie Bundren's drilled face. The evacuation of possessive pronouns in the following sentences causes "the eyes" to seem to float as much syntactically as visually.[113] Whose eyes? Whose reflection?

Then, in a flash, both faces merge with that of the woman at whom Enoch habitually peeps, from the bushes, while she swims:

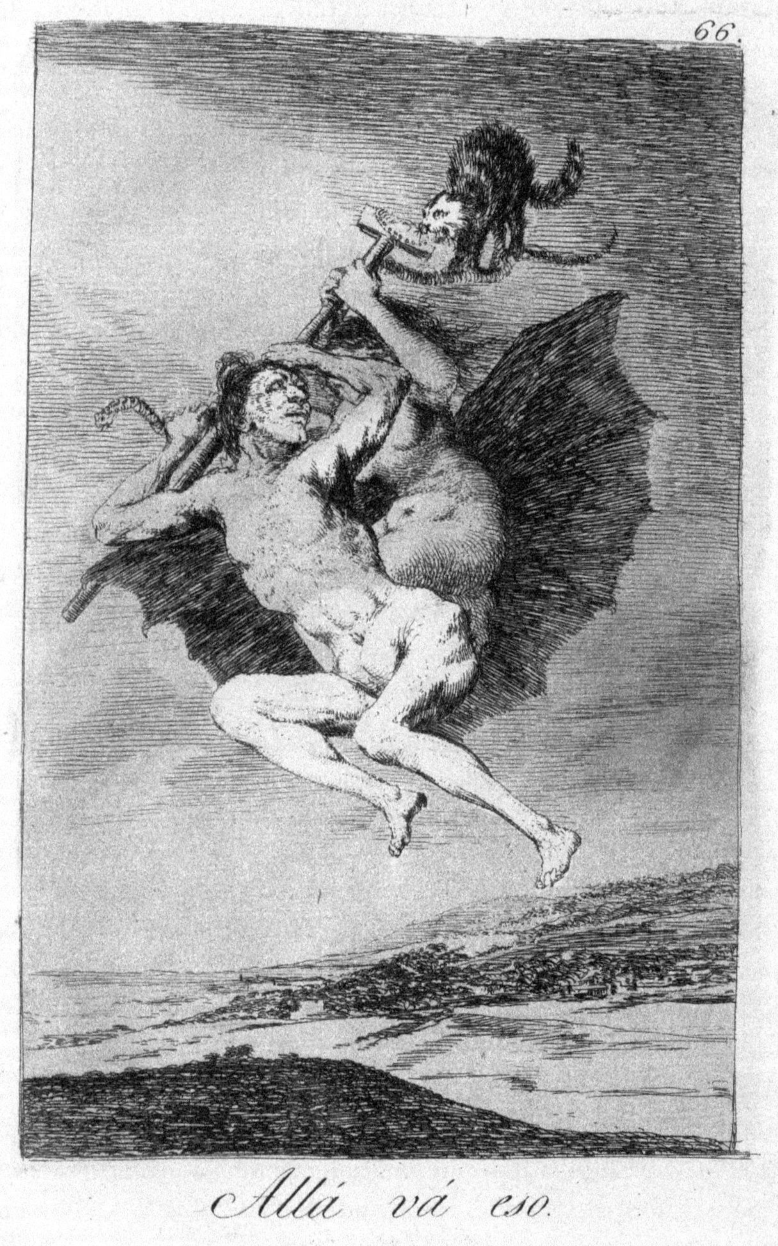

FIGURE 1.6. Francisco de Goya's "Capricho no. 66": *Allá va eso (There It Goes).*

Source: Met Museum.

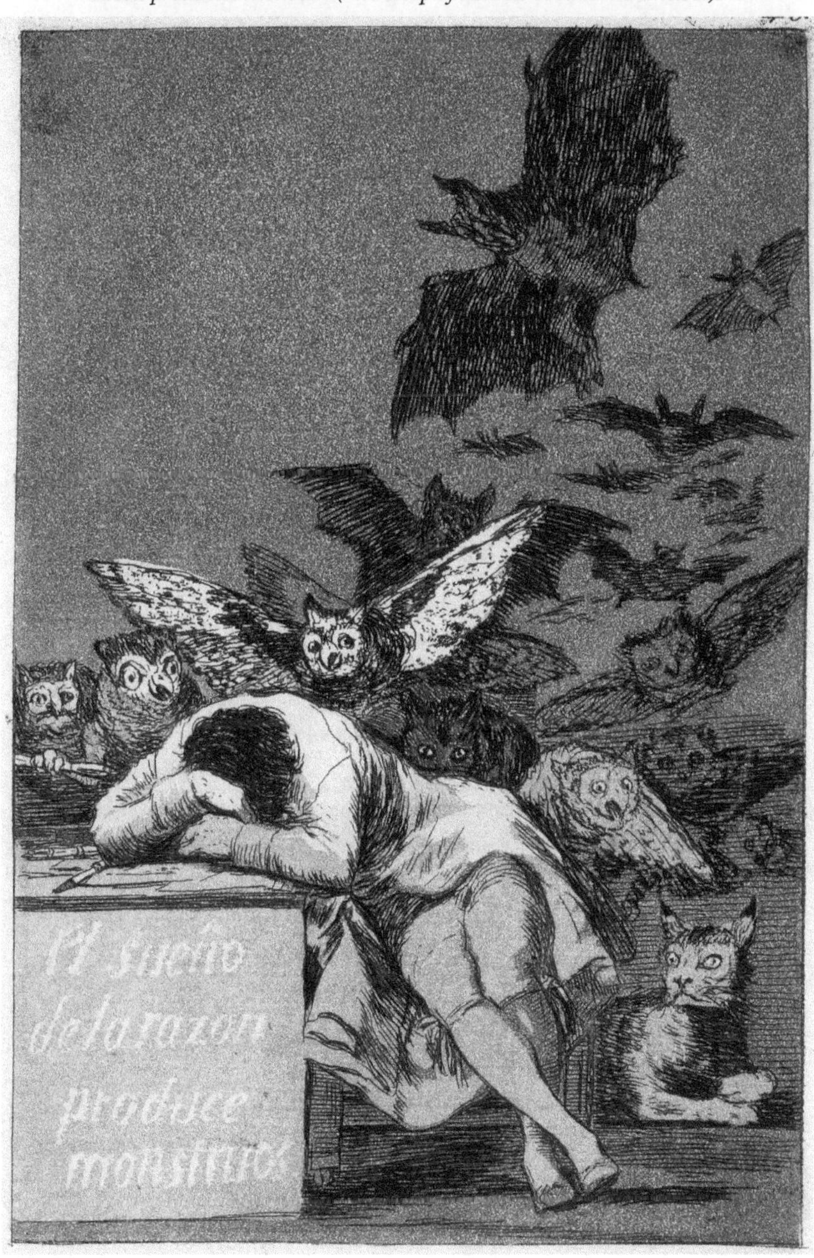

Source: Met Museum.

> She stopped on the other side of the case and looked down into it and the
> reflection of her face appeared grinning on the glass, over Hazel Motes's. . . .
> When Haze saw her face on the glass, his neck jerked back and he made a
> noise. It might have come from the man inside the case. In a second Enoch
> knew it had.[114]

The glass case, accompanied by a typewritten placard "telling all about" the
artifact, yet conveying none of the mystical knowledge that Emory desires,
wreaks havoc upon subject/object distinctions.[115] It flatly evacuates the visual
distance between them. While it is enshrined in the museum (or "M V S E V
M"[116]), that hallowed ground of classificatory scientific archiving, its glass case
works a sort of alchemy upon Motes and the object both, playing visual tricks
with distance and dimensionality. The face of the shrunken man confoundingly seems to produce the most affective charge of any visage in the novel,
right up until the moment that it punctures, empties, and flattens.

Nor is this the only time that a flat, reflective surface transposes Motes's
eyes onto those of the shrunken man. Sabbath Hawks is moved to a mock
maternal love of the thing. We begin with a description of the state of its face
after the ordeal of its theft from the museum case by Emory:

> One side of his face had been partly mashed in and on the other side, his eyelid
> had split and a pale dust was seeping out of it. . . . She had never known anyone
> who looked like him before, but there was something in him of everyone she
> had ever known, as if they had all been rolled into one person and killed and
> shrunk and dried.
>
> She held him up and began to examine him and after a minute her hands
> grew accustomed to the feel of his skin. Some of his hair had come undone
> and she brushed it back where it belonged, holding him in the crook of her
> arm and looking down into his squinched face. His mouth had been knocked
> a little to one side so that there was just a trace of a grin covering his terrified
> look. She began to rock him a little in her arm and a slight reflection of the
> same grin appeared on her own face. "Well I declare," she murmured, "you're
> right cute, ain't you?"[117]

Its off-kilter face seems to impel mimicry from Sabbath's own. Its composite
nature, "as if they had all been rolled into one person and killed and shrunk
and died," is reminiscent of the unsettling impersonality/universality of Mr.
Doyle's face in *Miss Lonelyhearts*.

And then Motes, wearing his mother's glasses, examining his own deeply lined face, spies it/himself/her/them in the mirror:

> There was a small white-framed mirror hung on the back of the door and he made his way to it and looked at himself. His blurred face was dark with excitement and the lines in it were deep and crooked. The little silver-rimmed glasses gave him a look of deflected sharpness, as if they were hiding some dishonest plan that would show in his naked eyes. His fingers began to snap nervously and he forgot what he had been going to do. He saw his mother's face in his, looking at the face in the mirror. He moved back quickly and raised his hand to take off the glasses but the door opened and two more faces floated into his line of vision; one of them said, "Call me Momma now."
>
> The smaller dark one, just under the other, only squinted as if it were trying to identify an old friend who was going to kill it.[118]

The novel continually stymies attempts to "identify"; this effort finally metastasizes in the figure of the shrunken man in the mirror. Filled only with "pale dust," a flat skin unnaturally stuffed, it seems to be the only body, and the only face, that other characters impute volition to, and feel any emotional draw towards, even as they consistently misclassify it. Motes—or, more accurately, his hand[119]—tries and fails to make contact with the flat face in the mirror. "The hand that had been arrested in the air moved forward and plucked at the squinting face but without touching it."[120] He settles, instead, for violence against the three-dimensional body:

> [I]t reached again, slowly, and plucked at nothing and then it lunged and snatched the shriveled body and threw it against the wall. The head popped and the trash inside sprayed out in a little cloud of dust.[121]

He throws the skin, emptied of its dust, out the door, a thirty-foot drop that used to house a fire escape.

Motes's interactions with the shrunken man in the mirror feel uncomfortably like the affective dynamics O'Connor sets up between her readers and characters. In these moments, Motes is an odd sort of reader surrogate, trying to identify and be identified with/by the grotesque figure coolly flattened out in the mirror, yet stymied by its impossible distance and dimensionality. At the end of the novel, a disillusioned Emory gives the shrunken man a racial epithet—"a dead shriveled-up part-nigger dwarf that had never done anything but get himself embalmed and then lain stinking in a museum the rest of his life."[122] This gives the political turn to the screw of this question of identification at the core of the novel's deployment of the grotesque.

The image of the faces of the racialized shrunken man, the luridly peeped-upon nameless woman, and Hazel Motes compressed in reflection upon the glass museum display case, bored through but not shattered by "the eyes [that] were like two clean bullet holes," captures the compounded difficulties of identification we find in moments of the double graphic. They show us that what is at stake in the affective ambivalence of the double graphic is the status of othered bodies—in a decidedly different, less cathartic way than in the grotesque.

The problem of affective distance and fraught identification that we see in Faulkner, West, and O'Connor is, ultimately a problem of dimensionality, surface, and depth; a series of topographic mismatches. The grotesque is an intensely three-dimensional, corpuscular, messy mode, preoccupied with protuberances, populated by people and things turned insides-out. Though its theorists have wrangled over its slipperiness—over the exact recipe of comedy and horror, carnival and uncanny that goes into creating its formal and thematic hybridity—they all agree that it evokes the affect of disgust and its action of gerundive release. The grotesque is repulsive, extreme, and in a constant state of "becoming" that violates boundaries and threatens established categories. If the grotesque was born in grottoes, however, then the double graphic transforms that dark, dank, fecund, and fearful cave into, confoundingly, both an opening and a Wile E. Coyote-esque *trompe l'oeil*—two-dimensional and three-dimensional at once, exposing tantalizingly gross interiors, baiting its would-be excavators to run violently headlong smack into unrelenting surface.[123]

The geometric faces qua topographic surfaces of *As I Lay Dying*, *Miss Lonelyhearts*, and *Wise Blood* coolly frieze/freeze the grotesque. In doing so, they arrest and render affectively ambivalent (even impotent) an aesthetic of disgusting, anarchic release by combining it with the classificatory, diagrammatic, cartographic gaze against which it was once an ostensible revolt. Graphic moments in American literature complicate the release theorists have argued is afforded by the disgust of the grotesque, leaving us caught up instead with the unresolved promise (and perversity) of a drive for identification that feels both too much and not at all.

2 The Ethnographic

IN *WHAT DO PICTURES WANT?*, W. J. T. Mitchell's study of the "libidinal fields" that pictures construct, he asserts that "images are like living organisms," infused with and inextricable from both desire and terror, "adoration and abomination."[1] Generated by and generating desire in "a mutually generative circuit," pictures themselves want, most of all, "to replicate themselves as images."[2] Mitchell explains the difference between pictures and images by appealing to both vernacular and scientific idioms: "[Y]ou can hang a picture, but you cannot hang an image,"[3] an image is to a picture as "species" is to "specimen."[4] The image is the abstracted, portable, replicable, symbolic content that is both distilled in and extractable from a singular picture. The picture, a solitary specimen of its species of image,

> wants to hold, to arrest, to mummify an image in silence and slow time. Once it has achieved its desire, however, it is driven to move, to speak, to dissolve, to repeat itself. So the picture is the intersection of two "wants": drive (repetition, proliferation, the "plague" of images) and desire (the fixation, reification, mortification of the life-form).[5]

The libidinal field of pictures is, in short, a thing of both frenzy and fixity. This intersection of seemingly paradoxical "wants" (meaning both lack and desire) is bound up with the oddly inanimate, yet animate-adjacent quality of images, those things that "can be lifted off the picture, transferred to another medium, translated into a verbal ekphrasis, or protected by copyright law."[6] Mitchell calls images "pseudo-life-forms":

> Thus when we talk about images as pseudo-life-forms parasitical on human hosts, we are not merely portraying them as parasites on individual human

beings. They form a social collective that has a parallel existence to the social life of their human hosts, and to the world of objects that they represent. That is why images constitute a "second nature." They are, in philosopher Nelson Goodman's words, "ways of worldmaking" that produce new arrangements and perceptions of the world.[7]

This chapter explores the pseudo-life-form that is the ethnographic image—in writing and in visual art—and the feelings that stick to and slide off of it. The ethnographic image is a creation of both fixity and frenzy, animated-yet-inanimate proliferation in American literature, eliciting unwieldy and ambivalent affective responses.

The particular mode of the double graphic that I am calling the ethnographic emerges when racialized bodies are violently transformed into flat figures—both in the sense of images and of calculable, manipulable quantities. The ethnographic is sentimental literature ghostwritten by the pseudoscientist—all the spectacle of violence and racially motivated brutality with none of the prescripted or prescribed affective release. To return to Eve Sedgwick's invocation of affective "texture" versus "texxture," the ethnographic figure is one that has been aggressively abraded of the latter, in which a racialized image becomes the sort of smooth object that "defiantly or even invisibly blocks or refuses" the tactile information "about how, substantively, historically, materially, it came into being."[8]

The nineteenth century, where this chapter begins, was both the heyday of sentimentalism and an age of increasing quantification. Good white female readers longed to weep at the grotesque tortures visited upon Black figures, while their husbands and brothers just as libidinally took to counting, graphing, and gridding as "sociology, ethnography, history, and the life sciences begin using quantitative methods."[9] Both sentimentalism and quantitative methods in the social sciences were, somewhat counterintuitively, exercises in abstraction.[10] To make bodies and feelings commensurable, either via the mechanisms of sentiment or statistics, "converts" (to borrow Joseph Entin's description of sympathy) "heterogeneity to homogeneity."[11]

At moments that embody this particular type of the double graphic, a text's "Africanist presence"[12] à la Toni Morrison becomes Mitchell's sort of image—libidinous, infectious, totemic; tantalizing, terrifying, and flat. In other words, a silhouette. The silhouette, as a technology, makes bodies into types—stereotypes and typefaces—ostensibly at once readily legible, accurate, and standardized. Silhouettes were traditionally images of absent—departed or dead—loved ones, displayed in the home as keepsakes and aide-mémoires. They hung on the walls of bourgeois homes as proof of want (both desire and lack) that nevertheless silently spoke to their possessors' relative economic comfort. As a technology of ostensibly objective transcription, the cut silhouette also held pride of place in racial science, vaunted as a different sort of self-evidence: that of the measurability of the essential internal inferiority of racialized types via the captured, graphic contours of the fixed profile. The silhouette is cut but can also cut.

An examination of the silhouette reveals how the identificatory bind of the double graphic, particularly when its subjects and objects are racialized others, derives from disconcerting mismatches between and across two- and three-dimensional figuration. Graphic feeling emerges when fully fleshed humans get flattened into two-dimensional geometry; or when what we thought were safely flat, fleshless diagrams and charts come to lumpy, grotesque life. The ethnographic silhouette both sharpens and subverts the structures of sympathy in unexpected ways. "Sympathy functions by establishing clear, virtually seamless lines of identification in which we understand other persons insofar as they represent what is most familiar and essential in ourselves."[13] In the doubly ethnographic texts that follow, lines of sympathetic identification become razor wire that are apt to catch and cleave us as we follow them.

Silhouettes are figures that can be both sentimental and statistical. Rich bodies of scholarship attest to the violence both sentimentalism and statistics have dissembled and disseminated when it comes to Black people who live, in Christina Sharpe's formulation, "in the wake" of chattel slavery in the United States. On the one hand, "sentimentalism," as Kyla Schuller argues, "in the midst of its feminized ethic of emotional identification, operates as a fundamental mechanism of biopower."[14] With its hallmark spectacles of violence and abjection, ostensibly aimed at cultivated fellow feeling and prompting morally upright political action, sentimentalism was at its effusively beating heart a "strategy of social control through embodiment . . . [a] mode of ideological management, [a] way of rhetorically containing potentially strange or threatening figures."[15] On the other hand, flattened statistics and diagrams, purportedly scrubbed of feeling, are often themselves violent in the way in which they make vulnerable human lives abstract and interchangeable and stand as the only archival traces we have of the victims of slavery. "The archive is, in this case, a death sentence, a tomb, a display of the violated body, an inventory of property, a medical treatise on gonorrhea, a few lines about a whore's life, an asterisk in the grand narrative of history."[16] In a perverse way the most violent part of this archive lies, according to Katherine McKittrick, not in the spectacular verbal recounting of violence, but in the antiseptic accounting of the horrific as the disinterestedly informational: "[T]his is where we begin, this is where historic blackness comes from: the list, the breathless numbers, the absolutely economic, the mathematics of the unliving."[17]

By tracing the figure of the silhouette through a canonically racist text, through the work of a contemporary visual artist, and finally through that original text's irreverent rewriting, this chapter explores what happens when the doubly sentimental and statistical scripts of the ethnographic collide and cut into one another, and the havoc it wreaks upon reading for and as identification. This chapter begins, as Toni Morrison prompts readers looking to unravel the way whiteness makes itself out of and against images of Blackness in American literature, with Edgar Allan Poe. His novel, *The Narrative of Arthur Gordon Pym of Nantucket*, exemplifies the inescapably flat, image-obsessed way in which the ethnographic makes raced bodies into objects of both clinical classification and visceral disgust—geometric and gruesome—at one and the same time. I then examine a contemporary reworking by an African American artist of the silhouetting mode of Poe's racist fever dream: Kara Walker's contemporary cut-paper silhouettes, which seem lifted from the pages of Poe's novel and set violently loose on gallery walls. And finally, I look at Mat Johnson's adaptation *Pym*, which retells, reverses, and refleshes Poe's text to discomfiting effect.

The Narrative of Arthur Gordon Pym of Nantucket

In her seminal 1992 work of literary criticism, *Playing in the Dark: Whiteness and the Literary Imagination*, Toni Morrison declares that "no early American writer is more important to the concept of American Africanism than Poe."[18] Edgar Allan Poe is Morrison's index case for "the ways in which a nonwhite, Africanlike (or Africanist) presence or persona was constructed in the United

States, and the imaginative uses this fabricated presence served."[19] She diagnoses Africanism as

> a disabling virus within literary discourse, [which] has become, in the Eurocentric tradition that American education favors, both a way of talking about and a way of policing matters of class, sexual license, and repression, formations and exercises of power, and meditations on ethics and accountability.[20]

As the "virus" spreads—following pathways set by early writers like Poe who were among the mad scientists, she asserts, that cooked it up—Africanism within American literature

> is the vehicle by which the American self knows itself as not enslaved, but free; not repulsive, but desirable; not helpless, but licensed and powerful; not history-less, but historical; not damned, but innocent; not a blind accident of evolution, but a progressive fulfillment of destiny.[21]

It is an engineered virus, in short, which inevitably reveals "the parasitical nature of white freedom."[22]

Poe's *The Narrative of Arthur Gordon Pym of Nantucket* was published in 1838, originally serially as an anonymous (and resoundingly unsuccessful) prank claiming to be an actual travelogue. It was Poe's only foray into the novel, a form that he despised. And it shows. The book is seemingly uninterested in continuity—of plot, time, or characters. As Cindy Weinstein puts it, "*Pym* operates according to a logic of what David Halliburton characterizes as 'bare seriality.'"[23] It also recycles, unattributed, large swaths of text from previously published travel narratives, such as Jeremiah N. Reynolds's *Voyage of the Potomac*.[24]

The story follows Arthur Gordon Pym, a blandly dissatisfied young white man who longs for adventure on the high seas. He nearly drowns on a drunken nighttime sail with his friend Augustus and stows away aboard Augustus's father's ship (*Grampus*). Then he nearly dies of starvation and rabid dog attack while hiding below deck, discovers that there has been a mutiny (led, in part, by the ship's Black cook), almost dies at the hands of the mutineers, gets shipwrecked again, cannibalizes one of the other survivors, gets rescued, sails toward the Antarctic, discovers a mysterious tropical island hiding amongst the ice floes and inhabited by a Blacker-than-Black race called the Tsalalians, barely escapes a massacre at the hands of these natives, and escapes in a canoe heading even farther south. The narrative abruptly ends when, still in the canoe, he sees an inexplicably immense, whiter-than-white humanoid figure looming in the distance. A postscript provides some unsatisfying explanations for a few of the phenomena Pym has witnessed on Tsalal and explains that the only survivor (Dirk Peters) cannot at present be reached for comment to corroborate or deny any of the preceding narrative. The novel's tone fluctuates as violently as does its plot, leaving readers temporally, narratively, and affectively disoriented.

Joan Dayan notes the affective whiplash effect of Poe's work in general. "All of Poe's fiction . . . moves rhetorically back and forth between extremes of affect (heartfelt devotion or undying love) and dispassion (cold mutilation or self-absorbed insensitivity)."[25] *The Narrative of Arthur Gordon Pym* is one of the most extreme examples of this characteristic oscillation. Affectively and temporally both, the novel showily rejects coherence. Many critics have commented on the chronological and geographic dysfunction of Poe's novel and have even tried to make painstaking sense of the capriciously inconsistent coordinates and dates that pepper the text.[26] I posit that the uncomfortably disjointed nature of the novel—emphasized time and again by its shifts into journal format, casually dispensing with norms of narrative causality—is of a piece with the two-dimensional ethnographic silhouettes that populate the text in lieu of characters. Texts like Poe's enable "the construction of a history and a context for whites by positing history-lessness and context-lessness for blacks."[27] This essentially ethnographic move narratively relies, in Michael A. Elliott's words, on the "ahistorical synchrony" of the present tense.[28] Part of the appeal of the silhouette as physiognomic evidence was the profile's ostensible imperviousness to time: "[T]he profile view served to cancel the contingency of expression; the contour of the head remained consistent with time."[29] The time of the silhouette, like the time of ethnography as a discipline, is defined by the disorientation of floating fixity.

Poe's text evokes, too, somewhat unexpectedly, the logic of the archive. As famously defined by Alan Sekula, the paradigm of the archive (in his case, collections of police photographs of criminal types) both eschews narrative and has the capacity to "reduce all possible sights to a single code of equivalence."[30] According to Sekula, the "pleasures" of archival reading are not the pleasures of narrative. There is, instead, a recombinant, even anagrammatic logic to what Sekula calls "archival play":

> The sequence could be rearranged; its temporality was indeterminate, its narrativity relatively weak. The pleasures of this discourse were grounded not in narrative necessarily, but in archival play, in substitution, and in a voracious optical encyclopedism.[31]

The Narrative of Arthur Gordon Pym qua archive is, in the ethnographic spirit of physiognomic and phrenological catalogues, structured along grid lines at once acquisitive, unbounded, playful, and violent.

"The Hybrid Line-Manager"

A character in Poe's novel comes to be a sort of composite ethnographic catalogue of one. Until the late arrival of the Tsalalians on the scene, the most static and racially marked character in the book is Dirk Peters, Pym's most faithful and persevering companion. Jared Gardner notes that he seems a "bizarre guide" for Pym to "explore the ultimate frontier of race" with, but, for that very reason, he is key to understanding the essentially chiaroscuro nature of race in Poe.[32] No other character, until we meet the Tsalalians, is described in such precise visual terms by the text. What Elliott writes of Melville's descriptions in *Typee* can as easily be applied to Poe's introduction of Peters here. "The scrupulous level of detail forces us to read the prose as an ethnographic account aspiring to mimetic accuracy":[33]

> This man was the son of an Indian squaw of the tribe of Upsarokas, who live among the fastnesses of the Black Hills, near the source of the Missouri. His father was a fur-trader, I believe, or at least connected in some manner with the Indian trading-posts on Lewis river. Peters himself was one of the most ferocious-looking men I ever beheld. He was short in stature, not more than four feet eight inches high, but his limbs were of Herculean mould. His hands, especially, were so enormously thick and broad as hardly to retain a human shape. His arms, as well as legs, were *bowed* in the most singular manner, and appeared to possess no flexibility whatever. His head was equally deformed, being of immense size, with an indentation on the crown (like that on the head of most Negroes), and entirely bald. To conceal this latter deficiency, which did not proceed from old age, he usually wore a wig formed of any hair-

like material which presented itself—occasionally the skin of a Spanish dog or American grizzly bear. At the time spoken of he had on a portion of one of these bearskins; and it added no little to the natural ferocity of his countenance, which betook of the Upsaroka character. The mouth extended nearly from ear to ear; the lips were thin, and seemed, like some other portions of his frame, to be devoid of natural pliancy, so that the ruling expression never varied under the influence of any emotion whatever. This ruling expression may be conceived when it is considered that the teeth were exceedingly long and protruding, and never even partially covered, in any instance, by the lips.[34]

Poe describes this "singular being" using a veritable catalogue of ethnographic analogy. Peters's skull is indented like "most Negroes," his countenance "bet[akes] of the Upsaroka character," his hairpiece could be made of "Spanish dog" or of "American grizzly bear," his amalgamated form "hardly . . . retain[s] a human shape." Despite the text's emphasis on Peters as the product of active and repeated intermixing—the son of an "Indian Squaw" and a "furtrader"—his defining physical characteristic is uncomfortable, unnatural stasis. His legs are inflexibly bowed, his mouth "devoid of natural pliancy." He seems permanently fixed—both in expression and, following a classic sense of ethnographic temporality, in time.[35]

Hinging on the mention of the "Upsaroka character" of Peters's face, the mode of description shifts halfway through the paragraph. The body parts the narrator taxonomizes are suddenly described not as Peters's own ("his hands . . . his arms"), but rather as those of a general type ("the mouth . . . the lips"). Peters's parts dislodge from the man as a whole and take on a classificatory identity of their own, a move that is particularly jarring as it lingers over his face, the ostensible site of individuality and ethical identification both. This change from the genitive to the definite article evokes both ethnographic discourse in general and the "science" of physiognomy in particular. As soon as American Indians are evoked and the description moves to a reading of the features of Peters's face, the man becomes an object under a more clinical form of study. The description moves from feeling like a grotesque vignette describing a spectacularly unique chimeric beast to a systematically impersonal analysis of a man as a fixed type.

If this shift seems to be catalyzed by the mention of Upsaroka Indians, its urgency comes from the approach of Peters's face. Physiognomic analysis of the character of a person based on the contours and geometry of their face was pioneered by Johann Kaspar Lavater in his wildly popular *Essays on Physiognomy.* The first American edition of Lavater's book, plentifully illustrated with reproductions of paintings, diagrams, and silhouette portraits, was published in Boston in 1794. By the mid-nineteenth century, there were over 150 editions in print.[36] Physiognomy is an exemplary graphic discipline, "producing interpretive knowledge and social consensus in and through graphic representations."[37]As Emma Rutherford explains,

> [Lavater's] proposal that silhouettes captured the very essence of man, particularly when taken mechanically, sparked a rash of physiognotrace machines being used across the country. It is possible that Lavater's theories were embraced even more passionately in America than in Europe, as the country attempted to define a national identity—a difficult task in a land constantly flooded by émigrés, who were seen as imposters by those who considered themselves already part of an established society.[38]

Traced and cut silhouettes in particular were considered superior to painted portraits for those "looking to discern and understand the human soul from the appearance of the face"[39] because they "emphasized the solid and presumably unalterable features of the face."[40] The conventional wisdom was that, in silhouetted profile, it was impossible for a sitter to alter or dissemble, through emotion or guile, the true evidence of his or her countenance and, thus, character. Lavater encouraged applying lines and grids to the silhouette in order to measure and calculate all the truths of interiority and character that its fixity revealed. Silhouettes, in this mode, were treated as images made to be engaged with abstractly, and, enabled by their lack of extraneous surface details, read clinically for extractable informational content. "With its inherent flatness and lack of surface verisimilitude, the silhouette could conform ideally to [a] tradition of scientific imagery such as anatomical crosscuts and maps."[41]

The vaunted empirical—and real economic—value of the cut silhouette increased in America with the 1802 patenting of the physiognotrace machine by James Isaac Hawkins and Charles Willson Peale (Figure 2.1).[42] Peale in-

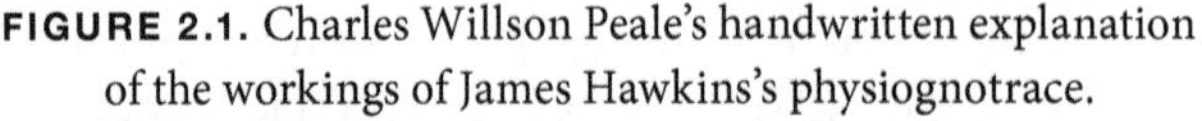

FIGURE 2.1. Charles Willson Peale's handwritten explanation
of the workings of James Hawkins's physiognotrace.

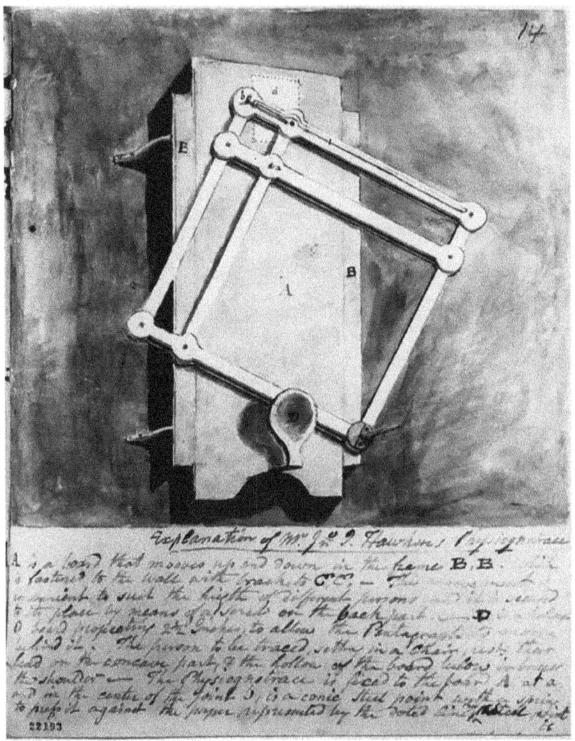

Source: Jefferson Papers, Library of Congress.

stalled the machine in his eponymous museum in Philadelphia, which was also distinguished by its early adoption of Linnaean taxonomy. Notably, the machine was frequently operated by Moses Williams, a Black man who was enslaved in the Peale household until his manumission at the age of twenty-eight.[43] In his mastery of the machine, as well as his other work within the museum, Williams was treated more as a curiosity than a craftsman (Figure 2.2). Positioned at the end of "The Long Room," whose walls were lined with neat grids of display cases, "he cut his silhouettes in a room where distorting mirrors provided the visitor with momentary amusement as a respite from science. His presence oscillated between display and performer."[44] When the museum hosted its now-famous 1802 exhibit of mastodon bones, Peale sent Williams dressed as an American Indian to pass out handbills on the streets of Philadelphia. Ellen Fernandez Sacco argues that Williams was put up, in these ways, "for the same scrutiny as the displays," consistently and carefully given a "subordinated status within a practice of visual order."[45] The archive ravenously ingests both commodified silhouette and its cutter.

Because Dirk Peters's face doesn't move, he is, in his unnatural rigidity, already perfectly primed for physiognomic analysis. Mary Douglas writes in *Purity and Danger* that

> the yearning for rigidity is in us all. It is part of our human condition to long for hard lines and clear concepts. When we have them we have to either face the fact that some realities elude them, or else blind ourselves to the inadequacy of the concepts.[46]

Peters embodies, in a grotesque three-dimensional form, the fulfillment of both the desire for rigidity and its inadequacy. In Poe's ethnographic fantastic, Peters is the unsettling, ossified product of the crossing and compounding of racial boundaries.

FIGURE 2.2. This silhouette, attributed to Raphaelle Peale, is of Moses Williams, "cutter of profiles."

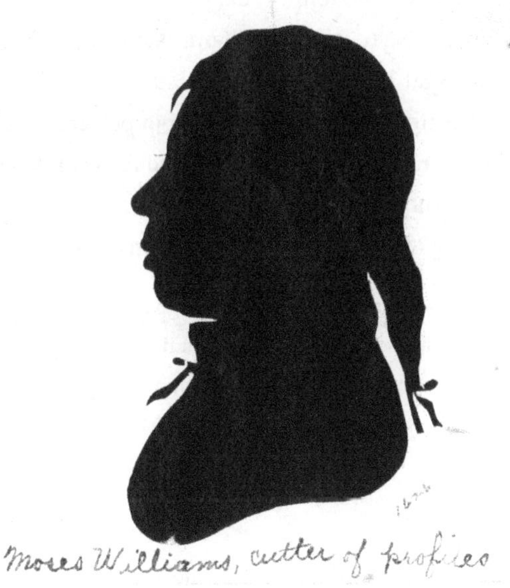

Source: Library Company of Philadelphia.

Peters confounds by seeming to compound too many racial types in one body. He is both too static ("devoid of natural pliancy") and too animated ("the conduct of the hybrid appeared to be instigated by the most arbitrary caprice alone"). This ambivalence is constitutive of the stereotype not in spite of, but rather because of, its emphasis on "fixity." As Homi Bhabha suggests, "fixity, as the sign of cultural/historical/racial difference in the discourse of colonialism, is a paradoxical mode of representation: it connotes rigidity and an unchanging order as well as disorder, degeneracy and daemonic repetition."[47] The stereotype, as the "major discursive strategy" of colonial fixity, is "a form of knowledge and identification that vacillates between what is always 'in place,' already known, and something that must be anxiously repeated."[48] Racial stereotypes, like precariously animate silhouettes, are anything but self-sufficient. They must be propped up and (shadow) puppeted: "The colonial stereotype is a complex, ambivalent, contradictory mode of representation, as anxious as it is assertive."[49] An image par excellence, à la Mitchell, the stereotype forms its own libidinal field, following its own not-quite-biological imperative to replicate.

Peters, in his "arbitrary caprice" (which Pym loves to assert verbally, though we as readers rarely actually see in action) and with physical features seemingly frozen in a state of emotive extremity that renders them illegible, is also an exemplar of what Sianne Ngai calls "racial animatedness." In her description of this "ugly feeling," Ngai lingers on puppets, suggesting that animatedness is "the translation, into affect, of a state of being 'puppeteered.'" This is evinced in "the disturbingly enduring representation of the African-American as at once an excessively 'lively' subject and a pliant body unusually susceptible to external control."[50] This feeling is an "ugly" one, she explains, because

> as an exaggerated responsiveness to the language of others that turns the subject into a spasmodic puppet, in its racialized form animatedness loses its generally positive associations with human spiritedness or vitality and comes to resemble a kind of mechanization. At the same time, the minimal affect is turned into a form of emotional excess, and similarly stripped of its intentionality.[51]

The animated figure is both too full of flesh and feelings and too mechanistic. Schuller largely reiterates Ngai's argument through the framework of impressibility, which racialized people were purported to lack within what she terms the nineteenth-century American "biopolitics of feeling." "The racialized were assigned the condition of unimpressibility, or the impaired state of throwing off affects but being incapable of being affected by impressions themselves."[52] Dirk Peters embodies, in a fairly literal way, unimpressibility. His face is a mask of violent expression that seems not to change in reaction to external stimuli.

Dirk Peters is often called simply "the hybrid," or because of his job on the soon-to-be-shipwrecked *Grampus*, "the hybrid line-manager." When Augustus, Pym, Peters, and Richard Parker (a fourth survivor of the ill-fated vessel) are shipwrecked after the mutiny, Peters becomes nearly fatally tangled up in—and violently fixed by—the very material lines he ostensibly once managed. After the *Grampus* sinks, the survivors lash themselves to the shipwreck to keep from being tossed out to sea over the turbulent night.[53] While "this precaution alone saved us from destruction," it also imperils them when they wake to discover that the lines have been drawn dangerously tight overnight by the elements, even threatening to dismember Peters.[54] Setting aside for a moment the double meaning of "lashing" (at once securing and beating), what is most intriguing about the spectacle Poe gives us of Pym, Peters, Augustus, and Parker tied to the detritus of the shipwreck is how evocative it is of a sort of violent mapping. It's as if they've all been charted, inscribed with and by lines that cut too deep to be safely managed. Cut geometrically across at so many junctures, the men's bodies become analogous both to cadavers on the slab and territories on the map.

> My left arm had broken loose from its lashings, and was much cut about the elbow; my right was entirely benumbed, and the hand and wrist swollen prodigiously by the pressure of the rope, which had worked from the shoulder downward. I was also in great pain from another rope which went about my waist, and had been drawn to an insufferable degree of tightness. Looking round upon my companions, I saw that Peters still lived, although a thick line was pulled so forcibly around his loins as to give him the appearance of being cut nearly in two; as I stiffed, he made a feeble motion to me with his hand, pointing to the rope. . . . It had cut a deep gash through the waistband of his woolen pantaloons, and through two shirts, and made its way into his groin, from which the blood flowed out copiously as we removed the cordage.[55]

Pym's hands and wrists, lashed by the lines of the all-but-sunken ship, are grotesquely swollen, making them physically akin for a moment to Peters's ("so enormously thick and broad as hardly to retain a human shape").[56] Peters, meanwhile, is himself excruciatingly nearly bisected by the lines, his "hybridity" made graphically literal as the rope threatens to rend him asunder.

This scene of men bound to the wreckage evokes Mitchell's reflections on the double meaning of "drawing":

> [A]s an act of tracing or inscribing lines, on the one hand, and an act of pulling, dragging, or attracting, on the other, as when we talk of a horse-drawn buggy, drawing water from a well, drawing back a bowstring to release the arrows of desire, or "drawing and quartering" a human body in that most grotesque form of capital punishment.[57]

Poe draws (and quarters) his characters with ruthless, impersonal specificity as they float amidst the wrecked *Grampus*, anticipating the manner in which they will be called upon, in a matter of pages, to do the same to each other (when the time comes for cannibalization). Mitchell's parsing of drawing as tracing, attraction, and punishment brings up, too, in this context, the double meaning of "lashings." Poe plays out an odd frieze of a whipping scene on the nearly sunken decks of the *Grampus*. The character who is the most violently lashed is Dirk Peters.

Even in this context, the nonwhite Peters seems to attract a unique intensity of both description and violent inscription; the line cuts a "deep gash" starting at his genitals, leaving him graphically more passive and prone than his fellow survivors. Bhabha describes the action of the racist gaze as a similar type of flaying, "Black skin splits under the racist gaze, displaced into signs of bestiality, genitalia, grotesquerie, which reveal the phobic myth of the undifferentiated whole white body."[58] Peters's potential castration can't help but evoke, too, assertions by Poe's contemporaries about the biological analogies between mulattoes and mules vis-à-vis sterility.[59] Pointing to the (probably apocryphal) etymological origin of the word "mulatto" in "mule,"[60] Josiah Nott in fact defined "mulatto" as a "hybrid" and asserted that this meant "the offspring of two distinct species—as the mule from the horse and the ass," going on to warn his peers in the nineteenth-century medical establishment about the threats of degeneration and sterility in this "stock."[61] The plotting of the latter half of the novel requires Peters to become white (more on this in a bit), and so never to have had any Black blood in him, yet here (as with the analogy to "the heads of most Negroes" in the earlier description) Poe draws Peters in a way that suggests otherwise.[62] As the novel progresses, Peters becomes both an ostensible wrench in and an invaluable tool for grasping Poe's binary racial logic. He is the consummate, conglomerate other until, faced with an even more confounding Blackness, he suddenly isn't. Peters's journey towards provisional whiteness begins with a gruesome (shadow) puppet show.

"A Large Hermaphrodite Brig": Shadow Puppetry at Sea
When Pym et al. manage to get free of the constraints of their lashings, they find themselves adrift, alone, and starving on the high seas. In the distance, heading toward them, they spy what seems like salvation: "a large hermaphrodite brig, of a Dutch build, and painted black, with a tawdry gilt figure-head." Pym couches his account of the encounter with "I relate these things and circumstances minutely, and I relate them, it must be understood, precisely as they *appeared* to us," implying, not subtly, that appearances are soon to betray them.[63] The men spy a welcoming figure on the deck of the ship:

> This last was a stout and tall man, with a very dark skin. He seemed by his manner to be encouraging us to have patience, nodding to us in a cheerful although rather odd way, and smiling constantly, so as to display a set of the most brilliantly white teeth.[64]

The first sign that something is off is the waft of "a smell, a stench, such as the whole world has no name for—no conception of—hellish—utterly suffocating—insufferable, inconceivable."[65] The narrative zooms in on the smiling, nodding, apparently black-skinned figure:

> His arms were extended over the rail, and the palms of his hands fell outward. His knees were lodged upon a stout rope, tightly stretched, and reaching from the heel of the bowsprit to a cathead. On his back, from which a portion of the shirt had been torn, leaving it bare, there sat a huge sea-gull, busily gorging itself with the horrible flesh, its bill and talons deep buried, and its white plumage spattered all over with blood. As the brig moved farther round so as to bring us close in view, the bird, with much apparent difficulty, drew out its crimsoned head, and, after eyeing us for a moment as if stupefied, arose lazily

from the body upon which it had been feasting, and, flying directly above our deck, hovered there a while with a portion of clotted and liver-like substance in its beak. The horrid morsel dropped at length with a sullen splash immediately at the feet of Parker. . . . The body from which it had been taken, resting as it did upon the rope, had been easily swayed to and fro by the exertions of the carnivorous bird, and it was this motion which had at first impressed us with the belief of its being alive. As the gull relieved it of its weight, it swung round and fell partially over, so that the face was fully discovered. Never, surely, was any object so terribly full of awe! The eyes were gone, and the whole flesh around the mouth, leaving the teeth utterly naked. This, then, was the smile which had cheered us on to hope! this the—but I forbear.[66]

The nodding Black body begins, Dominic Mastroianni argues, as a figure of welcome, evincing a "provocatively Emersonian form of hospitality— 'encouraging . . . patience' in a 'cheerful' but 'odd' way."[67] He is also, with "very dark skin" and "smiling constantly, so as to display a set of the most brilliantly white teeth," an image trafficking in racial stereotype—a seemingly perfect Sambo, the "omnibus stereotype, the original and continuing basis for the myriad of black stock figures that arose during the nineteenth-century."[68] Cassuto notes that the Sambo, "at the root of all slave stereotype . . . represented a clear object (the happy slave) surrounded by blurry, but recognizably southern, outline."[69] This dark figure on the deck of the brig might be read as Poe's white nightmare of the duplicitous Sambo doll, puppeteered by a ravenous whiteness (the gull) that embodies the violent needs and desires of Pym and his ilk.

Both the ship's welcoming committee and the brig itself have uncomfortable resonances with Peters, too. A "hermaphrodite brig" is its own sort of hybrid: "a sailing vessel that combines the characters of two kinds of craft."[70] And the constant smile of the black figure, revealed to be the product of the gull having devoured "the whole flesh around the mouth, leaving the teeth utterly naked," is not unreminiscent of Peters's own "exceedingly long" teeth "protruding, and never even partially covered, in any instance, by the lips."[71] If Peters is fixed via the lines by which he lashes himself to the sunken ship, the tall, stout, dark figure that seems to beckon from the Dutch hermaphrodite brig is an image of Ngai's ugly feeling of racial animatedness brought to its gruesome extreme. "The connection between animation and affectivity is surprisingly fostered through acts resembling the practice of puppeteering, involving either the body's ventriloquism or a physical manipulation of its animatedness parts."[72]

The cadaver puppet is animated by Pym's desire for welcome, by his own affect, while being functionally unable to provide its own.[73] This affective puppeteering (akin, in some ways, to the "caprice" Pym constantly assigns to Peters) grotesquely materializes in the bloody gull's uncanny animation of the line-lashed body. The appalling puppet of the blackened cadaver on the hermaphrodite brig is the three-dimensional grotesque counterpart to the silhouette's two-dimensional diagrammatic geometry.

Shadow puppetry is an integral part of the material history of the silhouette. They are related through the mechanics of projection. Descriptions of the shadow puppet resonate with those of stereotypes: "The thinnest of puppets, the poorest, the least substantial, is the puppet of shadow theater. . . . This is a puppet all of surface, with no back to it, no depth."[74] Mitchell uses Du Bois's figure of the veil to explicate the visual, material, and ethical flatness of stereotypes, writing that "The stereotype is an especially important case of the living image. . . . It forms a mask, or what W. E. B. Du Bois called a 'veil,' that interposes itself between persons." Stereotypes, "insinuat[e]" themselves into everyday life and constitute[e] the social screens that make encounters with other people possible—and, in a very real sense, impossible."[75] The puppeted dead man on the brig later gets projected on the "social screens" of Pym's racism into the animate ethnographic silhouettes of the Tsalalians.

The text isn't clear about whether the "smiling" sailor is dark skinned by phenotype or from corporal decay, and various critics have taken one or the other reading for granted without commenting upon the ambiguity. Gardner, for instance, asserts that the primary horror of the hermaphrodite brig is that "the white European crew has turned black, cannibalized by white birds."[76] Mat Johnson, in *Pym*, pointedly calls attention to the "smiling" sailor's marks of Blackness.[77] What matters for an analysis following Morrison, however, is not what this dark figure essentially is, but how its darkness is instrumentalized by the white characters who see it and the white author who describes it. This is the troubling catalytic quality of the "dark, abiding, signing Africanist presence" in white American literature.[78] The "acute and ambiguous moral problematic" that the appearance of the zombie puppet Sambo on the hermaphrodite Dutch brig directly activates is one of the most anxious nineteenth-century travel narrative taboos: cannibalism.[79]

"Bloody and Cannibal Designs"

The logic of the silhouette is one not just of flattening, but also of draining and cutting. Silhouettes are emptied of their innards, evacuated of internal differentiation, and sliced up into bare outlines. They are images of humans reproduced for quick consumption and easy digestion. When viewed this way, then, it is hardly a surprise (though it still comes as a visceral shock) when Poe's novel takes a turn toward cannibalism. Geoffrey Sanborn argues that Pym's encounter with the hermaphrodite Dutch brig is a turning point in the novel.[80] The scene of cannibalism that immediately follows marks a moment of racial anxiety and peril for Pym, who, as a white man eating human flesh under the pressure of famine, hazards being "branded with the racial epithet 'cannibal.'"[81] But Pym emerges, Sanborn argues, remarkably not racially marked, and not even identified as a "cannibal." Seeing the positive desire for human flesh in Augustus's eyes, Sanborn says, is what saves Pym.[82] In the protracted moments leading up to cannibalism, Poe has Pym look steadily into the eyes of the perverse limit case of humanity, and, by remaining rational and keeping desire and bloodlust out of his own eyes, he manages to retain his "whiteness." After this, he evinces a commitment to "the advancement of a knowledge that belongs not to any one individual, but to the universal human subject conjured up by the philosophers of the Enlightenment."[83] This transformation is one of identification, a definitional shift from one mode of identifying to another. Pym ceases to empathize and starts to categorize:

> Augustus, with whom Pym had once identified, putrefies, dies, and goes to pieces; the universal human subject, with whom Pym now identifies, is eternally clean and whole. . . . Now that he identifies with what is, quite literally, a body of knowledge, Pym can disidentify with the perverse fleshly body that had moved of its own accord toward the ensanguined spot.[84]

Sanborn asserts that in Poe's racial schema, the rational pursuit of disinterested knowledge, "the universal human subject"—significantly as a means of denying identification with putrefying flesh—*is* whiteness.

I would argue, however, that the most graphic moments of the novel reveal that this empirical, calculating assumption of the ability to measure and chart other humans universally is the most violent and affectively ambivalent force of the text—not apart from, but a part of, the "perverse fleshly body" and its desire for "the ensanguined spot." The actual description of the act of cannibalism is overshadowed in length by the deliberations and eventual drawing of straws that lead up to it. When it comes to eating Richard Parker, Pym's account is short, exact, and self-effacingly explicit. Despite his handwringing about how he "must not dwell upon the fearful repast," he provides a potent concentration of specific procedural details about how he, Augustus, and Peters dispatched Parker's body (hands are indeed wrung):

> I must not dwell upon the fearful repast which immediately ensued. Such things may be imagined, but words have no power to impress the mind with the exquisite horror of their reality. Let it suffice to say that, having in some measure appeased the raging thirst which consumed us by the blood of the victim, and having by common consent taken off the hands, feet, and head, throwing them together with the entrails, into the sea, we devoured the rest of the body, piecemeal, during the four ever memorable days of the seventeenth, eighteenth, nineteenth, and twentieth of the month.[85]

Pym and company drain, disembowel, and dismember the body of Parker. Harkening back to the initial ethnographic description of an otherwise grotesque Peters, the narrative attempts to temper, yet succeeds in making more unsettling, the way its narrator acts towards another's body by adopting the definite article to refer to Parker's parts. Pym sips and snips not Parker's blood or limbs but "the blood of the victim," and "the hands, feet, and head . . . the entrails."

As they prepare to draw straws and kill and eat one of their own, Pym and company face a double-edged danger—loss of life or, alternately, loss of "humanity" qua whiteness. Kyla Wazana Tompkins, citing Peter Hulme and Stuart Hall, writes that

> [A]cross modernity cannibalism has signified the total primitive otherness against which Western rationality—and its installation of the putatively ungendered and deracinated "human" as its subject—measured itself. This dialectic—between what Stuart Hall has called "The West and the Rest"—points to the ways that the imperial project underpins European Western modernity as a whole.[86]

The detached manner—distilled into the definite article—with which the other men prepare and consume Parker's body is also key, in nineteenth-century racial logic, to maintaining a claim on whiteness.

> [I]f this inner cannibal did not appear in their eyes, if the survivors exhibited nothing more than a piteous physical need, then their acts could be reconciled with a putatively natural, rational white identity. As long as they held off until "the last extremity," wrestled with the morality of the act, drew lots when someone had to be killed, and divided the body equally, their cannibalism was merely situational, and therefore not really cannibalism at all.[87]

For Poe and Pym, nineteenth-century white men, graphic detachment towards/from a grotesque act is a way of maintaining racial categories.

In fact, "cannibal" is only used once in the novel—to describe the man Pym ends up eating, who is consumed with "bloody and cannibal designs" before his flesh is literally consumed by the ever-white Pym. By labeling Parker the "cannibal" before they eat him, Pym et al. both justify and distance themselves from the action they take, constructing him as their own (provisionally nonwhite) uncanny "monstrous double." René Girard develops the concept of the "monstrous double" in his book *Violence and the Sacred*, cited here by Kathleen Donegan in her discussion of cannibalism in the Jamestown colony:

> [A] monstrous double [is] a figure who emerges at the height of crisis as other subjects "watch monstrosity take shape within [them] and outside [them] simultaneously." Girard argues that monstrous doubles, who absorb the dangerous excesses of the community, belong both inside and outside of it: "They thus occupy the equivocal middle ground between difference and unity that is indispensable to the process of sacrificial substitutions—to the polarization of violence onto a single victim who substitutes for all others." These monstrous doubles must be destroyed as sacrificial victims, but they are then displayed and destroyed over and over again.[88]

In a command performance of ethical (and ethnic) shadow puppetry, Parker is made linguistically into the monstrous double of his erstwhile shipmates in preparation for the moment at which, themselves exorcized of monstrosity by projecting it onto the doomed Parker, they can then materially drain, flatten, and consume his body. Yet Parker's body is not the ultimate shadow-puppeted monstrous double at the heart of the novel's ethnographic anxiety.

"These Were Black": The Silhouettes of Tsalal

Tsalal is an inexplicably tropical island located at the far southern reaches of *Pym*'s globe. It is "a country differing essentially" from any Pym or the rest of the crew of the *Jane Guy* have ever encountered.[89] Its rock formations, the trunks of its trees, and the bodies of its inhabitants—human and animal alike—are all of the blackest black. These "Africanist" characters are not just stereotypes or caricatures, but silhouettes—flat, matte, black; they are at once constitutively opaque and seemingly readily legible to the nineteenth-century gentleman-scholar's "scientific" eye. And they deliver a nasty cut.

> Their complexion [was] a jet black, with thick and long woolly hair. They were clothed in skins of an unknown black animal, shaggy and silky, and made to fit the body with some degree of skill, the hair being inside, except where turned out about the neck, wrists and ankles. Their arms consisted principally of clubs, of a dark, and apparently very heavy wood. . . . There were a great many women and children, the former not altogether wanting in what might be termed personal beauty. They were straight, tall, and well formed, with a grace and freedom of carriage not to be found in civilized society. Their lips, however, like those of the men, were thick and clumsy, so that, even when laughing, the teeth were never disclosed. Their hair was of a finer texture than that of the males.[90]

Not only are the Tsalalians "a jet black" in skin, hair, and clothing, but, as we learn later, even their teeth are black.[91] They greet the crew of the *Jane Guy* with shows of hospitality and solicitousness, some of which are, in line with racist stereotype, suggested to be sexual—"the women especially were most obliging in every respect."[92] If Peters seems like a frozen animation, the Tsalalians are, at least initially, an army of flat, racist silhouettes simultaneously brought to obliging life.[93] After the racial confusion of the episode of cannibalism, it seems a relief both to Pym and Poe to conjure these animate outlines, textbook dark others.

The Tsalalians appear to invite being treated as objects as they themselves have only a passing and naïve understanding of the difference between animacy and inanimacy: "They believed the Jane to be a living creature, and seemed to be afraid of hurting it with the points of their spears, carefully turning them up."[94] When the Tsalalian chief, Too-wit, observes the cook of the *Jane Guy*, in an act reminiscent of the mutinous Black cook on the *Grampus*,[95] accidentally making a gash with his axe in the deck of the ship, "the chief immediately ran up, and pushing the cook on one side rather roughly, commenced a half whine, half howl, strongly indicative of sympathy in what he considered the sufferings of the schooner, patting and smoothing the gash with his hand, and washing it from a bucket of seawater which stood by."[96] Finally, in what is almost a mock performance of the book's own quaking at two-dimensional boogey-men it has itself conjured, Too-wit balks at his own infinitely regressing reflection in the facing mirrors of the captain's cabin:

> Upon raising his eyes and seeing his reflected self in the glass, I thought the savage would go mad; but, upon turning short round to make a retreat, and beholding himself a second time in the opposite direction, I was afraid he would expire upon the spot. No persuasion could prevail upon him to take another look.[97]

This moment alludes, too, to an episode from the mutiny—when Pym dresses himself up as a dead man in order to terrify and overtake the mutineers and is "seized with a violent tremour" upon spotting himself "in a fragment of looking-glass" on the wall.[98]

It's when the Tsalalians become "systematic" in their actions that Pym most distrusts them, presaging their shift from one sort of flat racial stereotype to another: "In the whole of this adventure we saw nothing in the demeanour of the natives calculated to create suspicion, with the single exception of the systematic manner in which their party was strengthened during our route from the schooner to the village."[99] Animated stereotypes acting systematically is a central racial terror of Poe's *Pym*. The allusion to the axe work of the Black cook who masterminded the mutiny on the *Grampus* should prime readers for the pendulum swing that follows. The abrupt switch of the Tsalalians from one sort of stereotype of Blackness (subservient, childlike, hospitable) to another (savage, violent, barbarous) again evinces Bhabha's ambivalent "fixity" of the colonial stereotype. Creatures both of "rigidity" and "daemonic repetition," the Tsalalians, drawn as static, internally undifferentiated silhouettes, flatly embody the paradox Bhabha describes. This ambivalence is perhaps nowhere more evident than after the Tsalalians massacre the crew of the *Jane Guy*, via a carefully engineered rockslide: "We alone had escaped from the tempest of that overwhelming destruction," Pym declares as he and Dirk Peters emerge from being buried alive and realize the extent of the destruction wrought by the Tsalalians' machinations. Then he goes on with the simple statement: "We were the only living white men upon the island."[100] Exposed under extreme conditions against a backdrop of murderous Blackness, Peters casually jumps categories in Pym's mind, ceasing to be hybrid and becoming white. This line in the novel is the clearest indicator of the chiaroscuro binary racial logic of the American ethnographic. Out of fear and self-preservation, everyone solidifies their identities against the darker, flatter Africanist presence of the Tsalalians. Peters's racial identity as a character shifts, but the racial schematics of the novel as a whole—at once recombinant and unyielding—lock into place.

When Peters becomes a white man, it raises the question of what sort of silhouette Poe has been cutting. In other words, what or who is the negative space in the novel? And what or who is the subject being carved into or out of that background?

Hollow Cutting and the White Cataract

There are two types of cut silhouettes: cutout and hollow-cut. In cutout silhouettes, an artist removes the paper surrounded an outlined profile of the sitter. The positive shape is retained and mounted upon a background. The paper that made up negative space surrounding it is discarded. In the hollow-cut silhouette, the figure is cut out from the center of the paper and thrown away. The "hollow" negative space is then backed with paper or black silk to show the resultant silhouette. The hollow-cut, which was often the result of machine-cutting, predominated in America in the eighteenth and nineteenth centuries, particularly in New England.[101]

The silhouette is thus, on both thematic and material levels, always begging questions of interiority and exteriority, negative and positive space: Who or what is cutting or being cut? Which figure produced by that cutting is discarded/discardable? Thinking of the ethno- double graphic through the figure of the silhouette both recalls and adds new weight to Sara Ahmed's argument: "The surfaces of bodies 'surface' as an effect of the impressions left by others."[102]

We might think of Morrison's critical project in *Playing in the Dark* as a reassessment, à la the famous optical illusion known as Rubin's vase, of negative space in American literature (Figure 2.3).[103] Morrison calls us to read against the grain of American classics like Poe's *Pym* by resurfacing the black objects qua characters that others had been overlooking as mere background detail, vacant negative space. She asks what happens when you sort through the scrapheap of the discarded innards of "hollow-cut" silhouettes. She makes readers and critics grapple with the fact that the white faces, which we see brought together in myriad scenes of modest, lip-grazing sentiment, could not and do not exist without the backing of that black vase.

Poe, it seems, would just as soon douse the entire archive in bleach. The end of *The Narrative of Arthur Gordon Pym* is a wildly successful failure, arguably one of the primary reasons the book has garnered such relentless scholarly attention over the years—and so many remakes.[104] Henry James famously calls it, in his preface to the New York edition of *The Turn of the Screw*, "the would-be portentous climax of Edgar Poe's 'Arthur Gordon Pym.'" He argues that the ending fails by trying to dispense with the necessary work of establishing "the indispensable history of somebody's *normal* relation to something." The horrific events and mysterious phenomena, delivered like this, he argues, become "immediate and flat."

> [The] climax fails—fails because it stops short, and stops short for want of connexions. There *are* no connexions; not only, I mean, in the sense of further statement, but of our own further relation to the elements, which hang in the void: whereby we see the effect lost, the imaginative effort wasted.[105]

FIGURE 2.3. Examples of Rubin's vase or "figure and ground."

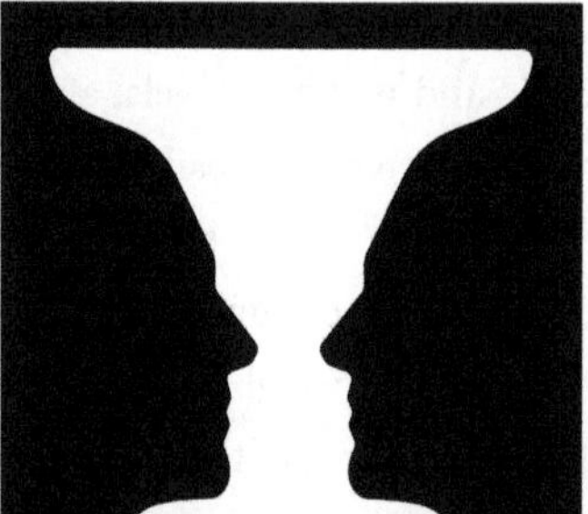
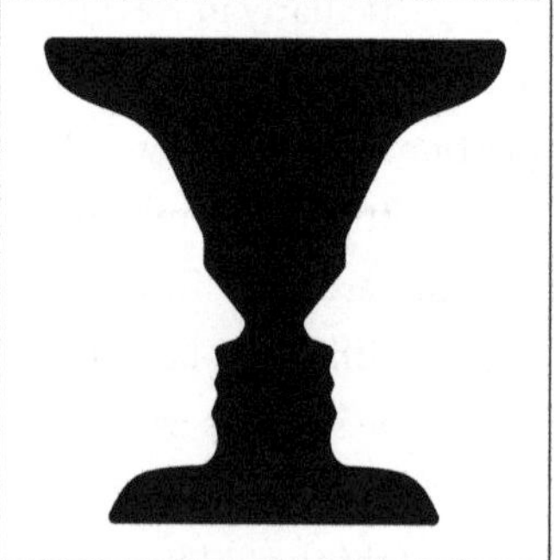

Source: iluslab / Alamy Stock Vector.

James takes exception not just to the narrative, but to the affective disorientation and dissatisfaction afforded by the end of the novel. He ascribes its failure to a sort of sensationalist laziness. For James, when Poe writes of the supernatural or shocking "with its 'objective' side too emphasized the report (it is ten to one) will practically run thin. We want it clear, goodness knows, but we also want it thick, and we get the thickness in the human consciousness that entertains and records, that amplifies and interprets it."[106] In sum, James faults Poe for producing a text that is "objective," "immediate and flat," in which not just characters and plot, but readers and their feelings "run thin."

Identification with and through "thickness" of characterization or consciousness is not what Poe's text affords. The mode of identification that runs most relentlessly through the novel, rather, is classification. Sanborn, borrowing from Gérard Genette, calls this Poe's investment in "an aspectual attention to elements of experience that hang, successively, in a void."[107] Aspectual attention resides in the perpetual vague historical present of ethnographic time. It is the anti-narrative domain of the archive, or proto database. Aspectual attention is also the pseudoscientific use to which the nineteenth-century technology of the silhouette was put. As Sanborn points out, the novel seems to "want to halt our awareness of what surrounds us and hold it, as long as possible, in an attention to aspect," which has the effect of "naturaliz[ing] a cultural system in which differences of physical features—particularly those features associated with sex and race—are tacitly equated with differences of capacity and status."[108] Sanborn argues that this "rapt attention to aspect is a form of quietism, a luxurious immersion in the warm milk bath of the representational status quo."[109] He argues, too, though, that aspectual attention is affectively volatile, it

> provides more time for associations and feelings to cluster around the image. Stare too long at the wonder of whiteness, as Ishmael does in *Moby-Dick*, and it may begin to accrue a degree of horror. Stare too long at the horror of blackness, as Pym does on Tsalal, and it may begin to accrue a degree of wonder.[110]

It is whiteness that looms before Pym at the end of the novel:

> The darkness had materially increased, relieved only by the glare of the water thrown back from the white curtain before us. Many gigantic and pallidly

> white birds flew continuously now from beyond the veil, and their scream was the eternal *Tekeli-li!* as they retreated from our vision. Hereupon Nu-Nu stirred in the bottom of the boat; but upon touching him we found his spirit departed. And now we rushed into the embraces of the cataract, where a chasm threw itself open to receive us. But there arose in our pathway a shrouded human figure, very far larger in its proportions than any dweller among men. And the hue of the skin of the figure was of the perfect whiteness of the snow.[111]

Morrison calls the shrouded figure a "figuration of impenetrable whiteness."[112] Its whiteness is both impenetrable and insurmountable, even by the figure itself, vying and failing to be the subject of its own sentence. If blackness is a violently fixed silhouette in Poe, whiteness is visually, syntactically, narratively, racially a cataract—a sight-obscuring opacity and a violent onrush—that eventually blots out blackness (Nu-Nu dies) and then snuffs itself out because there's no more "play of difference" against which to articulate "the representation of the subject."[113] Poe throws out the vases and the faces, figure and background, both. And we're left wondering which was the "hollow" after all, or whether it even matters, since neither catalogued, flattened, classified racialized figures nor rationally hysterical, cannibalizing white men were possible to read for anything recognizable as empathic identification anyway.

Toni Morrison writes of Poe:

> The act of enforcing racelessness in literary discourse is itself a racial act. Pouring rhetorical acid on the fingers of a black hand may indeed destroy the prints, but not the hand. Besides, what happens in that violent, self-serving act of erasure to the hands, the fingers, the fingerprints of the one who does the pouring? Do they remain acid-free?[114]

I am drawn to the way that Morrison's "acid-free" evokes both paper and archives. "Acid-free" resonates both with the figure of the silhouette and the logics, aesthetics, and affects of informational administration and conservation. Poe's archival whiteness, which plays at endless recombinant acquisition (à la the mid-text opportunistic and contingent incorporation of Dirk Peters into the category), seems existentially to need Blackness to be flattened into silhouetted stereotype (or burned smooth into deindividuated anonymity). The silhouetted images of Blackness that Poe and his ilk help to create take on, as Mitchell argues that images do, a quasi-life of their own. They desire, they parasite, they "form a social collective that has a parallel existence to the social life of their human hosts, and to the world of objects that they represent."[115] They create libidinous fields. These particular images are render via cutting, but most violent perhaps in their schematic abstraction, their diagrammatic distillation and reduction of individuating detail.

What happens when, 150 years later, the scissors—and the cool, crisp, taxonomizing, pseudoscientific trappings of scopic mastery that accompany them—end up, quite literally in the hands of the other(s)? Does the most famous contemporary creator of silhouette tableaux "evade and simultaneously register the cul de sac, the estrangement, the non-sequitur that is entailed in racial difference"[116] in same manner as Poe? Is she slicing through archival-grade paper? Is it the ethnographic images themselves who are now spitting acid?

Kara Walker's Paper Cuts

Walker is like De Sade crossed with Edgar Allan Poe.

   —JERRY SALTZ, "An Explosion of Color, in Black and White"

How can her figures be so fleshed out and yet so abstract? . . . [T]he silhouette is simultaneously carnal and categorical.

   —ALESSANDRA RAENGO, *On the Sleeve of the Visual: Race as Face Value*

In the early 1990s, a young, female African American visual artist sliced her way onto the international art scene. Her favored mode: the nearly life-sized black cut-paper silhouette, adhered directly onto gallery walls. Much has been said by critics and Kara Walker herself about her signature medium. In her own words, "it's a blank space, but it's not at all a blank space, it's both there and not there."[117] This aggressive coexistence of absence and presence perfectly encapsulates ethnographic feeling. Walker's tableaux take Poe's flattened forms, in all of their violent affective ambivalence, into the twentieth and twenty-first centuries. Her compositions lift the Tsalalians and their ilk from the pages of *The Narrative of Arthur Gordon Pym*, blow them up, and set them dancing across gallery walls and through the landscapes of a phantasmagoric American South (Figure 2.4).

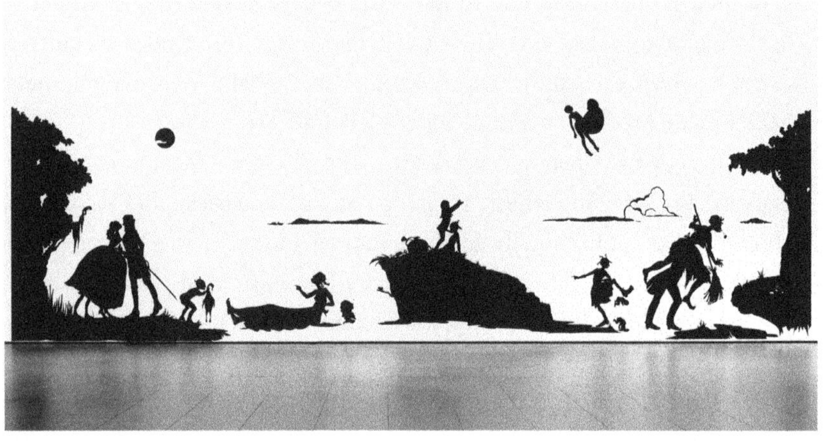

FIGURE 2.4. Kara Walker's *Gone: An Historical Romance of a Civil War as It Occurred b'tween the Dusky Thighs of One Young Negress and Her Heart*, exhibited first in 1994 in New York.

Source: The Museum of Modern Art / Licensed by SCALA / Art Resource, NY, © 2022 Kara Walker.

"Fixing the Shadow"

Ancient legend has it that the art form began as a "silhouette of the beloved."[118] The art of "fixing the shadow," silhouette drawing traditionally "expresses the wish to deny death or departure, to hold on to the loved one, to keep him present and permanently 'alive,'" both in and as the face of absence.[119] As much, though, as the silhouette traces its origins to the sentimental keepsake, it is, too, part of the genealogy of racial pseudoscience.

Lavater's bestseller *Essays on Physiognomy* valued the silhouette because it was an ostensibly objective record that—by marshalling all legible detail into the graphic specificity of a single crisp, clean, exterior outline—purged the figure of all ambiguity and deception, precipitating interiority into exteriority through strategic opacity (Figure 2.5).[120] The "shade," as Lavater referred to it, "evacuated a subject's bothersome interiority while at the same time inscribing 'character.' . . . Shades were a space whose margins contained all pertinent information and whose centers were spaces of blank, yet readable, negative interiority."[121] Lavater encouraged his armchair physiognomist readers to map for themselves the tangents of the flattened facial planes that the silhouette revealed in order to, in turn, geometrically chart the newly exposed terrain of the sitter's character.

FIGURE 2.5. Silhouette with measurements from frontispiece of Johann Kaspar Lavater's *L'art de connâitre les hommes par la physionomie*, published in 1806.

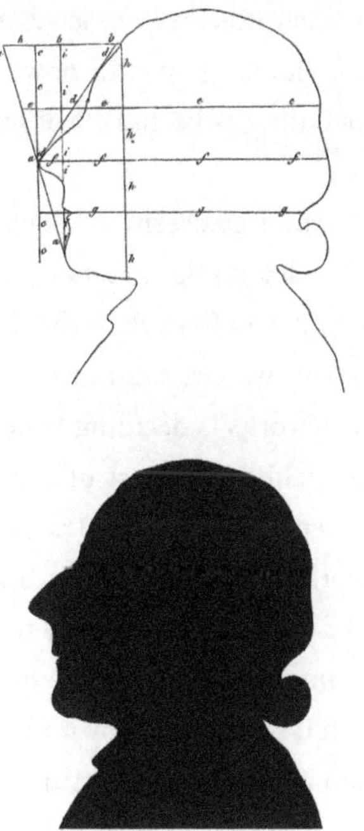

Source: Paris,1806 (frontispiece).

Kara Walker cites both of these lineages—the bourgeois sentimental portrait and the pseudoscientific record (what Alessandra Raengo calls the "shadow archive" of race science[122])—in her revival of the silhouette. By throwing her crisp cutouts into all manner of carnal contortions and cringe-worthy encounters with one another—framed, always, by hints at the saccharine conventions of the plantation romance—she also animates the violence inherent in both genealogies. The "violent collision" of abstract form and grotesque content in Walker's silhouettes places viewers uncomfortably in the position both of amateur scientist and nostalgic commissioner of a keepsake portrait.[123]

Walker's work viscerally reminds viewers that neither diagrammatic abstraction nor sentimental portraiture are divorced from the function of social and political power. As Sekula writes, "Every portrait implicitly took its place within a social and moral hierarchy. The private moment of sentimental individuation, the look at the frozen gaze-of-the-loved-one, was shadowed by two other more public looks: a look up, at one's 'betters,' and a look down, at one's 'inferiors.'"[124] Walker's silhouettes, forever looking away from their viewers, confront us with how we each position ourselves within Sekula's menu of scopic identification—are we looking up at or down upon these graphic grotesqueries formally masquerading as keepsakes of somebody's long-lost loved ones?

Her narratively evocative tableaux seem to ask viewers both to taxonomize the vacant dark figures they see doing imaginative/unimaginable things to one another and to fabricate stories to explain the sharply outlined yet narratively withholding assignations we see. An inescapable part of the narrativizing we do while viewing her works is deciding which black figures are white and which are Black. The opaque blackness of her figures calls attention to how epidermalized race essentializes and abstracts people, by making us as viewers casually do that work ourselves.[125] "In putting the visual signification of race at a remove from the bodies it is supposed to differentiate and administer, they succeed in showing how the language of black and white remains seemingly intact, even when it is supported by nothing behind it."[126]

The guiding preposition of Walker's unsettlingly depthless cut-paper silhouette is, by necessity, *beside*. For Eve Sedgwick:

> *Beside* permits a spacious agnosticism about several of the linear logics that enforce dualistic thinking: noncontradiction or the law of the excluded middle, cause versus effect, subject versus object. Its interest does not, however, depend on a fantasy of metonymically egalitarian or even pacific relations, as any child knows who's shared a bed with siblings. *Beside* comprises a wide range of desiring, identifying, representing, repelling, paralleling, differentiating, rivaling, leaning, twisting, mimicking, withdrawing, attracting, aggressing, warping, and other relations. . . . Invoking a Deleuzian interest in planar relations, the irreducibly spatial positionality of *beside* also seems to offer some useful resistance to the ease with which *beneath* and *beyond* turn from spatial descriptors into implicit narratives of, respectively, origin and telos.[127]

Much of the affective impasse of the ethnographic, as a phenomenon both grotesque *and* geometric, derives from how aggressively "planar" it is. In the ethnographic we find three-dimensional human bodies translated into what

Sedgwick calls the agnostic, though hardly "metonymically egalitarian or even pacific" relationality and spatiality of *beside*. This *beside*ness of Walker's tableaux has implications for the possibilities and problematics of identification—as both a descriptive/classificatory and sentimental/empathic endeavor.

Identification and Insurrection!

Identification as description—what do we see being done, and to and by whom—ought to be the simplest way of engaging with Walker's silhouettes, yet it becomes one of the most fraught. I will focus here on an installation exhibited in 2002, entitled *Insurrection! (Our Tools Were Rudimentary, Yet We Pressed On)*. In the tableau, which spans two walls, we see a naked woman (Black) beside a clothed man (white), followed by a woman (Black) wearing a noose and carrying a decapitated head (Black?) next to a small child (white?) carrying a hat, beside a girl (Black) carrying a head on a pike (white). And that is just one wall. All of these figures, arrayed beside one another, appear to be in front of, but are actually behind a number of colorful transparencies emanating from overhead projectors situated throughout the room (Figures 2.6 and 2.7).

"Describing" what's going on in the images requires the viewer to decide some things, or to project them upon what we see. The museumgoer becomes an amateur physiognomist—something that Walker uncomfortably seems to encourage by pulling her profiles from the archives of stereotype. The medium enforces the sharp optic division between the background (white) and the figures (black). Walker cuts the dualistic ideology of American race into—out of?—the inflexible black space of one half of that already inflexible binary. The onus for sussing out and enforcing any further Black/white binary then lies with the viewers and the physiognomic analysis they do along the razor-thin edges of the figures' profiles.

Take, for instance, the brief, seemingly straight description the Guggenheim gives of *Insurrection!* in its online catalogue.

> In *Insurrection! (Our Tools Were Rudimentary, Yet We Pressed On)* (2000), a series of grisly scenes unfold. A plantation owner propositions a naked slave behind a tree and a woman with a tiny baby on her head escapes a lynching, while a group of people eagerly torture a victim. In this piece, Walker expands

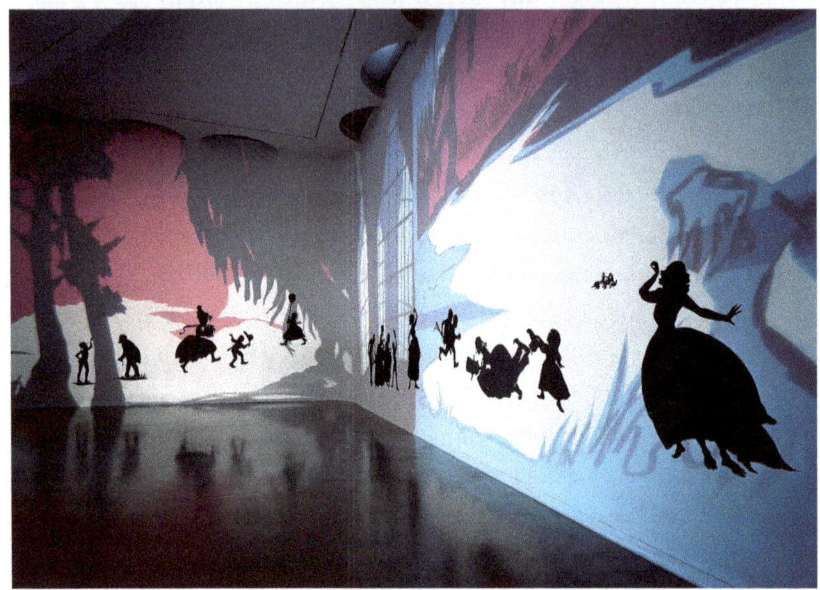

Source: Production still from the *Art in the Twenty-First Century* season 2 episode, "Stories." © Art21, Inc. 2003.

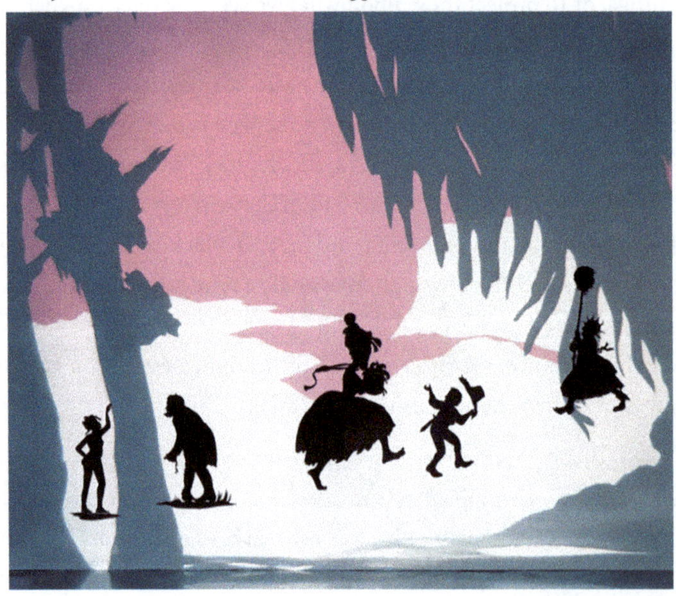

Source: © Kara Walker, courtesy of Sikkema Jenkins & Co., New York; Sprüth Magers, Berlin.

the vocabulary of her shadowy forms to include projected silhouettes and colored lights. When viewers walk in front of these projections, their shadows are introduced into the scene, denying them the comfortable position of spectator and implicating them in the unfolding events.[128]

The description names one woman a "slave," decides that she is being propositioned by "a plantation owner," demurs on assigning either race or legal status to the "group of people" who perform dissection via soup ladle upon "a victim" behind the gridded windowpanes but does choose to characterize their ministrations as "eager." The Guggenheim's description of *Insurrection!* exemplifies the obstacles that Walker's tableaux pose to simple description.

There is no innocent, nonimplicated way to describe what one sees, what is "going on" in Walker's tableaux. The figures demand interpretation, even as their form implies simplistic self-evidence. In order to "ground" what we see—in space, in narrative, in affect—one must "seriously overdetermine the visual information provided."[129] What seem at first blush like scenes of extravagant excess soon reveal themselves as stubbornly ambiguous scenarios of informational paucity (there is certainly no way of knowing if anyone is doing anything akin to blushing). If the pseudoscientific conceit of the Lavaterian silhouette was to draw interiority out and into exteriority, Walker animates that hubristic premise to its horrific extreme, giving us a carnival of silhouetted stereotypes in which, with all insides precipitated outside—or rather, the two terms collapsed to the point of nonsense—there is no longer any safe or possible way of standing blamelessly outside of what one sees. Description is always a guilty act. "In fact, such an encounter ['to tell a story about these figures'] very nearly becomes do-it-yourself slavery. With each viewing, Walker's botched antebellum narratives engender new tellings of the period, new turns on its truths."[130] Or, as Mitchell puts it, "the fact that the vignettes are all too legible and recognizable, makes it very difficult to deny that we, as spectators, feel that we have seen this before. But where? The only answer can be that they come out of our own dream life, not just Kara Walker's."[131]

Insurrection! materializes, using overhead transparency projectors, the sort of interpretive projections in which viewers themselves must guiltily participate. And it uses a historically weighty, yet easily overlooked, visual motif to do so: the grid. Walker projects a backdrop of gridded windowpanes upon the central scene of cannibalistic dissection-by-kitchen-utensils, bringing questions of self-evidence, scientific objectivity, and abstraction formally front (and/or back?) and center (Figure 2.8).

In interviews, Walker has cited the realist painter Thomas Eakins as an inspiration for *Insurrection!*:

> The idea at the outset was an image of a slave revolt at some point, prior to me. And it was a slave revolt in the antebellum South, where the house slaves got after their master with their instruments, their utensils of everyday life. And really, it started with a sketch of a series of slaves disemboweling a master with a soup ladle. My reference, in my mind, was the surgical theater paintings of Thomas Eakins and others.[132]

The allusion to Eakins's surgical theater paintings, paired with the gridded "background" overlaid by overhead projectors, further emphasizes one effect of the silhouette: holding up the contours and characters of human bodies as objects of disinterested schematic study.

Art critic Michael Fried compares Eakins, particularly his *Gross Clinic* (Figure 2.9), to Caravaggio, equating the "aggression" of a shocking overexpo-

FIGURE 2.8. Detailed installation view of Kara Walker's
Insurrection! (Our Tools Were Rudimentary, Yet We Pressed On)
at the Guggenheim Museum in New York in 2002.

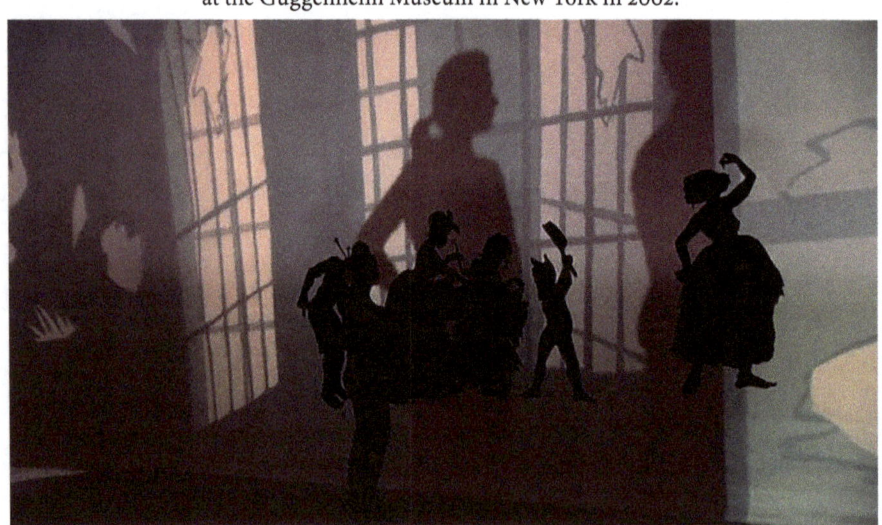

Source: Production still from the *Art in the Twenty-First Century* season 2 episode "Stories." © Art21, Inc. 2003.

sure of bodily gore in the portrayal of dissection with the extreme withholding of visual information in chiaroscuro shadows:

> As often in Caravaggio, there is in those aggressions, as well as in the blackness and opacity of Eakins's chiaroscuro, an applied affront to seeing—a stunning or, worse, a *wounding* of seeing—as if the definitive realist painting would be one that the viewer literally could not bear to look at, or as if the ultimate realist undertaking consisted in the effacing of seeing in the act of looking (cf. Caravaggio's *Medusa*).[133]

Fried puts the "blackness and opacity of Eakins's chiaroscuro" on par with the "aggressions" of the realist tradition—"when tactics of shock, violence,

FIGURE 2.9. Thomas Eakins's *Portrait of Dr. Samuel D. Gross (The Gross Clinic)*, 1875.

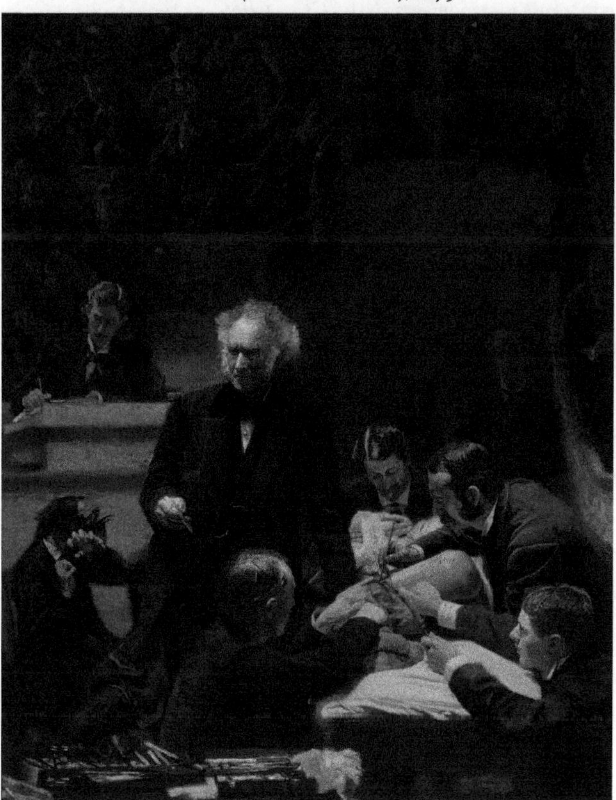

Source: Philadelphia Museum of Fine Art.

perceptual distortion, and physical outrage were mobilized against prevailing conventions of the representation of the human body specifically in order to produce a new and stupefyingly powerful experience of the 'real.'"[134] Both forceful opacity and violent exposure are "a *wounding* of seeing" that also enact "the effacing of seeing in the act of looking." Chiaroscuro, however, effaces seeing not by creating a spectacle that "the viewer literally could not bear to look at" but rather by conjuring an illusion of weight and depth that is all flatness and no information—by giving the viewer something to look at that itself cannot bear the weight of further scrutiny. There's nothing more to see in the opacity of a jet-black shadow. The affront to seeing in those shadows is that as closely as you peer, the only data that can be gleaned are the optical illusions or mental projections you, as viewer, bring to bear on the flat and unyielding surface. Fried concludes that

> what confronts us as viewers in the *Gross Clinic*, as repeatedly in Caravaggio, is an image that is painful to look at and all but impossible, hence painful, *to look away from*, and that it is above all the conflictedness of that situation that grips and excruciates and in the end stupefies us before the picture.[135]

I think we find this sort of stupefaction in affective responses to Walker's work as well: a conflictedness tied to being shown both too much and not enough aggressive visual information. But "blackness and opacity" have an added weight in Walker's tableaux. Her weaponization of opacity evokes Édouard Glissant's polemic against the "requirement for transparency" in Western thought's approach to the racialized other. "In order to understand and thus accept you, I have to measure your solidity with the ideal scale providing me with grounds to make comparisons and, perhaps, judgments. I have to reduce."[136] Against demands for knowability, commensurability, and perpetual sentimental availability, Glissant instead sues for opacity. "The opaque is not the obscure, though it is possible for it to be so and be accepted as such. It is that which cannot be reduced, which is the most perennial guarantee of participation and confluence."[137] To be for opacity is to be staunchly against what Xine Yao decades later calls the "coloniality of sympathy."[138] Glissant avers "it is not necessary to try to become the other (to become other) nor to 'make' him in my image."[139] He offers an ethics of understanding the other that privileges the sanctity of mutual opacity over the proprietary "grasping" of an invasive need for fellow feeling, the lust for intimate emotional knowledge qua territorial occupation.

Christina Sharpe's version of Glissant's opacity is what she calls "black redaction," which she offers as a methodology of obscuring, withholding, and protecting Black interiority in service of a move "toward seeing and reading otherwise; toward reading and seeing something in excess of what is caught in the frame; toward seeing something beyond a visuality that is . . . subtended by the logics of the administered plantation."[140] It remains frustratingly (though perhaps fittingly) unclear whether "seeing and reading otherwise" sully the game that Walker's ethnographic silhouettes are playing. Walker baits her viewers with the opacity of her figures, tempting us to populate their textureless interiors with the tactile stuff of feeling, to try if we might to feel with and as them. What remains perhaps most unsettling is the suspicion that the aggressive opacity of her figures is following neither the simpering script of sentimentality nor a wholly redemptive or resistant one in line with Glissantian opacity. What if it's all (just for) shits and giggles?

The grid against which Walker's Eakins-esque surgical/cannibal theater is shown is a racially significant form in America, Phillip Harper argues, precisely because it protests so vehemently that it is not. Referring to Benjamin Franklin's famous "thirteen virtues" chart of self-perfectibility, Harper says:

> Recruited to the project of figuring the moral perfection of the proto-republican citizen, [the grid] . . . figures the absolute exclusion of blacks (and other non-white-male persons) from the polity, inasmuch as they were considered incapable of either sublimating their particular interests or eradicating their vicious tendencies (both of which were held to be intractable elements of their blackness itself), and deemed wholly devoid of the capacity for reason. . . . Considered in this way, the ostensibly innocuous grid construct is effectively an avatar of the white-masculine form itself, whose own supposed generic-representative character has made it the archetypal image of everything from the citizen-soldier to the prospective consumer.[141]

Walker's *Insurrection!* wreaks multiple forms of havoc on these aspirations to abstraction, using the window of the "white-masculine form" as a backdrop to the dissection and cannibalism of the body that grids like Franklin's worked so hard to render generic and rational—and then smashing it (Figure 2.10).[142]

FIGURE 2.10. Chart of the thirteen virtues from the *Autobiography of Benjamin Franklin*. The vertical column lists the abbreviated virtues: temperance, silence, order, resolution, frugality, industry, sincerity, justice, moderation, cleanliness, tranquility, chastity, and humility.

Form of the pages.

TEMPERANCE.						
EAT NOT TO DULNESS; DRINK NOT TO ELEVATION.						
	S.	M.	T.	W.	T.	F.	S.
T.							
S.	*	*		*		*	
O.	* *	*	*		*	*	*
R.			*			*	
F.		*			*		
I.			*				
S.							
J.							
M.							
C.							
T.							
C.							
H.							

Source: Franklin, *The Autobiography of Benjamin Franklin* (1868; repr., New York: Vintage / Library of America, 1990), 79.

Meanwhile, the figure of white-masculine scientific expertise (à la Eakins's *Gross Clinic* or *Agnew Clinic*) is usurped by a headscarf-wearing Black woman taking a dainty sample of the dish her able assistants are carving up (Figure 2.11). The pale blank squares of the partially smashed window mimic the white faces of Eakins's painted clinic audiences, and perhaps mirror, too, the majority of Walker's viewers (Figure 2.12).[143]

The grid is graphic in a way that seems to be the polar opposite of the grotesque cannibalism it backs. But if, as Harper argues, it protests its racelessness too much (Morrisonian acid bath, anyone?), its petition for exception from the realm of violated flesh is also nearly as quickly crumpled up and discarded as

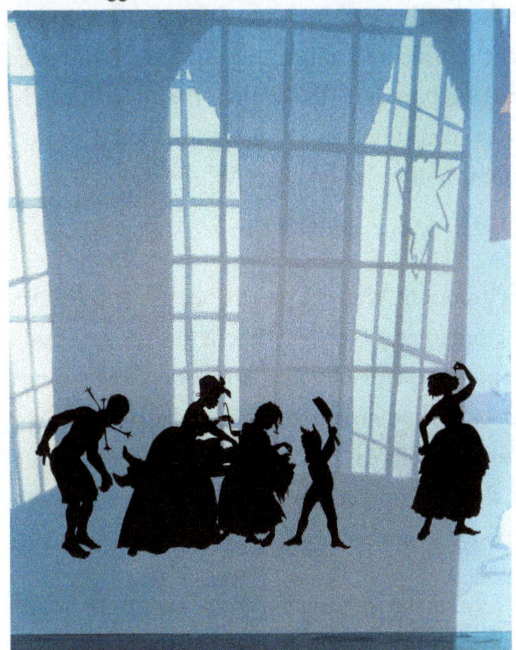

Source: © Kara Walker, courtesy of Sikkema Jenkins & Co., New York; Sprüth Magers, Berlin.

FIGURE 2.12. Thomas Eakins's *Agnew Clinic*, 1889.

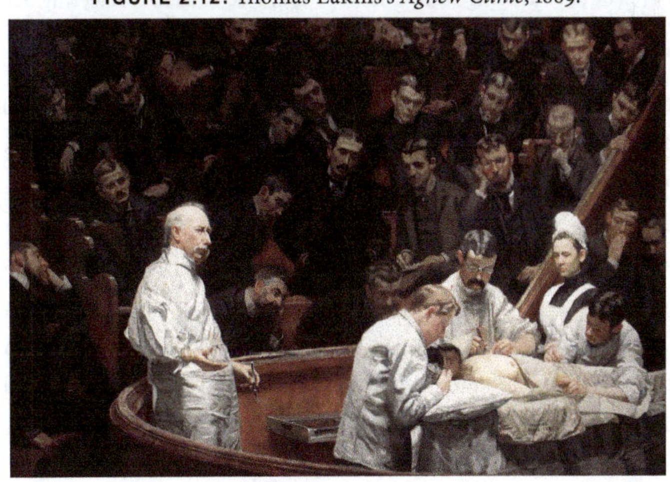

Source: Philadelphia Museum of Fine Art.

a hollow-cut silhouette's absent center—particularly, as with Franklin's guide to perfectibility, in an American context. Gridded ledgers, Saidiya Hartman reminds us, contain the traces of irreclaimable lives of enslaved people.[144] In the context of the "settlement" by white colonists of already occupied land in North America through mechanisms like the Land Ordinance of 1785, Harper shows how, in the way that it "looks more than anything else like *emptiness* packaged for easy consumption . . . the grid actually produces the notional emptiness that it simultaneously orders."[145]

Projection

Insurrection! is unique in Walker's oeuvre because it is the first work in which she used projectors to cast over her silhouettes the gridded windowpanes of the plantation house, the diaphanous creepers of the swamp that surrounds it, and, of course, the bodies of her viewers who themselves creep ever closer to the figures on the walls to try to suss and out make sense of what they are seeing. Asked about her choice to incorporate overhead projectors into the piece, first exhibited in 2002, Walker said:

> I wanted to activate the space, in a way, and have these overhead projectors serve as a kind of stand-in for the viewer, as observers. And my thinking about the overhead projectors connected with my thinking about painting—as far as creating an illusion of depth, but in a very mundane, flat, almost didactic way. . . . Overhead projectors are a didactic tool; they're schoolroom tools. So, they're about conveying facts. The work that I do is about projecting fictions into those facts.[146]

The projections are not just stand-ins for the viewer, though. They also make the viewer's shadows stand in amongst the ones that Walker has affixed to the wall. It is in that fixity, however, to return to Bhabha's formulation of the stereotype, that viewers and their shadows stand apart from and are denied (or spared) full identitification with the silhouettes. The insurrectionists and insurrectionees on the wall are fixed opaquely there while our shadows move across and through the scenes. We are made into shadow puppets. And even in their saturation, the shades of the viewers are not identical to the paper cut-outs on the wall. "The light of the projectors reproduces us as, and enmeshes us with, the silhouettes. Though not indistinguishably: our shadows are waterier, less substantially black."[147] We are neither seamlessly incorporated into, nor safely extricable from, the frieze. "To be suspended in such riotous scenes—bathed in colored light and screened—is to renounce the possibility of dissociation from the work."[148]

The scene is also cannibalistic—the images implying that the bodies *beside* one another are soon to be or have been bodies *inside*--consumed by—one another. The grotesquely melding and joining figures in the right-hand wing of the *Insurrection!* triptych—in which bodies mount each other in various permutations or occupy the same set of clothes—mirror and distort the intimacy of cannibalism. Walker says that

> "[C]annibalism is wanting to have everything of the other person, body and soul. . . . There is a little bit of masochism, I think, involved . . . so much love and hate involved in eating something; to kill something and eat it. It's very sexual, very sensual."[149]

Walker extravagantly mixes and multiplies transgressions, following the logic of the "presexological mapping of the erotic and alimentary pleasure in the antebellum period."[150] Tompkins asserts that this mapping of the erotic and the alimentary "had its corollary in the literal, that is, geographic, mapping of the nation, and it was at the overlap between the two that the mouth, as a doorway into the consuming body, first became a site of biopolitical intensity in the United States."[151] It is telling that mouths are one of the sites of greatest intensity in the ethnographic silhouetting practiced by both Poe and Walker. "Thick and clumsy lips" mark the Tsalalians as racially other to Pym even before the revelation of their black teeth firmly annexes them from the map of the human. Though Walker's tableaux remove the signifier of skin color, the size of lips gains outsized significance even before they begin gorily and gleefully to eat—cannibalize and fellate—each other.

One of the most disquieting effects of the flat *beside*ness of Walker's silhouetted figures is that, amidst all of these acts of interpenetration and consumption, it can seem like many of the figures are actually enjoying themselves. Pleasure plays an unsettling role in Walker's work, which defies, at every turn, not just narrative but affective expectations.[152] She says of the silhouette that it's a "blank space that you [can] project your desires into. It can be positive or negative. It's just a hole in a piece of paper, and it's the inside of that hole."[153]

Yet the holes themselves seem have a lot of desires, too, usually for other holes. Walker's figures are orgiastically, complicatedly *beside* one another, even as we long to see how exactly they get inside one another. This *beside*ness makes interiors beside the point as it circumvents "the topos of depth or hiddenness, typically followed by a drama of exposure."[154] The silhouettes are as exposed as they ever will or can be, stubbornly "resistan[t] to the ease with which *beneath* and *beyond* turn from spatial descriptors into implicit narratives of, respectively, origin and telos."[155] Tactilely, their texture is smooth. Emotionally, they both attract a swarm of contradictory feelings—delight, disgust, horror, humor—and blithely, smoothly, swat them all away.

Walker's work is unsettling less because of the taboo nature of the bodily excesses it shows, its "compulsive penetrations,"[156] and more because of the double bind of the participation it requires of and the identification it denies to its viewers. Viewers become collaborators in, but never full inhabitants of, the scenes she cuts and pastes. The silhouettes elicit involvement, interpretation, and projection, but these interactions can never reach the point of empathic identification, or even the proper too-closeness of full-throated disgust. In part, this is because of what silhouetted profiles can never fully be: faces. Emmanuel Levinas avers that the face is "inviolable; these eyes absolutely without protection, the most naked part of the human body," and offers, in its nakedness, "an absolute resistance to possession."[157] Adam Newton reminds us that, according to Levinas, "violence succeeds precisely by avoiding the face, by angling away from the 'no' which is inscribed on it."[158] Walker's silhouettes materialize the fraught ethics of "avoiding the face" by giving us only the profile.[159] The ethnographic affect of her work is a product of how silhouettes, iconic of a chiaroscuro American attitude toward race, violently turn identification via empathy into identification of categories—a dynamic that the visual overlay of the shattered window grid in this particular tableau exemplifies even farther. Though Newton, in his analysis of Stephen Crane's *The Monster*, draws heavily upon Levinas, he also notes the limitations of the transcendent power the philosopher gives to the face: "Indeed, perhaps nothing more graphically contests the prophetic or religious force Levinas ascribes to intersubjective relation—the Face says, 'You shall not kill'—than that stark symbol of racial violence, a lynched body with a black face."[160] Black faces have not historically been the inviolable guard against violence that Levinasian ethics would wish. Walker refuses scripts of sympathetic identification, intersubjective ethical engagement, and the refined debasement of suing for sentimental humanization by giving her viewers only flat optic blackness.

Her work vehemently goes beyond what Lauren Berlant terms "postsentimentality": "An author's or text's refusal to reproduce the sublimation of sub-altern struggles into conventions of narrative satisfaction and redemptive fantasy . . . a resistant strain of the sentimental domain," which, however, in the end "does not involve an aesthetic disruption to the contract sentimentality makes between its texts and readers—that proper reading will lead to better feeling and therefore to a better self."[161] Because this refusal still acknowledges and adheres aesthetically to the formal contraints qua contract of sentimentalist, Berlant argues that "[p]ostsentimental narratives are lacerated by ambivalence: they struggle constantly with their own attachment to the promise of unconflictedness and intimacy with which the U.S. sentimental tradition gifts its politically exhausted and cynically extended citizens."[162] Walker's images are materially lacerated, yes, but they revel in conflictedness, at the very level of their cut-paper medium.

By denying us access to faces, and, with them, an expected mode of affective identification with her geometric grotesqueries of pleasure and pain, Walker takes an unforgiving scalpel to the scripts of Levinasian ethics and American literary sentimentalism both.

Refleshing Poe's Silhouettes: Mat Johnson's *Pym*

Where Walker allows only projection upon her cut-paper figures, Mat Johnson, with his chatty first-person narration, both allows and demands that his readers inhabit and identify with his Black male protagonist. His 2011 novel *Pym* is a pithy, satiric rereading and rewriting of Poe's *Narrative of Arthur Gordon Pym of Nantucket*.

Told in the first person and bookended, like Poe's *Pym*, with explanatory notes from the "editor," Johnson's novel follows the adventures of Chris Jaynes, a professor of African American literature at a small East Coast liberal arts college. Jaynes, who teaches an underenrolled course called "Dancing with the Darkies: Whiteness in the Literary Mind," is obsessed with rooting out the origins of racial whiteness—"this odd and illogical sickness"—in the pages of early American texts like Poe's. After he is denied tenure for refusing to join the college's diversity committee or for not teaching the courses they expect of their "Professional Negro,"[163] he buys the manuscript of a slave narrative that turns out to have been written by Dirk Peters. It reveals that *The Narrative of Arthur Gordon Pym of Nantucket* was actually a factual account of a real voyage to Antarctica and gives the tantalizing promise that he, Chris Jaynes, might discover the land of Tsalal.

After finding one of Peters's descendants (coming into possession of the diseased skull of the supposedly fictional character) and rallying an all-Black crew that includes his best friend (an overweight recently-laid-off bus driver named Garth Frierson), Chris sets off for the Antarctic. They discover, not Tsalal, but the very race of large whiter-than-white humanoids (the Tekelians) whose appearance precipitously ends Poe's book. They also find a miraculously alive Arthur Gordon Pym, living amongst them. Planning on taking a few of the creatures, King Kong–style, back to the mainland for display and profit, all but one crew member of the Creole Mining Company ends up, instead, enslaved to them. Chris and Garth escape with Pym and discover an equally improbable bioDome, where famous mass-market schlock painter Thomas Karvel, "The Master of Light" (a thinly veiled Thomas Kinkade) is hiding out, trying to live inside of one of his own paintings. A showdown with the Tekelians ensues, ending in a genocidal Last Supper and a generator explosion that together wipe out the race. The novel ends with Chris, Garth, and Pym (now expired) in a canoe, approaching a land populated by "a collection of brown people, and this, of course, is a planet on which such are the majority."[164]

This summary implies, and Johnson lets his readers believe, for a time, that *Pym*'s game is a virtuosic, slightly heavy-handed inversion of Poe's narrative—a clever photographic negative of the nineteenth-century narrative, dropped playfully into the early twenty-first century. The young white man yearning for maritime adventure (Pym) is now the middle-aged light-skinned Black professor (Chris Jaynes) leaving the stifling comforts of the eastern seaboard of the United States to encounter, at the far end of the world, the flat, terrifying essence of the other—this time the monstrously white Tekelians instead of the savagely Black Tsalalians. Whiteness is the horrific monolith, blackness the privileged norm. But that schematic sort of one-to-one inversion of flat stereotypes doesn't hold for long. The graphic lines of Poe's narrative come to lumpy life over the course of Chris's adventures.

The book begins, however, deeply steeped in schematism, committed to the geometric side of the graphic. The most affectively charged identification we see Chris express, at the beginning of the novel, is not with another flesh and blood human, but with his abused books—dumped unceremoniously on the porch of his house when the college's moving service empties out his office.

> My books, my treasure. Sitting in the rain, bloated with a week's worth of water and dirt and mold. Pages bursting open like they were screaming. . . . I picked one up, threw it down, started screaming. Jumping.[165]

Chris is his books. They "scream," figuratively; he screams, literally. He finds comfort in their pristine flatness, and their buckling and bloating presages the havoc his journey will wreak on his safely distant classificatory academic pose (and prose).

Chris's proclivity is to maintain a sharp-edged anthropological stance towards the people and places he encounters. During his exposition of the literary portrayal of Dirk Peters in Poe's novel, Chris notes, with some degree of disdain, the bind of the binary racial logic of America's "one drop" rule. It bothers him that Poe fudges Dirk Peters's identity, both sidestepping it and having it both ways:

> Narratively, Dirk Peters needs to be half Indian despite his Negroid traits because there is no such thing as a half Negro, according to the American "one drop" social reality. Either you are a Negro, containing some African ancestry, or you are not; half whiteness is not allowed. Peters must be at least half white because it is his shred of white decency that leads him to abandon the mutineers and assist Augustus in taking back control of the ship.[166]

Chris brings a similar degree of disdain to the members of the "Native American Ancestry Collective of Gary (NAACG),"[167] whose roster includes Mahalia Mathis, one of Dirk Peters's descendants. "To my eyes, they looked like any gathering of black American folks, some tan and most brown," he notes, as he witnesses their hopes dashed in real time by the revelation of DNA tests that disprove their claims to Native American heritage. Garth reprimands him:

> "So that's it, everybody has to play their roles, right? Black people can't be Indians, don't matter what's in their blood or how they was raised or what

the freedman did for red folk. You just got to be on Team Negro if you got any black in you. Even your octoroon ass." Garth took a bite of a Little Debbie fudge roll so big it seemed to end the conversation right there, as a matter of physics.

. . . "You so scared someone's going to kick you off Team Negro that you think everybody's got to stick to some crazy one-drop rule."[168]

Garth accuses Chris, with his "octoroon ass," of defensively ethno-categorizing everyone around him to compensate for feeling like a precarious benchwarmer on "Team Negro." As Jennifer Wilks points out, Chris's "struggle with race is not only a question of escaping demands that he play the part of the 'Professional Negro' but also of recognizing his own desire to categorize identity."[169] If Poe and Walker both trade in the sharply cut ethnographic of violent binary visual racialization, Johnson gives us a protagonist who can't quite admit to himself he has those same proclivities, even as he navigates through a fictional world that makes an ever-shifting mockery of them.

While Johnson recovers and fleshes out Black characters from Poe's racist schema, he doesn't exactly flatten or frieze whiteness in turn. In the first encounter with the Tekelians, their bodies are "mountainous and hidden, covered in hooded capes that hung broadly from the shoulders and concealed their bulk in folds."[170] The garb of Tekelians initially evokes, as Wilks aptly points out, the white hoods of the KKK. "All the cloth was off-white, composed of what appeared to be the rawhide of skinned animals. In the dim light it was difficult to make out depth and distance."[171] At first, "depth and distance" are difficult to establish, given both the "dim light" and the undifferentiated off-whiteness of their clothes. What "freezes" Chris and the rest of the Creole Mining Company, however, making them involuntarily mimic the continent in which they are trapped, are the faces of the Tekelians, which are then described at length.[172]

Both characters and racial groups in Johnson's work have internal distinctions, individuation, and thus, the possibility of evoking readerly identification. One can ostensibly inhabit, sympathize with, breach the opacity of Johnson's black-and-white figures in a way that is impossible with the silhouette forms of either Poe or Walker. There is textural detail there to which emotions can, à la Ahmed, stick. Even the whiter-than-white abominable snowmen, who seem to be Johnson's inverse of the ethnographically flattened "savage" Tsalalians, eventually become individuals as Chris learns to differentiate amongst them. In his initial description of them, even, phenotypic profiling gives way to a more nuanced assessment of facial feature, the Levinasian gateway to identification:

> What I at first glance had assumed to be horrific masks proved instead to be *their actual faces.* The color, or lack of it, was striking. Albino, it seemed clear, but their eyes contradicted that. Looking into them as they stared intently back at my own, I realized that I had never truly seen pale blue eyes before. I had seen blue but never in this shade, the lightest possible variant, which had more in common with the snow around us than with any accepted form of ocular pigment. These darting, acute, haunting orbs bobbed over noses that were so long and pointy I assume they served some sort of evolutionary purpose that was at the moment unclear. The nostrils were cavernous stretches of ovals, from which gusts of steam—the sole visual evidence that these were actually hot-blooded creatures—pulsed. Also from the holes in their noses came hair, straight and brittle, that fed into their beards, thick corn silk completely devoid of coloring, pouring out of their ponchos. The only pigment attached to them was a yellowing around the mouths and noses, presumably from feeding or bodily fluids.[173]

Chris tries his hand at anthropological classification, wondering what "sort of evolutionary purpose" the monsters' long and pointy noses might serve. But his description also quickly gives lie to the idea that they are creatures of undifferentiated whiteness. They have breath and heat and fluids, causing them to yellow, somewhat ickily, around the edges.

Chris develops a relationship with one particular Tekelian, Krakeer (a play on "cracker," a derogatory term for poor southern whites), who purchases him. Chris's "owner" is an unusual individual. Renamed "Augustus" by Chris ("in honor of Pym's fallen shipmate and my own morbid passive aggression"), he is "probably the only Tekelian I could whup." Crooked of teeth, balding ("the skin [his hair] failed to cover was the gray of dog bellies"), and prone to anxiously chewing his fingernails (apparently usually "long talons" that other Tekelians "clearly took pride in"), Augustus is pathetically individuated.[174]

Johnson characterizes Augustus as a sad outcast mongrel of the Tekelians, but that he characterizes Augustus at all marks a break from Poe's treatment of the Tsalalians. Named after Pym's friend in Poe's novel, Augustus's outsider status amongst his race ("perpetually alone"[175]) begins to forge an almost sympathetic bond between him and Chris. "Staring across at him, watching his pale, watery eyes looking at me, I actually felt a moment of pity. Perhaps in response to this empathy, Augustus did the most human of things: he rolled his marble eyes at me."[176] Rather than simply reversing, then, Johnson refleshes Poe's ethnographic silhouettes.

Eating Little Debbie

"Come on, take a bite of the white girl. It'll make you feel good."
 —GARTH, encouraging Chris to eat a Little Debbie cake

Cannibalism is rampant in the ethnographic worlds of Poe and Walker, but what is its fate in Johnson's text, in which a spectrum of contemporary African American archetypes replaces the monolithic racist stereotypes of his predecessor? [177] Faithful to Poe, people still eat people in *Pym*. After a fashion.

As Chris suffers from starvation during his enslavement to Augustus né Krakeer, he has a hallucinatory vision of saccharine salvation:

It was a human head. It was a child's head. A white girl, no older than four years by my estimate, whistling and skipping with curly chestnut hair billowing out of her blue summer bonnet. All that protected her from the freezing air was a blue and white, checkered sundress, but she seemed fine. There were no signs of hypothermia at all, in fact her cheeks were quite rosy (and not from frostbite). She just whistled along, pausing only to take a bite out of the Swiss roll snack treat in her lovely little hand, the pastry's delicate chocolate covering falling like ebony snow to the ground.

"Little Debbie," I called to her, but my delusion just giggled and kept skipping around. Skipping and chewing, swallowing then whistling. This was a girl whose feet didn't touch the ground. Literally, they didn't touch the ground, floating a good two inches above it yet still managing to make those lovely tapping sounds. Little Debbie's shoes may have missed the floor, but her crumbs didn't, and the more she skipped around, the more her crumbs fell where I could come eat them later. Skip, Little Debbie. Dance! If it would help, I would be her beige Bojangles. For that pastry good stuff, I would bug out my eyes and hop up and down the stairs with her in blackface just like

Louis Armstrong had done for Shirley Temple. I didn't care about principles, and I didn't even care that this was surely all a hallucination. I wanted some of that sweet stuff too. Bite off her head and scoop the cream filling out of her neck with my hands.[178]

Johnson translates Arthur Gordon Pym's cannibalization of Parker into Chris Jaynes's fantasy of scooping the innards out of a hallucinated Little Debbie, who easily takes on the cream-filled attributes of her namesake snack cake by the end of the passage (Figures 2.13 and 2.14).

Pym sees cannibalism shining, with "intense and eager meaning" in the eyes of Augustus after the seagull throws a liver-like clot of human offal at their feet. Chris, enticed by the saccharine purity of Little Debbie, admits to himself that he is just as disconcertingly ready to "bug out my eyes and hop up and down the stairs with her in blackface just like Louis Armstrong had done for Shirley Temple."[179] The savagery that Pym abhors but succumbs to—cannibalism—is translated in Johnson's text into Chris's starvation-fueled willingness to be consumed—appropriated and eaten up—by racial stereotype in order to satisfy a ravenous sweet tooth and gorge himself on sweet empty-calorie whiteness. This fantasy consumption is, of course, tainted too by both the material history of sugar and enslavement (compare with Kara Walker's 2014 installation, *A Subtlety, or the Marvelous Sugar Baby*[180]), and an uncomfortable history of the alleged sexual violation of white female bodies justifying actual violence against Black men.[181] In a footnote, the text expands upon the Little Debbie/Shirley Temple connection (Figure 2.15) and its sexual connotations:

Shirley Temple was America's biggest star during the twentieth century's Depression, but she was a national obsession that from a distance of time now seems quite disturbing. Just a little girl, Temple was the ultimate symbol of purity: the sacred virgin, worshiped by all. There is an innocence to the virgin icon, but at its center it is still a sexual role. Little Debbie, I must say, was beyond such considerations, her purity unassailable. You don't talk about Little Debbie.[182]

Little Debbie becomes Shirley Temple for Chris Jaynes, but the figure's lineage just as easily dates farther back to *Uncle Tom's Cabin* and Little Eva, equally "the ultimate symbol of purity: the sacred virgin, worshiped by all."

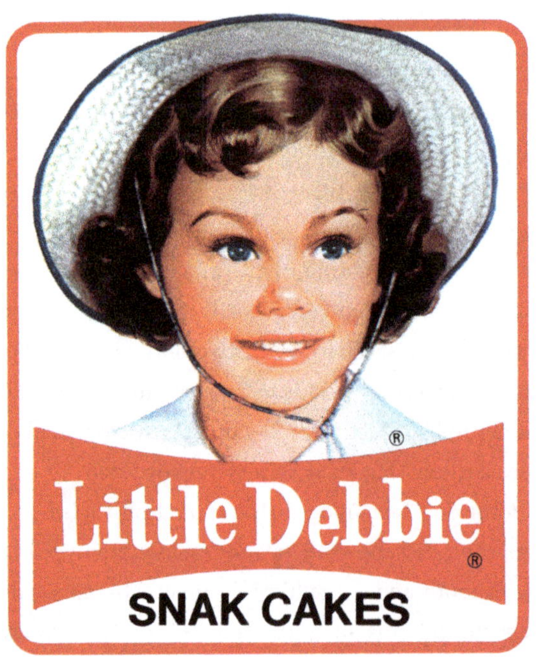

FIGURE 2.13. Little Debbie "Snak Cakes" logo.

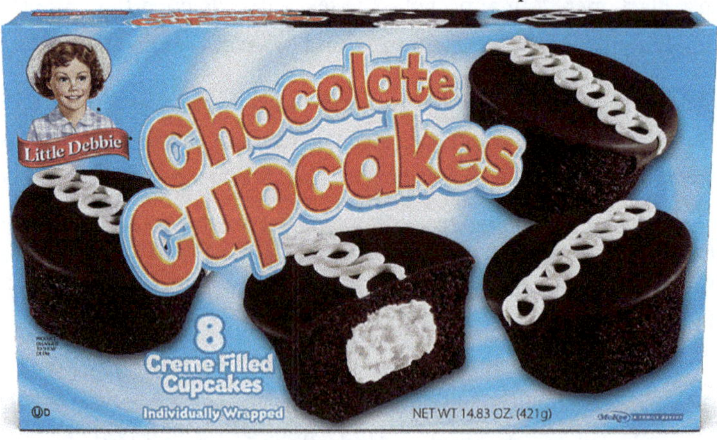

FIGURE 2.14. Little Debbie chocolate cupcakes.

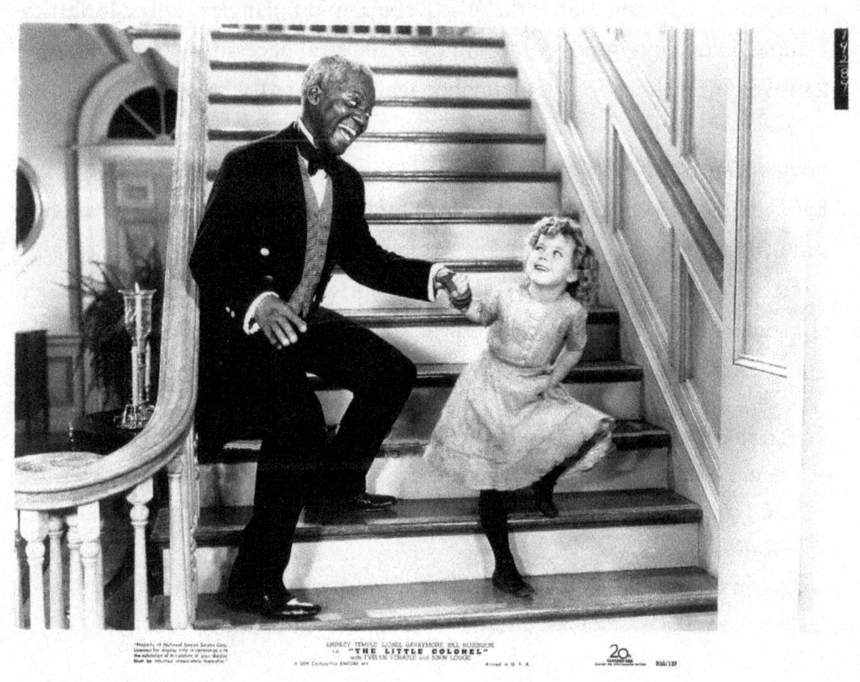

Source: 20th Century Fox press photo.

Whiteness, in the avatar of Little Debbie, is a thing of surfaces—flat advertisements and empty calories. Tim Christensen argues that Little Debbie "comes to signify the primary mechanism through which the ideology of whiteness is disseminated: consumerism."[183] In the figure of Little Debbie, "Whiteness, addiction to the empty calories of junk food, and the attempt to achieve fulfillment through the passionate engagement with consumer culture are inextricably bound" up in one another.[184] And Chris salivates for, longs to fill himself up with, this seductively saccharine emptiness. But in conjuring Shirley Temple alongside Little Debbie, and Bojangles alongside Shirley Temple, Johnson reminds readers of the structural necessity, in formulating a figure of pure whiteness, of setting her against a dark background.

Another One Bites the (Cheetos) Dust

Before it goes up in smoke, though, perhaps the best single image of how Johnson inflates, interrupts, and makes flamboyantly fleshy Poe's mode of silhouetted blackness is when Chris wakes up, disoriented, in what he will discover is Thomas Karvel's Dome of Light, face to face with the naked distended belly of his friend Garth, dusted with a fine film of Cheetos powder.

> Tracing their path off into the horizon, I saw that right before the farthest clouds disappeared past a blooming cherry tree, there were black letters written right onto the blue sky. It was a signature, the autograph of this land's creator.
>
> In my terror I realized that this was not my h-eaven, this was Garth's. This was my hell. I was trapped inside a Thomas Karvel painting.
>
> "Dog, you up?"
>
> I rolled over onto my side and saw my friend.
>
> Garth stood buck naked. Eating a bag of Cheetos.
>
> "Where the hell are we?" I managed, taking him in. Orange cheese dust powdered Garth's various bodily hairs from his goatee down, his overhanging belly covering his genitalia, fortunately.[185]

Chris wakes up and tries to read the inscrutable, oversaturated landscape. His old friend, the written word, further confounds him by showing up where it doesn't belong, hovering just above the horizon. His gaze finally lands upon the contours of another old friend, the most incongruently illegible figure of them all: the overweight, unclothed, orange-dusted body of Garth. This black-and-orange body is hardly the ethnographic silhouette of Poe's novel or Walker's collages. Chris's first gloss on the words in the sky is actually not that far off. He is trapped within the flat fantasy world of a Thomas Karvel painting, a place born of "the fevered Caucasian dreams of Tolkien and Disney."[186] Karvel's Dome of Light is "a stunning example of a simulacrum, the self-contained image world that is both the dream and the nightmare of postmodern culture."[187] And reading this simulacrum for sense—or, for that matter, sensibility—confounds Chris.

This episode purposefully echoes, in a decidedly different tonal register, the moment during the *Grampus* mutiny when Poe's Pym frenziedly attempts to read Augustus's handwritten note, scrawled in blood on a tattered scrap of white paper, illuminated by the faintly glowing dust of his last phosphorous match, in the dark hull of the ship.[188] Johnson comically recasts Pym's vital but withholding sheet of paper as Garth's corpulent body, illuminated this time by the alchemy not of glowing phosphorous fragments, but of neon-orange cheese puff dust. And communicating just as little useful information. (Poe's Pym admits that "In my anxiety, however, to read all at once, I succeeded only in reading the seven concluding words, which thus appeared—'*blood—your life depends upon lying close*'"—missing much of the point of the letter, which was to explain that a mutiny had occurred above deck.[189]) Garth's body, in black and orange, also cites (hinted at with "Dog, you up?") Pym's own canine companion, Tiger, in Poe's novel. Throughout Johnson's *Pym*, what had been the flat, violently detached surfaces of Poe's original text bloat out into multidimensional space—in the forms of fleshed-out characters and inhabitable bioDomes alike.

Rearranging and inflating Poe's text (both the letter and the novel) of Black savagery and mutiny into the Cheeto-dusted belly flesh of an out-of-work bus driver who fervently loves to consume the whitest, emptiest of saccharine delights, both culinary and cultural—the cakes of Little Debbie and the kitsch painting of Thomas Karvel—Johnson does something satirically unsettling. On the one hand, in his gleeful manhandling of Poe's original text, he gives us a skewed version of Sekula's definition of "archival play": a frenzy of "substitution and . . . voracious optical encyclopedism."[190] He also tests the limits of what Sharpe calls "anagrammatical blackness":

the moments when blackness opens up into the anagrammatical in the literal sense as when "a word, phrase, or name is formed by rearranging the letters of another" (*Merriam-Webster Online*). We can also apprehend this in the metaphorical sense in how, regarding blackness, grammatical gender falls away and new meanings proliferate; how "the letters of a text are formed into a secret message by rearranging them" or a secret message is discovered through the rearranging of the letters of a text. *Ana-*, as a prefix, means "up, in place or time, back, again, anew."[191]

What Sharpe means most directly in her own text is the way in which, in the wake of slavery, "the meanings of words fall apart, we encounter again and again the difficulty of sticking the signification" when it comes to blackness, "the ways that meaning slides, signification slips, when words like *child, girl, mother,* and *boy* abut blackness."[192] These slippages are what rearrange a Black mother into a monster, a Black boy into an adult threat. We can see anagrammatical blackness at play certainly in Poe's ethnographic racism, and in many of the fraught descriptions of Kara Walker's stubbornly and suggestively opaque silhouettes. But we also see Walker and Johnson playing *with* the anagram and its violence, daring audiences to try to read what Sharpe calls blackness's "signifying surplus"[193] for the powerful (meant many ways) pleasures of identification, when perhaps the only pleasures it wants to yield up are purely scatological.

"The View Up a Care Bear's Ass"

Rather than just swapping Black for white, and vice versa, almost exactly two-thirds of the way through the book, Johnson gives us the queasy technicolor dreamscape of Thomas Karvel's Antarctic habitat, his Dome of Light,—a three-dimensional, habitable version of paintings that "look like the view up a Care Bear's ass."[194] Johnson presents Karvel's bioDome as an oversaturated vision of a "fantasy of whiteness realized."[195] It's a fantasy that isn't aggressively chiaroscuro, but rather, and just as violently, prismatic.

Karvel's "life-size terrarium" transforms his romantic Anglo-European mass-market kitsch paintings into his own personal habitat. His vision delivers a shock to the ice-inundated systems of Chris and Garth:

The overall look of the room was utterly unreal. The grass we walked on was green, but it was too green. The water that ran through the rambling stream that went diagonally through the space was actually blue. The azaleas and roses and tulips that appeared across the space were all, simultaneously, in the most vivid bloom. It was as if we were walking through a world that had been colorized with markers by an enthusiastic eight-year-old.[196]

Karvel's Dome of Light refracts Morrison's description of Poe's "impenetrable whiteness" into a technicolor rainbow of oversaturated, utterly artificial hues. Like the optical action of a geometric prism, Karvel's fantasy is synthetically produced and fans out its dazzling display of "otherworldly blooms" and sickly-sweet scents from a carefully isolated beam of whiteness. As Wilks argues, "in Karvel's case, decontextualization serves as a means of bolstering, not diluting, his identity."[197] The flat worlds of his paintings are places where "it wasn't just that there were no black people present, it was also that Karvel's world seemed a place where black people couldn't even exist, so thorough was its European romanticization."[198]

His Antarctic hideaway also eschews blackness with an obsessive scrupulousness. The flora and fauna alike within the Dome of Light are carefully "maintained" and "managed." Rabbits, doves, and Karvels: "all the animals were white: I heard some scurrying in the walls while sleeping on my mat and half expected to see a white lab mouse run by."[199] This carefully curated, mechanically managed prismatic terrarium of white fantasy ends up not being entirely sustainable. But it poisons and dynamites Poe's original whiter-than-snow vision of white utopia before it takes its final bow. "While the Tekelians figure whiteness as a prehistoric barbarism, Karvel fantasizes a multi-colored, self-contained techno-paradise."[200] The final conflagration both wipes out and effectively collapses the difference between the two, as Chris et al. serve the Tekelians a poisoned feast, suddenly becoming guilty archival bedfellows with early European settlers of the Americas.

Morrison asserts that "an Africanist character is used to limn out and enforce the invention and implications of whiteness."[201] Thinking about the ethnographic through the image of the silhouette in Poe, Walker, and Johnson forces a serious consideration of the low-hanging (tantalizing) pun of "limn" with "limb." The presumably reparative refleshing of Johnson's *Pym* does not make for a more affectively comfortable or legible read. The ambivalent pull between disinterestedness and disgust remains. The script of sympathetic identification remains staunchly unyielding (no matter how much phosphorous or Cheeto dust we rub across its stubborn surface, it's still all Wingdings to me). Grotesquerie yields neither cathartic release nor empathetic occupation. Opacity reigns, even (or especially) when prismatically projected in "Caucasian fever dream" technicolor. The doubly graphic dynamic of this sort of ethnographic resides, it turns out, not so much in mere flattening as in the proliferation of racialized images qua "pseudo-life-forms" that are, in the mode of Bhabha explication of the stereotype, full of both fixity and frenzy. These ethnographic images are dimensionally disjointed. We don't know how to react to geometric two-dimensional cutouts that start disgorging three-dimensional viscera, just as we find ourselves in an affective bind when three-dimensional flesh is fixed and flattened into two dimensions.

The Pornographic

Sexual desire interweaves *eros* and *thanatos* in the way that Freud works at
without ever being able quite to work out in *Beyond the Pleasure Principle*—
life hanging on for dear life in the deferral of the death drive, which is
simultaneously the dilatory effort of death to get a life, or live itself off through
life. . . . The desires aroused and satisfied by dolls are desires that oscillate
between life and death in the same way. It is in this sense, perhaps, that all
sexuality is idolatrous, and all dolls are sex dolls.

 —STEVEN CONNOR, "Guys and Dolls"

I ran my tongue back and forth over the slivers, back and forth over the words
"copyright 1966 Mattel Inc., Malaysia" tattooed on her back. Tonguing the
tattoo drove Barbie crazy. She said it had something to do with scar tissue being
extremely sensitive.

 —A. M. HOMES, "A Real Doll"

"I'M DATING BARBIE." SO BEGINS A. M. Homes's "A Real Doll," the final
story in a collection entitled *The Safety of Objects*. The story recounts, in first-
person and graphic detail, a sexual affair the narrator—an unnamed, presumably just-pubescent boy—has with his younger sister's Barbie doll. What does
he do to/with Barbie?

> We fucked, that's what I called it, fucking. In the beginning Barbie said she
> hated the word, which made me like it even more. She hated it because it was
> so strong and hard, and she said we weren't fucking, we were making love. I
> told her she had to be kidding.[1]

Barbie seems to talk to and flirt with the narrator. He drugs her (with Valium-
spiked Diet Coke), sucks her plastic feet, pops her head into his mouth and

bites her neck, buys her gifts, and ejaculates both all over her and, twice, into the hollow torso of a temporarily decapitated Ken doll. Meanwhile, Jennifer, the boy's sister and Barbie's owner, has a penchant for chewing off the doll's feet and eventually brings the story to an end by giving it/her a gruesome, molten DIY double mastectomy.

The logistically fraught question of how to have sex with Barbie is the story's subject.[2] The first time the narrator "fucks" Barbie, it goes like this:

> I was on top, trying to get between her legs, almost breaking her in half. But there was nothing there, nothing to fuck except a small thin line that was supposed to be her ass crack.
>
> I rubbed the thin line, the back of her legs and the space between her legs. I turned Barbie's back to me so I could do it without having to look at her face.
>
> Very quickly, I came. I came all over Barbie, all over her and a little bit in her hair. I came on Barbie and it was the most horrifying experience I ever had. It didn't stay on her. It doesn't stick to plastic. I was finished. I was holding a come-covered Barbie in my hand like I didn't know where she came from.
>
> Barbie said, "Don't stop," or maybe I just think she said that because I read it somewhere. I don't know anymore. I couldn't listen to her. I couldn't even look at her. I wiped myself off with a sock, pulled my clothes on, and then took Barbie into the bathroom.[3]

Both the boy and the story seem intent upon fucking (with) many a "small thin line"—between Barbie's legs, between people and things, play and porn, humor and horror. The story is unflinchingly sexually explicit, but equally unsettling because the object of desire is just that: a (sexless) object. The image of the narrator's horror at his semen not adhering to the inanimate surface of the Barbie doll exemplifies the affective ambivalence of the sex doll as a pornographic object—arousingly explicit, and, by being coolly abstracted, equally appalling. Barbie's plastic curves, seemingly begging for rough play, turn the boy on; Barbie's plastic curves, stubbornly slick and impenetrable, likewise horrify him. The moment is also, for readers "watching" this pubescent boy stare with terror at his sister's cum-slick Barbie doll, somewhat queasily hilarious, as it toggles between the gross and geometric poles of being graphic.

The gag of Homes's story—a boy trying to figure out the logistics of how to fuck a Barbie—amplifies these dynamics of the pornographic (or, possibly, the porno-graph-ick). The titillation/trepidation of sexy/sexless plastic becomes even more explicit when, while trying to reassemble Barbie after Jennifer has swapped her head with Ken's, the narrator finds himself fondling, then ejaculating into the hollow torso:

> I started rubbing Ken's bump and watching my thumb like it was a large-screen projection of a porno movie. . . . In the second before I came, I held Ken's head hole in front of me. I held Ken upside down above my dick and came inside of Ken like I never could in Barbie. I came into Ken's body and as soon as I was done I wanted to do it again. I wanted to fill Ken and put his head back on, like a perfume bottle. I wanted Ken to be the vessel for my secret supply. I came in Ken and then I remembered he wasn't mine. He didn't belong to me. I took him into the bathroom and soaked him in warm water and Ivory liquid. I brushed his insides with Jennifer's toothbrush and left him alone in a cold-water rinse.[4]

The boy gets off on Barbie's plasticized surfaces, the signs of her manufacture—he loves to tongue the raised "tattoo" of the graphic inscription of the Mattel copyright on her neck, while he quickly and disdainfully spits upon and rubs away the defacement of pubic hair Jennifer has drawn on with a marker.[5] Each of his sexual encounters is mediated by, and explicitly cribs from, other pornographic texts he's read or seen ("Barbie said, 'Don't stop,' or maybe I just think she said that because I read it somewhere" and "watching my thumb like it was a large-screen projection of a porno movie"). But he can only come in the space—made grossly literal—of male interiority—inside Ken's hollow torso. This puts him in cozy—perhaps claustrophobic—literary company with many a man who has lusted after a doll. The dynamics of this doll play, and how it coolly embodies doubly pornographic feeling, is the subject of this chapter.

Sex Dolls and Porn Studies

The sex doll is the pornographic object par excellence. Histories of the sex doll often take as their starting point the myth of Pygmalion, who so loved his own sculptural creation, the marble statue Galatea, that Aphrodite brought it/her to life for him to consummate his desire. In Ovid's version of the story,

Pygmalion and Galatea then marry and have children. Pygmalion lives on in the psychological profession via the disorder dubbed "pygmalionism," first discussed at length in Iwan Bloch's 1908 *The Sexual Life of Our Time in Its Relations to Modern Civilization* and defined today as "the condition of loving a statue, image, or inanimate object; sexual attraction towards such an object. Also: love for an object of one's own making."[6]

The history of the sex doll is shrouded in rumor, speculation, and myth. In the seventeenth century, French and Spanish sailors would take crude fornicatory dolls made of cloth or leather and known as *dames de voyage* or *dama de viaje* on long sea voyages.[7] The Japanese, who encountered these dolls through frequent trading with the Dutch East India Company, called them *datch waifu* or "Dutch wives." By 1908, Bloch refers to French sex dolls made of rubber and plastic, replete with "a 'pneumatic tube' filled with oil" used to imitate "the secretion of Bartholin's glands" and lubricate the artificial female genitals.[8] A popular urban legend holds that during the Second World War, Nazi Germany's "Borghild Project" engineered the first modern sex dolls—perfect Aryan specimens—in order to both train and contain the sexual appetites of its invading armies, tempted as they were on all sides by contamination from foreign prostitutes of "inferior races."[9] Himmler's "traveling army of gynoids" was intended "to follow the conquering Wehrmacht across the battlefields of Europe. The dolls were to be housed in a series of 'disinfections-chambers.'"[10] What we know for sure is that in the 1960s, the now-iconic inflatable sex doll first appears in the United States in mail-order advertisements printed in men's magazines.[11]

Anthony Ferguson describes the contemporary sex doll as "woman in her most objectified form . . . never more than the sum of its fully functional parts . . . immobile, compliant, and perhaps most importantly, silent."[12] Debates surrounding sex dolls tend to be analogous to those around the bodies and actions depicted in hard-core video pornography. Are these depictions of women as sexual objects inherently violent themselves? Do they encourage their users to enact or mimic (following Robin Bernstein's notion of scriptive things) certain violent actions?[13] Some argue it's just good dirty fun. The sex doll focuses these myriad debates about pornography and the pornographic to more specific questions about the interplay between guts and geometry, flesh and fabrication, that are at the heart (pulsing or plasticized) of the affective ambivalence of the double graphic when its content is sexual, when the sympathetic drive to intimately inhabit the other's feelings gets penetratively literal. The sex doll can be uncanny, repulsive, titillating, or hilarious (the open question its gaping openings beg is what—or who—is the true butt of the joke). It is a form at once sensuous and antiseptic. It is a pornographic object that is graphic in multiple and seemingly contradictory ways—at once explicit and abstracted, sexy and schematic, disgusting and disinterested.

The sex doll seems to aim at a verisimilitude—visual, tactile, and functional—in which "the aim of the image is to displace reality."[14] It's a representation—or replacement—however, that is always skirting the pitfalls of both the "uncanny valley" and ethical censure.[15] Sex dolls depict women too well for comfort while turning a mirror back unflatteringly upon the men who consume them. "The image may be of a woman," Steven Connor argues, "but what it unmistakably shows is male desire, objectified and made immediately recognizable and mechanically predictable."[16]

There is some debate in scholarship on sex dolls, though, about whether reality or verisimilitude are really the aim of the object at all or are only the source of its titillation. In a study that focuses on the fetish of the "erotic doll" in both the context of commercial sex dolls and the work and lives of prominent twentieth-century artists—including Oskar Kokoschka, Hans Bellmer, and Marcel Duchamp—Marquard Smith argues that "the erotic doll or mannequin is held up not as a site of verisimilitude and mimeticism but as a fabricated form organized or arranged, and understood to draw attention to its own distorting, fragmentary, partial and anagrammatical nature"[17] (Figures 3.1 and 3.2). Smith's description of getting off on distortion, fragmentation, and fabrication laid brazenly bare vibrates tantalizingly with many popular theorizations of the playful, antirealist promiscuity of literary postmodernism. The allure of the "erotic doll" isn't that it can be mistaken for a flesh and blood woman, but that it infinitely accommodates and enables the self-gratifying creative manipulations of men. The man aroused by the sex doll's openness to being manipulated is also recursively aroused by his own ability to make an object arousing.

There's something—slightly skewed—of Sianne Ngai's formulation of "the cute" to the sex doll, too. According to Ngai, cuteness is "an aestheticization of powerlessness ('what we love because it submits to us')."[18] She suggests that

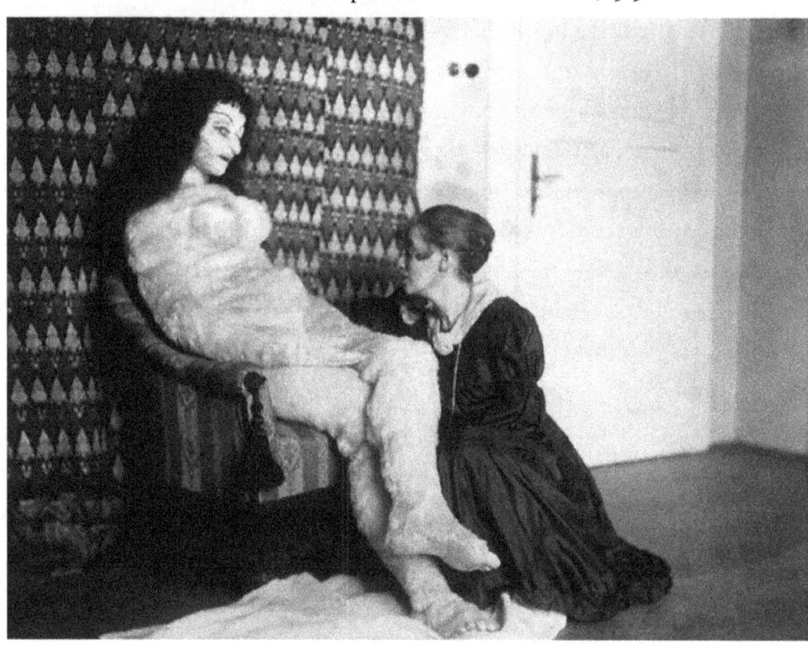

FIGURE 3.1. Dressmaker Hermine Moos and the life-size doll she was commissioned to make of Alma Mahler, who was the ex-lover of painter Oskar Kokoschka, 1919.

Source: Wikipedia Commons, Public Domain.

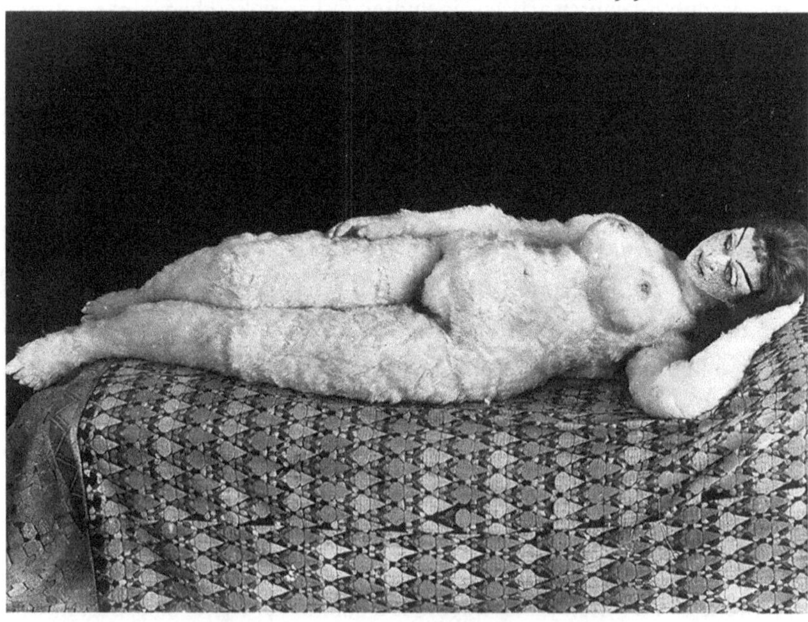

FIGURE 3.2. Oskar Kokoschka's "Alma doll," 1919.

Source: Wikipedia Commons, Public Domain.

"since soft contours suggest pliancy or responsiveness to the will of others, the less formally articulated the commodity, the cuter."[19] Even if the sex doll is imperfectly cute—too lifelike and firm to suit that aesthetic's ideal, which Ngai epitomizes with the example of a baby's bath sponge in the shape of a smiley frog face—it seems to hold, in its passivity and muteness,[20] an analogous affective force, an "exaggerated passivity" that "seems likely to excite the consumer's sadism or desire for mastery as much as her desire to protect and cuddle."[21] The sex doll thus captures the gendered aspects of a certain kind of writing that combines a detached, sterile pose with explicit, upsetting, and/or arousing content. It shows how the desire to know and have through fixation/fixity produces confusion between subject and object, person and thing, natural and artificial. And it intimates how this uncanny, gendered, and sexed dynamic—with its attendant preoccupations with texture, surface, and access to interiors—might emerge in pornographic texts.

Linda Williams's *Hard Core*, the first book-length assessment of the form and function of hard-core adult films, in many ways inaugurated the academic field of porn studies. Drawing on Foucault's observations in *History of Sexuality* about the "modern compulsion to speak incessantly about sex," she defines and analyzes hard-core film and video pornography "as one of the many forms of the 'knowledge-pleasure' of sexuality."[22] While this chapter is not primarily about video pornography or porn as a genre, it is about moments within primarily linguistic literary texts that share hard-core's drive to "knowledge-pleasure." This epistemological imperative subtends the "graphic" in these texts, as they revel in being at once clinical and visceral in how they divulge sex.

Recent contributions to porn studies have looked to expand the field both within adult entertainment films and beyond those generic constraints. Helen Hester argues that "adult entertainment and the pornographic should not be viewed as one and the same thing."[23] She is invested, instead, in articulating "a distinction between pornography as a representational genre and pornography as a capacious cultural concept."[24] Hester notes the "slippage," that the term "pornographic" has undergone in recent years (see popular coinages from "war porn," to "food porn"). She argues that these newly porn-appended works and more generic pornography share affective charges of "disgust and disapproval," even as they are rarely explicitly about the sexual body. She posits that, instead:

> [T]he concept of the pornographic has migrated away from adult entertainment and become attached to other, less rehabilitated forms of prurience—a lascivious curiosity regarding war, for example, or abuse, or torture, or any other type of representation that depicts authentic scenes of psychic or bodily intensity in a culturally denigrated fashion.[25]

My look at the pornographic intervenes in similar fashion in what Williams has dubbed the "weedy field" of porn studies. Like Hester, I want to return to pornographic linguistic texts as objects of study, and to think about the application of the term to moments in works that fall outside of the traditional generic constraints of adult entertainment.[26] While Hester focuses on the slippage of "the porn suffix," I attend to the -graphic of the pornographic. Williams asks, decades after *Hard Core*, in her contribution to the 2014 volume *Porn Archives*, about the tendency of academic "porn studies" to generally eschew the more formal "pornography" in favor of the vernacular "porn," which indeed graces that very tome's title. "How have we come to designate a field of academic study by this term? Why have we lost the *graph* in *pornography*?"[27] Indeed, parsing the dual meanings of the "graphic" helps clarify the affect that Hester finds in her expanded notions of the pornographic:

> Porn cannot be characterized as merely "a sex thing" . . . even if adult entertainment can; it is not preoccupied with eliciting a genitally sexual response but with provoking more general forms of queasy *jouissance*—horror, anger, sorrow, and a certain nauseated fascination.[28]

Not losing the -graphic emphasizes this affective ambivalence, the oddly easy simultaneity of disgust and detachment, of explicit grossness and geometrical exactitude, that emerges more and more in information-age portrayals of sex.

This chapter explores (and expands) this question of the pornographic's "queasy *jouissance*" by taking up a twentieth-century classic of male-focalized obscene doll play (Vladimir Nabokov's *Lolita*), followed by two more contemporary works by Black women in which the dolls disconcertingly play back: Fran Ross's 1974 postmodern picaresque *Oreo*, and the avant-porn burlesque performances of Narcissister. Along the way, I'll examine a key register of doubly pornographic affect that Hester's description notably misses: the humor that emerges when the soft and sensual is translated through and into the mechanical and mass produced—and, in doing so, becomes the gag (quip, prank, retch, choke).

Articulating *Lolita*

Lolita is an exemplary porno-graphic novel, a tale about lust and geometry, desire and diagrams, flesh and paper. Lolita, Humbert Humbert's pet name for Dolores Haze, the nymphet of his creation, is—in many senses—a real doll. Humbert is obsessed with the texture of his Dolly's skin and the manual manipulation of her limbs. He plays rough with her. Dozens of pages before he introduces Lolita as a body, Nabokov's Humbert famously dismembers and rebuilds her name as an almost coercively sensuous, molded, and masticated word:

> Lolita, light of my life, fire of my loins. My sin, my soul. Lo-lee-ta: the tip of the tongue taking a trip of three steps down the palate to tap, at three, on the teeth. Lo. Lee. Ta.
>
> She was Lo, plain Lo, in the morning, standing four feet ten in one sock. She was Lola in slacks. She was Dolly at school. She was Dolores on the dotted line. But in my arms she was always Lolita.[29]

In these first lines of the novel, Humbert takes apart and fondles Lolita's name piece by piece. He disassembles the word along syllabic joints in a way that makes it/her, even before the hint of "she was Dolly at school," into an articulated plaything. It is in this dollification of Dolores Haze, through which Humbert's lust turns her into a squeamishly special sort of object, that the truly pornographic moments of *Lolita* lie.

"A pet form of the name Dorothy. Hence given generically to a female pet, a mistress," "doll" also signifies "an image of a human being (commonly of a child or lady) used as a plaything," and "a dummy used by a ventriloquist, or by a puppeteer."[30] The name "Lolita" is Humbert's coinage for the nymphet he sees in Dolores Haze, but her nickname, "Dolly," is uncomfortably close to what he wants out of the flesh and blood girl he adores and abducts: a pet, a mistress, an image, a plaything, a mute dummy. Analyzing the work of the German artist Hans Bellmer, Marquand Smith ties the eroticism of a certain type of doll to its "anagrammatical nature," in which titillation lies in the inanimate body's very potential for clean disassembly: "where the body is a sentence dismantled and put back together differently" the "logic to such assembling" is "erotic."[31] Bellmer wrote about and created life-sized dolls in which myriad legs and breasts and heads could be attached to a central "ball joint" of a stomach and pelvis (Figure 3.3). He avowed that

> [T]he sentence is comparable to a body that appears to invite you to disarticulate it, so that its true contents may be recomposed through an endless series of anagrams. The body is comparable to a sentence that appears to invite you to disarticulate it, so that its true contents may be recomposed through an endless series of anagrams.[32]

This elision of body and sentence found its physical form in Bellmer's work, as I argue it does in Nabokov's, through and in the erotic and linguistically caressed doll (Figure 3.4).

FIGURE 3.3. Hans Bellmer, *La Poupée (The Doll),* from his exhibition *Les jeux de la poupée* (The Games of the Doll), 1935–1938. Silver gelatin print.

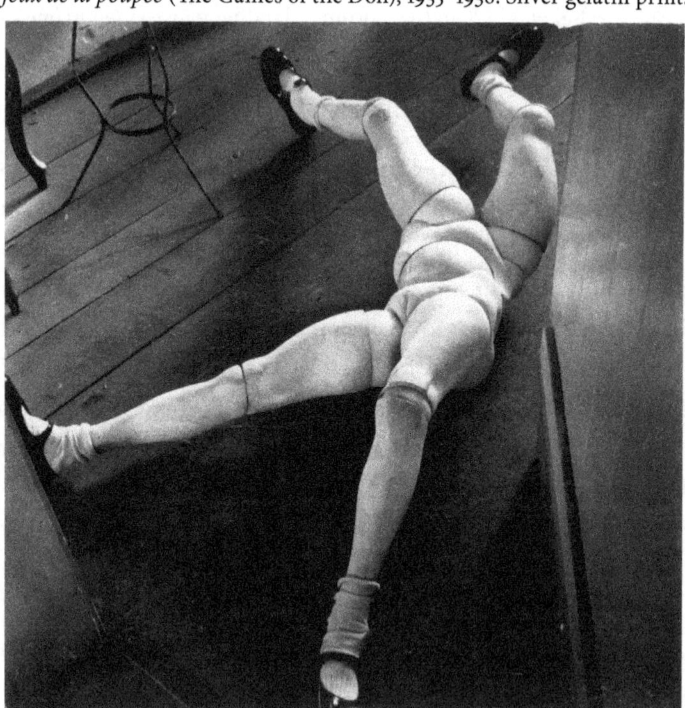

Source: Repro-photo: Philippe Migeat. Digital Image © CNAC/ MNAM, Dist. RMN-Grand Palais / Art Resource, NY.

FIGURE 3.4. The cover of *Lolita* for the 1997 Vintage edition, designed by Megan Wilson.

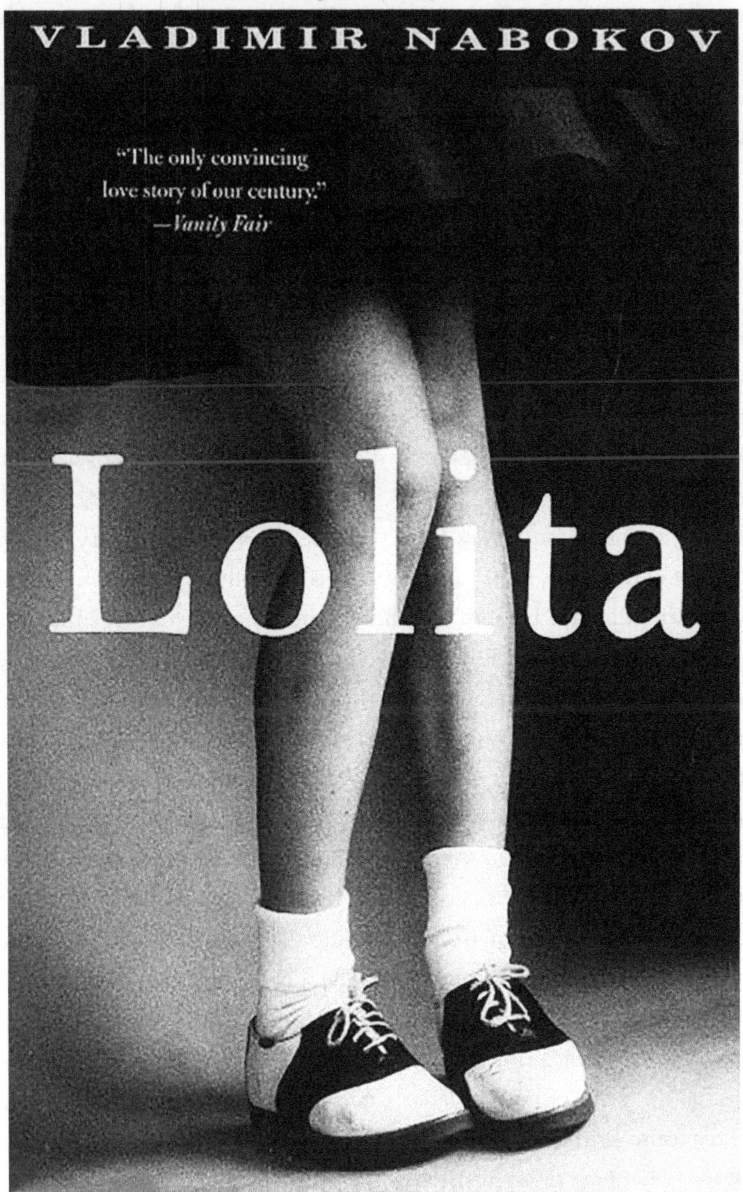

Source: Bertram and Leving, *Lolita: The Story of a Cover Girl: Vladimir Nabokov's Novel in Art and Design*, 29.

By the end of the novel's first famous paragraph, Lolita has been declared, dismantled, and resequenced, much like any doll with removable parts. There is an emphatically recombinant logic to Humbert Humbert's obsession with Lolita, the ideal nymphet, the second coming of "a certain initial girl-child." The name "Lolita" itself is an anagrammatic mutation of Dolores, in which the ball joint of the central "Lo" gets shuffled to the front of the name and appended to a "li/ly" borrowed from the generic pet name "Dolly." Once he fixes/fixates on the name Lo-lee-ta in its tri-syllabic recombination, though, the erotics of the dissection of Lolita becomes as much about the grossly titillating fixity of sequence and repetition as the Bellmer-esque acrobatics of being "put back together differently" and "recomposed through an endless series of anagrams." "Lolita, Lolita, Lolita, Lolita, Lolita, Lolita, Lolita, Lolita, Lolita. Repeat till the page is full, printer."[33] There is something at once evocative of doll play and essentially, obsessively diagrammatic about the novel's opening lines.

Eugenie Brinkema argues for a violence inherent in the very sequential structure of diagrams in her analysis of the 2009 film *The Human Centipede*. Written and directed by Tom Six, the infamous horror film tells the story of a German surgeon who kidnaps three hapless tourists, two women and one man, and joins them together surgically, mouth to anus, in order to form a "human centipede" with a single digestive tract. Brinkema cites Jacques Bertin's *Semiology of Graphics*, in which he "distinguishes a diagram from a network from a map from a symbol with the crucial notation that a diagram establishes divisions of one component and another; the diagram explicitly turns on the separation of parts, and is always, in some way, about the elemental."[34] Humbert's move from "Lolita" to "Lo-lee-ta," through the diligent but eventually discarded taxonomy of "She was Lo, plain Lo, in the morning" through "Lola," "Dolly," and "Dolores," to, finally, "Lo. Lee. Ta." is diagrammatic in the extreme. This first paragraph "explicitly turns on the separation of parts," in terms of both syllables and roles that the girl will come to play. The diagram, Brinkema argues, is the essence of the violence of *The Human Centipede* because of its insistence on unmodifiable sequence, "a rivetedness to a certain notation" that elides individuals into a thing and forecloses escape: "the formality of a written bondedness violent in excess of any order stained with blood, vomit, pus, piss, shit, agony, weeping, terror. The diagram is what poses the formality of the problem of escape from the sequence that it is."[35] Though there is much that is sensual and luxurious and recombinant about Nabokov's articulation of Lo-lee-ta, it is in its diagrammatic insistence on sequence, element, and formal instruction—the pedagogy of the speech pathologist with a lurid flourish—that this initial assembly of the girl's name holds perhaps the germ of the violence to come. "The tip of the tongue taking a trip of three steps down the palate to tap, at three, on the teeth" is also a visceral description of a biting, chewing, hinged, dexterous maw.

In these first few lines, Humbert Humbert virtuosically articulates and masticates "Lolita." The "articulate," to mine the *OED*, consists of "clearly distinguishable parts (usually words and syllables) capable of conveying meaning," is "expressed in clear and eloquent language," "clearly structured," and "set out in articles, particularized, specified." The word's definition also oscillates, as the entire book does, between language and ligament, that which is "distinctly jointed or marked," or "composed of segments that are linked or united by joints."[36] Articulation, then, being as much about the diagrammatic anatomy of a sentence or word as of a "downy" or dolly limb, is key for thinking about the doubly graphic relationship between Humbert and Lolita.

Barbara Johnson argues that a person-like thing's "realness" has something to do with whether the articulation of its joints is evident or erased. "The principal sign of Pinocchio's 'realness' is the disappearance of the signs of his articulation: in a puppet, the joints are marked; in a 'real boy,' they are erased."[37] When the "signs of his articulation" disappear—meaning the signs both that he is peg-jointed together and that he was spoken into being by someone more real than he—Pinocchio becomes "real himself." In other words:

> Pinocchio becomes a real boy when his body is entirely smooth. Organic form is thus, among other things, an erasure of articulation. This may be why Western cultures are intolerant of any lines on the body—any wrinkles or signs of experience—especially in a love object.[38]

By over-articulating Lolita's linguistic joints from the very beginning, Nabokov subverts any claims to the "realness" of the nymphet Humbert constructs throughout the rest of the novel. Despite protestations to the contrary, Humbert always wants Lolita to be more doll than real girl.[39]

"She Was Dolly at School": Knowledge-Pleasure and Measurement Grids

Nabokov's novel is as much about knowledge—a scholarly or schoolroom impulse to document, taxonomize, and make the desired thing telegraph its secrets—as it is about eroticism or even sex. Humbert's over-articulated nymphetmania shares with hard-core pornography what Williams calls "the 'knowledge-pleasure' of sexuality."[40] Humbert explains, "I am not concerned with so-called 'sex' at all. Anybody can imagine those elements of animality. A greater endeavor lures me on: to fix once and for all the perilous magic of nymphets."[41] Humbert's obsession with halting, capturing, and possessing the nymphet at her magical, illusive moment of peak (under)development is structurally similar to hard-core pornography's fixation on the equally slippery task of fixing, in a moment, "the visual 'knowledge' of women's pleasure."[42] Williams argues that the defining drive—and frustration—of hard core has always been a need to document, know, and *see* incontrovertible proof, or "authentication,"[43] of the withheld and wily moment of female orgasm, "the out-of-control confession of pleasure, a hard-core 'frenzy of the visible.'"[44] This desire to arrest—to fix—moments and physiognomies that resist this sort of suspension is a hallmark of the pornographic. Pornography tries to render unruly and evasive flesh and blood individuals with their own mental interiority into objects examinable at and as leisure.

Lolita is, of course, not hard-core pornography. Eric Naiman argues that, because it eschews any portrayal of Lolita's own sexual pleasure, it isn't even soft core.[45] But the novel does trade in and linger over moments that are distinctly *pornographic* in the doubled sense of this book. Humbert's will to knowledge-pleasure entails both the geometric and the grotesque sides of the "graphic," as he figuratively both measures and disembowels Lolita. Much critical emphasis has been put on emphasizing the "-ick" of Nabokov's uneasily, notoriously, and disputedly pornographic literary masterpiece, so I will begin with how it relies upon the "graph."

In her discussion of the relationship between Eadweard Muybridge's proto-cinematic photographs of bodies in motion and pornography's "frenzy of the visual," Williams argues:

> The principle of maximum visibility operates in the hard-core film as though Muybridge's measurement grids were still in place, trying to gauge with in-

creasing exactitude the genital equivalent of "at / which point in a leap the female breast / is highest."[46]

Throughout Nabokov's novel, Humbert surveys his Lolita in a surprisingly similar way, through constant recourse to "measurement grids" of various ilk. The first grid against which Lolita is measured is that of the overdetermined dead childhood love, Annabel. When Humbert first sees Lolita, he "recognizes" a doppelganger, detail for detail, point for point, of Annabel. As his "glance slithered over the kneeling child . . . the vacuum of my soul managed to suck in every detail of her bright beauty, and these I checked against the features of my dead bride."[47] Diagrammatically, Humbert confirms her correspondence to the dead ideal. Foucault characterizes the "pure optical system," the Panopticon as "the diagram of a mechanism of power reduced to its ideal form; its functioning, abstracted from any obstacle, resistance or friction."[48] Brinkema suggests that as neither an archive nor a repository, "the diagram is a cartography of an ideal."[49] As his gaze "slithers" over her in this split blazon, the frictionless vacuum of Humbert's set of abstracted nymphet protocols consumes and catalogues the body of Dolores Haze, who becomes more object-like with each checked detail, down to "the tiny dark-brown mole on her side."[50]

Later in the novel, Humbert relishes being able to confirm his mental cartography of Lolita's body, before he has physical access to it at the Enchanted Hunters lodge, when he selects clothes for her. He studiously consults a reference text, the now-deceased Charlotte Haze's "Know-Your-Child" book:

> One of my guides in these matters was an anthropometric entry made by her mother on Lo's twelfth birthday (the reader remembers that Know-Your-Child book). I had the feeling that Charlotte, moved by obscure motives of envy and dislike, had added an inch here, a pound there; but since the nymphet had no doubt grown somewhat in the last seven months, I thought I could safely accept most of those January measurements: hip girth, twenty-nine inches; thigh girth (just below the gluteal sulcus), seventeen; calf girth and neck circumference, eleven; chest circumference, twenty-seven; upper arm girth, eight; waist, twenty-three; stature, fifty-seven inches; weight, seventy-eight pounds; figure, linear; intelligence quotient, 121; vermiform appendix present, thank God.

Apart from measurements, I could of course visualize Lolita with hallucinational lucidity; and nursing as I did a tingle on my breastbone at the exact spot her silky top had come level once or twice with my heart; and feeling as I did her warm weight in my lap (so that, in a sense, I was always "with Lolita" as a woman is "with child"), I was not surprised to discover later that my computation had been more or less correct.[51]

The meticulous catalogue of measurements is slightly numbing (too many numbers, easy to skip right over) but it also invites the reader to join Humbert in the calculus of translating dimensions on paper into the "hallucinational lucidity" of mind's-eye photographic visualization. It is also another iteration of Humbert toying with, articulating, and separating Lolita by her parts.

Nabokov emphasizes the resonance between his first sight of her and this moment of measurement via the absurd flight of fairytale fancy that briefly accompanies each. Humbert describes the department store's "touch of the mythological and the enchanted," echoing the saccharine ecstasies of first surveying Lolita from afar "as if I were the fairy-tale nurse of some little princess (lost, kidnapped, discovered in gypsy rags through which her nakedness smiled at the king and his hounds)."[52] The act of measuring, assessing, and diagramming Lolita as a body against abstract rubrics, with increasing exactitude, seems to be its own arousal for Humbert. It is at moments when she is abstractly transposed onto flat surfaces, legible yet tangibly impenetrable—displayed and di-splayed both, put up for visual consumption, duplicated, cracked open, sexually prone—that *Lolita* is most graphic.

Having cast her in visual flatness at various moments in the novel—most famously as "a photographic image rippling upon a screen"[53]—Humbert reincarnates Lolita as an image in a mirror toward the end of the novel:

There was the day when having withdrawn the functional promise I had made her on the eve (whatever she had set her funny little heart on—a roller rink with some special plastic floor or a movie matinee to which she wanted to go alone), I happened to glimpse from the bathroom, through a chance combination of mirror aslant and door ajar, a look on her face . . . that look I cannot exactly describe . . . an expression of helplessness so perfect that it seemed to grade into one of rather comfortable inanity just because this was the very limit of injustice and frustration—and every limit presupposes something beyond it—hence the neutral illumination.[54]

The expression Humbert glimpses on her face "through a chance combination" of opaque surfaces set at revealing angles is so extreme and charged that it loops back into neutrality. It is the look of someone utterly captured—by the light that glances off the mirror, by the man who glances at the mirror through the bathroom door. Brinkema writes that "the diagram is what poses the formality of the problem of escape from the sequence that it is."[55] She also glosses Foucault's exegesis of the mirror in *Las Meninas* as "'that enchantment of the double,' what restores the visibility of what had remained invisible."[56] This image of Lolita in the mirror too wreaks havoc with doubleness and invisibility, though Humbert here narrates the *dis*enchantment of the double. This startling realization is available to him only through the flattening and distance provided by her image being transposed onto a mirror and observed unawares. After Humbert has denied Lolita her own chance to skate smoothly over surfaces ("some special plastic floor"), it is another shiny flat plane that captures her, helpless, in a moment of vulnerable, visual, intimately stolen revelation, a cruel parody of the helpless "out-of-control confession of pleasure" of Williams's "frenzy of the visible."[57]

Earlier, Humbert, maudlin, laments: "Oh, my Lolita, I have only words to play with!"[58] And he fondles them lustily. His narration provides constant reminders that "graphic" means also "of or pertaining to writing; fit to be written on." The physical and mental act of writing—the visual, oral, and aural shape of words—is the very fabric of his fixation:[59] "Lolita exists as a subject and object somewhere in Humbert's prose, but nowhere beyond that text."[60] The novel is Lolita. Lolita is the novel. Within the grid-like text, even something as staid as her name in an elementary school class list, which he transcribes in its entirety, name for name, becomes lyrically lascivious:

> What is it that excites me almost to tears (hot, opalescent, thick tears that poets and lovers shed)? What is it? The tender anonymity of this name with its formal veil ("Dolores") and that abstract transposition of first name and surname, which is like a pair of new pale gloves or a mask? Is "mask" the keyword?[61]

Throughout the novel, Nabokov has his readers see uncomfortably through Humbert Humbert's eyes. As we are inevitably bored by the dull parade of unmoored labels (forty in all) that don't belong to our Dolly, Nabokov seems to ask, or perhaps authorize, us to scan the "poem" of Lolita's class roster until, with satisfaction and relief, we alight on her name. The impersonal self-evidence of the list form attains a tint, then a taint of guilty eroticism in the next paragraph under Humbert's gloss. He feels, or feigns, surprise that such a drily objective text produces in him such an arousal—"hot, opalescent, thick tears."

How is it, he asks, that "anonymity" and "abstract transposition" pump from him these ooey gooey feelings, this ejaculatory weeping?[62] But what Humbert styles as anomalous about this excitation is in fact one of the novel's most naked displays of the pornographic dynamic at play throughout the book. Lolita, over-articulated as a word and as a sex doll, is Humbert's creature/creation of "tender anonymity" and "abstract transposition." His sexual objectification of her is a thing of both "downy" disgust and cold hard calculation. This ambivalent pornographic bent is figured by how Humbert handles, so to speak, the literal dolls scattered everywhere in the novel, an army of Lolita dummies.

Could You Be a Doll And . . . ?

One of Humbert's early attempts to find a stand-in for Annabel in a brothel ends abortively when he flees at the sight of "a monstrously plump, sallow, repulsively plain girl of at least fifteen with red-ribboned thick black braids who sat on a chair perfunctorily nursing a bald doll."[63] The exclusion of the "plump, sallow, repulsively plain girl" from Humbert's island of the nymphet seems to be as much signaled by the baldness of the doll and the "womanly" act of nursing it as by the girl's own physical appearance. The doll, too inanimate to suckle, has already been worn bare and bears the evidence of past use and abuse. By the calculus of an implicit, cringingly facile transitive property, so too has the girl who, with a futile and premature mechanical gesture, performs a sort of care that disgusts Humbert, gesturing toward a future womanhood he wishes to be forestalled. Every overdetermined object in the tableau Humbert paints—girl and doll alike—fails its ostensible category. And for a man who lusts after the pseudo-anthropological identification of the rarest of categorical "discoveries," classing himself as one of the "lone voyagers" bound for the "enchanted island haunted by those nymphets of mine and surrounded by a vast, misty sea,"[64] this is the most repulsive thing there is—misclassification.

When he touches Lolita, by contrast, he luxuriates in describing, yet again, how she checks all of the boxes of nymphetdom. His "perfunctory" encounter with the plain girl is countered later by one of his first covert caresses of the "downy" Lolita, as she sits playing with "a ballerina of wool and gauze":

> [A]nd finally, when I had completely enmeshed my glowing darling in this weave of ethereal caresses, I dared stroke her bare leg along the gooseberry fuzz of her shin, and I chuckled at my own jokes, and trembled, and concealed my tremors, and once or twice felt with my rapid lips the warmth of her hair as I treated her to a quick nuzzling, humorous aside and caressed her plaything. She, too, fidgeted a good deal so that finally her mother told her sharply to quit it and sent the doll flying into the dark, and I laughed and addressed myself to Haze across Lo's legs to let my hand creep up my nymphet's thin back and feel her skin through her boy's shirt.[65]

The analogic structure—girl to doll—of this later encounter is chillingly similar, but here it attracts Humbert because there is concordance. Caresses of Lolita and caresses of "her plaything" easily flow one into another. Indeed, his caresses of the doll's body provide cover for his fondling of Lolita's. Her mother's tossing of the doll reminds us, as Steven Connor asserts, that "to be a toy is to be able to be injured as well as caressed. There is a kind of deathliness in play—not the simple deathliness of the inanimate object, but the impulse that all play releases and allows, of putting the toy to death."[66] This "impulse . . . of putting the toy to death" also, of course, works as a double entendre with *la petite mort*. Humbert wants to put Lolita to death (orgasm) but only succeeds in hastening the actual death of Dolores Haze.

Waxing Waxen: Lusting to "Turn My Lolita Inside Out"
Mortification subtends several of Humbert's elaborate bodily fantasies. At the Enchanted Hunter, he initially declares: "I was still firmly resolved to pursue my policy of sparing her purity by operating only in the stealth of night, only upon a completely anesthetized little nude."[67] Even after he has raped her while she is fully conscious, however, he feels a perverse quasi-surgical desire: "My only grudge against nature was that I could not turn my Lolita inside out and apply voracious lips to her young matrix, her unknown heart, her nacreous liver, the sea-grapes of her lungs, her comely twin kidneys."[68] This graphically literalizes the knowledge lust of hard-core porn while also invoking the long

history of prone, semi-ecstatic, waxen medical mannequins à la *The Anatom-ical Venus* (Figure 3.5).

In Marquand Smith's history of the "erotic doll," he remarks of the anatomical wax figures popular in Italy in the seventeenth and eighteenth centuries:

> Following the graphic conventions of drawings and woodblocks from the late Middle Ages and Renaissance depicting the opening up of women's bodies, these wax figures as systems of knowledge are a supposed antidote to women's withholding in life of inaccessible knowledge: of generation, reproduction, and sexuality. . . . Here, hidden, uncertain and concealed knowledge—the specialized knowledge that makes up the "secrets of women"—is finally revealed and mastered and is comprehended, perhaps because it is in death, as titillating, sexual, erotic.[69]

Humbert, even as he congratulates himself for proprietarily "attending to the wants of my little auburn brunette's body," lusts for that body to expose its secrets more completely to him. It is from the desire for knowledge's victory over withholding nature—against which, Smith argues, more men than Humbert have held a grudge—that the pedagogical tool of the wax anatomical figure gains its erotic charge:

> Notwithstanding such barbaric anatomizing, and more likely because of it, these female anatomical figures are figured as erotic, pornographic even. The waxes' pathology as a spectacle of display is, I would argue, recognized as all the more erotic because of it prone, corpse-like posture.[70]

The Anatomical Venus, the star attraction of Peter Leopold's Royal Museum of Physics and Natural History in late eighteenth-century Florence,[71] is a model par excellence of this sort of wax doll, itself a prime object of what Foucault famously calls the "*scientia sexualis*," which "constructs modern sexualities according to a conjunction of power and knowledge that probes the measurable, confessable 'truths' of a sexuality that governs bodies and their pleasures."[72] One of the most notable attributes of *The Anatomical Venus* was her layered, removable abdomen, which allowed viewers—and touchers (she was made to be palpated)—to examine her internal reproductive organs from all sides by removing them and holding them in hand.[73] Humbert seeks the same access (and then some) to Lolita's "young matrix." "Matrix" evocatively means "a supporting or enclosing structure," "a point of origin and growth,"

FIGURE 3.5. *The Anatomical Venus* by the Workshop of Clemente Susini and Giuseppe Ferriani c. 1789. Composed of wax, human hair, rosewood, and venetian glass.

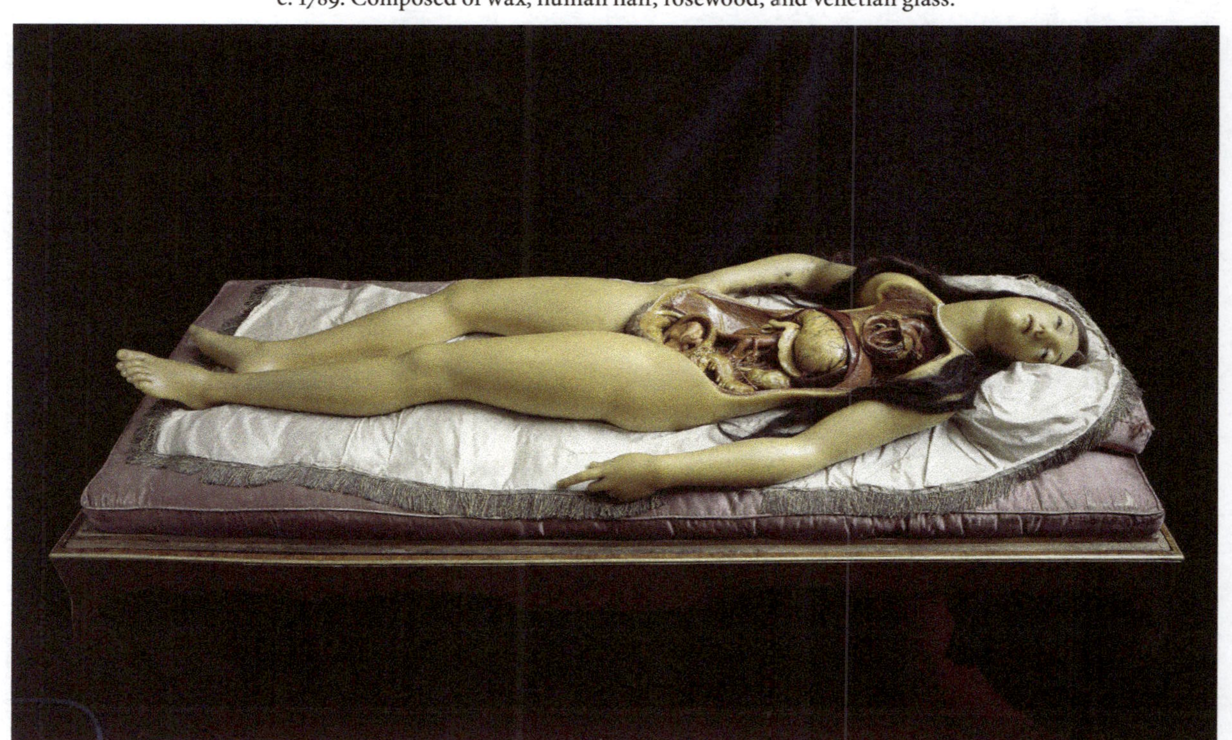

"a rectangular array of symbols or mathematical expressions arranged in rows and columns," "an array of symbols representing truth values," and also historically, "the womb; the uterus of a mammal."[74] Humbert's grudge against nature is that Lolita isn't more like the immaculately aestheticized waxwork *Venus*. He wants to lip her grids and her gooey innards both. And he collapses both desires into the same graphic term, "matrix."[75] He dreams not just of applying grids to his Lolita, but also of the vindicating idea that such measures were natural and internal all along.

There is something decidedly obscene about Humbert's desire to lick Lolita's innards. Earlier, he actually does press his tongue to one of her eyeballs, ostensibly to remove an irritant, and is about to taste the other eye when she tires of the game and leaves the room.[76] During their first road trip, Humbert sucks Lolita's blood out of bug bite: "a raised purple-pink swelling (the work of some gnat) which I eased of its beautiful transparent poison between my long thumbnails and then sucked till I was gorged on her spicy blood."[77] And the book begins, of course, with him licking her name, piece by articulated piece.

The graphic discomfort, in these moments of not-quite-explicitly-sexual bodily obscenity, partially derives, like his treatment of Lolita as a doll on the whole, from an uneasy/too-easy elision of person with thing. Only here, especially in the case of his desire to "turn my Lolita inside out," it is her parts, as things, that are articulated, via personification, as their own independent entities ("her unknown heart, her nacreous liver, the sea-grapes of her lungs, her comely twin kidneys.") It's an indecency that recalls Jean Baudrillard's argument in "The Ecstasy of Communication":

> [O]bscenity begins precisely when there is no more spectacle, no more scene, when all becomes transparence and immediate visibility, when everything is exposed to the harsh and inexorable light of information and communication. . . . it is the obscenity of the visible, of the all-too-visible, of the more-visible-than-the-visible.[78]

Humbert's alarming and eloquent image of Lolita turned inside out, made "all-too-visible," oddly enacts his desire to see Lolita herself in the throes of sexual ecstasy, a word whose Greek root *ekstasis*, an irrational state associated with lovers and poets, literally means "to be or stand outside oneself." The only way that Humbert can access the "unknown heart" of his doll-like object of desire being in ecstasy, however, is by taking the term too literally and clinically, by imaginatively making her insides stand outside herself—and addressing the individually characterized organs as he (orally) removes them one by one from her body.

The next few lines of the novel attest to this failure to produce any spark of (orgasmic) ecstasy within her.

> On especially tropical afternoons, in the sticky closeness of the siesta, I liked the cool feel of armchair leather against my massive nakedness as I held her in my lap. There she would be, a typical kid picking her nose while engrossed in the lighter sections of a newspaper, as indifferent to my ecstasy as if it were something she had sat upon, a shoe, a doll, the handle of a tennis racket, and was too indolent to remove.[79]

Naiman references this scene when describing teaching *Lolita* to undergraduates. One of his students, he paraphrases, argues that the book is misogynistic less because of its portrayal of pedophilia than "because Nabokov could not bring himself to represent female sexual pleasure. Were *Lolita* to portray its heroine enjoying her sexual encounters with Humbert, the novel would risk toppling into the genre of at least soft-core pornography."[80]

It is not entirely accurate that the novel cannot bring itself to represent female sexual pleasure, however. Humbert's note that Lolita is "indifferent to my ecstasy" recalls another, earlier instance when Nabokov does "bring himself" to represent, in purple prose, the sexual pleasure—nay "solitary ecstasy"—of Humbert's "initial girl-child" Annabel:

> Her legs, her lovely live legs, were not too close together, and when my hand located what it sought, a dreamy and eerie expression, half-pleasure, half-pain, came over those childish features. She sat a little higher than I, and whenever in her solitary ecstasy she was led to kiss me, her head would bend with a sleepy, soft, drooping movement that was almost woeful, and her bare knees caught and compressed my wrist, and slackened again; and her quivering mouth, distorted by the acridity of some mysterious potion, with a sibilant intake of breath came near to my face.[81]

When the adult Humbert is having sex with the girl he constructs as Annabel's double (re)incarnate, however, "ecstasy" becomes a euphemism for his penis, which in turn becomes analogous to "a shoe, a doll, the handle of a tennis racket" in Lolita's indifference to it.

Although Humbert bemoans Lolita's lack of ecstatic feeling towards or from him (her unwillingness to resuscitate Annabel's "dreamy and eerie expression, half-pleasure, half-pain"), he also structurally needs her to be object-like for the reincarnation to work. Henri Bergson notes that repetition always suggests the mechanical—a truly living life never repeats itself.[82] In a similar vein, Barbara Johnson argues that "only the inanimate has the fixity, the lack of feeling, the lack of need that corresponds to the unchanging idea."[83] In order for Lolita to be "the unchanging idea" of the nymphet, or of the second coming of the dead Annabel, she must remain sensibly "inanimate" (Humbert makes sure repeatedly to assert that nymphets are not really children but "demoniac"[84]) and, so, necessarily excluded from "feeling," "need," and ecstasy. Here, the ostensible incompatibility of the two sides of the pornographic emerges as the classificatory impulse toward fixity—an unchanged and exact duplication—comes up against the soft-core animation of the original. Again, Nabokov embodies this paradox in Humbert's fondleable yet impassive Dolly.

"Two Large Dummies"

In the accusatory poem qua death sentence that Humbert forces Clare Quilty to read at gunpoint, he at last calls Lolita the doll, as he has always treated her:

> *a little downy girl still wearing poppies . . .*
> *because you stole her*
> *from her wax-browed and dignified protector*
> *spitting into his heavy-lidded eye*
> *ripping his flavid toga and at dawn*
> *leaving the hog to roll upon his new discomfort*
> *the awfulness of love and violets*
> *remorse despair while you*
> *took a dull doll to pieces*
> *and threw its head away*
> *because of all you did*
> *because of all I did not*
> *you have to die*[85]

As his dubious verse displaces onto his double, Quilty, all culpability and agency in taking "a dull doll to pieces," he yet lingers, as throughout the novel, upon surface and texture. Humbert himself interrupts the parade of progressively less animate textures—"downy girl"[86] to "wax-browed . . . protector" to "dull doll." His waxiness—a medium valued in the creation of lifelike eighteenth-century medical dolls and twentieth-century celebrity portraits alike—comes to seem a textural catalyst for Lolita's transformation from "downy girl" to "dull doll," even as his poem accuses Quilty of being the violent agent who "stole her" and "took [her/it] to pieces." Humbert's surfaces incriminate him even as his words equivocate.[87]

By calling himself "wax-browed," he aligns himself, too, with the other victim of the car crash that kills Charlotte Haze: "an old gentleman with a white mustache, well-dressed—double-breasted gray suit, polka-dotted bow-tie—lay supine, his long legs together, like a death-size wax figure." This victim is not only collateral damage, dying from a heart attack as Charlotte is hit by a car, but also left out of the "grotesque diagram" with which his son painstakingly documents the accident.[88] As Humbert convicts Quilty of his own crime, he figures himself akin to that "old man-doll,"[89] positioning himself as a hapless bystander qua civilian casualty, while also sliding conveniently into the same thing-like category as the dismembered, decapitated "dull doll" that was Lolita. Indeed, as the second half of the novel progresses, circling towards Clare Quilty's murder, a strange thing happens to the figure of the doll: It becomes Humbert. Humbert becomes it.

Absent a Dolly Haze to articulate about, over, and with, Humbert figures himself, more and more, as the pornographic plaything of the novel's pages. This shift is presaged by a moment, shortly before Lolita runs away, in which Humbert and his charge survey a collection of mannequins in a store window:

> One figure was stark naked, wigless and armless. Its comparatively small stature and smirking pose suggested that when clothed it had represented, and would represent when clothed again, a girl-child of Lolita's size. But in its present state it was sexless. Next to it, stood a much taller veiled bride, quite perfect and intact except for the lack of one arm. On the floor, at the feet of these damsels, where the man crawled about laboriously with his cleaner, there lay a cluster of three slender arms, and a blond wig. Two of the arms happened to be twisted and seemed to suggest a clasping gesture of horror and supplication.
>
> "Look, Lo," I said quietly. "Look well. Is not that a rather good symbol of something or other?"[90]

The "something or other" that dolls may or may not symbolize in the novel starts soon after to fracture and slip. Dolls—not all of them direct analogues to Lolita—litter the book, in tantalizing symbolic-ish excess. For instance, on the diagram that maps out Charlotte Haze's fatal accident, "Mrs. H. H.'s trajectory was illustrated at several points by a series of those little outline figures—doll-like wee career girl or WAC—used in statistics as visual aids."[91] Once she is safely dispatched and silenced, Humbert perversely bestows on "the Haze woman" the honorific of "doll-like." Soon after Charlotte's death, as he shops in his fairytale mall for clothes for Lolita, the enchantment is enhanced, perhaps even conjured, by the "life-size plastic figures of snubbed-nosed children with dun-colored, greenish, brown-dotted, faunish faces float[ing] around me."[92] As he and Lolita then snake their way across the country by car, dolls again impel and enhance consumption: "If a roadside sign said: VISIT OUR GIFT SHOP—we had to visit it, had to buy its Indian curios, dolls, copper jewelry, cactus candy."[93] One of Lo's high school friends, who tells Humbert that Lolita is "a doll," is herself named Mona Dahl.[94] This cumulative piling on of dolls is reminiscent of the unsettling recombinant frenzy of Bellmer's creations, each feeling like "a rather good symbol of something or other," begging you to try to rearrange them, reaching out clasping limbs in ways that "seem to suggest" but can never actually say.

Before Humbert finally articulates himself as a doll, the unifying characteristic of each iteration is an unsettling muteness and opacity, a seeming openness to being passively put to vaguely symbolic use. As Sianne Ngai writes of the cute object: "'giving face'" in cuteness seems to amount to denying speech."[95] Humbert starts speaking himself into doll-like-ness soon after he draws Lolita's attention to the tangle of mannequin limbs in the shop window. Though hardly cute, giving himself a doll's lifeless limbs seems to be Humbert's attempt to face up to what he has done, through what in the end amounts to an unsettling effacement of his own culpability and Lolita's subjectivity both.

Limbs re-emerge in Chapter 32, which might be considered an ethical turning point in the novel. Humbert begins to recall scenes from his time on the road with Lolita that are anything but rose-tinted: "I have still other smothered memories, now unfolding themselves into limbless monsters of pain."[96] In one, he casts himself as a mechanical plaything:

[I]t struck me, as my automaton knees went up and down, that I simply did not know a thing about my darling's mind and that quite possibly, behind the awful juvenile clichés, there was in her a garden and a twilight, and a palace gate—dim and adorable regions which happened to be lucidly and absolutely forbidden to me, in my polluted rags and miserable convulsions.[97]

Lolita's erstwhile downy limbs are replaced by Humbert's "automaton knees" clad in "polluted rags and miserable convulsions" as his pornographic will to knowledge unravels. Yet even at this moment of potential ethical clarity, he returns to his own version of "awful juvenile clichés" with the line "there was in her a garden and a twilight, and a palace gate"—the same ilk of saccharine fairytale analogizing that marked Lolita's first bodily entrance into the novel, where it was she in "gypsy rags"—suing still for the safe unreality of his erstwhile plaything.[98]

A page later, Humbert unearths another "smothered memory":

[W]hen after having had my fill of her—after fabulous, insane exertions that left me limp and azure-barred—I would gather her in my arms with, at last, a mute moan of human tenderness (her skin glistening in the neon light coming from the paved court through the slits in the blind, her soot-black lashes matted, her grave gray eyes more vacant than ever—for all the world a little patient still in the confusion of a drug after a major operation)—and the tenderness would deepen to shame and despair, and I would lull and rock my lone light Lolita in my marble arms, and moan in her warm hair, and caress her at random and mutely ask her blessing, and at the peak of this human agonized selfless tenderness (with my soul actually hanging around her naked body and ready to repent), all at once, ironically, horribly, lust would swell again—and "oh, no" Lolita would say with a sigh to heaven, and the next moment the tenderness and the azure—all would be shattered.[99]

Holding a girl rendered more doll-like than ever ("skin glistening in the neon light," "grave gray eyes more vacant than ever") in his arms, Humbert too, in his "shame and despair," is markedly more thing than person. Rocking her in his "marble arms," he is both a pedophilic Pygmalion and a Galatea before transformation. Connor, analyzing the dynamic between female sex dolls and their male "lovers," argues that "the male lover is turned into a dummy or automaton by the force of the desire excited by the doll—a desire which hardens him into a petrified object."[100] Though Humbert proclaims himself "at the peak of this human agonized selfless tenderness," his "marble arms" belie the claim, and indeed all but summon the moment when "lust would swell again," which, one assumes, then "hardens him into a petrified object." Just as Lolita is neither true doll nor automaton, Humbert is no mere comic "dummy," but human and inhuman, humane and inhumane, at once.

Lust, tenderness, shame, and despair are the affective quartet Humbert retrospectively identifies in this darkly representative postcoital scene. Shame might be the most interesting of the four to explore as a feeling that, 285 pages into the novel, readers are now perhaps expected to share uncomfortably with their narrator. Citing Emmanuel Levinas, Brinkema writes that shame

> involves the fact of being riveted to oneself. It is the confrontation with that need to get out of oneself, and the realization that this desire is unfulfillable. . . . Accordingly, shame is not linked to a limitation of being (weakness, vulnerability, lack) but rather resides in the inability to break with oneself, a fullness of one's presence to oneself.[101]

Levinasian shame is, in other words, the feeling of "being annexed to oneself as a pulsating presence."[102] As he sits under throbbing neon lights with his human doll in his marble arms, Humbert seems to capture Levinasian shame as well as the too-closeness of the graphic, particularly when it forces us to face coolly rendered acts that do, or ought to, disgust.

For Eve Sedgwick, however, "[shame] is not at all . . . the place where identity is most securely attached to essences, but rather . . . the place where the *question* of identity arises most originarily and most relationally."[103] Shame's affective weight, she argues, is not anchored in being anchored to oneself. Instead,

> As best described by [Silvan] Tomkins, shame effaces itself; shame points and projects; shame turns itself skin side out; shame and pride, shame and dignity, shame and self-display, shame and exhibitionism are different linings of the same glove. Shame, it might finally be said, transformational shame, *is* performance.[104]

This understanding of shame—as not the solidification, but the cracking open and questioning of the self-containment of identity—helps explain why

Nabokov's novel summons a double for Humbert, Clare Quilty, in an uncomfortably and inappropriately slapstick "dramatic" encounter between the mirrored man-dolls at the end of the novel.

As Humbert and Quilty wrestle for Chum, the gun, on the floor of Quilty's mansion, they become first children and then those children's crude rag dolls:

> We fell to wrestling again. We rolled all over the floor, in each other's arms, like two huge helpless children. He was naked and goatish under his robe, and I felt suffocated as he rolled over me. I rolled over him. We rolled over me. They rolled over him. We rolled over us. . . . He and I were two large dummies, stuffed with dirty cotton and rags.[105]

With all this rolling and stuffing, Humbert and Quilty enact Connor's argument about the essentially, absurdly self-objectifying nature of the sex doll. Nabokov dramatizes the idea that

> [T]the objectifying male is always reduced by his doll-making to the condition of a guy, dummied by his dummy desire. . . . In being roused from insentience by the desire of the male user, and then in its turn arousing that user, the doll may also serve to figure tauntingly for the male what is impersonal, mechanical and thinglike in his own sexuality.[106]

The difference, of course, is that Lolita wasn't "roused from insentience by the desire of the male user," but rather rendered "vacant"-eyed, "neutral[ly] illuminat[ed]," and "comfortab[ly] inane" by a crisp, cutting calculus, by the violent impersonality of both the category of the nymphet and its creator.[107] Doll was never a doll. She was always a real girl.

Shame, attached to the uneasy translation of humans into objects, pervades the end of *Lolita*. Taking up and literalizing Sedgwick's assertion that "shame effaces itself," masked performance artist Narcissister gleefully flaunts herself as an object, a doll who is no dummy, for whom smooth-surfaced thingness becomes a site for the performance of "radical narcissism."

The Topsy-Turvy Titillation of Narcissister

Narcissister is a Brooklyn-based artist, photographer, and "avant-porn" burlesque performer. She protects her anonymity by always wearing (at least one) Barbie-style plastic mask but has informed interviewers that she is a former Alvin Ailey dancer and the child of a Moroccan Jewish mother and an African

American father. She was also briefly a contestant on the televised talent show *America's Got Talent.* The routine, called "Upside Down," which brought her to television screens across the country, begins with Narcissister walking onto a stage that has been set with a roughly 6-foot-tall doll house.[108] She is wearing her customary mask and a floor-length blue velvet hooded cape over a long red dress with full skirts. As the music plays Diana Ross's "Upside Down," the burlesque begins (Figure 3.6). Dancing, Narcissister removes the cape and turns around to reveal another face and a blue floral print on the other side of her dress. Then she flips into a handstand—skirts now covering her head, faces, and torso—to reveal, between her legs, another head with yet another plastic face. Her legs are clad with long satin gloves, like her arms. She cartwheels during the rest of the song, over and over, removing more and more clothing from her two pseudo-torsos in the process. By the end, she stands before the judges, on her feet, her red-satin-bra-clad back facing them while she holds the microphone up to the mask on the back of her wigged head and thanks them for their applause and kind words.

The *AGT* number was a PG-13 version of stage pieces like "This Masquerade," which Narcissister has performed in various Brooklyn burlesque clubs (Figure 3.7). In those pieces, she ends up completely naked aside from the harness that loops around her neck and down her torso to her crotch to keep her other "head" in place. Other performance pieces include a reverse striptease entitled "Every Woman" in which she starts out entirely naked aside from wig and merkin and re-dresses herself with items of clothing that she removes, one by one, from various bodily orifices.[109] Throughout these performances, though, the mask remains constant.

Narcissister's signature mask, and her commitment to never being seen without it, places her in the mold of just the sort of life-sized plaything Marquand Smith theorizes: erotic because, not in spite of, its obvious fabrication. The plastic mask promises anonymity, replicability, mass production, interchangeability; in short, the protections and provocations of abstraction. In concert with her solo performances, Narcissister also launched a community project in 2013 entitled *Narcissister is You,* which her website describes as

> many different sisters (including male sisters) embodying the Narcissister character. Fundamental to this project is the idea that Narcissister can

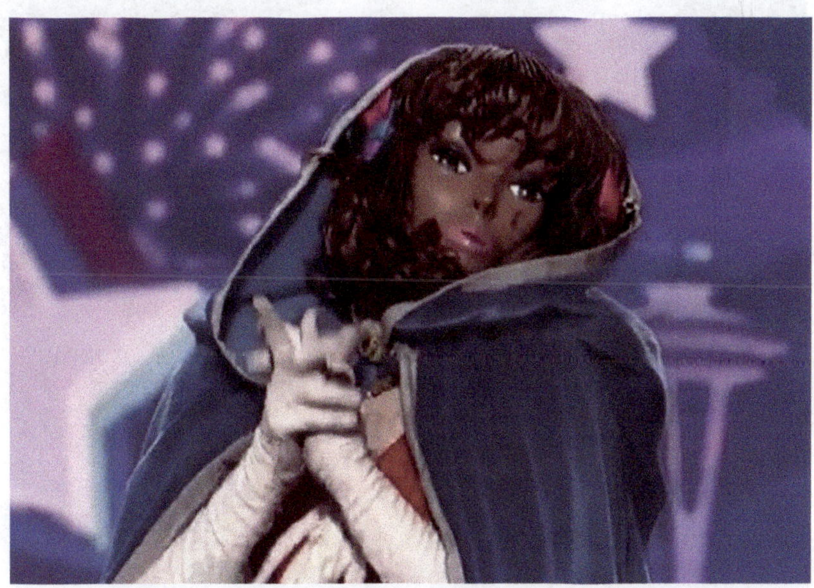

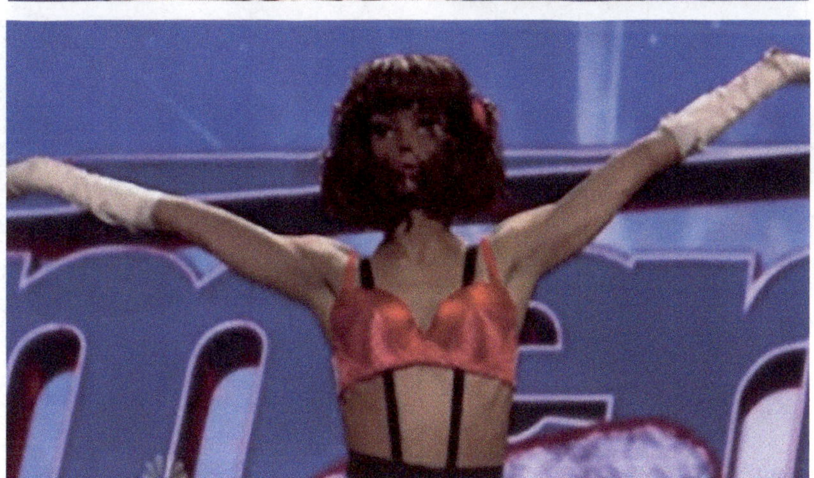

Source: Narcissister.

 Narcissister performing "This Masquerade" at Abrons Art Center in New York City in 2012.

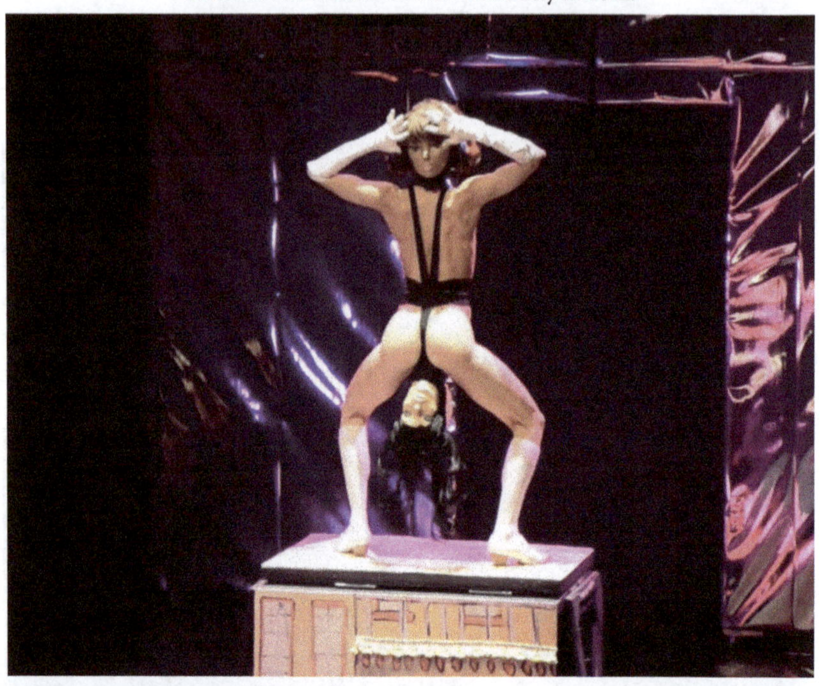

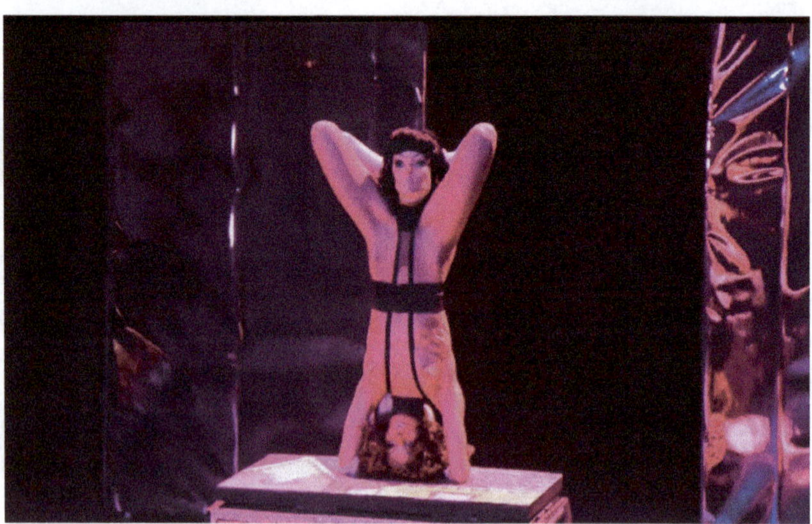

Photo: Rob Roth. Source: Narcissister.

be anyone, she is universal, reflecting that on some level we are all one, that radical narcissism/radical self-love can be found in our quotidian existence and that it is a concept worth cultivating. Participants are asked to document themselves and their friends wearing the Narcissister mask and doing anything that feels radically narcissistic or radically self-loving. The video installations are comprised primarily of these self-shot video clips which are edited together and set to original music by Narcissister and Earthmasters.[110]

The function of the mask in the *Narcissister is You* project feels like a fleshed out version of comics scholar and cartoonist Scott McCloud's theory of the cartoon face: that the more simplified or abstracted a drawn face, the easier it is for readers to identify both with and as the drawn character. When the cartoonish characters then inhabit more realistically drawn settings (as is common in Japanese manga), McCloud evocatively argues that readers "mask themselves in a character and safely enter a sensually stimulating world. One set of lines to see. Another set of lines to be."[111]

Narcissister's wearable, circulating mannequin mask seems to offer similar sorts of lines (guidelines, scripts, even lifelines), letting the various Narcissisters who wear it both hide and expose themselves. It revels in the vexed dynamics between flesh, face, and fabrication, particularly for bodies usually not granted a default universalism or abstraction (those not white, cis, male)—offering no solution of or for this mixture, but, rather, a medium for temporary, ecstatic suspension. Narcissister's description of the mask and its power plays against the ways in which, in Brian Phillip Harper's words,

> [A]bstraction itself has historically been detrimental to black people, both directly and collaterally, constituting them as a dehumanized generality thus eligible for enslavement (among other things) and underwriting an exalted generic national personhood from which they have typically been excluded.[112]

The mask's power seems to work by an alchemy of incomplete anonymizing, somewhat paradoxically providing its wearers the cover to uncover, access to a luxurious sort of abstraction through an emphasis on their own fleshy particularity as they engaged in "radically self-loving" acts. Uri McMillan notes the relationship between this "universal" mask and the doll in Narcissister's "Upside Down": "she wears her signature double-faced mask—eerily resembling a lifeless Barbie—on her head as well as over her nether regions, repeatedly contorting her body to reveal all four mask faces; in swirling petticoats, she resembles a modern-day topsy-turvy doll come to life."[113]

Each of Narcissister's two different, yet overlapping lineages noted by McMillan—Barbie and the topsy-turvy doll—has her/its own discomfiting sexual associations. First appearing in 1959 (four years after the publication of *Lolita*), Barbie was named after the daughter of its creator, Ruth Handler, but modeled off a German doll based on a comic strip prostitute named Lilli:[114]

> Barbie . . . possessed the secrets of adult femininity seemingly without any of the awkwardness, messiness, or embarrassment experienced by her human owners. The flavor of her past as a sex toy for men doesn't damage her appeal; on the contrary, it seems to guarantee her heterosexuality.[115]

With neither nipples nor anything but smooth plastic at her crotch, Barbie is a thing of sterilized stereotyped white womanhood, ready to teach girls how to dress, accessorize—and possibly, at that sweet spot of preteen backlash—dismember her.[116] The provenance of the topsy-turvy doll—a two-in-one with full skirts that hide not legs but another torso of the opposite color, revealed only when you flip her over—is far older and harder to pin down, but most scholars agree that she/they/it was originally sewn by enslaved African American women in the antebellum South.[117] The topsy-turvy doll predated the Topsy of *Uncle Tom's Cabin* but, after the success of Harriet Beecher Stowe's novel, it was for a time commercially produced as the Topsy-Eva doll, training young girls in both sentimental iconography and naughty skirt-flipping that flirts with the imagery of miscegenation. Many have argued that the topsy-turvy doll is both unsexed—no legs, much less genitals, to go between them—and obscene.

The sinister, subtly sexual "cuteness" of the topsy-turvy doll evokes Ngai's assertion that "cuteness is a way of sexualizing beings and simultaneously rendering them unthreatening."[118] Citing Lori Merish, Ngai notes that "if cuteness is a 'realm of erotic regulation (the containment of child sexuality) that offers "protection" from violence and exploitation,' it is clearly also a way of bringing that sexuality out."[119] This comic and sexualized cuteness has, according to Merish, also been "consistently racialized" in America, long associated with, and arguably evolving in tandem with minstrelsy.[120] Though its lack of genitalia can be read as "prudish,"[121] the topsy-turvy seems to beg to have its skirts lifted regardless of whether Black or white torso is being displayed on top, and its very alternation of Black and white—separate but mirroring—alludes to even as it polices "racial mixing, sex, and rape within the plantation system."[122] In this way, the topsy-turvy "has been read as enslaved women's polyvalent representation of their experiences of sexual violation."[123] Robin Bernstein argues that the cute/vulgar topsy-turvy dolls yet historically voiced a sort of resistance that "unwittingly smuggled enslaved women's thoughts and anger into the inner sanctum of southern domesticity."[124] At the same time that the doll signifies "illicit sexual contact, including rape," "the doll's symbolism is endlessly complicated, for in the mermaid-like absence of a crotch, African-American women figured un-rape-ability, sexual safety."[125]

Combining hard and soft, then, both in her physical materials and her citational precursors (Barbie and the topsy-turvy doll), Narcissister dares her viewers to pick a script for how to play with her. Her performances seem creepy, cold, floppy, confrontational, awkward, and titillating all at once. They are also hilarious. Sex is funny and sex dolls are particularly funny. The most graphic (or graph-ick) depictions of sex, in the dual senses of both explicit and graph-like, are also those in which bodies engaged in or contemplating sex are rendered most doll-like, their actions most mechanically scripted. These are frequently moments, as in the Homes story with which this chapter opens, of often quite dark and unsettling humor. The comedy of Narcissister's performances is that of the (re)animated sex doll, a category incongruity à la Schopenhauer that also embodies Bergson's famous definition of the comic as "something mechanical encrusted on the living."[126]

Ariel Osterweis characterizes Narcissister's surface and texture play in just this way: "By donning hard masks and inserting doll heads into various orifices . . . Narcissister places the brittle surface of the racist kitsch object . . . onto—and into—the mutable, muscular surface of a live fleshly body."[127] This insistence on surface is key to the pornographic, where a lust for knowledge of interior sensations morphs into an obsession with applying various epistemological grids to more visible exteriors. Just as Narcissister constructs her persona from objects that demand to be played with, she also plays with us, presenting herself as an object both sinewy and smooth, starkly naked and stubbornly illegible: "within this space of simultaneous objectification and agency: her criticality is founded upon spectacles of sexual excess."[128]

Narcissister thus harnesses what Walter Benjamin calls "the vital nerve" of the consumer fetishism that many have tied to the commodification of female bodies in hard-core porn and fashion photography alike:[129] "the sex appeal of the inorganic."[130]

What is the affective valence of this combination of hard and soft? Wilhelm Worringer claims that "just as the urge to empathy as a pre-assumption of aesthetic experience finds its gratification in the beauty of the organic, so the urge to abstraction finds its beauty in the life-denying inorganic, in the crystalline or, in general terms, in all abstract law and necessity."[131] Narcissister's grafting of "the life-denying inorganic" onto the "beauty of the organic" yields an incongruous Frankenstein's monster of empathy and abstraction. But the monster isn't having a particularly bad time. Worringer suggests further that "aesthetic enjoyment is objectified self-enjoyment. To enjoy aesthetically means to enjoy myself in a sensuous object diverse from myself, to empathize myself into it."[132] From her name to her *Narcissister is You* project manifesto, this avant-porn performer is all about self-enjoyment in just this sense. The crux of the emotional toggling between excess and anemia in her work is that it emphatically insists on the self-enjoyment of the inorganic. What, she asks us, happens when a sex doll learns how to masturbate?

The last section of this chapter analyzes a text that is, in many ways, Nabokov turned topsy-turvy. *Oreo* plays all the postmodernist linguistic games—and then some—of *Lolita*, but places a savvy, inviolate, polyglot Black female body in the driver's seat. If Nabokov's Humbert plays with Lolita as a doll, and Narcissister makes us watch while she plays with her doll-self, Fran Ross's *Oreo* makes her readers into the text's plaything. She shows us what happens to the double graphic's dynamics of power and abstraction, its interpenetration between flesh and data, when the pornographic sex doll talks back.

Fran Ross's "Head Equations"

I discovered *Oreo* through a 2011 review on NPR, which proclaimed it ahead of its time and one of the funniest works ever written. I agree that it's funny, but not that funny. I downgraded my rating due to one chapter of explicit pornography which added little to the story.

—AMAZON REVIEW, 4.0 out of 5 stars

Fran Ross's 1974 *Oreo* is a trip—of a decidedly different sort than the one taken by Humbert and Lolita. Riffing on the voyages of Theseus, the novel tells the story of its eponymous protagonist, a young woman (half Black, half Jewish) from Philadelphia, who sets out with a set of cryptic clues on a quest to find her father in New York City and learn the secret of her birth. The novel overflows with polyglot wordplay, satirical diagrams galore, and an encyclopedic knowledge of slang and scientific words for genitalia both male and female. Perhaps the first thing a reader, or even a casual page flipper, of Ross's novel will register (and possibly with some flutters of trepidation) is that there's even some suspiciously mathematical notation in the book.

For instance, the novel narrates the fateful first meeting of Oreo's mother Helen Clark, "Singer, pianist, mimic, math freak (a 4 on the color scale)," and her father Samuel Schwartz, "Just another pretty face," like so:[133]

> As Helen sang her part in the chorale chorus *Jesu, Joy of Man's Desiring*, she constructed one of her typical head equations, based on the music's modalities and hers:
>
> $$BTU = \frac{3 \times 10^8}{\sqrt{\epsilon/\epsilon_0}} \ \mathrm{m/sec}$$
>
> where B = Bach
>
> $\quad T$ = time
>
> $\quad U$ = weight of uric acid, ml
>
> Simple, she conceded, compared with the overlapping fugal subject-answer-countersubject head equations that were her favorites—elegant, in fact, but not quite absorbing enough to keep her mind off the fact that she was perspiring and wanted desperately to pee.
>
> Samuel, passing through the rehearsal hall, caught a glimpse of Helen's face and, mistaking her expression of barely controlled anguish for religious fervor, was himself seized with an emotion that mystics have often erroneously identified as ecstasy-*cum*-epiphany (*vide* Saul on the road to Damascus, Theresa of Ávila every time you turn around): the hots. His accounting books fell to the floor.[134]

As Helen calculates, in her head, the urgency with which she needs to hit the head, this first comically inadequate equation in the novel sends up any presumptions of graphic self-evidence through abstraction. Not only is Helen's "head equation," which we are told is more "simple" and "elegant" than usual, mystifying to the mathematically expert and illiterate alike, but her facial expression is also ludicrously misread by Sam. Neither cool equations nor impassioned facial expressions communicate all that clearly. For both, an obscure calculus transubstantiates, or mistranslates, the ecstatic, the uric, and the sexual with one another. Bach's ode to the holy desire for Jesus only exacerbates Helen's need to pee; Samuel, in turn, reads Helen's bodily urge as an orgasmic "ecstasy-*cum*-epiphany," and proceeds to spill his own numbers all over the floor.

From their first appearance in *Oreo*, then, "head equations" (as the very name suggests), are inextricable from the body and its euphemistically unmentionable bits and procedures. Ross's mathematical formulae embody as they abstract the twofold nature of the graphic. Given the novel's interracial preoccupations, they also cite an ethnographic history of grotesquely rendering bodies as chartable, quantifiable, calculable, and thus expendable or easily violable. After Helen breaks up with Samuel, she compiles a list of her skills and contemplates which one might be viably translated into a source of income in order to support her children:

1. Mimicry
2. Making head equations
3. Singing
4. Piano playing[135]

She tellingly quickly removes number 2 from consideration. "As for her head equations, she refused to commercialize them."[136] Helen's decision to take private control of own numbers can be read as a round rejection, through a subtle acknowledgment, of the cycles of quantification, monetization, and exploitation that might otherwise fall on her beloved head (equations).

Likewise, *Oreo*'s humor often works through extravagant excess that hides a pointed rejection of certain kinds of historical baggage. Helen decides to support her children by playing piano: "operating on numbers 3 and 4 were all the pluses and minuses of cliché, but she picked number 4."[137] Harryette Mullen writes of Ross's play with cliché that her "witty reconfigurations of hackneyed phrases are sometimes just for the fun of it, but frequently her visual-verbal puns and transliterated metaphors also expose and break down petrified stereotypes in the clichés and commonplaces of familiar expressions."[138] We learn, for instance, that the nickname "Oreo" (her given name is Christine) came to her grandmother Louise in a dream as "Oriole," but no one could understand what she was saying through her thick southern accent and so "Oreo," which seemed an apt enough comparison, stuck.[139] Aural information lost in translation is easily filled in with a convenient, clichéd racial slur ("an Oreo is an insult before it is a cookie in black America"[140]—Black on the outside, white on the inside) and "Oreo" replaces the other saccharine nicknames of her youth ("Brown Sugar and Chocolate Drop and Honeybun") for good. This explication of the book's title is its own commentary on the facile false equations of racial stereotyping and gives a taste of the multilayered nature of the humor—homonyms upon puns upon cultural in-jokes upon physical comedy—that distinguishes the novel as a whole.

Of the three basic theories of humor—superiority, relief, and incongruity—Ross's novel is largely a virtuosic performance of the last two. Briefly, superiority theory, espoused by the likes of Plato, Aristotle, and Hobbes, says that we laugh at the misfortunes of others, or former versions of ourselves. Freud was the maven of relief theory, asserting that laughter offers a valve-like release of the pent-up pressures of sexual or violent urges. Incongruity theory, finally, attached to names like Immanuel Kant, Arthur Schopenhauer, and Søren Kierkegaard, says that we laugh at things that violate our mental patterns and expectations. Schopenhauer specified that we laugh when the incongruity between abstract categories and real things becomes evident, like the fact that a Chihuahua and a St. Bernard are both in the category "dog."

> [The] very incongruity of sensuous and abstract knowledge, on account of which the latter always merely approximates to the former, as mosaic approximates to painting, is the cause of a very remarkable phenomenon which, like reason itself, is peculiar to human nature, and of which the explanations that have ever anew been attempted, as insufficient: I mean laughter. . . . The cause of laughter in every case is simply the sudden perception of the incongruity between a concept and the real objects which have been thought through it in some relation, and laughter itself is just the expression of this incongruity.[141]

In *Laughing Fit to Kill*, Glenda Carpio celebrates the creative generativity of the incongruity theory, which "allows us to appreciate the fact that, far from being *only* a coping mechanism, or a means of 'redress,' African American humor has been and continues to be both a bountiful source of creativity and pleasure and an energetic mode of social and political critique."[142] The incongruity theory of humor also best describes the setup/punch line model of stand-up comedy, which I will argue is a prevailing structure in *Oreo* and generic pornography both. Schopenhauer's formulation of the "incongruity of sensuous and abstract knowledge" is thus a good way, too, of understanding the double graphic in the pornographic, as it toggles between incongruent abstract and corporeal dimensionality.

The World-Wide Wedge

Sex is a wedge issue in *Oreo*. The book's pornographic relationship with sex begins with, and continually references, a geometrically inclined extended etymological joke. The precocious Oreo is homeschooled, and her English tutor is "Professor Lindau, renowned linguist and blood donor . . . He spoke in roots."[143] In order to understand anything her teacher says, Oreo must become adept at hunting down the linguistic lineage of the words he uses until she can suss out what he means—an operation similar to, though in the end perhaps more rewarding than, her search for her own absent father. Conversations with Professor Lindau tend to go as follows:

> One day, Professor Lindau came in, in a bad mood. He ranted fitfully about his girlfriend. "That wedge!" he shouted. "What can one do with a wedge like that?" he asked rhetorically.
>
> Oreo was puzzled, so the professor tossed her the desk copy of Partridge. After following a trail of false roots and camouflaged cognates, she came to Partridge's assertion that *cunt* (or, as Partridge put it, "*c*nt*") derived from the Latin *cunnus*, which was related to *cuneus*, or "wedge." Eric went on to say that the word had been considered obscene since about 1700, adding that "the dramatist Fletcher, who was no prude, went no further than 'They write *sunt* with a C, which is abominable', in *The Spanish Curate*. Had the late Sir James Murray courageously included the word, and spelt it in full, in the great O.E.D., the situation would be different; . . . (Yet the O.E.D. gave *prick*: why this further injustice to women?) . . . (It is somewhat less international than *f**k*, q.v.)
>
> Oreo fell off her chair laughing at this witty entry in Partridge. When she got herself together, she shook her head. Her *sprachgefühl* told her that

Eric was stretching a point (or, rather, a wedge) and that the professor was perpetuating Partridge's error by persisting in this pie-eyed usage. She had never been misled by her *sprachgefühl*, and as she thumbed through a later edition of Partridge, she found that that worthy had corrected himself in a supplement: "*cunt* (p. 198) cannot be from the L. word but is certainly cognate with O.E. *cwithe*, 'the womb' (with a Gothic parallel); cf. mod. English *come*, ex O.E. *cweman*. The ~*nt*, which is difficult to explain, was already present in O.E. *kunte*. The radical would seem to be *cu* (in O.E. *cwe*), which app. = quintessential physical femineity . . . and partly explains why, in India, the cow is a sacred animal."

Oreo fell off her chair laughing at the part about the cow. She was, after all, just a child in her mid-units. Then she pointed out the passage in the supplement to the professor.[144]

Despite her *sprachgefühl* ("linguistic instinct," *OED*) and subsequent proof that "Eric was stretching a point (or, rather, a wedge)," the coinage sticks. The satisfying abstract geometric fit of the thing overpowers its etymological flimsiness. There's something sexy about its aggressive, diagrammatic sleekness, somehow both vulvic and phallic. As the professor retorts: "'I know, I know,' he said, dismissing her quibble. 'But I like the idea of wedge. It whips.'"[145] At once pseudoscientific and obscene, "wedge" as code for "cunt" is a hilarious riff, too, on the pornographic as an exercise in "knowledge-pleasure." Oreo's circuitous search through various dictionaries, trying to get to the root of—or grow from the root up—what ends up being an elaborate vaginal obfuscation puts her in the comical position of a sexual-epistemological explorer. She even experiences, like any good pornographic sleuth, two moments of involuntary convulsion—falling off her chair laughing. And we, in turn, laugh at the oscillation between abstract wordplay, dirty jokes, and bodily pratfalls.

In one of the surprisingly few scholarly treatments of the novel, William W. Cook and James Tatum remark that, "We remember not so much the plot of *Oreo*, as its great lines. We often have the sense that an entire scene is set up to clear the way for some outrageous one-liners."[146] There is a structural resonance between stand-up's setups—which lead to and dissipate in the abrupt release of either the one-liner or punch line—and common complaints about the narrative structure of pornography, or the lack thereof. In "The Pornographic Imagination," Susan Sontag notes Adorno's critique that "a piece of pornographic fiction concocts no better than a crude excuse for a beginning; and once having begun, it goes on and on and ends nowhere."[147] The stand-up set as a whole, in its multiple iterative ends, is similar in this way to the pornographic film—a series of climaxes strung together in what could very well be an infinite series, really only constrained and brought to a final end by an arbitrary time limit. As John Limon writes, "the problem with seeing a stand-up performance (five or twenty or ninety minutes) as a single aesthetic object is that stand-up is dominated by miniclimaxes—the series of punch lines—that are not readily convertible into straight lines for a metaclimax or punch line of the whole."[148] Though it's hard to attest to Ross's personal experience as a viewer of pornography, she was intimately acquainted with the miniclimaxes of stand-up comedy, having worked as a ghostwriter in the 1960s for a Jewish comedian.[149]

Oreo, more of a picaresque than a novel, less a traditional plot than a series of elaborately contrived one-liners, is structurally as well as thematically akin to both the stand-up comedy set and the lowly porno. This raises some questions about the relation of the comic to the pornographic: How different is the punch line (or gag) from the money shot?[150] And do they rely on similar sorts of formulae and displacements, similar sorts of performed abjections, similar dynamics of embodiment and abstraction?

Oreo, as a character and as a novel, dramatizes and satirizes what Limon characterizes as the "Jewish approach" to comedy. Limon lauds the "beautiful abstract geometry of stand-up," whose appeal "is akin to the appeal of math, except that the formal abstraction of a gag retains as its subject matter the pollution of the liminal."[151] Stand-up comedy, he argues, puts abjection—in both colloquial and Kristevan terms[152]—upright and on display. "Stand-up makes vertical (or ventral) what should be horizontal (or dorsal)."[153] In other words, "the appeal of comedy may be traced to its imposition of geometrical perfectionism on compounded liminality."[154] This "compounded liminality" has much to do with the historical relationship in America of Jewishness to whiteness and so, necessarily, to its definition through opposition against Blackness, homosexuality, and femininity. "American abjectness taken to its extreme is a craving for abstraction,"[155] which Limon reads as extreme whiteness:

> [T]he Jewish approach to white America—as in *The Jazz Singer*—was made through blackface. It was made, in sum, through the black body, the homo-

sexual body, and the female body. "Through" them means "by way of abjecting" them . . . On behalf of the American suburb, heretofore Protestant, Jewish comedians took the body and turned it into a gag, which is not the same as expressing it or repressing it. It is abstracting what is the essence of the concrete.[156]

On behalf of the Black, female, and queer body, *Oreo* gags right back. All bodies become intensely linguistically abstracted and toyed with. The small thin line distinguishing human sexual agents from inanimate sexual object becomes increasingly hard to trace. If the novel is her extended stand-up set, in the grand tradition of Mel Brooks and Carl Reiner, *Oreo* is unabashedly all the bodies they use to court and create the abstraction they crave.

In *Oreo*'s sexual situations, though—the ones in which people become distinctly and uncomfortably doll-like—a more specific dynamic of comic incongruity is at play. Ross's comic genius evokes, time and again, Henri Bergson's theory of laughter. All laughable objects and moments, he asserts, give us some version of the image of "*something mechanical in something living*."[157] Bergson theorizes that "The rigid, the ready-made, the mechanical, in contrast with the supple, the ever-changing and the living . . . in a word, automatism in contrast with free activity, such are the defects that laughter singles out and would fain correct."[158] What I argue *Oreo* shows us, through the figure of the sex doll, is the way in which the pornographic and the comic share this combination of liveliness grafted onto mechanism, flesh controlled by unrelenting formulae, "in a single combination, the illusion of life and the distinct impression of a mechanical."[159] In conventional comedy and pornography, in other words, bodies act like abstract machines—for our pleasure.

It's important, in this context, that the humor of *Oreo* is both intensely bodily and intensely heady: gross, linguistic, allusive, and mathematic-ish to the point of abstraction. As Cook and Tatum point out, "by running black English and everything else through her conceptual wringer of lexicography and philological analysis, everything that might be considered sacred or profane in the 1960s and 1970s becomes weirdly distant, defused, impossible to take seriously."[160] "Weirdly distant, defused, impossible to take seriously" could just as easily be a description of the figure of the sex doll as Ross's prose. And indeed, it is by translating herself into that pornographic object that Oreo unexpectedly stages a topsy-turvy escape from the novel's climactic attempted rape.

A Slapstick Bed Trick

Before Oreo evades rape by becoming doll-like, though, she treats herself to her own climax by getting herself off, in an unusual way. The bodies Ross plays with hardly stay upright and isolated, as purely auditory and scopic spectacles on a spot-lit stage. Their gagging gets gross, tactile, and unexpectedly participatory. Unfolding in a section titled "Half-WIT" within the chapter "Pets, Playmates, Pedagogues," the first sex scene of the novel is a bed trick with a twist. Ross sets the scene:

> Oreo's tutors were on vacation. She needed something to do to occupy her fourteen-year-old mind for a few weeks, so she put an ad in the papers. Three days later, she received a phone call from what sounded like a young white man.[161]

The man who calls in response to her ad in the "Situations Wanted column of the Inquirer" identifies himself as "Dr. Jafferts. I'm the medical examiner for district five. I was wondering if I could interest you in a job?" After some bureaucratic foreplay, covering Oreo's college certificates, hourly pay, and gas mileage money, Jafferts asks, à la Williams's "knowledge-pleasure" and reminiscent, in a slightly different key, of Humbert Humbert's fantasy of caressing Lolita's internal organs—"Would you submit to a medical examination for the job?" The game is on. Jafferts asks Oreo's age, whether she's a virgin, what color her underclothes are ("all white") and if she'd mind "telling me all the words you know that mean sexual intercourse?" "With a wicked smile, Oreo said, 'Certainly. *Procreation, cohabitation, coition, coitus.*'"[162] Her tutors are, after all, on vacation. Sounding "terribly disappointed," Jafferts then asks Oreo, over the phone, to undress and masturbate. She obliges, after her own fashion:

> After a few moments he said, "Are they off?"
>
> "No," said Oreo, "I'm having trouble with my wedgies." The doctor continued, oblivious to her anachronistic answer. "Rub along the inside of your thigh and tell me when you get wet."
>
> Oreo put down the phone and went over to water her begonia, then she came back and coughed into the phone to let the doctor know she was there.
>
> "Are you wet yet?" he said wistfully.
>
> Oreo said, "You know, doctor, the trouble with masturbation is you come

too fast. There's no one for you to give directions to. You know, like 'No, not like that, like this. No, yes, no, harder, softer, up, down. No, no. I'm losing it. Yes, yes, that's it, stay there, right there. No, no, not like that—the way you were doing it before. Yes, that's it.' And there's no one for you *not* to give directions to. You know what I mean, doctor"?"

There was a moan at the other end of the line. "I'd like to come over and give you a complete examination," said the moaner hoarsely.

"Why don't you do that," said the moanee sweetly. . . .

The doctor let out a gasp as big as Masters and Johnson and said he could be at her place in an hour. Oreo told him that she would wait for him on her front porch and that she would be wearing a begonia leaf.[163]

After her initially disappointingly dry, scientifically graphic dirty talk of "*Procreation, cohabitation, coition, coitus,*" the scene gets a little wetter. While watering her own begonia, Oreo linguistically whets the sexual appetite of the hapless "medical examiner." Throughout the novel, but particularly at this moment, Ross revels in making it titillatingly tricky to tell what is euphemism and what isn't. In a postmodern novel that, as Kathryn Hume has pointed out, has scant use for a Barthesian "reality effect" and the extraneous details that create it, there's little against which to check a claim that "she went over to water her begonia"—and what that might actually mean.[164] Is Oreo really watering a houseplant or is she actually masturbating? Ross might as well have written "wouldn't *you* like to know?"—with the begonia leaf at the end a possible shorthand for "well what did you *think* she was doing?"

By making staid sexual clichés ambiguously literal, Ross leverages language's ability to linger indefinitely in the ambiguity of euphemism—a privilege it holds above its sister arts. At the same time, she suggests that it doesn't really matter what Oreo is or isn't doing at this point in the novel with her nethers. Oreo's elaborate pranking of "the moaner" is its own—and better— kind of slick, satisfying self-gratification. Aesthetic and linguistic stimulation here are sexier than genital. Meanwhile, Ross's readers find themselves with their own sort of mounting . . . anticipation for the gag or punch line that this extended setup promises. Oreo bemoans to her moaner that "the trouble with masturbation is you come too fast" because "there's no one for you *not* to give directions to." She seems, though, to have solved that problem, using the "doctor," in some ways, as her own sort of "Dutch wife" or masturbatory aid, a convenient rag doll she moves diagrammatically through a particular satisfying bed trick in order to mete out some punishment, but mostly prolong her own self-gratification.

Diagrammatic is a particularly apt way to think about both the figure of the sex doll and the structure of the humor in *Oreo*. The diagram, straddling representation and abstraction, is defined by its two-dimensionality. It delivers information by flattening it, similar to *Oreo*'s characterization of sex as a binary "yes/no" game. According to Jakub Zdebik, writing on Deleuze and the diagram, "the diagrammatic process could be imagined as a physical state or system being atomized into incorporeal abstract traits and then reconfigured into another state or system."[165] *Oreo* disassembles (or, maybe, dismembers) the game that the "doctor" thinks he'll be playing with the object of his desire, atomizes the system of sex into its various "incorporeal abstract traits" (both "*Procreation, cohabitation, coition, coitus*" and the joke about the begonia), and then reconfigures them into a different system, one in which the doctor has become the doll and Oreo pleasures herself. The sneaky implication, too, is that the reader herself, just along for the ride, is not there so much to get off on the spectacle as to serve as another "one for you *not* to give directions to," another sex toy for the brash and boundless heroine, and the author who penned her.

Eve Sedgwick, most famously, argues of female masturbation that while under the "modern, trivializing, hygienic-developmental discourse . . . auto-eroticism not only is funny . . . but also must be relegated to the inarticulable space of (a barely superseded) infantility," masturbation, especially by women, "can seem to offer—not least as an analogy to writing—a reservoir of potentially utopian metaphors and energies for independence, self-possession, and a rapture that may owe relatively little to political or interpersonal abjection."[166] Oreo is, I argue, a slightly different sort of masturbating girl. What makes the comedy of the novel's pornographic scenes both more ambivalent and more hilarious—in other words, more essentially graphic—than the dreamy lyricism of masturbation as a utopian metaphor of independence and empowerment is how much it derives its pleasure not in opposition to, but through a virtuosic embrace of "the modern, trivializing, hygienic-developmental discourse." Much of the novel's humor comes from overlaying this mode of mechanical, abstracted language onto situations that owe very much indeed to "political or interpersonal abjection." And then getting off not in spite of, or rapturously freed from that mechanistic gaze or that abjection, but because of them.

After watering her begonia, whatever it may be, Oreo hangs up on Dr. Jafferts and goes down the block to ask Betty Williams for help:

> Betty was the neighborhood nymphomaniac. For two cents she would fuck a plunger. In fact, the story of Betty and the plumber's friend was a West Philadelphia legend. Anyone who thought that the shibboleth *friend* referred to a person was known to be an outsider and was therefore the object of xenophobic ridicule and scorn. Betty agreed to help her young friend Oreo.[167]

Betty seems particularly equipped, in a number of ways, to make use of men as objects, objects as men. The scene then moves to Oreo's house, where, watching from a hiding spot, she lets Betty toy with the "medical examiner":

> Sitting on a high stool, Betty began a rhythmic opening and closing of her legs, revealing and concealing a tangle of pubic hair. The sweat stood out on the doctor's head after the first two open-close, open-close beats. After a while, he seemed in danger of drowning in his own juice.
>
> But Oreo's plan was without mercy. Simultaneously with the rhythms she was laying down from her stool, Betty began telling the doctor one of her favorite jokes. "It's about this man and woman who go down to Florida on their fifteenth wedding anniversary. They get up in their room, and the first thing they do is take off all their clothes."
>
> The doctor licked his lips in anticipation, his eyes fixed on Betty's open-close, open-close.[168]

The man who asked Oreo over the phone to get herself wet is now mired helplessly "in his own juice." The "open-close" mirrors the "No, not like that, like this. No, yes, no, harder, softer, up, down" oscillation that Oreo uses earlier over the phone to describe sex as a primarily linguistic enterprise of vaguely ineffective binary instruction-giving. The merciless "open-close" beat seems to be as titillating to the doctor as the "tangle of pubic hair." This unyielding mechanical alternation—graphically undeviating and explicit both—is what nearly drowns the doctor.

Embedded within the physical comedy of Ross's bed trick gag, and key to its pacing, is Betty's recitation of her favorite joke, which ups the slapstick ante of the scene. In the joke, a married couple, in a bid to spice up their love life, decide to stand naked in opposite corners of a room and run at and into each other:

> "... But they miss and run right past. The man is going so fast, he goes sailing out the open window. His room is on the tenth story, but he's lucky 'cause he falls in the swimming pool. But he's afraid to come out 'cause he don't have no clothes on. Everybody seems to be running to the hotel and nobody's paying him no mind, but he's still afraid to come out the pool buck naked. Then he sees this bellhop ready to go in the hotel, and he calls him over. He says, 'Say, bellhop, I want to get out the pool, but I can't 'cause I ain't got no clothes on.' The bellhop don't even look surprised. He says, 'That's all right, sir, nobody'll pay no 'ttention to you. You just come on out.' The man says, 'What do you mean nobody'll pay no 'ttention to me? I'm buck naked!' The bellhop says, 'I know, sir, but most of the people are up on the tenth floor trying to figure out a way to get a woman off a doorknob.'"[169]

The punch line—"trying to figure out how to get a woman off a doorknob"—is a slight inversion of the Bergsonian comedic dictum of "something mechanical encrusted on the living."[170]

It captures perfectly, though, Bergson's elaboration of his theory that "the laughable element . . . consists of a certain *mechanical inelasticity*, just where one would expect to find the wideawake adaptability and the living pliableness of a human being"—both in physical and linguistic comedy.[171] The diagrammatic plausibility—and inflexibility—of the couple's plan is foiled by their own human foibles, even as it gets one of them stuck on a very materially inelastic piece of home furnishing.

Betty's favorite joke is pure physical comedy—and slapstick at that.[172] Slapstick, many have argued, is funny because people get hurt. But you know that those people aren't you, and that you won't get hurt, so you laugh. Both the titillation and the slapstick sense of personal security that follow Betty's favorite joke are short-lived for her male audience, however:

> Oreo came out of hiding and gave him a quick *shu-kik* to the groin, then got his jaw in the classic *nek-brāc* position. With his life but a *blō* away,

he promised Oreo he would never again annoy innocent young women by phone or in person with his snortings and slaverings. With a half-force *bak-bop* she propelled him off Betty's porch and watched as he shmegeggely fled the street.[173]

The "medical examiner" abruptly realizes he's misjudged where the frame of the shtick is, and that his own stick is suddenly in very real physical danger—his life but a (not that kind of) "*blō* away." It's a nightmare scenario for a slapstick audience—to be a sudden participant when you thought you were a mere listener/observer.

Donald Crafton argues that "slapstick cinema seems to be ruled by the principle of accretion: gags, situations, costumes, characters, camera techniques are rehearsed and recycled in film after film, as though the modernist emphasis on originality and the unique text was unheard of."[174] Or, put another way, "in slapstick nothing is discarded."[175] Betty's joke is not a new joke, nor is the bed trick a new form of prank (though this one never quite makes it to bed).[176] Novelty has nothing to do with the humor here. This "principle of accretion" is an apt way of thinking about the graphic humor in *Oreo*, which trades so heavily in making light of (but never cathartically purging) heavy historical baggage and functions via the rapid accumulation of seemingly incongruent forms of excess—excessive diagrams, equations, puns, euphemisms, wetness, wit, and WIT. The silent slapstick film has had the same narrative structure critiques leveled against it, too, as pornography, called "flawed" because "the elements of slapstick are not 'integrated' with other elements (characters, structure, vision, cinematic style . . .). In this reading of film comedy, slapstick is the bad element, an excessive tendency that it is the task of the narrative to contain."[177]

In the phone sex/bed-trick section's own excessive ending, Oreo punching the doctor—"his life but a *blō* away"—isn't even its final punch line. In a move that has been the crux of some criticism on the limits of Ross's feminism, especially when it comes to the sexuality of women in the novel who aren't Oreo, the section ends with:

She turned back just in time to hear Betty saying plaintively, "But what about me?"

Oreo realized that it had been very brave and self-sacrificing of Betty to participate in this little hoax. But her face brightened when she saw what time it was. She gave Betty the good news. "What about you? It's five-thirty. Your father will be home any minute now. Do what you usually do in these circumstances. Fuck *him*."[178]

Stick it to the patriarchy—(literally?) fuck your father? Tru Leverette argues that "the text's feminist narrative . . . falters when confronted with the reality of female sexual desire and prostitution." She claims that

> [T]he novel characterizes Betty, the woman who helps Oreo trick the obscene caller, with malice and contempt. . . . [I]t is clear from her characterization that Betty shares none of Oreo's indignation with the man's attempt to molest women over the phone and in person; additionally, she is characterized singularly in terms of her body and her physical desires, a mindless entity, the "Half WIT" of the section's title.[179]

I think this is a misreading of the novel's attitude towards Betty, one that reveals the subtlety of the section by missing that, even when it doesn't consummate in sex, it is all about self-pleasure. The "Half WIT" section, I would argue, is more about a female Narcissisterian "radical narcissism" than it is about "indignation." The novel isn't prurient or preachy about sex, but the detached doubly graphic comedic register in which it narrates all of its content—sexual and otherwise—has tempted such a misinterpretation.

Having denied Betty one form of sexual relief by sending the phone harasser showily on his way, Oreo encourages her to find another member with which to pleasure herself. This one just happens to be a member of her family. The dig is less at Betty than at the slate of objects Ross makes interchangeably available for her to fuck. Plunger, prank caller, father—none of the rods are all that appealing, but Betty is welcome to them if she wants, and Oreo delights in offering her a quick and easy (and the implication is almost completely fungible) swap. Oreo (the book and the character both), it seems, prefers a queerer, less penetrative pleasure.

Maidenhead®

The novel's action comes to a head in a graphic depiction of a would-be rape foiled by a futuristic super-strong rubber-like false hymen called a Maidenhead®, which Oreo pragmatically wedges into her "wedge." In this chapter, our super-savvy hyper-verbal protagonist strips and splays, turning herself into a (sex) doll with a vengeance in order to repel, quite literally, the unwanted sexual advances of a well-hung man named Kirk.

After Oreo has left Betty and Philadelphia behind to follow her father's clues through the streets of New York City, she sees "A black pimp and ten prostitutes, five white, five black, in alternating colors, wend[ing] toward her in a ragged V, a checkerboard wedge of wedges."[180] Oreo observes a ritual in which "Parnell," as she dubs the pimp, demands a shoe shine from and gives out a boot in the rear to the assembled "wedges," at which point, as comeuppance, she gives "him a grand-slam clout across the ass" with her cane and runs away. The Maidenhead scene begins with Oreo having been brought to Parnell's lair for punishment, in the form of rape, in front of an audience of prostitutes. She is to be raped not by the pimp himself, but rather by "a man, virtually on all fours, caparisoned in a black loincloth," named Kirk, who Parnell calls his "some kinda way-out instrument of torture." As Kirk approaches Oreo, and *Oreo* approaches its attempted rape scene, Ross reverses the appraising, taxonomizing, pornographic gaze. After the amply endowed Kirk's junk is unsheathed, "unfurled like a paper favor blown by Gabriel at the last party in the history of the world," Oreo digresses into a flight of euphemistic excess:

> Oreo was impressed. Male genitals had always reminded her of oysters, gizzards, and turkey wattles at best, a bunch of seedless grapes at worst. On the other hand, most marmoreal baskets (e.g., the David's) resembled the head of a mandrill (a serendipitous pun). An inveterate crotch-watcher, she had once made a list of sports figures whom she classified under the headings "Capons" and "Cockerels." The capons (mostly big-game hunters, bowlers) were men whose horns could be described by any of the following (or similar) terms: *pecker, dick, cock, thing, peter, prick, dangle, shmendrick, putz, shmuck.* The cockerels (gymnasts, swimmers) sported any of the following: *shlong, dong, rod, tool, lumber.* Neutral words (*member, penis*) were applicable in cases where the looseness or padding of the standard uniform made definitive as-

sessment impossible (baseball, basketball, football, hockey, and tennis play-ers). But Kirk's stallion was a horse of another collar, of such dimensions that he could have used a zeppelin for a condom.[181]

In an epic catalogue of phallic nomenclature, Ross makes euphemism itself somewhat appalling, bringing the nausea back to ad nauseum. The true object of admiration, however, is clearly not the various peckers, dongs, and rods that Oreo ogles, but, rather, as always, her own polyglot verbal virtuosity. With the appraising eye of a collector, she neatly populates a linguistic cab-inet of cock-and-ball curiosities, carefully chopped off from the extraneous bodies to which they were once attached and preserved as specimens for later use and appreciation. Much of the humor of the passage comes from Ross's ballsy insistence on turning, against gender type, an appraising eye on male physiognomy in a flourish of extravagant objectification.[182] If the male gaze transforms women into sex dolls, her rebuttal pares all men down, with a hard-edged linguistic flourish, into dildos.

This power play is an important part of a setup in which Oreo seems (tem-porarily) to embrace prostration and passivity before the punch line reveals how she has weaponized her own sex. Parnell directs Oreo to strip, and Oreo directs Parnell (who deputizes a prostitute) to clean up Kirk (an inspection reveals that "Kirk had cornered the market on smegma"[183]). Oreo returns from the bathroom clad only in sandals, a brassiere, and a mezuzah. Then the action begins:

> Kirk came out of his corner with his nose wide open. As he advanced, his stallion did an impressive caracole right, a no-slouch caracole left, then ma-jestically reared its head. He threw the unresisting Oreo to the floor, stretched her legs wide in the ready-set position of a nutcracker, took aim, tried to jam his pole into her vault and—much to his and everyone else's surprise—met with a barrier that propelled him backward and sent him bounding off the nearest wall.[184]

Splayed like one sort of tool (nutcracker), Oreo seems magically to repel an attempted penetration by another (Kirk's "stallion") at the behest of yet a third (the pimp, Parnell). Of course, the inanimate object to which Oreo's body is first compared ends up being a fairly apt description of what she does to Kirk:

> The look of astonishment on Kirk's face as he gave the dullard's flat-eyed stare
> to his bruised cock and muscles would warm her heart's cockles for all the
> time she was alive, alive-o. The puzzlement of Parnell, the hoaxing of the
> whores—oh, Oreo could do nothing but smile her cookie smile.[185]

Ross again reminds us of her heroine's perpetual association with visual objectification as she smiles "her cookie smile," an allusion to her name and susceptibility to consumption. Her nickname brings us back, in this otherwise antirealist romp, to the real fact that as a woman, and particularly a Black woman, Oreo would be perceived by others as a hypervisible hypersexualized object first, especially in the eye of a white man like Kirk. Though critics are right to note that "the only thing the novel doesn't target is Oreo herself," making sure she remains not only "omnicompetent" but sexually inviolate, Ross knows and shows that the world in which Oreo lives would like nothing better than to make her as ready for disintegration and consumption as her namesake prepackaged confection.[186]

After these two setup paragraphs during which the reader shares in the puzzlement of Kirk, Parnell, and the prostitutes at this "cookie smile," Ross lets us in on the secret of Oreo's impressive powers of repulsion.

> The barrier Kirk had come upon (but not come upon) when he tried to pull
> a 401 (breaking and entering) was a false hymen made of elasticium, a newly
> discovered trivalent metal whose outstanding characteristic was enormous
> resiliency. Elasticium's discovery had been made possible by a grant from
> Citizens Against the Rape of Mommies (CAROM), an organization whose
> membership was limited to those who had had at least one child (or were in
> the seventh to ninth month of pregnancy) before being attacked (usually by
> their husbands, an independent survey revealed). CAROM's work was a clear
> case of mother succor (and thus an aid to rhymesters). Vindictiveness would
> soon lead CAROM's leadership to share false hymens with the world ("Maid-
> enheads® are available in your choice of Cherry pink, Vestal Virgin white,
> or Black Widow black"), but Oreo had been able to get hold of a prototype
> because of her acquaintanceship with its inventor, Caresse Booteby.[187]

In the Maidenhead scene, Ross both riffs on and largely denies her readers the titillations of a more traditionally pornographic episode of debasement. She enacts a version of the abject dynamics of stand-up comedy—even as Oreo spends much of the scene more or less lying down. Limon notes that

> [S]tand-up itself has the structure of abjection insofar as comedians are not allowed to be either natural or artificial. (Are they themselves or acting? Are they in costume?) . . . All a stand-up's life feels abject to him or her, and stand-ups try to escape it by living it as an act.[188]

If Ross's badass mixed-race heroine qua stand-up comedian is, in her state of "compounded liminality," "not allowed to be either natural or artificial," she'll double down and arm herself with an elasticized hymen made out of a material not only artificial but entirely made up.

Maidenhead in place, Oreo has bridged her own gap and made herself into a no-sex doll. Though she's been playing Theseus throughout the novel, here she seems, at a moment of crisis, to be pulling a Daphne, "the most famous story of a person transformed into a thing."[189] But whereas the Daphne-turned-laurel-tree of Greek myth is rooted, organic, and beholden to her father, Oreo, the doubly graphic object of the 1970s, is decidedly none of those things. She is free-standing, inorganically equipped, and, though on a quest to find her father and the secret of her birth, utterly uninterested in paternal salvation. Rather than a piece of shrubbery who will remain sexually inviolate while having no choice but to see her leaves used in victory wreaths and savory stews alike, Ross's beset heroine becomes a mezuzah-clad, afro-sporting Black Barbie, who bucks not only the attempted rape by Kirk but an expected script of what she, as an African American female protagonist of a novel published in the 1970s should expect to have visited sexually upon her.[190] As Danzy Senna writes in the foreword to the novel's republication:

> *Oreo* resists the unwritten conventions that still exist for novels written by black women today. . . . The character is never violated, sexually or otherwise. The characters are not from the South. Oreo is sincerely ironic, hilarious, brainy, impenetrable at times.[191]

Rather than appealing to a father river god to save her from rape by turning her into an inarticulate—voiceless and jointless both—tree, Oreo embraces the elasticity of a self-imposed, self-gratifying artificiality. Ross's doubly graphic object—gross and geometric at once—is both pleased with and pleasures itself.

Ross's doubly graphic objectification of her protagonist paradoxically refuses to make Oreo available for what Hortense Spillers termed "pornotroping,"[192] or, in Alexander Weheliye's words, "the enactment of black suffering for a shocked and titillated audience."[193] Daphne Brooks expands on Spillers by noting that "born out of diasporic plight and subject to pornotroping, this body has countenanced a 'powerful stillness.' "[194] Turning prone stillness into unexpectedly slapstick movement is, in part, the hinge of the comedy of the Maidenhead scene. As attempted rape CAROMs somewhat jarringly into gag, Ross refuses the pornotropic and instead gives us an unexpected bit of pornographic humor, in which the sex doll pleasures herself by becoming a gleefully graphic object. This move to the masturbatory for the minoritarian subject allows, as Summer Kim Lee writes of Ocean Vuong's 2016 poem "Ode to Masturbation," bodies that "bear the marks of violent history" to "evade narratives reducible to either injury or resilience through the pleasures felt from within."[195] It's a "within" that we, as readers, are unable to penetrate—casting us in an uncomfortable confederacy with Kirk.

An abstracted linguistic humor—begonia, cunt, cockerel, etc.—meets the physicality of slapstick again and again in *Oreo*, without ever really melding comfortably. Kirk rebounding off of the linguistically overdetermined surface of the Maidenhead in this scene evokes what Crafton calls "the gag's status as an irreconcilable difference."[196] Crafton argues, against critics of the slapstick film who deem the gag's lack of integration into narrative a failure, that easy, seamless integration was never the point. Rather, "while other genres work to contain their excesses, in slapstick (like avant-garde, a kind of limit-text), the opposition is fundamental. Furthermore, it is carefully constructed to remain an unbridgeable gap."[197] This trifecta of unbridgeability, resistance to epistemological comprehension, and unintegrated excess is key to Ross's pornographic episodes.

The "unbridgeable gap" is a distance that exists not just internally, between gag and narrative, but externally, between reader and text. As Ngai writes of the related aesthetic of "the zany," "the zany object or person is one we can only enjoy—if we do in fact enjoy it or her—at a safe or comfortable distance."[198] Unlike Williams's characterization of pornography as "body genre," whose "success . . . is often measured by the degree to which the audience sensation mimics what is seen on screen,"[199] Ngai's zaniness "does not seem to call forth a subjective response in any way mimetic of itself. This lack of accord between aesthetic subject and object seems all the more surprising given zaniness's unique history as a style explicitly about mimetic behavior."[200] The sex doll is an object that seems to remain both zanily distant from and pornographically close to the bodies it mimics—making it an exemplary figure for a queasily double graphic mode of penetrative flattening.[201]

The often-gleeful failure—or refusal—of various disparate elements "to integrate" in *Oreo*'s slapstick humor is also a notable feature of Ross's treatment of race.[202] The novel, with its mixed-race heroine, is decidedly not about a utopian ideal of seamless and emancipatory racial amalgamation. Her name is Oreo, not caramel. Instead, it insists on graphic boundaries—reminiscent of the "checkerboard wedge of wedges,"[203] or the cartwheeling skirt-flipping of the topsy-turvy/Topsy-Eva doll—between various racial and ethnic groups and flaunts, but hardly romanticizes its heroine's virtuosic ability to code switch and temporarily hop between the stubbornly chiaroscuro planes of Black and Jewish identity that make up her world. "An equal-opportunity satirist, Ross hits African American phobias as cheerfully as Jewish ones."[204] But she never facilely collapses them into each other. Oreo briefly becomes one sort of mechanical thing, but a bridge across racial divides isn't exactly it.

The reason for this refusal might have something to do with the history of the stage and film practice of slapstick itself in the United States, which is inextricable from both Jewish vaudeville and minstrelsy. Carpio notes the persistent "challenge of creating an embodied, physical comedy given the lasting power of the specter of minstrelsy."[205] Blackface minstrelsy was, long preceding Al Jolson's star turn in *The Jazz Singer*, an avenue for "Americanizing ethnics"—Irish and Jewish performers—to make a living and access whiteness.[206] As Bernstein points out, drawing a connection between blackface performance and the topsy-turvy doll, "The white performer in blackface, like the topsy-turvy doll, gained form from what showed and what hid, from whiteness-and-blackness, from the promise and threat of racial flip-flops."[207] Melting into or with performed "blackness" was never the point of blackface. And neither, with very different politics, does a (post)racial melting pot seem to be an option entertained (or entertaining) in the world of *Oreo*, infused as it is with both Jewish and Black traditions of verbal and physical performance that Ross stages as infused with animosity towards each other (Oreo is conversant in Yiddish not because of her Jewish father but because her Black grandfather, James Clark, hating Jews, sells mail-order items to them at an outrageous markup[208]). Boundaries and barriers are real things, even if the materials that make them up are as artificial as Elasticium, and neither uplift nor utopia are things Ross's novel cares much about. "Unbridgeable gaps" get laughs.

With the Maidenhead, Oreo transforms herself via temporary implant into a sexless toy that plays at once on the plastic sex doll, the cloth topsy-turvy doll, and the black gutta-percha doll. These black rubber dolls were most often modeled wearing permanent grins, "and their smiles suggested that violent play was acceptable, even enjoyable."[209] The elasticity of the rubber, gutta-percha, was not only key to the ways in which play was scripted for the children who used them, but also alludes to a sinister nexus of race, innocence, and pain in American culture. Robin Bernstein argues that "the materiality of black rubber dolls configures blackness as an elastic form of subjectivity that can withstand blows without breaking."[210] Particularly in the nineteenth century, children were trained through these dolls to experience the battering of black bodies as play, their grins and limbs imperturbably, even giddily holding up under treatment that would easily shatter their more fragile white porcelain counterparts.

Oreo's transformation cites at once the plastic Barbie, the cloth topsy-turvy, the black gutta-percha, and the inflatable sex doll. Aligning *Oreo* with these playthings also signals the novel's complicated awareness of the kind of fun, familiarity, and unfettered access that has been expected of minoritarian subjects in the United States. As Kim Lee again writes, "minoritarian subjects must also bear and navigate the burden of relatability from which a compulsory sociability emerges; one must not only be legible and transparent but also accessibly and accommodatingly so."[211] When the minoritarian subject-as-sex-toy becomes autoerotic, though, it suddenly jumps the shark of compulsory sociability, legibility, and transparency. The masturbating sex doll gives us instead, à la Sedgwick, "the vision of a certain autoerotic closure, absentation, self-sufficiency."[212] The Maidenhead, moreover, materializes Sedgwick's formulation of "autoerotic closure" and turns it into a pun, a performance, and a provocation: in short, a gag.

———

Ross incorporates the scripts of these various objects of rough play and transforms the doll herself into the heroine of her own brand of roughhouse retribution.[213] Just as Ross reverses the male gaze earlier in the chapter, Oreo's repulsion of Kirk takes the passivity, muteness, and anagrammatic proneness of the doll as a pornographic figure and turns it on its (Maiden)head. In doing so, she trades *Lolita*'s mode of claustrophobic readerly complicity for an aesthetic of bravura, defiant, inorganic, elasticity. Though Oreo embraces, temporarily, the role of the animated nonliving entity, the gag of the scene quickly becomes the dummying of Kirk and his cock, in their repetitive, fruitless assault—and the solitary pleasure Oreo takes in it.

The artificiality of linguistic bodies puts them on the same shelf, in key ways, as the sex doll. Do with dolls and words what you like—"real" bodies aren't really at stake. Embracing bodies as linguistic constructions and their attempted knocking together of parts as Bergsonian slapstick, the sex scenes of *Oreo* tacitly acknowledge and sharply satirize the fact that bodies like Oreo's—Black and female—have seldom been considered "real" either. Comedy may be a "man in trouble,"[214] but the punch lines of the post-45 canon are disturbingly often a woman being raped. The sex doll is both a figure and figurine—a rich analogy and a functional object. Centering it in this book's discussion of how identification works and is unworked in post-45 narratives and performances that do grossly diagrammatic and/or diagrammatically gross things with sex helps us see how not only both the comic and pornographic, but also the double graphic at large, function through a logic of overarticulating, abstracting, and mechanizing human bodies.

Thinking the pornographic through the (topsy-turvy) sex doll also allows us to finesse Linda Williams's theorization of pornography as "the frenzy of the visual" by taking touch and dimensionality seriously. Nabokov, Narcissister, and Ross all knowingly use, abuse, and make palpably unnerving the classically visual vocabulary of the pornographic gaze by lingering on the stickily slick surfaces and ambivalently inviting orifices of the uncannily (in)animate sex object. In other words, the dummy that dummies. Read through and for the doubly graphic figure of the sex doll, the crux of the obscenity of Nabokov's *Lolita* becomes a libidinous drive for identification qua classification, an insatiable fixation on coercively articulating—speaking, manipulating, parsing—a person into a thing. Both flattened and hollowed out—emptied of both internal organs and human interiority—*Lolita*'s dolls embody a doubly graphic misalignment of two- and three-dimensionality, along with their attendant modes of identification. Narcissister's citation-rich combination of organicism and inorganicism, meanwhile, evokes the disruption of "any dualistic understandings of agency and passivity"[215] that Sedgwick assigns to touch; yet the performance artist, by reveling in the unyieldingly dualistic form of the topsy-turvy doll, also seems to balk at a cozily reparative reading of her pornographic play. Delighting, too, in self-objectification, Ross's *Oreo* rescripts the male gaze and recasts the recombinant masturbatory aid as the epic heroine—elastically weaponizing both fetishization and flatness, as apt to repel as compel intimate contact, be it sexual or sympathetic. In the doubly pornographic, the frenzy of the visual fondles the plasticized roundness of sex dolls—some of whom discomfitingly, aggressively touch us (and themselves) back.

The Infographic

As a cultural form, database represents the world as a list of items which it refuses to order. In contrast, a narrative creates a cause-and-effect trajectory of seemingly unordered items (events). Therefore, database and narrative are natural "enemies."

—LEV MANOVICH, "Database as a Symbolic Form"

Most information visualizations are acts of interpretation masquerading as presentation.

—JOHANNA DRUCKER, *Graphesis: Visual Forms of Knowledge Production*

AMERICAN GRAPHIC'S FINAL CHAPTER EXAMINES the distinctive form of the double graphic evident in post-45 novels that are structured by tangential revelations of, or casual contact with, trauma. The rendering of violence and viscera into data characterizes the "cool" of a particular type of information-age graphic. Instead of the ethnographic silhouette, or the pornographic sex doll, bodies in these texts become dimensionless data points—the raw material conglomerated and transubstantiated into information visualizations. Tangential plotting and parasitic incorporation are the propulsive forces behind these database-inflected texts. Lee Manovich writes that, "Indeed, if, after the death of God (Nietzsche), the end of grand Narratives of Enlightenment (Lyotard) and the arrival of the web (Tim Berners-Lee), the world appears to us as an endless and unstructured collection of images, texts, and other data records, it is only appropriate that we will be moved to model it as a database."[1]

I focus here on database-inflected novels in which bodies, particularly minoritized bodies, are treated as the raw stuff of data, and in which trauma inflicted upon them populates the information visualizations qua plots of the texts. Both Thomas Pynchon's *The Crying of Lot 49*, written towards the beginning of the digital age, and Teju Cole's *Open City*, steeped in the ethos of Wikipedic pastiche, unfold via the rapid proliferation of tangential information, usually sparked by physical contact between their protagonists—Oedipa Maas and Julius, respectively—and other, usually fleetingly minor, characters. Each contact is quickly followed by Oedipa's or Julius's either paranoid or parasitic incorporation of those others' stories into their own. Both novels revolve, too, around moments of attempted ocular mastery, often belatedly accompanied by revelations of occluded histories of violence. How, these texts prompt us to ask, does the flattening that we think of as characteristic of the postmodern lend itself to, or even demand, a clinical pose towards and a computational mastery over violence? How does the logic of the mathematic tangent relate to the structure and function of the narratological one as these protagonists graph and graft others' stories onto and into their own? How do the aesthetics and affects of data visualization inflect or infect literary narrative in post-45 literature? What is the calculus of identification when texts read people as tangentially connected data points?

I will discuss "points"—coordinates, conclusions, and punctures—in the context of the paranoia of *The Crying of Lot 49* and explore theories of parasitism in my reading of the (graphic) revelation toward the end of *Open City*, while reading the affective dynamics of both novels through Alan Liu's notion of "cool." My readings of each text hinge on moments of sexual violence, which bring out the grotesque dimension of the infographic's particular form of graphic exposure.

Thomas Pynchon's Striptease

Beloved of twentieth-century American literature survey courses, *The Crying of Lot 49* is often taught as a (mercifully short) example par excellence of the postmodern novel. Within its modestly numbered pages, space and time flatten, expand, and contract with ostentatious ironic detachment, while characters and readers alike all seem to be auditioning for the band The Paranoids. Early reviews of the novel were quick either to trumpet or turn up their noses at the book's flamboyant form of flattening. Harkening back to Nathanael West's original subtitle for *Miss Lonelyhearts* ("a novel in the form of a comic strip"), a *Time* magazine review entitled "Nosepicking Contests" declared *The*

Crying of Lot 49 "a metaphysical thriller in the form of a pornographic comic strip."[2] Another contemporary review called it "a step backward to the art of the emblem books, a patchy collection of images propped up by claims of significance in terms which the artist hasn't proved the right to use."[3] Another way of viewing the patchy collection of images would be as not a step backwards to emblem books, but as a slide forwards into database aesthetics, which, in Manovich's words, "represents the world as a list of items which it refuses to order."[4] Each reviewer seemed to latch on to the book's peculiar mix of affective detachment and visually evocative—even aggressive—distastefulness. Few moments in the novel exemplify this pose of a "pornographic comic strip" better than the game of Strip Botticelli.

The novel's protagonist, Oedipa Maas, who recently has been named executrix of the estate of her late ex-beau Pierce Inverarity, begins a quest that will morph into a dizzying dive into the mysterious world of underground postal carriers and the elusive Tristero. Early on she meets the lawyer Metzger at the Echo Courts hotel. As the two watch an old movie starring a young Metzger, who turns out to be the erstwhile child actor Baby Igor, the lawyer responds to Oedipa's questions about how the film will end by instigating a game he calls "Strip Botticelli." "Go ahead," said Metzger, "ask questions. But for each answer, you'll have to take something off. We'll call it Strip Botticelli."[5] Oedipa, in turn, has her own "marvelous idea." She excuses herself to the bathroom and proceeds to don "as much as she could of the clothing she'd brought with her." One of the novel's most amusing and, perhaps, unsettling episodes ensues. Oedipa, swaddled in countless layers of clothes, spies herself in the mirror and falls over laughing, knocking over a can of hairspray, which proceeds to go rogue and destroy the bathroom, shattering mirrors and glass shower doors before it finally loses steam and clatters to the ground. Though Oedipa begins drunkenly to kiss and embrace Metzger, the scene dubiously climaxes with an unconscious Oedipa awaking to "find herself getting laid."

The graphic surfaces of *The Crying of Lot 49* are all tinted, as Christopher McKenna points out, with an unshakeable, uncanny ambiguity:

> Just as the Strip Botticelli scene, though simultaneously funny and sexually charged, is inevitably colored both by the dangerous flight of the broken spray can and by the predatory sexual advances that frame the scene (Miles's menacing advance on Oedipa at its start and Metzger's virtual date-rape of her at

its end), the primary thematic element of the novel, Oedipa's quest for the Tristero, is also characterized by an ambiguity that resists any simple explication.[6]

McKenna, in his broader analysis of the novel, analogizes the idea of modern computers' GUIs (graphic user interfaces) with the seeming accessibility and sense of "game-playing," via wit and irony, that Pynchon's style gives to his novel. McKenna uses "graphic" in the sense of the pieces of stylistic flair in Pynchon's writing that mimic the tricks of computer programs' user interfaces, both of which mask the objects' underlying alienating complexity and make interacting with, and returning to, the text, program, or game fun and appealing for the lay user or reader. McKenna notes that "the distinguishing characteristic of the 'graphical' elements in Pynchon's novels is ambiguity (where comedy is never entirely funny, nor sex sexy)."[7] I argue that fun and accessibility might not be quite the game that Pynchon is playing, but would like to take McKenna's attention to graphic surfaces and styles farther in discussing the ambient ambiguity that I agree defines the novel's key moments, especially this scene of "virtual date-rape."

Almost none of the abundant criticism of Pynchon's novel names this scene as rape—notice how McKenna, even, couches it as "virtual" date rape. Yet, when teaching this novel to undergraduates, I've noticed that one of the first comments about this scene is reliably an observation about consent, and the fact that an inebriated and incapacitated Oedipa has notably not given it when she wakes up to find herself being penetrated by a virtual stranger. In 2018, the homework help site Shmoop, which brags "we speak student," commented on the scene in its "Steaminess Rating" section (now tellingly removed) of its study guide to *The Crying of Lot 49*:

> In Pynchon's world, sex is weird, weird, weird. If you don't believe us, just read up through the end of Chapter Two when Metzger and Oedipa begin their affair. Metzger thinks he has convinced Oedipa to play a stripping game, but then she slips into the bathroom and puts on every piece of clothing she can find until she looks like "a beach ball with feet" (2.78). When she finally agrees to have sex with Metzger, it takes him so long to take off her clothes that she falls asleep several times—only to wake up in the middle of the act. Like we said: deeply weird. And kind of rape-y.[8]

I bookend this chapter with episodes of rape that are narratively elided but key to the affective dynamics of both Pynchon and Cole's novels and of the infographic at large. The tendency of these novels to overload us with information, all delivered in the same flat register of the "cool" or the "interesting," becomes uncomfortably grotesque when it intersects with their equally marked obsessions with trauma, violence, and bodily transgressions, particularly sexual.

The slapstick of the Strip Botticelli debacle is set off, significantly, by an act of looking. After layering an extensive closet's-worth-catalogue of clothing over her body in preparation for her game of burlespionage, Oedipa

> made the mistake of looking at herself in the full-length mirror, saw a beach ball with feet, and laughed so violently she fell over, taking a can of hair spray on the sink with her. The can hit the floor, something broke, and with a great outsurge of pressure the stuff commenced atomizing, propelling the can swiftly about the bathroom. Metzger rushed in to find Oedipa rolling around, trying to get back on her feet, amid a great sticky miasma of fragrant lacquer.[9]

Oedipa has rendered herself a "beach ball with feet" in an attempt to insulate herself against potential contact with her would-be seducer. She finds herself suddenly and unexpectedly threatened instead both by the bone-shattering bombardment of a crazily "caroming" can of hairspray and by suffocation and immobilization at the hands of its vaguely unseemly "outsurge" of "stuff." In becoming spherical, Oedipa becomes ripe and ready for a fast and loose radiation of interpretive tangents. The aerosol assault is easily a comic trivialization of a violent airstrike; or a send-up of the proliferation, not of nukes, but of the paraphernalia of the femininity-industrial-complex; or, with its miasmic dispersion of noxious fumes made of unspecified "stuff," a figure for the atmosphere of dread that Oedipa's tryst with Tristero soon conjures in the novel. Abundant analogies dissipate into the mist, leaving us to think, instead, about the sticky relationship between form and affect in the scene, wondering what, following Sara Ahmed, are the objects to which feelings will stick—or slide off of—and how, and why.

Like Oedipa's search for the secretive organization Tristero, the Strip Botticelli game unfolds in and as a series of suspensions. "So it went: the succession of film fragments on the tube, the progressive removal of clothing that seemed to bring her no nearer nudity, the boozing, the timeless shivaree of voices and guitars from out by the pool."[10] A single moment is dilated[11] and, through a combination of the prose's temporal stretching and the aerosol can's spatial movement, also diagrammed.

> She looked up past his eyelids, into the staring ceiling light, her field of vision cut across by wild, flashing overflights of the can, whose pressure seemed inexhaustible. The can knew where it was going, she sensed, or something fast enough, God or a digital machine, might have computed in advance the complex web of its travel; but she wasn't fast enough, and knew only that it might hit them at any moment, at whatever clip it was doing, a hundred miles an hour.[12]

The movement of the aerosol can effectively maps the contours—lines and planes—of the bathroom as it makes destructive contact with each of them in turn—cutting again and again across Oedipa's field of vision in its "wild, flashing overflights;" colliding with the mirror; destroying the frosted glass of the enclosed shower, the tiles of its three walls, the ceiling itself. This process of spatial definition through violent temporal contact seems to point to a telling phenomenon of the infographic in general.

What makes this scene doubly graphic, especially if we read it as a figure for reading, is its elision of cool shiny, ricocheting, map-making, inanimate violence with sticky fleshy seduction. Elided, too, are the actions and attitudes of us, the readers, with those of Metzger, the man attempting to remove an eventually unconscious Oedipa's layers. In this dilated moment, disinterest and disgust coexist uncomfortably against a framework of binary information gathering. Even as the slick surfaces of irony and aerosol-lacquered bathroom floor seem to promise us ethical and aesthetic distance, the structure of analogy and the fact of eventually nonconsensual sex attach an uneasy guilt and grime to our acts of interpretation, with a stickiness that recalls Ahmed's analysis of disgust.

"Disgust," Ahmed argues, "operates as a contact zone; it is about how things come into contact with other things."[13] Wrapped up in this contact theory of disgust, a chilled version of which seems to be generated by the uneasy climax of Strip Botticelli, are the dynamics of stickiness, which Ahmed explains via Sartre as being "about what objects do to other objects—it involves a transference of affect—but it is a relation of 'doing' in which there is not a distinction between passive or active, even though the stickiness of one object might come before the stickiness of the other, such that the other seems to cling to it."[14] The confusion of active and passive is key to the discomfort of Oedipa's lack of consent to the actual act of sex when it finally comes.

> She sank with an enormous sigh that carried all rigidity like a mythical fluid from her, down next to him; so weak she couldn't help him undress her; it took him 20 minutes, rolling, arranging her this way and that, as if she thought, he were some scaled-up, short-haired, poker-faced little girl with a Barbie doll. She may have fallen asleep once or twice. She awoke at last to find herself getting laid; she'd come in on a sexual crescendo in progress, like a cut to a scene where the camera's already moving.[15]

Oedipa is the "Barbie doll" to Metzger's "poker-faced little girl," and the prose cuts out the moment of possible consent or lack thereof by cutting to a flat celluloid analogy—"like a cut to a scene where the camera's already moving." The messiness of rape is metaphorically plasticized into Barbie dolls and film strips. It is leveled out under analogy.

Eugenie Brinkema, writing of the formal features of disgust in film, cites Darwin's definition of the affect: "Darwin figures revulsion as the 'not' or 'no' in any system by grouping his discussion of disgust with other 'signs of affirmation and negation.' Disgust is a binary toggle that accepts or rejects food as a defensive and protective gesture for a vulnerable biology."[16] The Strip Botticelli scene turns rape into a grotesque sort of child's play, denying both its victim and the reader an ability to discern a clean "binary toggle"—and with it both a clear ethics of consent or a pure affective response of disgust, even as the game's initial structuring logic seems to demand clear "signs of affirmation and negation." What the infographic texts in this chapter each seem to ask, in different ways, against the amorphous backdrop (ambiguous grid?) of the information age is how (or if) a binary system of switches (or contacts, or *touches*) can produce a complex network of meaning. How can points have dimension? Or binaries attain complexity? And, are those contacts always necessarily somehow violent or violating, are those switches always also or already the "binary toggles" of disgust?

Cool Walkings

One way to understand the particular identification crisis, the oversaturated affective shrug of this book's final iteration of the double graphic—what I'm calling the "infographic"—is by turning to Alan Liu's account of the rise of the contemporary aesthetic category of the "cool." Liu's "cool" is adjacent to, but not identical with Sianne Ngai's "interesting." Ngai makes this distinction.

> [T]he epistemological aesthetic of the interesting is cool, both in the sense of the ironic detachment Friedrich Schlegel attributed to the "*interessante*," an aesthetic of eclectic difference and novelty embraced by his circle as part of a larger romantic agenda calling for literature to become reflective or philosophical, and in the technocratic, informatic sense Alan Liu conveys in his book on postmodern knowledge work.[17]

In the introduction to *The Laws of Cool*, Liu describes this category in distinctly geometric, visual terms, not so different from the "inexhaustible" pressure of the high-speed "caroming" of the ever-vectoring aerosol can foreplay of Pynchon's Strip Botticelli. "Cool," Liu writes, "is the techno-informatic *vanishing point* of contemporary aesthetics, psychology, morality, politics, spirituality, and everything. No more beauty, sublimity, tragedy, grace, or evil: only cool or not cool."[18] Cool, in the information age, is a flattening, binary category that doesn't quite erase, but rather lacquers over, all other possibilities for aesthetic experience or affective adherence. Cool also, if only figuratively, seems to realign us with a sense of Cartesian perspective, with its standardized grids, horizon lines, vanishing points, and self-contained ostensibly objective viewers.

Liu explains cool's relationship to information as one, interestingly, of withholding. He points to an early Netscape website in 1996–97 that answered the question "What's cool?" with a breezy: "Someday, we'll all agree on what's cool on the Net. In the meantime, the Netscape cool team will continue to bring you a list of select sites that catch our eye, make us laugh, help us work, quench our thirst . . . you get the idea."[19] The ellipsis of ". . . you get the idea" encapsulates, for Liu, the complex aesthetic relationship the information age has with information itself:

> At once gesturing toward the "idea" of cool and withholding that idea, such an ellipsis is a uniquely paradoxical inexpressibility topos—one whose full-

ness of implied content (site after site after site) is constrained by a silence that is more than simply neutral or practical. The silence is also a proscription, an interdiction. The proscriptive ellipsis may be taken to be the elementary rhetoric, the mental pixel, of information cool.[20]

The tantalizing approach and withdrawal that Liu argues characterizes this "mental pixel" of information cool is not, structurally, all that different from the simultaneous dynamic of attraction and repulsion that marks the disgusting.

The difference is that disgusting objects give too much affective information;[21] cool ones give too little. Both seem to be social tags that require a certain sort of negative confirmation. Declaring an object disgusting, Ahmed argues, essentially makes it so—and calls on others to share in its rejection.[22] Declaring an object cool might, on the other hand, effectively negate its ability to be so.

> Cool is the aporia of information. In whatever form and on whatever scale (excessive graphics, egregious animation, precious slang, surplus hypertext, and so on), cool is *information designed to resist information*—not so much noise in the information theory sense as information fed back into its own signal to create a standing interference pattern, a paradox pattern. Structured as information designed to resist information, cool is the paradoxical "gesture" by which an ethos of the unknown struggles to arise in the midst of knowledge work.[23]

This description of cool bears more than a passing resemblance to the sort of miasmic paranoia surrounding the everywhere and nowhere of information about Tristero in *The Crying of Lot 49*—or, maybe too, the famously glib Supreme Court definition of pornography.[24] Cool is self-evident/self-sufficient information, you know it when you see it; unlike porn, though, if too many other people agree, it might just vanish again. Cool insists on a sort of "correct distance" (with all the disdain that implies), yet, its attempt to cultivate an "ethos of the unknown . . . in the midst of knowledge work" retains the essential binary logic of computer-age data. What happens, then, when novels seem to adopt or adapt the ethos of cool in a world that remains as sticky as ever?

Bright Lights, Grid City

The Crying of Lot 49 is famously one of the first novels to compare a cityscape to a computer chip, and much literary critical data has been crunched on how and why Pynchon used and abused, in 1966, the newly familiar paradigms of information technology.[25] As Oedipa, en route to Metzger and as yet blissfully unaware of Tristero, steps out of her car and looks down upon the planar grid of the fictional city of San Narciso, the harsh sunlight and her "high angle" allow the city to strike her as strangely reminiscent of a circuit card she first saw in a transistor radio.

> She looked down a slope, needing to squint for the sunlight, onto a vast sprawl of houses which had grown up all together, like a well-tended crop, from the dull brown earth; and she thought of the time she'd opened a transistor radio to replace a battery and seen her first printed circuit. The ordered swirl of houses and streets, from this high angle, sprang at her now with the same unexpected, astonishing clarity as the circuit card had.[26]

Faced with a nearly incomprehensible sprawl of human habitation, Oedipa turns to metaphor qua data visualization. She refigures a new and daunting landscape (and, implicitly, the innumerable people who occupy it) into a diagrammatic abstraction (a grid) that she resolidifies as a new object she can imaginatively hold in hand. Dipping her toe into what Lev Manovich calls the "anti-sublime" of data visualization, Oedipa briefly attempt to "map" the incomprehensible "into a representation whose scale is comparable to the scales of human perception and cognition."[27] This image of city as chip collapses macro and micro, startles Oedipa with both the promise and impossibility of legibility ("there were to both outward patterns a hieroglyphic sense of concealed meaning, of an intent to communicate"), and quickly slides (back, perhaps, towards a sort of sublime) into a hazy flirtation with religious-ish revelation.

> There'd seemed no limit to what the printed circuit could have told her (if she had tried to find out); so in her first minute of San Narciso, a revelation also trembled just past the threshold of her understanding. Smog hung all round the horizon, the sun on the bright beige countryside was painful; she and the Chevy seemed parked at the center of an odd, religious instant. As if, on some other frequency, or out of the eye of some whirlwind rotating too slow for her

heated skin even to feel the centrifugal coolness of, words were being spoken. She suspected that much.[28]

Oedipa, from her elevated vantage point, both graphs and grafts disparate grids onto one another. Once again, as with the Strip Botticelli scene, a look at a three-dimensional reality made suddenly and alarmingly flat—Oedipa's bulbous reflection in the mirror, San Narciso's "swirl of houses and streets" rendered orderly from far above—catalyzes a dilated moment of suspended action and failed communication. Oedipa's temporary scopic mastery translates cityscape into printed circuit into inarticulate, inarticulable religious revelation.

These layered grids—cityscape and circuit card—offer a distilled image for the geometric sense of the graphic. Exponential information made flat, transferable, visualizable, and abstract. A "disarticulated surfeit . . . rendered knowable and usable through some kind of systematic processing."[29] Lisa Gitelman and Virginia Jackson go so far as to offer as a basic "precept" that "not only are data abstract and aggregative, but data are mobilized graphically."[30] One of the most basic graphic mobilizations of data is the grid. Rosalind Krauss, describing the significance of the grid in twentieth-century visual art, writes:

> Surfacing in pre-War cubist painting and subsequently becoming ever more stringent and manifest, the grid announces, among other things, modern art's will to silence, its hostility to literature, to narrative, to discourse. As such, the grid has done its job with striking efficiency. The barrier it has lowered between the arts of vision and those of language has been almost totally successful in walling the visual arts into a realm of exclusive visuality and defending them against the intrusion of speech.[31]

As Oedipa's "high angle" makes her visually privy to a new and startling analogy between grids of different ilk but similar structure, she also finds herself adjacent to, but emphatically cut off from, some sort of linguistic communion. "Words were being spoken," but the silent grids she both sees and recalls each tempt her with yet cut her off from understanding what is, or might be, being said. Pynchon's prose itself, rather than being of a piece with "literature . . . narrative . . . discourse," instead places Oedipa on the side of visual grids, walled off from verbal revelation.

Grids, for all their seeming self-evidence and hostility "to literature, to narrative, to discourse," admit, in Krauss's analysis, a number of irreconcilably contradictory, simultaneously available interpretations. Krauss charts how both practitioners and interpreters of grids have found themselves, much like Oedipa, unable to resolve a fundamental "ambivalence about the import of the grid, an indecision about its connection to matter on the one hand or spirit on the other."[32] She argues that the grid was visual artists' attempt to short-circuit the seemingly binary choice of the secular versus the sacred, somewhat unexpectedly through the unforgiving geometry of lines uniformly arranged along two perpendicular axes. "Given the absolute rift that had opened between the sacred and the secular," she writes, "the modern artist was obviously faced with the necessity to choose between one mode of expression and the other. The curious testimony offered by the grid is that at this juncture he tried to decide for both."[33]

What does it mean, then, for a narrative—the very thing against which the grid arrays itself—to not just represent but somehow phenomenologically reproduce the "will to silence" of the visual grid through the form of the novel? And if, as Nico Israel claims of contemporary life, "the grid in all its globalizing geopolitical manifestations, including that of surveillance (think 'Google Earth' and drone weaponry), has proved ever harder to escape,"[34] what are the stakes of this kind of translation? Pynchon's engagement with the grid is, to return to the novel's contemporary reviews, not that different from West's perhaps equally hostile attempt to create "a novel in the form of a comic strip." The literary/verbal graphic seems to be trying, in some ways, to *grid* literature, and thereby gird it against certain sorts of interpretive intrusions, sheathing it in ambiguity, rendering it "flattened, geometricized, ordered, . . . antinatural, antimimetic, antireal."[35]

The inherent ambiguity to the grid is evident, too, in the competing feelings with which it seems aligned. As already noted, Alan Liu's definition of cool owes much to grid-like analogy. The grid also seems like the natural visual companion and vehicle for Ngai's aesthetic category of the interesting, which is all about the "desire to know reality by comparing one thing with another, or by lining up what one realizes one doesn't know against what one knows already."[36]

Even as they seem naturally aligned with the cool and calculating epistemology of the interesting, grids have been theoretically tied, too, to the affect of disgust. Taking Peter Greenaway's *The Cook, the Thief, His Wife, and Her Lover* as her primary text, Eugenie Brinkema argues that

> [I]t is in the grids, the lexicons, the encyclopedias—to which I would add: the rooms and menus in sequence, the iterations and repetitions, entrances and exits, patterns and foldings, colors and rhythms—that affect saturates Greenaway's work. It is not the case that the more formalist the film, the more distanced it is from affect: rather, the more rigorously structured the text, the more affective it is.[37]

Echoing and extending, in many ways, William Ian Miller's assertion, building on the work of Mary Douglas, that pollution (and with it, the disgusting) does not exist without the "conceptual grid[s] that structure particular domain[s],"[38] Brinkema makes a rigorously formal claim that grids not only allow for, but actually produce a saturating affect of disgust in Greenaway's work.

Brinkema warns her readers against the temptation of reducing disgust to a catalogue of disgusting objects. She focuses, instead, on the form of the affect, *before* it becomes attached to an object. Key to this form, for her, is in fact the denial of an object, the refusal of representation. Disgust is all about "the promise of worsening, this possibility of something more disgusting than the disgusting."[39] This formal reading of disgust echoes debates about whether the grid in visual art is to be experienced as a self-contained whole or as a gesture toward infinity—what Krauss terms the "centripetal" versus the "centrifugal" reading. "By virtue of the grid," is a work of art "structured as an autonomous, organic whole," or, instead, experienced as "a tiny piece arbitrarily cropped from an infinitely larger fabric"?[40] The grid, viewed centrifugally, promises, like the affect of disgust, the prospect of never-ending expansion and continuation into realms unseen and unimaginable.

As Oedipa nears the end of the novel,[41] she finds herself not surveying from above, but now tracing and treading on the ground level the grids of the novel's fictionalized San Narciso, alternately fighting and flirting with a sense of illegible infinity. She becomes aware of the city itself as a system of overlapping grids—rail lines, streets, bus lines, street cars, telephone cables—whose vertices all seem to be marked with the Tristero symbol. Liu names the proliferation of grids as "one of postmodernism's most common motifs: the image of a world structured at both infra- and superstructural levels as laby-rinthine network or grid—a sort of deconstructive structure or what . . . I have called the *disturbed array*."[42] As Oedipa meanders through her "infected city" at night, attempting to plot—narrate, diagram, and map—appearances of the Tristero "post horn" within the "disturbed" urban "array," she finds a sort of mesmeric refuge on buses.

> She stayed with buses after that, getting off only now and then to walk so she'd keep awake. What fragments of dreams came had to do with the post horn. Later, possibly, she would have trouble sorting the night into real and dreamed.
>
> At some indefinite passage in night's sonorous score, it also came to her that she would be safe, that something, perhaps only her linearly fading drunkenness, would protect her. The city was hers, as, made up and sleeked so with the customary words and images (cosmopolitan, culture, cable cars) it had not been before: she had safe-passage tonight to its far blood's branchings, be they capillaries too small for more than peering into, or vessels mashed together in shameless municipal hickeys, out on the skin for all but tourists to see.[43]

Her description of the city as "made up and sleeked" evokes the Strip Botti-celli rape scene, making the surfaces of San Narciso into primped and polished flesh, its transit lines into its circulatory system, its congestions and intersec-tions into "shameless municipal hickeys." Even as Oedipa is transposed into the possessor/aggressor role à la Metzger, "the city was hers," her body, in its "linearly fading drunkenness" is the one that still plausibly carries hickeys past and, so, is akin too to the newly sexualized cityscape. Oedipa's nighttime jour-ney along the city's gridlines is then, perhaps, one of a not entirely un-violent sort of self-possession. Riding on buses along the transit axes qua city capillar-ies makes Oedipa feel a strange, maybe even numbed sense of safety.

> Nothing of the night's could touch her; nothing did. The repetition of symbols was to be enough, without trauma as well perhaps to attenuate it or even jar it altogether loose from her memory. She was meant to remember. She faced that possibility as she might the toy street from a high balcony, roller-coaster ride, feeding-time among the beasts in a zoo—any death-wish that can be consummated by some minimum gesture. She touched the edge of its volup-tuous field, knowing it would be lovely beyond dreams simply to submit to it;

that not gravity's pull, laws of ballistics, feral ravening, promised more delight. She tested it, shivering: I am meant to remember. Each clue that comes
is supposed to have its own clarity, its fine chances for permanence. But then
she wondered if the gemlike "clues" were only some kind of compensation.
To make up for her having lost the direct, epileptic Word, the cry that might
abolish the night.[44]

The equivocation of the "perhaps" in "The repetition of symbols was to be
enough, without trauma as well perhaps to attenuate it or even jar it altogether
loose from her memory," inevitably imbues the buses, the gemlike "clues," and
the woman who rides and collects each respectively, with a sheen of recursive
violation. Oedipa wonders whether riding the grid, as it promises an ever-
expandable infinity of "gemlike 'clues'" is also possibly an uneasy "compensation" for a lack—whether, to return to Krauss's discussion of the grid's refusal
of language and all it entails, this proliferation of symbols is in fact a manifestation of some sort of "will to silence,"[45] the loss of the "direct, epileptic
Word, the cry that might abolish the night." The more information the griddy
city yields up to Oedipa, the less power language seems to have. Information
merely overloads and fatigues her own organic circuitry.[46] She faces the possibility that "she was meant to remember," by panning imaginatively outward
and upward to the visual, occupying again the position of ostensible scopic
mastery and detachment that marked her circuit card revelation. "She faced
that possibility as she might the toy street from a high balcony, roller-coaster
ride, feeding-time among the beasts in a zoo—any death-wish that can be
consummated by some minimum gesture."

Invasive Inscriptions and Tristero Tangents

As Oedipa looks out on the city become circuit card become site of unspeakable revelation, she is experiencing it as if it were a piece of visual art. The
city becomes a flat aesthetic object, explicitly evocative of a circuit card, while
implicitly akin to the contemporaneous 1960s grids of an Agnes Martin or
Robert Ryman painting. Both analogies trade in an ambiguous mix of affects
and incommunicabilities. Both seem to bespeak a need in Oedipa and perhaps
the novel as a whole analogically to rescale the sprawling three dimensional
into a manageable two-dimensionality.

In "Visualization and Cognition," Bruno Latour recasts power as a function of this very kind of rescaling via "paper shuffling," or the question of how, specifically in science and technology, "inscriptions and their mobilization . . . help small entities to become large ones."[47] Power, for Latour, is all about the ability to dominate others through the persuasive power of inscriptions that are at once "mobile, immutable, presentable, readable, and combinable."[48] Inscriptions become shuffle-able through what he calls "optical consistency," a trait of translating complex material realities into two dimensional traces—maps, charts, records, diagrams, drawings, etc.—that can be transposed upon or made analogous to one another. This "entails the 'art of describing' everything and the possibility of going from one type of visual trace to another."[49]

A proliferation of inscriptions with optical consistency, Latour argues, historically enabled disparate data, objects, facts, and figures to be seen side by side at the same time, allowing most of the sorts of "discoveries" that previous studies of the scientific revolution attributed more speculatively to shifts in cognitive abilities. "Most of what we impute to connections in the mind may be explained by this reshuffling of inscriptions that all have the same 'optical consistency.' The same is true of what we call 'metaphor.'"[50] Once traces are optically consistent, connections can be made, equivalencies "discovered," complexities reduced, and control—over people, places, things—captured. "[D]omains which are far apart become literally inches apart; domains which are convoluted and hidden, become flat; thousands of occurrences can be looked at synoptically."[51]

The dual implications of the word "capture"—evocative of detainment and description—gets to the heart of Latour's argument. Only once someone has captured (described) vast territories on a map can they then capture (detain, claim) them in reality. Even as optical consistency generatively catalyzes innovation, discovery, and creativity, it also facilitates dominion and dispossession. As Drucker writes of information visualization, "all bar charts, line graphs, and scatterplots bear the imprint of that administrative agenda through the assumptions their metrics naturalize in images."[52] The crux of many of these obscured assumptions that inhere in all data visualizations is the question of which bits of data qua "*capta*"[53] can (or should) be made (or allowed) to share a coordinate plane. In other words, which qualities and quantities, taken from the world and its inhabitants ought to be rendered extractable and comparable. The question, to a large extent, is one of the ethics of commensurability (which brings us, perhaps unexpectedly, back to debates about sympathetic reading and the sentimental literary tradition).

This interest in data visualization is key to the type of literary graphic I see becoming increasingly prevalent in a post-45 milieu. According to Orit Halpern , as design philosophy changed following the Second World War, experience was increasingly "based on data inundation as a form of truth and moral virtue":

> Objectivity here was associated with the power of recall. The human eye might possess "errors" as a result of its archival limitation, but the machinic eye does not. . . . Objectivity was redefined in terms of the production of algorithms, methods, and processes that facilitate interaction, based on the assumption of an infinitude of stored information always/already readily available.[54]

Data points became synonymous with moral truths, recall with objectivity. Database waged, and looked like it was winning, a war on narrative. In this sort of postwar landscape, points and tangents—and the modes of contact they demand, and perhaps even the sorts of feelings they can formally produce—take on a new and complicated narrative and ethical significance.

The Crying of Lot 49 wreaks havoc, with its own rampantly mobile inscription, upon this vision of the morally and epistemologically clarifying power of safely capturing objects from the real world in two dimensions. Indeed, the novel doesn't just verbally describe, but visually shows its readers its own icon of "simple geometrized two-dimensional shapes": the muted post horn that symbolizes the shadowy Tristero, an underground postal delivery service that becomes Oedipa's obsession. Soon, the novel is littered with appearances of the symbol, which marks, among other things, the W.A.S.T.E. ("We Await Silent Tristero's Empire") receptacles to and from which they make their deliveries. The first appearance of the Tristero symbol in the novel is on the wall of a bathroom stall (Figure 4.1). The Tristero icon's inclusion in *The Crying of Lot 49* provides information that would have been more laboriously and less exactly delivered through words alone. It's a "graphism" in Latour's sense of the word, a geometrically efficient inscription that creates connections that could not have existed otherwise.[55] Without this image, given as image, would its paranoid proliferation through the plot and its many tangents be as effective? Would Pynchon's readers, like his protagonist, be able to find themselves seeing it everywhere?

Scott McCloud, in *Understanding Comics*, argues that the more cartoonish a face is in a comic, the more "universality" it possesses. "In the nonpictorial icons, meaning is fixed and absolute. Their appearance doesn't affect their meaning because they represent invisible ideas. . . . In pictures, however, meaning is fluid and variable according to appearance. They differ from 'real-life' appearance to varying degrees."[56] The Tristero symbol skirts the line between icon and picture. It is a representation of a muted postal horn taken to a level of geometric abstraction that makes its mimetic resemblance to it its "real-life" subject tenuous at best. McCloud defines this extremely simplified form of picture as a cartoon. The cartoonish rendering of objects emphasizes "the concepts of objects over their physical appearance."[57] What, then, does the graphically simplified muted post horn amplify? The fact of (muted) amplification itself?

FIGURE 4.1. Tristero symbol.

"Maybe a late shift?" But Metzger only frowned. "Be back," Oedipa shrugged, heading for the ladies' room.

On the latrine wall, among lipsticked obscenities, she noticed the following message, neatly indited in engineering lettering:

"Interested in sophisticated fun? You, hubby, girl friends. The more the merrier. Get in touch with Kirby, through WASTE only, Box 7391, L. A."

WASTE? Oedipa wondered. Beneath the notice, faintly in pencil, was a symbol she'd never seen before, a loop, triangle and trapezoid, thus:

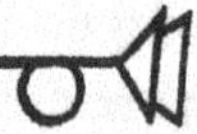

It might be something sexual, but she somehow doubted it. She found a pen in her purse and copied the address and symbol in her memo book, thinking: God, hieroglyphics. When she came out Fallopian was back, and had this funny look on his face.

Source: Pynchon, *The Crying of Lot 49*, 38.

The Tristero symbol is both a simple picture of a muted post horn and a recursive representation of mathematical tangents. In it, a tangent line radiates from a circle and connects to the 90-degree angle of a right triangle, each of whose angles have tangents calculable as the ratio of the length of the opposite side to the length of the adjacent side—in other words, the Tristero symbol is tangent upon tangent. I want to now take seriously the narrative implications of the mathematical tangent. A tangent line is one that touches a curve, without crossing it, at a single point. Only one possible line can touch but not break the curve at any given point.[58] The tangent is in fact the line that passes through a *pair* of points that are infinitely close together on the curve. Thus, the single point whose derivative we take, and whose slope we then determine, can computationally stand in for both points, while still theoretically relying on the fiction that two have not been collapsed into one. The tangent line imaginatively attaches itself to a curve and extrapolates outward to give a lonely point both direction and duration, by conjuring for it a phantom companion point.

One could argue that mathematically plotting tangents is thus also an oddly *narrative* act of plotting. *The Crying of Lot 49* bombards its readers with an embarrassment of "points,"—of plot, possible explanations, geographic locations, rhetorical claims, and accusing fingers alike—even as it aggressively resists coalescing around any one in particular. As we try, like Oedipa, to be good readers by keeping tally and catching hold of these points qua projectiles, the frequency and freneticism of their aerosol-can-like flight lends the plot a sense of violence, beyond even the often-blood-soaked content of its revelations, relocations, and recriminations. The "point," even as it eludes us, is a productive way to think about what's happening in the book and how. The word "point" itself conjures mathematical tallying, geographic positioning, punning, and semiotic gesturing all at once.

Each potential meaning of a point implies, even demands, some sort of *contact*. In *The Practice of Everyday Life,* Michel de Certeau defines two different types of contact zones that in turn, he argues, define space and narrative in fiction: "the frontier and the bridge." For de Certeau, "stories are actuated by a contradiction that is represented in them by the relationship between the frontier and the bridge, that is, between a (legitimate) space and its (alien) exteriority."[59] Frontiers make and organize spaces, establishing differences and creating separations, but only through *points* of commonality, moments of *contact*. De Certeau continues:

> Thus, in the obscurity of their unlimitedness, bodies can be distinguished only where the "contacts" ("*touches*") of amorous or hostile struggles are inscribed on them. This is a paradox of the frontier: created by contacts, the points of differentiation between two bodies are also their common points. Conjunction and disjunction are inseparable in them. Of two bodies in contact, which one possesses the frontier that distinguishes them? Neither.[60]

This contact point or *touche* model of distinguishing bodies resonates with Oedipa's oscillating, paranoid detective work qua foiled close reading in and of Pynchon's California metropolises. Each point—both in terms of raw contact and belabored act of interpretation or argument—that Oedipa makes is an attempt to distinguish, categorize, and plot a narrative out of the "obscurity of the unlimitedness" of bodies in the world of the novel. Oedipa's engagements with plot points are thus inherently tangential.

And the narrative tangent functions by the same calculus as its mathematical analogue. Phantom others (points or persons) are summoned, exploited, and computationally discarded in order to give direction and duration to our chosen static, dimensionless point: our protagonist. When Oedipa encounters an old, tattooed sailor who clearly suffers from DTs (delirium tremens)—severe alcohol withdrawal—she does her own analysis of the mathematical tangent. She associates the upper-case DT of delirium tremens with the lower-case dt of the *differential* in calculus, which she remembers having learned about during a postcoital conversation with an old college boyfriend:

> "dt," God help this old tattooed man, meant also a time differential, a vanishingly small instant in which change had to be confronted at last for what it was, where it could no longer disguise itself as something innocuous like an average rate; where velocity dwelled in the projectile though the projectile be frozen in midflight, where death dwelled in the cell though the cell be looked in on at its most quick. She knew that the sailor had seen worlds no other man had seen if only because there was that high magic to low puns, because DT's must give access to dt's of spectra beyond the known sun, music made purely of Antarctic loneliness and fright.[61]

There is a decidedly fatalistic tenor to Oedipa's associative musings on the duration and direction—and with it the collapse of binaries like "projectile" and "frozen," "quick" and "dead"[62]—that the operations of calculus conjure for stationary points.[63]

Throughout the novel, Oedipa is trying to plot a narrative and a space for herself through this imaginative work of charting tangent upon tangent (as in the Tristero icon itself) from the myriad points she picks up along her way. Oedipa, as she tries to plot or map out potential plots, is trying to communicate (make contact) with an imaginary or hidden network of phantom points, absent interlocutors. In a world scaffolded on ever recursive, indeterminate grids, the novel begs the question of whether it is necessary to create for yourself an imaginary friend or monster or postal organization in order to plot a course forward. Is this imaginative, interpretive act ethical and hopeful, even redemptive—endowed with "high magic"—or, merely pitiful, paranoid, and intensely lonely?

Namwali Serpell argues that "the risk," in the way the narrative rapidly proliferates Oedipa's brief contacts with one-off minor characters is that "these minor characters are made into flimsy cartoons . . . [who] become the means toward self-discovery for privileged subjects like Oedipa."[64] Pynchon's novel becomes a narratively and affectively tangential catalogue, in which identification skews informational and all minor and/or minoritized subjects are reconfigurable, ultimately fungible and manipulable data points. Even at the moments that seem to want to smack of the most sympathetic sincerity. And indeed, this very same DT/dt suffering sailor, after being cradled somewhat perfunctorily to Oedipa's breast, is quickly narratively dispatched. After providing Oedipa an occasion to muse about calculus and indulge in a self-gratifying pieta tableau, the sailor is abandoned by the plot and its protagonist.[65] Oedipa tangents away. "But nothing she knew of would preserve them, or him. She gave him goodbye, walked downstairs and then on, in the direction he'd told her."[66]

Peripatetic Parasitism in *Open City*

Hosts and parasites are always in the process of passing by, being sent away, touring around, walking alone. They exchange places in a space soon to be defined.

—MICHEL SERRES, *The Parasite*

Julius, the first-person narrator of *Open City*, traces a tangential narrative path that uses contact with others in a similarly instrumental way. Teju Cole's acclaimed 2012 novel follows a young Nigerian immigrant and graduate student in psychology through his circumambulations of Manhattan. As he walks, the sights, sounds, and people of the city evoke Sebaldian, free-associative, quasi-encyclopedic musings on history, trauma, and memory for him. The book has received glowing critical attention, heralded as an exemplar of cosmopolitan honesty and hypnotic, peripatetic originality. Nicholas Dames includes Cole and his novel in his roster of a new class of writers he has dubbed the "Theory Generation," which includes the likes of Jennifer Egan, Jeffrey Eugenides, and Ben Lerner. Theory novels, according to Dames, are those that, written by authors with similar post-80s liberal arts educations, cannot help but be, more or less self-consciously, injected with "Theory" of a largely white, predominantly male canon of thinkers such as Foucault, Derrida, Adorno, Deleuze, Benjamin, Barthes, and Jameson.[67] "These novels don't entirely regret, nor do they entirely accept, Theory; they satirize it with unease."[68] Theory becomes part of the internal content of that which it was originally developed to evaluate from the outside.

> Theory is judged from within the forms it tried to dismantle (psychological realism; the bildungsroman), by criteria Theory could only recognize as regressive or naïve: What kind of a person does Theory make? What did it once mean to have read theorists? What does it mean now? How does Theory help you hold a job? Deal with lovers, children, bosses, and parents? Decide between the restricted alternatives of adulthood?[69]

Theory is naturalized in these novels, familiarity with it taken as a given, its praxis so relentlessly modeled by its own characters from the inside that its application to the books from the outside becomes both inevitable and strangely impossible.

Cole's narrator, Julius, is no exception. The protagonist and narrator of *Open City* has been called many things. *Flâneur, fugueur,*[70] cosmopolitan, "productively alienated" outsider,[71] dreamer, diarist,[72] "peculiar fellow."[73] I will add to that list by asking if he might also properly, and productively, be labeled a parasite. The figure of the parasite encapsulates pathology, hospitality, noise, embarrassment, discomfort, invisibility, paranoia. More than any broad-brush cosmopolitan ideal or disillusion that others have argued Julius might embody, does Cole offer him to us as, more than anything else, a narratological bedbug? In other words, might the type of consumption in which this particular Theory Generation novel protagonist engages be best classed as parasitic? And what might that mean for both a reading of the novel as a whole and the Theory Generation Novel as a genre?

The Birds and the Bugs

Nicholas Dames defines the "Theory Generation" narrator as "fundamentally *diagnostic.*"[74] The diagnostic bent of the Theory novel seems to demand of its narrator an objective, distanced, analytic view of the world and the other characters that populate it. The pose is, to return to Maurice Lee, "informational."[75] In de Certeau's discussion of walking in the city, he describes "the exaltation of a scopic and gnostic drive: the fiction of knowledge is related to this lust to be a viewpoint and nothing more."[76] In *Open City*, Julius's scopic and gnostic drive makes him long to be a (view)point and nothing more. His narration begins with a comparison between his own wandering and the migratory patterns of birds. "Not long before this aimless wandering began, I had fallen into the habit of watching bird migrations from my apartment, and I wonder now if the two are connected."[77] The book ends, too, with birds, this time in the form of statistics on the number of wrens "fatally disoriented" by the light from the Statue of Liberty's torch, "all dead of the impact."[78] Julius, with this avian bookending of his story, longs for a birds-eye view.

Birds are associated with vision, open movement, and forward progress that requires no contact. The wafting, winged cosmopolitan creature of flight is the figure that the book begs (or baits) us to associate with Julius and his mode of narration. If Julius is a bird, then shouldn't his narrative point of view be not constraining and unreliable, as most first-person perspective narratives are, but instead lofty, aloof, and clear-eyed? Is not the bird the ideal image for a protagonist that has been widely received as "an early twenty-first-century update of the figure of the *flâneur*, an aesthete who uniquely manages to engage with the realities of the modern city without fully surrendering to them, and who exemplifies a cosmopolitan ethos that thrives on intercultural curiosity and on the virtues of the aesthetic"?[79]

The sweeping range of knowledge—or at least abundance of factoids—that Julius recalls at a moment's notice as he aimlessly wanders the city seems to mimic a bird's-eye view, a privileged perspective that can pan out to see, read, and map the whole, from a subject position of disinterested omniscience (or at least omni-vision). De Certeau describes (and pans) this sort of panning out through the figure of the man who ascends to the top of the World Trade Center:

> His elevation transfigures him into a voyeur. It puts him at a distance. It trans-forms the bewitching world by which one was "possessed" into a text that lies before one's eyes. It allows one to read it, to be a solar Eye, looking down like a god. . . . The voyeur-god created by this fiction, who, like Schreber's God, knows only cadavers, must disentangle himself from the murky intertwining daily behaviors and make himself alien to them.[80]

Julius, too, seems to see the city as his text. Likewise, he is somehow most comfortable with knowing its cadavers. As he walks with a crowd of commuters past the construction site of the new World Trade Center, he muses:

> But atrocity is nothing new, not to humans, not to animals. The difference is that in our time it is uniquely well organized, carried out with pens, train carriages, ledgers, barbed wire, work camps, gas. And this late contribution, the absence of bodies.[81]

Later on the same page, "pen" rings out ambiguously again—"I moved on with the other commuters through the pen."[82] This pun on the material means of dehumanizing captivity and a (perhaps nostalgic) instrument of writing, of containment with narrative, raises the question of what physical capture has to do with written transcription. The bird's-eye view is not just an idealization of a certain sort of freedom, a "potential association with open movement, un-impeded by the strictures of the ground,"[83] but also a tool of graphic perspective and circumscription that allows one sort of pen to create another. Julius seems eager to enact the "paradox" that Latour argues has allowed "paper shuffling" to enable large-scale acts of both scientific discovery and colonial domination:

> By working on papers alone, on fragile inscriptions which are immensely less than the things from which they are extracted, it is still possible to dominate all things, and all people. What is insignificant for all other cultures becomes the most significant, the only significant aspect of reality. The weakest, by manipulating inscriptions of all sorts obsessively and exclusively, become the strongest.[84]

Julius, who wishes he were a bird, pens others from a safe distance. Or believes he can. The bird's-eye view is schematic, "productively alienated" (to return to Wood's review).[85] As it floats freely above, it is able to evaluate people and position both from a vaunted point of objectivity.

But Julius isn't, in the end, wafting. He's walking. And the book doesn't soar in grand narrative arcs. It plods, meanders, veers, and stumbles on its narrator's own two feet. If birds suggest the possibility of consummating "the lust to be a viewpoint and nothing more"[86] (of taking flight through sight while transcending the constraints of site, of mapping and managing those below, of being the consummate data visualizer), the figure of the parasite (tied to contact, violation, and the specificities of place) offers an alternative analogue for Julius's mode of relation, not just as a narrator, but also as a character.

A Parasite Is . . .

Parasites have a history of association with the literary, especially when it comes to high theory. J. Hillis Miller's definition of a parasite emerged out of a debate about deconstruction and classification in critical theory. Miller originally penned his seminal article, "The Critic as Host," as a response to Wayne Booth's claim that the "deconstructionist" reading "is plainly and simply parasitical" on the "obvious or univocal" meaning of a text.[87] Miller responded by deconstructing the terms "host" and "parasite" in turn, in order to dismantle the binary logic that constructs them. In the process, he gives an oft-cited exhaustive tour of the etymology of the word "parasite." A Greek parasite, *parasitos*, meaning "beside the grain," was originally a guest who shared a meal with a welcoming host. Only later did the host himself become the food.

"The word 'Host' is of course the name for the consecrated bread or wafer of the Eucharist."[88] The parasite, then, Miller argues, in its very etymology, is a "guest in the bifold sense of friendly presence and alien invader."[89] It is both a companionate intruder and an invited infection.

The prefix para- means "beside, to the side of, alongside, beyond, wrongfully, harmfully, unfavorably, and among."[90] Miller emphasizes that a parasite can only be defined relationally—often oppositionally—to a host. Neither term signifies without its other. One might assume the relation of the two terms to be a simple alignment along either side of some sort of interior/exterior axis. But the exact positional relation of parasite and host—and even the certainty that this relation is based on a basic division—is, Miller argues, far more complicated:

> A thing in "para" is, moreover, not only simultaneously on both sides of the boundary line between inside and outside. It is also the boundary itself, the screen which is at once a permeable membrane connecting inside and outside, confusing them with one another, allowing the outside in, making the inside out, dividing them but also forming an ambiguous transition between one and the other.[91]

Looking to break down the distinction between host and parasite, and the analogies others have posited for the opposition between "obvious and univocal" and "deconstructive" readings, Miller argues "that the parasite is always already present within the host, the enemy always already within the house, the ring always an open chain."[92] Moreover, just as it is easier said than done to call one kind of criticism parasitic on another, or criticism itself parasitic on text, or vice versa, Miller asserts that "if the poem is food and poison for the critics, it must in its turn have eaten. It must have been a cannibal consumer of earlier poems."[93] A few years after Miller's essay, Michel Serres takes up this uneasy omnipresence of parasitic relationality in literature and beyond, with a vengeance.

Published in French three years after Miller's essay, arguably the most sustained exploration of the figure of the parasite as a universal concept, is Michel Serres's *The Parasite*. In this 1980 (in French, 1982 in English translation) book, Serres takes the French "parasite" in all of its semiotic range, arguing that the three meanings that the word evokes in his native tongue—infection, guest, and static (as in "*bruit parasite*" or "background noise")—have more than a merely coincidental connection. In fact, through their intrinsic relation, these valences make the parasite the ideal figure through which to understand many relational systems in the world today (for Serres, 1980). The uniting feature of the parasitic relational system for Serres is unidirectionality, an inherent lack of reciprocation. Human relations are only ever one-way streets:

> [A] human group is organized with one-way relations, where one eats the other and where the second cannot benefit at all from the first. . . . Man is a louse for other men. Thus man is a host for other men. The flow goes one way, never the other. I call this semiconduction, this valve, this single arrow, this relation without a reversal of direction, "parasitic."[94]

A man can be both louse and host, but never at the same time for the same other. Moreover, no man who has relations is exempt: "The parasitic relation is intersubjective. It is the atomic form of our relations."[95] All human relations are extractive.

The Parasite as a text moves in the same rambling, free associative mode as *Open City*, propelled less by strictly disciplined argumentation than by organically expansive augmentation. As the book wends its way, definitions of the parasite, appropriately enough, multiply at an alarming rate. The parasite is "the interrupter,"[96] "the repressed one, the chased entity that always returns,"[97] the "essence" of "relation" as and through "nonrelation,"[98] "being and nonbeing at the same time,"[99] and—under a heading that proclaims it "The Best Definition"—"the parasite is a thermal exciter."[100] Anders Gullestad argues that what makes this last definition truly "The Best" is that "by focusing on what the parasite brings about, rather than on how it differs from non-parasites, Serres . . . allows us to come to terms with a problem that the parasitologists of today have inherited from their predecessors: that of the low status of their object of research."[101] By avoiding questions of magnitude and moral judgment, Gullestad posits, Serres opens the field for appreciating "the properly *creative* element involved in [the parasite's] work."[102]

This work is modest. Parasites cause change through irritation, interruption, and excitation: "They do not transform the collective system as such, but they change its state. No, it is not a revolution, not even a reform; it is a little difference, a minimal action."[103] This attunement to change, however minute, is tied to Miller's definition of the boundary-crossing and boundary-confusion inherent in the para- prefix itself. Whether the parasite is manifest as insidious infection, flattering guest, or aural interference, its actions are *minimally* transforming, *marginally* exciting, *semi*conducting. This minimal, marginal action of the parasite only happens through the fact—concerned with margins—of touch: "The relation with a host presupposes a permanent or semipermanent contact with him."[104] In the world of biological parasites, this contact ideally happens not by overt assault but through covert camouflage:

> To avoid the unavoidable reactions of rejection, exclusion, a (biological) parasite makes or secretes tissue identical to that of its host at the location of contact points with the host's body. The parasited, abused, cheated body no longer reacts; it accepts; it acts as if the visitor were its own organ. It consents to maintain it; it bends to its demands. The parasite plays a game of mimicry. It does not play at being another; it plays at being the same.[105]

The biological parasite is a guest that doesn't quite crash the party. It forges its own invitation, or, more properly, makes the host believe it has been there all along.

As *Open City* progresses, Julius himself plays the role of invited guest until we learn of the unsettling moment in the past in which he wasn't. But even before this revelation, we begin to realize that he plays fast and loose with narrative boundaries. He collapses all of the stories he hears and retells them in his own affectively flat, unhurried univocality. At the same time, he freely and invasively diagnoses, deconstructs, and symptomatizes any and all narratives that are not his own. As Dames says of Theory novels: "These are novels about consumers. These are people who are given to consuming books, particularly books about other books. . . . These are receptive people—their characteristic act is taking in."[106] Julius enacts the collapsed binary para- of Miller: "the screen which is at once a permeable membrane connecting inside and outside, confusing them with one another."[107] As he feeds on the stories and "unacknowledged traumas" (real or projected) of those he sees and touches, public spaces become uncomfortably semi-private.

Of Touches *and Tangents*

James Wood argues that the events of *Open City* are propelled not by "event or contrivance, but a steady, accidental inquiry, a firm pressurelessness (which is to say, what moves the prose forward is the prose—the desire to write, to defeat solitude by writing)."[108] Contact is an uncomfortable question for the aloof, scopic Julius.

> Above-ground I was with thousands of others in their solitude, but in the subway, standing close to strangers, jostling them and being jostled by them for space and breathing room, all of us reenacting unacknowledged traumas, the solitude intensified.[109]

The solitude-in-a-crowd he constantly feels—and tries to counteract through syphoning and reciting others' stories—becomes "intensified" below ground. Here, touch becomes jostling and breathing (to say nothing of storytelling) is stifled to the point of near suffocation. Verbal contact becomes impossible, physical contact oppressively omnipresent. Julius is left even more by himself when he is physically barraged by others' rigidly bounded bodies.

Contact is key for a parasite's survival, but types of contact are many and varied and not all are equal. Parasitic contact dissolves certain frontiers while making actual contact points painfully, itchingly visible. This makes uncomfortably real de Certeau's assertion that contacts between bodies are events that establish frontiers at the instant of their violation: "[C]onjunction and disjunction are inseparable in them."[110]

This contact point or *touche* model of distinguishing bodies resonates with the encyclopedic, Sebaldian guidebook form of Cole's narrative. In short, both are inherently tangential. Contact creates points, which precipitate tangents, Julius's preferred mode of narrative progression. If we recall, a mathematical tangent extrapolates slope outward from a single point on a curve. When derived from "first principles," it is in fact the line that passes through a *pair* of points that are infinitely close together on the curve, the second of which effectively disappears in the calculus. Serres describes the parasite as "a differential operator of change. . . . the difference produced is rather weak, and it usually does not allow for the prediction of a transformation nor what kind of transformation."[111] A "differential" is the term for that—function, calculus, equation, coefficient—which is related to infinitesimal differences. In other words, tangents require a "differential operator of change," a phantom companion point.

Parasitism requires relationships. And protagonists, like Julius, require contact with others as means for their own self-discovery and as the starting points for narrative discursions. A few times in the book Julius seems to assign a trigonometric meaning to his own tangential digressions. "Generations rushed through the eye of the needle, and I, one of the still legible crowd, entered the subway. I wanted to find the line that connected me to my own part in these stories."[112] As Julius wanders, he really wants to plot lines not between himself and others, but between himself and his other self. He wants the "line that connected me to my own part." He walks through the city qua database longing for sympathy in the most sentimentalist sense, taken to its logical extreme—a "conver[sion of] heterogeneity to homogeneity" that cuts out the middle man of another body and reaches around to pure self-pleasure.[113] It is a mathematical, relational, parasitic necessity, however, that a point needs another point that is not itself—but can be computationally collapsed back into itself—to make a line.

This selfish primacy of the point and its calculating sleight-of-hand ability to define a line resonates with Julius's gnostic—and, to the extent he has one, narrative—drive. What Wood calls the narration's "firm pressurelessness" is thus more akin to what a biological parasite chemically concocts for itself to escape detection at its contact points. Where a parasite secretes tissue to combat its loneliness and connect with its meal, Julius, it would seem, spins stories instead. Julius does not transcend but in fact *requires* contact with others' frontiers, if only in the infinitesimally differential imaginary, if only in language. He needs others so that he can create and narrate his peripatetic yet solipsistic tangents. The competition between his lust for aloof bird-like viewing and his need for others' stories, which tend to come inconveniently attached to their bodies, is in many ways the central tension of the novel. This renders Julius less *flâneur* than flea, less promenader than parasite, less bird than bedbug.

"The Bedbugs Were on My Mind": Red Coats at Dawn

Bedbugs first enter Julius's mind, where they reside for a goodly number of pages, toward the beginning of the second half of the book, as he enters the apartment of his elderly friend and mentor, Dr. Saito.

We've had a rough time of it, Dr. Saito said, welcoming me in. I've been sleep-ing here in the living room, on this pallet. We've had an infestation of bed-bugs. Red coats they used to be called in this part of the country, do you know that name? We thought the exterminators had cleared it up, but it came back worse eight days later, and I've had to make an unpleasant choice between this room, with its noisy vents, and being eaten up by the little creatures. He ges-tured toward the slats above the window. They bite. Like this, one, two, three; breakfast, lunch, and dinner, along your arm; but I'm afraid I haven't much blood to spare anymore.[114]

Julius ignores much of what Saito says to him, tuning out of the conversation, transforming it mentally into *bruit parasite*, or static. Meanwhile, Julius ru-minates on the ascendency of this other more literal parasite: "The conversa-tions, as befitted a troublesome occurrence in the private arena, had remained private, and the bedbugs were having an unlikely success."[115] Bedbugs, in their elusive tenacity, their small-scale embarrassments, become emblematic to Julius.

One of the embarrassments of bedbugs, according to Julius, is their disre-gard for frontiers. "They did not discriminate on the basis of social class and, for that reason, were embarrassing."[116] Bedbugs refuse to respect distinctions of class, race, or erudition in their hosts. "Even as the terms of transnational conflicts had changed, a similar shift was happening in public health, where, too, the enemies were now vague, and the threat they posed constantly shift-ing."[117] Julius balks at his own feelings of sympathy and sadness about this, Professor Saito's most embarrassing and least fatal affliction:

[R]acism, homophobia, the incessant bereavement that was one of the hidden costs of a long life. The bedbugs trumped them all. . . . an example of how an inconvenience can, because of one's proximity to it, take on a grotesque aspect.[118]

After he leaves Dr. Saito's apartment, Julius, seeking respite from this feel-ing, takes recourse to books. "Later that night, looking through my medical textbooks for more on the bedbugs, I found only dry descriptions of etiologies, life cycles, and therapies."[119] Julius is searching not just for scientific knowl-edge, however, but also for affective access. He wants to experience the "sense of the disgust and awe in which *Cimex lectularius*" has been held through-out history. He finds this in a field report written by Charles A. R. Campbell in 1903.[120] Julius summarizes Campbell's observations, noting in particular detail the cannibalistic nature of bedbugs, whose young will sometimes "slit open and consume" their engorged progenitors. He goes on to catalogue Campbell's list of the "half dozen experiments he had carried out, ostensibly in the interest of scientific research but which gave the impression of an obstacle course designed to prove the bedbug's hardiness and intelligence." What gives Campbell's study the sense of access that *Julius* craves, what he calls "its real power," lies in its "gradual accumulation of assertions, which created an intense and oppressive image of the creature under study."[121]

This oppressively gradual, or gradually oppressive, sedimentation sounds not unlike the workings of a bedbug infestation. It also seems to be a sly description of *Open City*'s own peripatetic narrative structure. The open question is what—or who—is the "creature under study" in the novel? Are we as readers slowly being snowed in under "an intense and oppressive" composite image of New York or of the man at whose side/in whose head we walk its streets? There is no doubt that this novel parasitically and inescapably embeds its readers deep in the labyrinthine folds of its narrator. The lulling ebb and flow of Julius's encyclopedic (or at least Wikipedic) musings make logical continuity errors hard to catch. For instance, he concludes his bedbug philosophizing thus: "These tiny, flat creatures, which had sought out human blood since before Pliny's time, were involved in a kind of low-grade warfare, a conflict at the margins of modern life, visible only in speech."[122] He ends his digression on bedbugs with a statement that seems so poetically right, so metafictionally evocative, that one feels that all the specific facts and philosophical gestures he's been circling through must necessarily flow to that elegant and economic turn-of-phrase: "visible only in speech."

Only that's not true. Bedbugs aren't invisible. Dr. Saito has been telling him they aren't. Julius has admitted in his entomological exegesis they aren't. Bedbugs are visible in bites. "They bite. Like this, one, two, three; breakfast, lunch, and dinner, along your arm."[123] What's more, no one wants to talk openly about them. "The conversations, as befitted a troublesome occurrence in the private arena, had remained private, and the bedbugs were having an unlikely success."[124] In a move that mimics his parasitic action on the stories of others, Julius rhetorically flourishes a counterfactual conclusion into a heady cosmopolitan-ish rumination.

There is a tantalizing similarity, too, between Alan Liu's earlier-cited discussion of the "proscriptive ellipsis" and the gustatory calling card of the bed bug. Again,

> At once gesturing toward the "idea" of cool and withholding that idea, such an ellipsis is a uniquely paradoxical inexpressibility topos—one whose fullness of implied content (site after site after site) is constrained by a silence that is more than simply neutral or practical. The silence is also a proscription, an interdiction. The proscriptive ellipsis may be taken to be the elementary rhetoric, the mental pixel, of information cool.[125]

These three dots bespeak insider knowledge while refusing to let it actually be spoken. They resonate in evocative ways with the bedbug's signature bite pattern: three red points in a row, their own "uniquely paradoxical inexpressibility topos," implying sites upon sites upon sites, yet begging, through shame—or the desire to retain one's cool—their silence. The red ellipsis of bedbug bites promises untold—or perhaps untellable—horrors or wonders just beyond the edge of the frame. They straddle the visual and the verbal, signaling silence through sight.

Julius himself, our "low-grade" narrator, is more plausibly the one who is "visible only in speech." In short, he is a narrative parasite. There is something uncomfortably invasive about the way he uses others for story-making. It is not a stretch to say that Julius spends most of the novel telling other peoples' stories, feeding off of their personal trauma. Digesting others' unspoken wounds and making them "visible only in speech" are his parasitic actions. The visibility he seems to give to others' stories is tempered, even tainted, by a violation of the integrity of their otherness that renders them effectively invisible. To wit, there are no quotation marks in the book: There is nothing to set off the speech of other people, no identification of when they are speaking and when he is.

One can imagine a more optimistic reading of how Julius makes others' stories (selectively) visible (only) through speech. Perhaps he is realizing the creative, productive potential of parasitism as mode of contact. Maybe he's just a model empath, channeling, medium-like, the voices of the voiceless. But this reading also sounds a lot like psychiatry, the profession for which Julius is training. Damningly, his patients' stories, the only ones he is legally and professionally bound to protect, are also the only ones he shares publicly—makes into actual sounds—in front of an audience of others. Julius repurposes these professionally harvested stories to facilitate his private parasitism, to make himself a better guest, to ingratiate friends and gain further access to their own narratives:

> I indulged them, and told them stories about my patients, about the alien visitations and government surveillance, the voices in the walls, the suspicions of family conspiracies. There is always a fund of humorous tales from the horror of mental illnesses, particularly in the ranks of the paranoid. I called on these stories now, even passing off some of my colleagues' patients as my own.[126]

Julius sounds (voices, projects, penetrates, secures) the depths of others' traumas as he skates over the surface of his own. He cannot consume or confront his own story. But he can collect, catalogue, and ventriloquize those of others. The algorithmic action by which he processes these stories follows Manovich's description of the database: "[A]ny object in the world—be it the population of a city, or the weather over the course of a century, a chair, a human brain—is modelled as a data structure, i.e. data organized in a particular way for efficient search and retrieval (such as arrays, linked lists and graphs)."[127] Julius's habitual flattening and cataloguing is inextricable from both his preoccupation with scopic, graphic modes of understanding and from a lust for dominion that comes with it. Latour notes the power in rendering something—or someone—flat:

> There is nothing you can dominate as easily as a flat surface of a few square meters; there is nothing hidden or convoluted, no shadows, no "double entendre." In politics as in science, when someone is said to "master" a question or to "dominate" a subject, you should normally look for the flat surface that enables mastery (a map, a list, a file, a census, the wall of a gallery, a card-index, a repertory); and you will find it.[128]

There is a decidedly diagrammatic bent to the way Julius reduces and replicates his patients' narratives, extracting and flattening the contours of individual stories into the schematics of "the paranoid," making merely interesting, deindividuated archival entries in the annals of trauma and derangement. He levies the power of abstraction against those more vulnerable than he.

Cole seems to be in uneasy conversation with the familiar rhetoric of foreign immigrant as hostile invader qua parasite.[129] Saito's vernacular association of bedbugs with "red coats" further muddies the analogic waters of parasite/invader/insurgent/rebel. While in Brussels, on what proves to be a fruitless quest to contact his white maternal grandmother, Julius moves in quick succession through a series of other brown hosts. He can't record or broadcast their stories because he never exchanges words with them. This doesn't stop him, though. Where Julius can't transcribe, he projects, an act of twofold two-dimensionality. He imaginatively produces archetypical stories for the dancing Rwandans and the vacuuming woman he sees, then analogically transforms them in turn into flat works of visual art. "The realization that I had been with fifty or sixty Rwandans changed the tenor of the evening for me. It was as though the space had suddenly become heavy with all the stories these people were carrying. . . . The quiet faces surely masked some pain I couldn't see."[130] As Julius writes their generic scripts for them, the Rwandans' faces become masks. Likewise, as he acknowledges that he can neither access nor possess the secrets of a woman he sees vacuuming in a church, he still decides she must be "in Belgium as an act of forgetting," hiding from "what she might have seen in the Cameroons or in the Congo, or maybe even in Rwanda." She too becomes a nameless face on a commoditized canvas. "I would never find out, for she possessed her secrets fully, as did those women that Vermeer painted in this same gray, lowland light; like theirs, her silence seemed absolute."[131] Because she doesn't speak to him, Julius decides she cannot, projecting her onto a silenced two-dimensional canvas, safely backdated to the seventeenth century.

His insinuation of himself into other's memories and stories, between the world's traumatic sheets as it were, is unsettling. An ambivalent discomfort seeps more and more into the affective texture of the novel and its detached yet somehow too-close-for-comfort narrator. Everything and everyone that Julius encounters seems to be leveled out into information. The individual becomes, when touched and transcribed, encountered and ingested, by Julius, the merely interesting. An "epistemological aesthetic," Ngai's "merely interesting," is a discursive category that involves a new form of rapid circulation of information in the cultural economy of late capitalism.[132] As such, much like the "minimal action" of the parasite qua "thermal exciter" according to

Serres, the interesting is "always connected to the relatively small surprise of information or variation from an existing norm."[133] For Ngai, the interesting is an aesthetic category of documentary impulse and affective uncertainty, associated with "ambivalence, coolness, or neutrality," much in the way that both irony and "the modern scientific attitude" are.[134]

The affect associated with Julius's parasitic contacts, his cool, controlled (and controlling) "interest" in others and their stories, is less the class embarrassment he assigns to bedbugs and more the insidious discomfort they incite: "[T]he feeling was subconscious, contemptible." This affect is in line with how Ngai characterizes what she calls "ugly feelings": "affective gaps, illegibilities, dysphoric feelings," which, in the end, highlight the limits of both expressiveness and identification. When the grotesque is rendered as merely interesting, the affective result is ugly—unnerving discomfort rather than quaint embarrassment. What might be most unnerving is the suspicion that there is no affective import at all, that Julius's interactions with other humans give us all the structures of empathic identification but evacuated of any actual feeling—fellow or otherwise. And perhaps also that the book mocks or shrugs at its readers' consternation that there is no affective there *there* at all. Pieter Vermeulen doesn't go quite this far, arguing instead that the "event of reading" *Open City* does "not lead to an outright absence of emotion, but" quoting Ngai, "to a less comfortable and less tractable affective dynamics 'taking place outside of sensory and emotional codification.'"[135] The novel's "concern with different forms of mobility is cut across by an unruly and intractable affective dynamic that cannot be synchronized with the other movements it traces."[136]

Julius seems incapable of adopting any attitude but that of informational cool, of treating any person as anything but an expendable point, or any data or plot point as anything but a launchpad for a "merely interesting" tangent. Does Cole thus deny us, the readers, the narrative space to be viscerally appalled by the parasitic protagonist upon whom he has made us depend (parasites on parasites) for the story? Are we allowed the distance for disgust? Ahmed articulates the complex problem of distance when it comes to the affect of disgust:

> In disgust reactions, "words" are also cast out or vomited. The speech act, "That's disgusting!", can work as a form of vomiting, as an attempt to expel something whose proximity is felt to be threatening and contaminating. That

is, to designate something as disgusting is also to create a distance from the thing, which paradoxically becomes a thing only in the act of distantiation.[137]

Julius's parasitic tangenting not only collapses the distances between—and identities of—himself and his hosts, but it also muddies and mutes the possible distance between protagonist and reader. Where can we expel Julius as a disgusting object, if he is, claustrophobically, the entire verbal and narrative space of the text? What is the "correct distance" from which to appreciate this kind of infographic narrator?[138]

Vermeulen's analysis of the novel's discursive dissolution/digestion of boundaries inadvertently echoes Serres's parasitic trinity: of infection, guest, and static. He argues that *Open City* both "clearly privileges the contrapuntal principle of composition that is commonly associated with the musical fugue form," while at the same time consistently thwarting its successful realization by breaking down into "sheer noise."[139]

> The contiguity between the aesthetic success of a "fugue of voices" and the actuality of sheer noise is reflected in the novel's texture by the absence of quotation marks. This allows the different conjured voices to dissolve into a continuous discourse in which the lack of distinction between free indirect speech, interior monologue, and reported speech robs these voices of their dialogic, agonistic, or contrapuntal potential.[140]

All other voices and stories are assimilated into Julius's until everything is simply sound, simply *bruit parasite*, simply the static of atrocity.[141] Actual bedbugs, however, are silent, and the most traumatic revelation of the novel hinges not on an excess of noise and voices but instead on the silencing of one voice in particular.

Vermeulen works to parse out the experience of reading the novel through the lens of "demobilized" expectations:

> [T]he event of reading morphs from a frustrated occasion for empathetic cross-cultural identification to a protracted exposure to the unavailability of such emotional deliverance. *Open City*, in other words, refuses to offer the kind of gratifying and cathartic emotive transports that circumscribe the niche of literary migrant fiction in the global marketplace.[142]

The script we expect to follow when we as readers follow an upwardly mobile immigrant as he wanders through the cosmopolitan center is stymied by Julius's lack of progress. By the end of the novel, the stickiness of the revelation of certain effaced contacts in Julius's past ought to congeal its affect into a more codifiable sheen of disgust. The question is whether our inescapable narrative intimacy with Julius denies us the space for recoil, foreclosing the possibility of really feeling the disgust his actions ought to merit.

Traumatic Insemination

We are primed to note gaps and omissions in Julius's text through his own comment on what Dr. Saito taught him: "I learned the art of listening from him, and the ability to trace out a story from what was omitted."[143] For example, cannibalism is not the only routine violent "slitting" that happens in the bedbug lifecycle. There are the equally gory facts of bedbug mating. So, since Julius will not, let's talk about bedbug sex.[144] Bedbugs mate through a process called traumatic insemination, "during which the male pierces the female's abdominal wall with his external genitalia and inseminates into her body cavity."[145] It is a violent, occasionally fatal act. A male bedbug doesn't wait for an opening; he makes his own. If Cole offers his readers, as I argue, the bedbug as a less than flattering figure for his would-be *flâneur*, I would be remiss not to point out how this analogy anticipates even as it erases the novel's final revelation about Julius's rape of Moji.

This revelation makes the violence of the novel's mode of narrative contact disturbingly material and literal. Hamish Dalley calls it "the ethical flaw of [Julius's] attitude toward the *un*connectedness of place and person."[146] Julius's sort of parasitism is not merely an irritant—the instrumental erasure and incorporation of imagined others that goes into plotting his tangents not merely an incidental narrative tic/k. Parasitism is inextricable with a certain sort of harm. And Moji's rape makes that definitional fact inescapable. It is here that the geometrically graphic abstraction of the book's coolly plodding plot most suddenly vibrates uncomfortably with grossly graphic feelings of disgust and viscerality. The revelation penetrates and distends the two-dimensionality of Julius's diagrammatic database aesthetics. Moji confronts Julius as they sit alone on the balcony of her boyfriend's apartment, looking out over the Hudson River.

Then she turned to me and said, in a low and even voice, emotional in its total
lack of inflection, that there were things she wished to say to me. And then,
with the same flat affect, she said that, in late 1989, when she was fifteen and I
was a year younger, at a party her brother had hosted at their house in Ikoyi,
I had forced myself on her. Afterward, she said, her eyes unwavering from the
bright river below, in the weeks that followed, in the months and years that
followed, I had acted like I knew nothing about it, had even forgotten her, to
the point of not recognizing her when we met again, and had never tried to
acknowledge what I had done. This torturous deception had continued until
the present. But it hadn't been like that for her, she said, the luxury of denial
had not been possible for her. Indeed, I had been ever-present in her life, like
a stain or a scar, and she had thought of me, either fleetingly or in extended
agonies, for almost every day of her adult life.[147]

Julius's telling of Moji's telling is clinical. His description of her "flat affect"
even flatter. His only direct account of his own emotion is of his "relief" that
Moji didn't "begin to cry" (which makes us question just how affectively "flat"
she really is).

For his own relief, Julius quickly spins out a tangent, an anecdote about
Camus and Nietzsche. "At that moment—and I remember this as exactly as
though it were being replayed in front of me right now—I thought of how,
in his journals, Camus tells a double story concerning Nietzsche and Gaius
Mucius Cordus Scaevola, a Roman hero from the sixth century B.C.E."[148] Just
as the anecdote is about a "double story," his break with the balcony overlooking the Hudson—and the woman sitting there with him accusing him
of rape—is doubly mediated. The tangent is introduced by present-day Julius
self-consciously commenting upon his memory—a cinematically detached
"replay"—of his past self's tangential mental break with Moji on the balcony.
At this moment, the interesting—in all of its documentary, minimally differ-
entiating "affective uncertainty" —overtakes the individual. [149] Particularly
insidious and disturbing in this act of tangential digression is the very way in
which it flattens and diminishes trauma. Plotting a tangent from Moji's rape
to Camus's journal reduces one to the other, placing them on the same curve,
zeroing out their dimensions, leveling their distinctions. The emotional pose
of the interesting is "the low, often hard-to-register flicker of affect accompanying our recognition of minor differences from a norm."[150] Moji's rape, so

conspicuously subsumed into the book's larger structure of interesting tangential narration, wants to be a rupture but Julius tries to subsume it into yet another "minor difference from a norm" of flattened, distant, aestheticized, and indistinct accounts of the traumas of others.

This leveling effect—and affect—of the tangent is akin to what Latour terms the "'optical consistency' necessary for power on a large scale."[151] Julius's coolness, too, recalls Alan Liu's definition of the category as the "aporia of information." And indeed Julius, at this moment when he tries so hard to maintain his cool, rallies, what Liu calls *information designed to resist information.*[152] He veers into tangent and leaves his readers suspended ambivalently and uncomfortably between detachment and disgust.

Since the publication of the novel, a number of critics have attempted to reckon with this unsettling moment, and what it might mean for larger arguments about the novel as an exemplar of groundbreaking post-9/11 multiculti lit.[153] Madhu Krishnan ties the limits of Julius's self-knowledge to the novel's engagement with postcolonial spatiality and to its critique of neoliberal visions of cosmopolitanism. Moji's confrontation with Julius, staged, significantly, with a panoramic view of the Hudson River and the rest of New York City in the background, gives the lie to Julius's cosmopolitanism, which "masquerades as a universalism in which everything is connected and subjects are freed from the imperatives of local attachments." Obliquely summoning the ready bird analogy, Krishnan continues, "this very fiction of a free floating, open being in the world becomes an entrenchment of divisiveness through its inability to foster connectivities and multiplicity in being."[154]

Trauma is Julius's narrative obsession, and he sees and sows its seed throughout the streets of New York as he walks them. But the ease with which critics have folded Julius's rape of Moji into the book's "narrative pattern"—a move that the novel doesn't exactly discourage—points to something even more central about the all-too-easily-incorporated act of interpersonal violation. The proliferation of trauma to which Julius gives creative force in his wanderings is exactly what garnered the book so much critical praise, vaunted as the "productive alienation" of his scopic acumen.[155] Julius has quite successfully presented himself as a self-sufficient, Sebaldian, musing, promenading man of history-sipping free-associative leisure. One wonders, though, whether this ideal really has legs when it comes to the streets of New York City and the modes of trauma and community that exist for the nonwhite subject there. Wood applauds the fact that Julius

> is central to himself, in ways that are sane, forgivable, and familiar. And this selfish normality, this ordinary solipsism, this lucky, privileged equilibrium of the soul is an obstacle to understanding other people, even as it enables liberal journeys of comprehension.[156]

Understanding Julius as a parasite shows the complexity of the idea that "he is central to himself." Julius is anything but. He interrupts and irritates, generates peripatetic static, and violates the status of boundaries both fictional and physical. By subtly offering Julius as an unsettling analogue for an intimately dread urban pest, Cole seems to be pointing to the insufficiency of these critical appraisals of the novel, which elide violence just as eagerly as Julius does.

The book presents an intimate and grotesque connection between the mechanics of the mathematical and narrative tangent in the workings of diagnostic or high theoretical writing. Cole's lone point qua protagonist summons and discards computationally useful others. In turn, he searches for direction and movement, compulsively translating trauma into tangent. Does this speak to the form and function of Julius's "Theory Generation" classmates as well? Do we see in the post-45 Theory-saturated novel a proliferation of protagonists who, acting as sere, Serres-like parasites, move solipsistically through the world? Are they equally "differential operators of change," capable only of brief, semiconductive, one-way relations, subsisting in and on the static of the stories of others? Is Julius's elided rape of Moji an indication of the ethical failing, or even greater violence and violation, inherent in this mode of narration and relation? Is injecting narrative with Theory yet another form of violent insemination? By making available another biological metaphor (not a bird, but a bug), Cole also perhaps dangerously raises the question of whether, if it's all just analogically biological, forgiveness or blame can be meaningfully determined, or even become a permitted line of questioning at all. In this way, Cole, like his bedbugs, might just be leaving us, in the end, with an uneasy, ambivalent discomfort.

Sara Ahmed argues that disgust demands distance and only comes into being through its creation. At the end of the final chapter in this study of the double graphic, I want to return to Eugenie Brinkema's alternate view, which I cited in the introduction. This view, I suggest, ties together the geometric Julius of tangential plotting with the grotesque Julius of bedbug-esque violations, while also linking not only Oedipa's diagrammatically rendered rape but also her own paranoia-inflected mapping of tangents:

> Disgust is a spatial operator, delimiting zones of proximity that are discomforting versus acceptable, drawing lines in the thick muck. It is the forsaken outside that is nevertheless immediate and too close, a threatening proximity from which one recoils, but never with sufficient spacing, an exteriority without distance. . . . disgust is a problematic of geography, or geo-ontology. The map it draws puts objects, qualities, and people in their proper place. Destructive and generative, revolting and alluring, disgust is the inscribing agent of the map and the violence that commands one's adherence to its plan.[157]

The infographic combines of this sort of line-drawing, proximity-forcing, category-creating disgust with a contemporary pose of information-inundated cool. It overlays the grotesquely graphic schema of disgust with the planar graphicness of information visualization, making unexpectedly resonant and doubly applicable Johanna Drucker's pronouncement about the latter: "All graphical schema are built on the single principle of defining classes of entities and of relations."[158] In the infographic, people become finally not flat silhouettes or hollow dolls but in a sort of apotheosis of these processes of abstraction, just as violently, dimensionless data points.

CONCLUSION
Identification and Its Discontents

THE GRAPHIC, AT ITS ROOT (etymological and thematically), is about inscription: how, systematically, through words and images, we come to capture, convey, and store knowledge. And what happens when fundamentally texturally and dimensionally different structures of knowledge, particularly ways of knowing and recording other people, are conflated (inflated, and/or deflated) with each other. The increasing prevalence of the double graphic in post-45 American literature evinces a growing imbrication of (and friction between) how we attain and process different kinds of knowledge—emotional and informational—about other people in a cultural landscape structured by and as database. In other words, the double graphic forces us to grapple with our fundamental inability to know the other in all of their dimensions, even as our inundation with data seems to make capturing, cataloguing, and cathecting onto anyone and everyone a tantalizingly frictionless possibility.

In Jean Baudrillard's "The Ecstasy of Communication," now something of a historical artifact, he describes a "new" sort of obscenity that he calls "a whole pornography of information and communication":

> a pornography of all functions and objects in their readability, their fluidity, their availability, their regulation, in their forced signification, in their performativity, in their branching, in their polyvalence, in their free expression. . . . It is no longer then the traditional obscenity of what is hidden, repressed, forbidden or obscure; on the contrary, it is the obscenity of the visible, of the all-too-visible, of the more-visible-than-the-visible. It is the obscenity of what no longer has any secret, of what dissolves completely in information and communication.[1]

Pornography, we've seen, can be fun, and funny, and/or violent, and violating. So, too, the double graphic reveals, can "information." The obscenity of the double graphic arguably lies in various forms of overexposure, "the more-visible-than-the-visible." At the same time, though, one of the sneaking suspicions that thinking through the double graphic plants is that, oft-cited higher court decisions to the contrary, we might not actually know true obscenity when we see it. And if we do, we certainly won't know what it feels (like).

The double graphic exposes a potentially fatal error in the script (in terms of theatrical performance and computational programming both) of the aesthetic emotion of identification. And perhaps in long-held assumption that the ultimate value of reading is the empathetic education that it is sure to provide. Namwali Serpell writes, in an essay on "The Banality of Empathy," that "the empathy model of art can bleed too easily into the relishing of suffering by those who are safe from it. It's a gateway drug to white saviorism, with its familiar blend of propaganda, pornography, and paternalism."[2] Again and again, the texts this book examines make nonsense out of the presumed pleasures of reading as a way of inhabiting, knowing, intimately feeling (for, with, as) the other. The gateway drug has been swapped for an acrid placebo. And many amongst them seem, moreover, to be bidding a hardy good riddance to identification full stop. Don't let the door hit you on the way out, *Oreo* and Narcissister shout over their shoulders at sympathy. The archive of texts I've read across the ethno-, porno-, and infographic is purposefully ambivalent, in aggregate, about the uses to which the double graphic can be put. Or, perhaps more appropriately, about the ethical import of its affectively oscillating portrayals of scenes of violation. There is violence inherent in the graph-ick datafication of overexposed bodies. But there can also be a sort of perverse release in the reprieve from invasive sentiment.

The American graphic is in essence about bodies read into and against binaries—racial, sexual, computational. The ambivalent literary graphic that comes of age in mid-twentieth– century information culture coerces identification in moments of overexposure. Gregory Seigworth and Melissa Gregg call affects "integral to a body's perpetual *becoming*."[3] The seemingly impossible mapping of the aggressively flat affective forms of the diagrammatic graphic onto/over/into the texturally rich crevasses of the grotesque graphic confounds the process of emotional evocation itself. The double graphic names ostensibly affectively charged moments that seem to contribute not to "perpetual becoming," but instead to a paradoxically convulsive arrest of both being and feeling. Fully dimensional human beings are formally flattened, hollowed, compressed as they are figured as the silhouettes, sex dolls, and data points of the double graphic. What happens, though, when the figuration is both verbal and visual at once? Or, can a book called *American Graphic* really expect to get away with not reading any comics?

Comics: Robert Crumb, Chris Ware, Phoebe Gloeckner

Grids invade, subtend, and vivisect, either literally or figuratively, most of the texts that this book analyzes—from Nathanael West to Kara Walker to Thomas Pynchon. It feels only right, then, to conclude with a gesture towards, a brief dip into, the form of imagetext most indebted to that structure: comics. More specifically, I want to consider two canonical comics artists who sit stylistically at the extremes of the graphic spectrum: Robert Crumb, committed to "show it all"[4] with his LSD-fueled, explosive, often offensive grotesques, and Chris Ware, whose diagrammatic drawing style has been called everything from typographic to antiseptic.

R. Crumb, dubbed "the sugar-daddy of the comics renaissance"[5] by one critic, creates images that seem to relish their ability to outrage, wallowing in visual excess, unsavory sexual exploits, drug trips, violations of sexual and racial taboos, and the objectification of his prized brand of "big healthy girl." He describes the development of his style as a sort of opening of his psychic sluice gates:

> On LSD, I got flung back into this cruder forties style, that suddenly became very powerful to me. It was a kind of grotesque interpretation of this forties thing, Popeye kind of stuff. . . . Seeing S. Clay Wilson's work was a big breakthrough, because he just drew anything that came into his head, any violent, crazy, sexual thing. I saw that and I said, OK, anything goes, I'm just going to show it all, and reveal the dark side, everything.[6]

In Crumb's work, there are fluids and fellatio and degradations galore. Most panels are richly detailed and textured, with a signature emphasis on hatching and stippling—techniques that lend the images a sense of three-dimensionality—particularly in their abundantly bristling expanses of (especially Crumb's own) body hair. Very few surfaces within the visual field—be they floors, walls, ceilings, skin—are left smooth and unmarked. Everything seems rumpled or mottled, prickly or sticky with texture (Figure C.1).

There are also heavy doses of often heavy-handed satire in Crumb's work. The underground comix world out of which it emerged revolted against the 1954 Comics Code by being revolting, often purporting, in the process, to be about the liberated self—free to expel and extrude all manner of prurience onto the page in the name of entertainment, free expression, and experimentation. Crumb's work notably eschews the long form of the prestige "graphic novel" in favor of telling short tales that often feature recurring characters, including thinly veiled (or often fully naked) stand-ins for the cartoonist himself. He vomits sexual hungers and hang-ups at viewers/readers and expects complimentary explosions—of laughter, of disgust, of bodily fluids—back at the page in return. As Jared Gardner writes, though,

> Crumb's comix especially, but underground comix more broadly, underscore the degree to which the liberated self at the center of the stories being told was almost inevitably white, male, and straight—a liberation that often came explicitly, in the images on the page, at the expense of blacks, women, and homosexuals.[7]

The disgust reaction that Crumb's comix trades in (usually for laughs) is uncomfortable not least because of the extent to which the object of disgust (though it is frequently the Crumb stand-in characters themselves) is more often a series of gross caricatures of bodies markedly unlike his own.

Recalling Sara Ahmed and Sianne Ngai's focus on the sociality of disgust, we can see how when Crumb or his stand-ins declare their own thoughts or actions disgusting, they coerce their readers into an uneasy confederacy of the disgusted. As we take in the same exaggerated visual spectacles of female anatomy on which Crumb perversely fixates, the comix page asks us, too, to become the disgusting. Even as disgust is an affect of distancing and recoil, its unique form of sociality also trades in a guilty mode of empathy. The immediacy of visual media makes the potential disgust reaction all the greater. Crumb's characteristically amped-up approach to texture exaggerates the proximity of repellant surfaces, in which even the bodies drawn at a safe dis-

FIGURE C.1. Illustration from *R. Crumb's Sex Obsessions.*

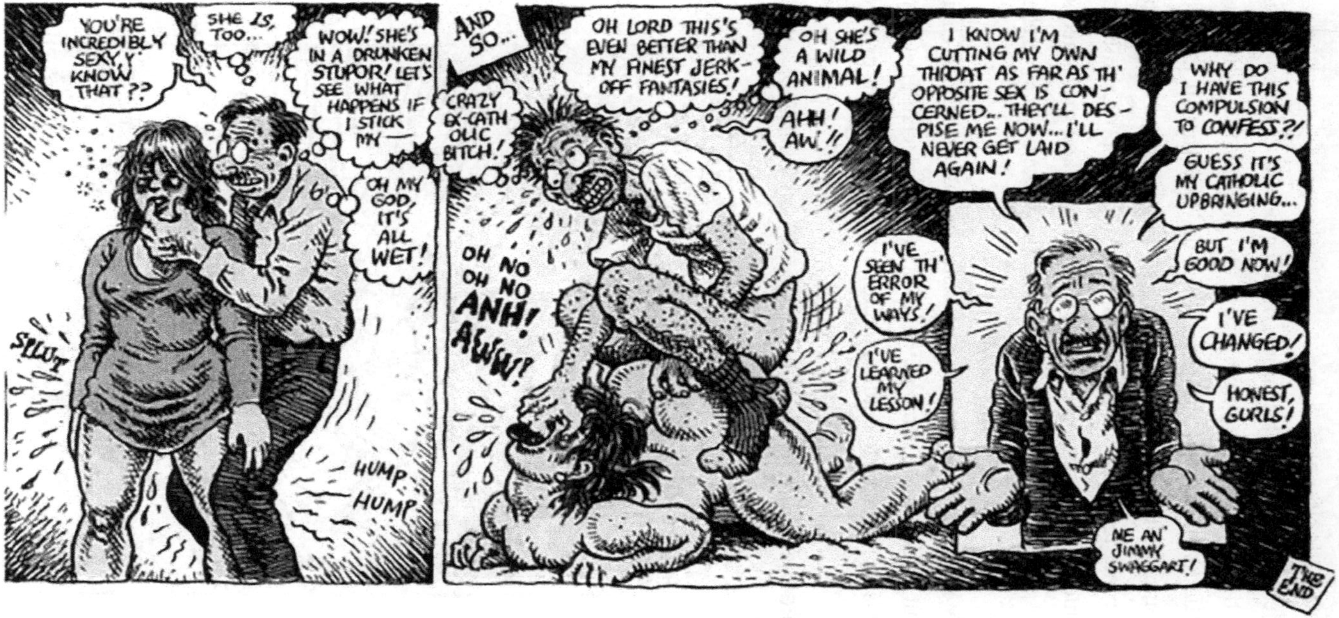

Source: Crumb, *R. Crumb's Sex Obsessions.*

tance feel zoomed in on, protuberant, uncomfortably too close, as if drawn in a trippy cinematic close-up.

Eugenie Brinkema expands upon the relationship between disgust as an affect and the notion of the filmic "close-up," writing that "disgust, in fact, mediates the two senses of the term 'close-up,' one that in English evokes proximity and in French (*gros plan*) suggests largeness and magnification . . . by both coming too close . . . and becoming too large."[8] Crumb's drawings of faces almost always combine both the proximate and magnified senses of the "close-up," through the amount of space they take up in a panel and their exaggerated attention to texture (Figure C.2).

Equally important for questions of distance, disgust, and sociality is the ever-present evidence of Crumb's own hand in his work. Hillary Chute argues that "there is an intimacy to reading handwritten marks on the printed page."[9]

FIGURE C.2. Illustration from Robert Crumb's *My Troubles with Women.*

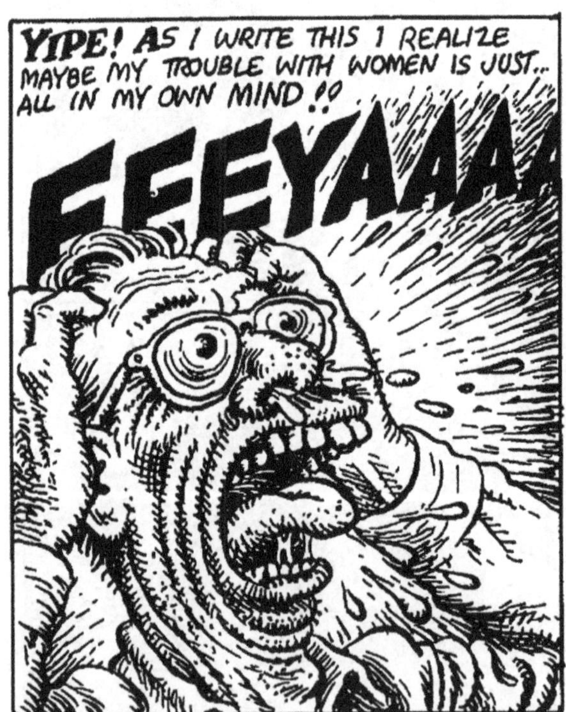

Source: Crumb, *My Troubles with Women.*

And Crumb's style is intimate in a number of ways. Not only are we always seeing Crumb as a character in his strips, but from the obviously hand-drawn lettering to the extravagantly irregular hatching and crosshatching, the style also conjures the phantom presence of the artist at the moment of creation. Jan Baetens, citing Phillippe Marion, calls this the work's "graphiation," a recognition of the time and labor that went into every page.[10] Baetens argues for the intimacy that overt evidence of a work's graphiation can produce:

> [T]he reader has the ability to redo, to remake, or at least to re-experience the enunciative work produced by the author for the very reason that this production is based upon gestures and mechanisms which every reader has known and practiced as a child, but which he or she has forgotten as an adult.[11]

We instinctively see and feel ourselves tracing—even making—the lines on the page when the graphiation is particularly gestural, embodied rather than mechanical. Eszter Szép argues, following Vivian Sobchak's discussions of experiencing film, that comics can be thought of "as a mediated interaction between three bodies: those of the drawer, reader, and object (the actual comic) . . . . Even though the final comic is printed and mass-produced, the reader feels the drawer's bodily trace in the drawings."[12] Crumb's sort of graphiation is sympathetic in this extremely tactile way.[13] We can feel, at least partially, the actions of his body as the actions of our bodies.

Just as the comics page evinces labor, so too does it demand it. Comics are made up of a series of panels divided by blank space known as the gutter. When we see a sequence of images, we pull them together into a narrative, filling in gaps of information, through what Scott McCloud calls closure: "the phenomenon of seeing the parts but perceiving the whole."[14] This comics gestalt renders "the audience . . . a willing and conscious collaborator."[15] Comics move through and across gaps, and we as readers fill them in from our own reserves of imagination. Kate Polak argues that closure "automatically has an ethical dimension; who you are and who you are prompted to identify with, how you are prompted to make inferences about what is and isn't depicted."[16] Much of this ethical import is vested in the spaces between the squares of comics grid: the negative space qua borderline qua limitless space of narrative and affective suturing. We'll recall that Julia Kristeva writes that in, abjection "the border has become an object,"[17] while Brinkema argues that "disgust is a beyond of any singular or objectal thing. It is the promise of worsening, this possibility of something more disgusting than the disgusting."[18] As we read and look at a Crumb page (as with most comics pages), the borders draft us as co-conspirators. And when the graphic edges into the Crumby grotesque, the gutter becomes an abject space potent with "the promise of worsening." To make the reading work, we must fill in the blanks, and, to repeat comics studies' favorite tired pun, get our minds into the gutter.

What happens, though, when "graphic" style turns from the opulently gross to the austerely antiseptic? How does it look and feel when we move from disgust to data—as in this dense, text-heavy image of a naked woman from Chris Ware's *Building Stories* (Figure C.3)?[19]

Let's begin by considering Ware's explanation of his own style, which I'm proffering as a comics exemplar of the geometric or diagrammatic graphic:

> I try to use the rules of typography to govern the way that I "draw," which keeps me at a sensible distance from the story as well as being a visual analog to the way we remember and conceptualize the world. I figured out this way of working by learning from and looking at artists I admired and whom I thought came closest to getting at what seemed to me to be the "essence" of comics, which is fundamentally the weird process of reading pictures, not just looking at them. I see the black outlines of cartoons as visual approximations of the way we remember general ideas, and I try to use naturalistic color underneath them to simultaneously suggest a perceptual experience, which I think is more or less the way we actually experience the world as adults; we don't really "see" anymore after a certain age, we spend our time naming and categorizing and identifying and figuring how everything all fits together. Unfortunately, as a result, I guess sometimes readers get a chilled or antiseptic sensation from it, which is certainly not intentional, and is something I admit as a failure, but is also something I can't completely change at the moment.[20]

Ware sees his work as governed by the "rules of typography." He explains the diagrammatic bent of his drawings as, somewhat unexpectedly, a formal technique of psychological realism, "a visual analog to the way we remember and conceptualize the world" via "naming and categorizing and identifying."

Reading Ware's often text-packed panels, which David Ball and Martha Kuhlman call "reminiscent of the wooden compartments in a typesetter's case,"[21] the eye quickly slips off of the slick, unyielding surfaces of his images

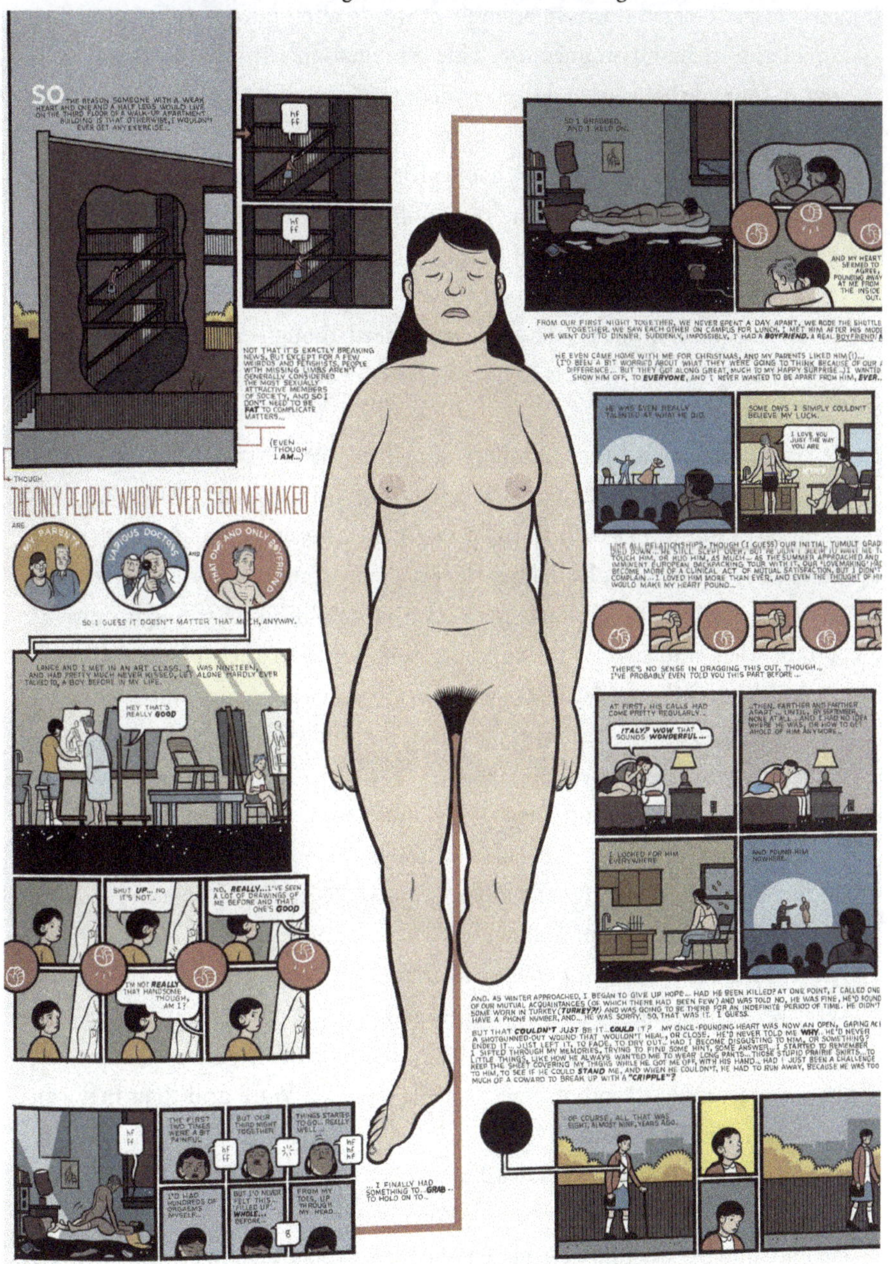

FIGURE C.3. Page from Chris Ware's *Building Stories.*

only to get bogged down in a tangle of words often purposefully printed so small as to demand an uncomfortable combination of squinting at and leaning in toward the page to decipher them (or, in digital form, picking up our virtual magnifying glasses to zoom in). Where the surfaces of Crumb's gross graphic are hairy, sticky, and haptically intimate, Ware's abstracted grids within grids within grids are more smooth, sterile, and scopic; a surface that has been Teflon-coated against lasting contact. Which sorts of emotions can or do, à la Ahmed, adhere to such objects? Ware's hand is nowhere to be seen in the line work or inking of his images. Indeed, though each page is painstakingly hand-drafted, Ware is frequently asked whether his comics are created on the computer.[22]

McCloud argues that the more simplified the portrayal of a person or object in a comics work, the more "universality" it possesses.[23] Using the juxtaposed examples of a realistically drawn man's face and a smiley face to make his point (Figure C.4), he defines the extremely simplified form of picture as a cartoon, which he explains as "a form of amplification through simplification" that emphasizes "the concepts of objects over their physical appearance."[24] According to McCloud, "when you look at a photo or realistic drawing of a face—you see it as the face of another. But when you enter the world of the cartoon—you see yourself."[25]

Is, then, a sort of cold universality and identification what Ware's iconic style yields? Does the assemblage of discrete cartoon data points, each individually rendered as flatly and simply as possible, encourage readers to enter the subjectivities these pages portray? Does Crumb's relatively realistic, heavily textural style limit the potential for identification, and perhaps, through its very realism (or naturalism) lay the groundwork for, even produce, a reaction of disgust by denying identification? Can viewers, in short, more easily inhabit the simple, iconic, symbolic faces and bodies of a Ware grid than they can those of a Crumb spread?

Isaac Cates argues that identification is hardly the whole story of Ware's smoothly detached style: "Whatever Ware is aiming at with his diagrammatic, iconic drawing, then, it isn't merely the reader's identification with the characters or any ease of access to the character's interiority."[26] Cates notes that many, if not most, of Ware's characters remain stubbornly impenetrable, the more so, somehow, for the many factoids and images, the plethora of "data,"

FIGURE C.4. Scott McCloud's explanation of the universality of the cartoon face.

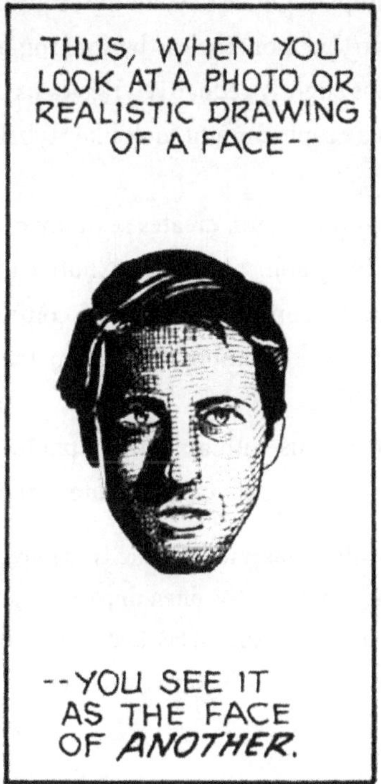

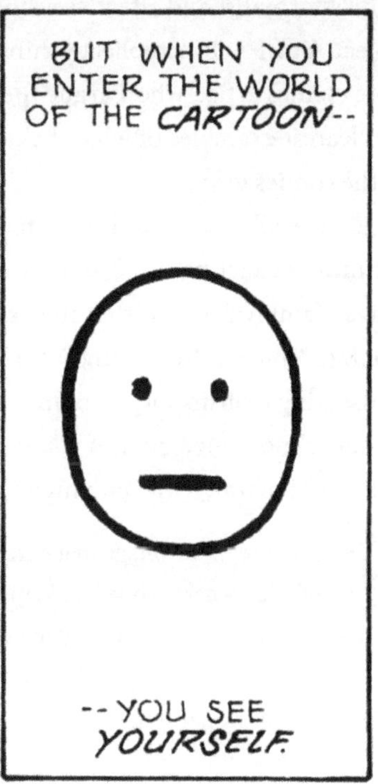

Source: McCloud, *Understanding Comics: The Invisible Art*, 31.

the "interesting" catalogues of "the relatively small surprise of information or variation from an existing norm," to quote Ngai's definition of that aesthetic category.[27] Contact remains elusive and interiority largely inaccessible even as information proliferates, producing, if anything, a pervasive sense of deadened melancholy. Not so much antiseptic as inadequately anaesthetized. Not stripped of emotion but sheathed from, or maybe even in it. Crumb, on the other hand, depicts and demands physically and affectively sticky contact of every sort on nearly every page. The frequently bluntly confessional mode of his narration, combined with the gross textural specificity of his visual style, pulls us into his particular interiority at the same time as we watch him fixate on—and often penetrate—the exteriors of others. This suggests that the polarity between these two kinds of graphic, and their relationship to questions of affect and identification are more complex than they might initially appear to be in comics. A theory of this complexity, in a medium with its own rich body of formalist and affective scholarship, might be beyond the scope of this project. But I will complicate things further nonetheless by looking at one more comics artist, who I argue (perhaps slightly reductively) gives us one of the clearest examples of what the double graphic might look like stylistically on the comics grid.

Phoebe Gloeckner, a trained medical illustrator, creates sexually explicit, technically exacting, unabashedly autobiographical comics. Chute calls her images "ambivalent" in that they are both "confrontational and confusing," evoking "intense foreboding" through their "combination of meticulous, painstaking realism and . . . nonrealism."[28]

Gloeckner's 1998 book *A Child's Life* begins with an author "photo" entitled "Self- Portrait with Pemphigus Vulgaris" (Figure C.5).[29] Chute argues that

> the repletion in the image that carries both disgust and pleasure is characteristic of Gloeckner's work. . . . While the content . . . is often unpleasant and discomfiting, this is countered not only by the pleasure of fascination with the revelation of the private and the disgusting but also by the visual abundance distinguishing her style.[30]

Gloeckner's self-portrait seems to script a mélange of the types of lingering that Ware and Crumb's work each respectively demand. The affective response to "Self-Portrait" toggles between disgust at the spectacle of the whole image and a sort of curious confusion at the coldly abstract specifics of the insets nested within it.

The Phoebe Gloeckner of the illustration looks down and away, brow ambiguously furrowed, concealing her right breast while displaying the ravaged and exposed subderma of her forearm, which tapers up into an intact, spot-lit right hand (presumably the primary tool of her craft). The open fissures on her forearm provoke a classic disgust response—a combination of repulsion and fascination. You want to lean in closer and see what's in there, what's being unnaturally revealed—even as you'd really rather not know. Stripped of words and context, the double inset, which conceals her other breast while revealing the microscopic workings of her ailment, is flummoxing. This anatomical evidence is hardly self-evident, for all of its stylistic clarity. In part, this inadequacy of evidence, of the facts themselves—the raw data of medical

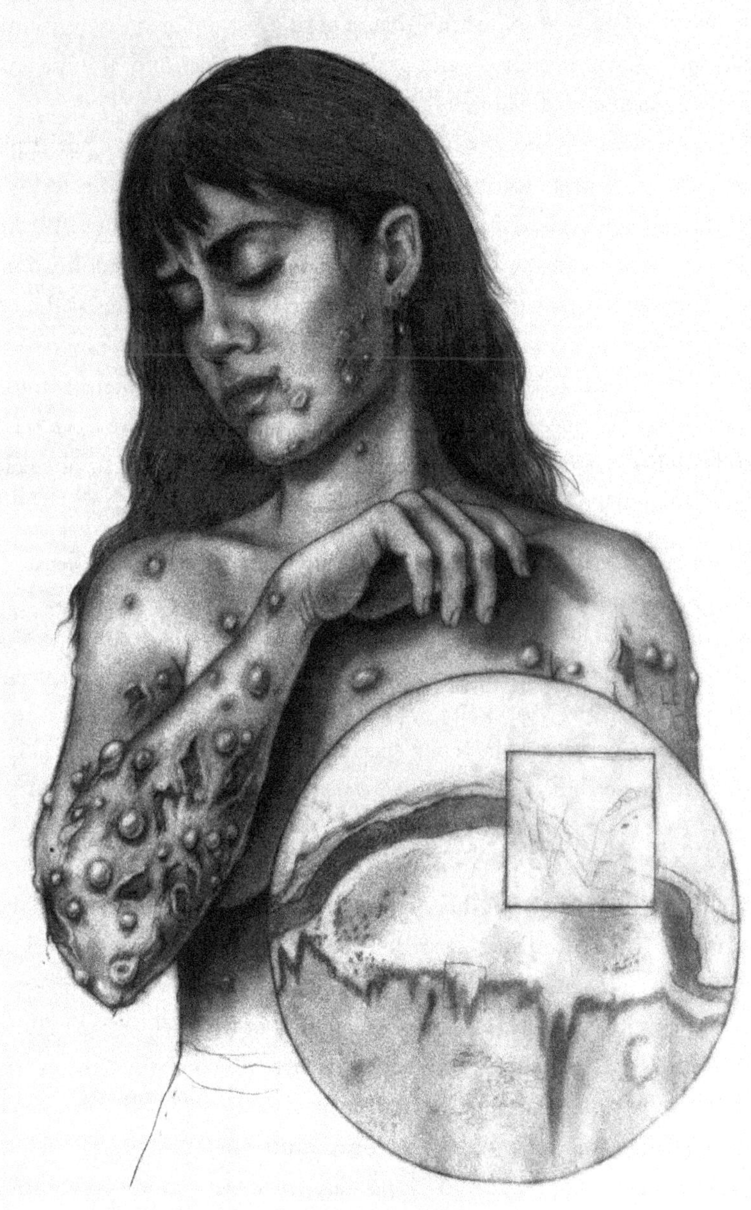

Source: Gloeckner, *A Child's Life and Other Stories*, 6. Reprinted with permission.

oddity or of personal trauma, however clinically delivered—thematically underpins all of the disturbing, sometimes unnervingly casual or even playful, stories of *A Child's Life,* which document Gloeckner's childhood filled with sexual abuse. Here, a graphic style that is both gross and geometric stymies a clear-cut affective response—and perhaps saves the victim of trauma from being a spectacular object of mere pity or disgust.

I also want to read Gloeckner's multiply graphic style here as a power play of sorts, not only in its technically virtuosic execution but also in terms of where she chooses to place this unusual self-portrait within the book. The first image of Gloeckner in the book is not this self-portrait of the adult woman with the fabricated skin disease (she makes a point of clarifying at the end of her foreword: "one more thing—I didn't <u>really</u> ever have Pemphigus Vulgaris"[31]), but instead a sketch by R. Crumb of a preteen Gloeckner, sitting on a couch, drawing, knees absentmindedly drifting apart (Figure C.6).[32] This latter detail becomes the focal point of his drawing only after, or as, one reads the accompanying text. On the facing page, Crumb bemoans:

> "I have to tell the truth. . . . I, too, lusted after the young, budding artist-cartoonist from the moment I first met her, when she was 16 or 17 years old. I, too, desired to subject the beautiful, intense young girl to all sorts of degrading and perverse sexual acts. The only difference was, I never got any further than a couple of piggyback rides. And why? Because I was *too nice a guy!* . . . But oh how I lusted after the young Phoebe in my heart! Did I get a blow job offa her? *Not even once! I got nothing!* I went home filled with self-pity, as usual. (Aren't men horrible??)"[33]

Following on the heels of this drawing and these words, Gloeckner's own gross and highly controlled image in her "Self-Portrait" can't help but feel like a pointed corrective in terms of both style and content. It seems to puncture Crumb's playfully self-effacing "I have to tell the truth" by delivering an image of devastating stylistic realism and clinical accuracy accompanied by text that strips it of any truth value whatsoever. At the same time, it both overexposes and desexualizes the body Crumb's words and image have grossly objectified, even as it puts on display fleshy openings galore. One of the provocations of Gloeckner's self-portrait is that there might be something paradoxically both exposing (or violating) *and* protective about becoming a figure of coolly graphic (self-)classification.

FIGURE C.6. R. Crumb portrait of young Phoebe Gloeckner.

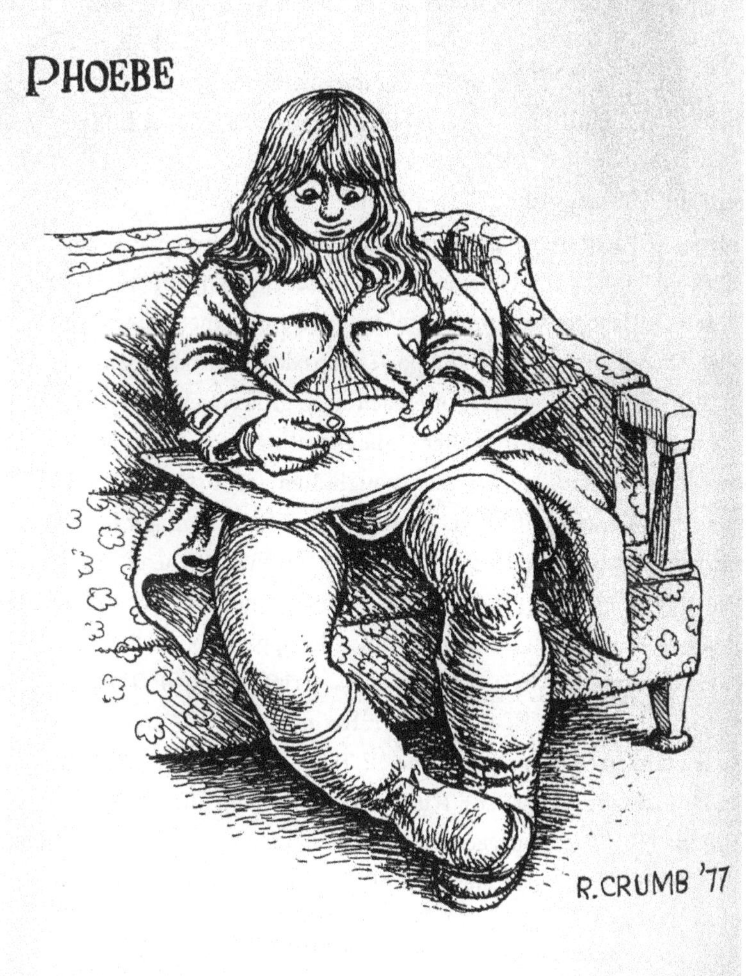

Source: Gloeckner, *A Child's Life and Other Stories*, 4. Reprinted with permission.

Gloeckner delivers a deadpan evisceration of Crumb's smugly not-quite-smutty imagetext portrait of her by drawing her own self-portrait that visits visual violence her own avatar. This response resonates with the way that Kara Walker and Fran Ross also seem to delight in countering structural vulnerability with performances of graphically irresolvable discomfort. It is a reminder that, as the double graphic kills (or at least mutilates) identification as we know, it often does it with an illegible smile on its mask-like face. And the ethics of that particular dispatching are anything but clear-cut or predetermined. Could the death of literary identification be a mercy killing?

Graphic Axes Galore

A sort of glitch in the aesthetic emotional matrix, the double graphic disrupts affect by surfacing the violence often inherent in sympathetic identification. Indexed by the prefixes ethno-, porno-, and info-, the chapters in this book have looked at some of the key power gaps across which sentimental hearts and their classificatory gazes often achingly, grotesquely feel, peer, and reach out, longing to palpate the other while placating themselves. This modest assemblage of prefixes feels to me, though, like just a start. I'll end by asking what other modes of affectively fraught identification might be productively examined through the lens of the double graphic? If the ethnographic, the pornographic, and the infographic all resonate unexpectedly in their affective structures, what about the topographic (the application of lines to surfaces)? The choreographic (charting movement, scripting steps)? The demographic (appalling portrayals of the democratic mob, the consumer, the fully abstracted citizen (*The Purge*, anyone?))? The polygraphic (instruments to measure physiological responses, truth as both fact and affect)? The holographic (thinking both about burgeoning debates about empathy, AI, and VR, as well as their resonance with questions of authenticity surrounding handwriting and replicas of manuscripts)?[34]

Could a category like the holographic, which evokes questions of replication and authenticity both in reproductions of handwritten manuscripts and the mechanical production of lifelike three-dimensional illusions (a revenant holographic Tupac Shakur "performing" in concert at Coachella in 2012, for instance), help us think about the proximity of empathetic identification, extraction, datafication, and violence in debates about what makes for ethical technological representations of the other? Empathy—which Xine Yao calls our historical moment's "update" of the concept of sympathy "in the continued hope for a better politics of feeling bound up with morality and justice"[35]—seems to be everywhere in discussions, both well meaning and sinister, of technology. Increasingly, too, critics, scholars, and even a few within the tech industry are questioning the facile and dangerous equation between the empathetic and the Good[36]—often by reminding us that the empathy-as-panacea bubble has long been burst in many disciplines, particularly by Black feminist scholars.[37] Lisa Nakamura, in a recent analysis of Facebook's bid to give VR "a new emotional identity as a technology of empathy" as a "curative for the digital industries' recently scrutinized contributions to exacerbating class inequality, violating users' privacy, and amplifying far-right fascist racism and sexism," concludes that, unsurprisingly, the tech behemoth doth protest too much.[38] Based on "toxic re-embodiment," VR as "empathy machine," she argues, aims at "making racial empathy pleasurable . . . [by] put[ting] the undercommons to work providing empathy content: their recorded 'experiences' become the alibi for VR's excesses and un-virtuous uses."[39] Might looking at doubly graphic holograms (broadly construed) add another sharpened blade to the toolshed of graphic axes that cleave identification, both with and against various grains?

Along, or with, what other axes do we, creatures of flesh and data, hew our literatures and our lives? I suspect that these briefly proposed categories and others have much to tell us about the dynamic relationship between reading, affect, form, violence, and identification in our contemporary world—ever more abstracted, ever more visceral, ever more graph-ick.

Notes

Introduction

1. "Graphic" entry in *Merriam-Webster* dictionary. Only selected portions of the entry are shown.

2. Ngai, *Ugly Feelings*, 6.

3. Brinkema, *The Forms of the Affects*, 38. Emphasis in original.

4. Brinkema explains that, for her, "the word 'affect'—far more so than synonyms 'emotion' or 'feeling' or 'sensation'—is redolent of a topology that de-privileges interiority, depth, containment, and recovery" (ibid., 23–24). See also Massumi, "The Autonomy of Affect."

5. Cvetkovich, "Affect," 15.

6. Seigworth and Gregg, "An Inventory of Shimmers," 2.

7. Brinkema, *The Forms of the Affects*, 25.

8. See Sara Ahmed's exemplary egg analogy (*The Cultural Politics of Emotion*, 210):

> The activity of separating affect from emotion could be understood as rather like breaking an egg in order to separate the yolk from the white. We can separate different parts of a thing even if they are contiguous, even if they are, as it were, in a sticky relation. We might have different methods for performing the action of separation. But we have to separate the yolk from the white because they are not separate. And sometimes we "do do" what we "can do" because separating these elements, not only by treating them as separable but by modifying their existing relation, or how they exist in relation, allows us to do other things that we might not otherwise be able to do. That we can separate them does not mean they are separate.

Or Sianne Ngai's characterization of the distinction as "a modal difference of intensity or degree, rather than a formal difference of quality or kind" (Ngai, *Ugly Feelings*, 27).

9. Sedgwick, *Touching Feeling: Affect, Pedagogy, Performativity*, 13.

10. Ibid.

11. Bora, "Outing Texture."

12. Sedgwick, *Touching Feeling*, 14–15.

13. Ahmed, *The Cultural Politics of Emotion*, 10.

14. Ibid., 209.

15. Ibid., 206.

16. Ibid., 208.

17. Ibid., 10.

18. Ibid., 8.

19. Ibid., 4.

20. Ibid., 11.

21. Ibid.

22. Ibid., 10–11.

23. Sedgwick, *Touching Feeling*, 15.

24. Ahmed, *The Cultural Politics of Emotion*, 214.

25. Schuller, *The Biopolitics of Feeling: Race, Sex, and Science in the Nineteenth Century*, 13.

26. Massumi, "The Autonomy of Affect," 31.

27. See Hemmings, "Invoking Affect: Cultural Theory and the Ontological Turn"; Garcia-Rojas, "(Un)Disciplined Futures: Women of Color Feminism as a Disruptive to White Affect Studies"; Palmer, "'What Feels More Than Feeling?': Theorizing the Unthinkability of Black Affect." Palmer argues that "affect theory as an academic discourse has yet to substantially account for the problematic of blackness, the particular affective dispositions that emerge in reaction to processes of racialization and racial subjugation, or the ways in which affect serves as an exploitable tool of racial domination and anti-blackness" (35).

28. Hemmings, "Invoking Affect," 557.

29. Ibid., 551. Emphasis in original.

30. See Berlant, *The Female Complaint*; Berlant, "Structures of Unfeeling: 'Mysterious Skin'"; Yao, *Disaffected: The Cultural Politics of Unfeeling in Nineteenth-Century America*.

31. Yao, *Disaffected*, 13. Emphasis in original.

32. Ibid., 4.

33. Da Silva, *Toward a Global Idea of Race*.

34. Yao, *Disaffected*, 4.

35. Ibid., 5.

36. Berlant, *The Female Complaint*, 56.

37. Yao, *Disaffected*, 22.

38. Berlant, "Structures of Unfeeling."

39. Yao, *Disaffected*, 11.

40. Ibid., 16.

41. Ngai, *Our Aesthetic Categories: Zany, Cute, Interesting*.

42. Stephens, *The Poetics of Information Overload: From Gertrude Stein to Conceptual Writing*, 7.

43. Ibid., xi.

44. Lee, *Overwhelmed: Literature, Aesthetics, and the Nineteenth-Century Information Revolution*, 4.

45. Entin, *Sensational Modernism: Experimental Fiction and Photography in Thirties America*, 35.

46. The informational is "characterized by instrumentalism, objectivity, transparency, bureaucratic impersonality, calculation, and reconfigurable data." Lee, *Overwhelmed*, 4.

47. Stephens, *The Poetics of Information Overload*, 7.

48. Manovich, "Database as a Symbolic Form," 81.

49. Vesna, *Database Aesthetics: Art in the Age of Information Overflow*, iii.

50. Manovich, "Database as a Symbolic Form," 86.

51. Ahmed, *The Cultural Politics of Emotion*, 11:

> Drawing on Marx, I argue that emotions accumulate over time, as a form of affective value. Objects only seem to have such value, by an erasure of these histories, as histories of production and labor. But whilst Marx suggests that emotions are erased by the value of things (the suffering of the worker's body is not visible in commodity form), I focus on how emotions are produced. It is not so much emotions that are erased, as if they were already there, but the processes of production or the "making" of emotions. In other words, "feelings" become "fetishes," qualities that seem to reside in objects, only through an erasure of the history of their production and circulation.

52. Sack, "Aesthetics of Information Visualization," 139: "Scientific and engineering pragmatics . . . dematerialized the body over the course of the invention and development of contemporary information technologies."

53. Drucker, *Graphesis: Visual Forms of Knowledge Production*, 2.

54. Ibid., 6.

55. Bertin, *Semiology of Graphics: Diagrams, Networks, Maps*, 2.

56. Ibid., 3.

57. Drucker, *Graphesis*, 128. Emphasis in original.

58. Lee, *Overwhelmed*, 12.

59. Drucker, *Graphesis*, 27.

60. See Houser, *Infowhelm*.

61. Manovich, "Data Visualization as New Abstraction and Anti-Sublime," 7. Sianne Ngai makes this argument too, in her analysis of the "ugly feeling" of "stuplimity." Ngai, *Ugly Feelings*, 248.

62. Foster, *The Return of the Real: The Avant-Garde at the End of the Century*, 221.

63. Stephens, *The Poetics of Information Overload*, 7.

64. Lee, *Overwhelmed*, 5.

65. Ngai, *Ugly Feelings*, 337.

66. Di Renzo, *American Gargoyles: Flannery O'Connor and the Medieval Grotesque*, 5.

67. Ngai, *Ugly Feelings*, 335.

68. Miller, *The Anatomy of Disgust*, xii.

69. Ngai, *Ugly Feelings*, 337.

70. Ahmed, *The Cultural Politics of Emotion*, 87.

71. Bakhtin, *Rabelais and His World*, 310.

72. Chaouli, "Van Gogh's Ear: Toward a Theory of Disgust," 58.

73. "Identity" meaning both "a distinct impression of a single person or thing" and "The quality or condition of being the same in substance." See "Identity, n." entry in *OED Online*.

74. Bakhtin, *Rabelais and His World*, 310.

75. Ahmed, *The Cultural Politics of Emotion*, 92.

76. Ibid., 91.

77. Kristeva, *Powers of Horror*, 2.

78. Ibid., 4.

79. Ahmed, *The Cultural Politics of Emotion*, 86.

80. Limon, *Stand-up Comedy in Theory, or, Abjection in America*, 4.

81. Brinkema, *The Forms of the Affects*, 170. See also Kolnai, *On Disgust*.

82. Brinkema, *The Forms of the Affects*, 130.

83. Ibid., 131. See also Menninghaus, *Disgust*.

84. Brinkema, *The Forms of the Affects*, 131.

85. Lancaster, "Feeling the Grid: Lorna Simpson's Concrete Abstraction," 135.

86. Higgins, *The Grid Book*, 6.

87. Israel, *Spirals: The Whirled Image in Twentieth-Century Literature and Art*, 210.

88. Zdebik, *Deleuze and the Diagram: Aesthetic Threads in Visual Organization*, 1.

89. Bender and Marrinan, *The Culture of Diagram*, 33.

90. Ibid., 10.

91. Zdebik, *Deleuze and the Diagram*, 1.

92. Ibid., 17–18.

93. Latour, "Visualisation and Cognition: Drawing Things Together," 7. Emphasis in original.

94. Ibid., 15.

95. "In politics as in science, when someone is said to 'master' a question or to 'dominate' a subject, you should normally look for the flat surface that enables mastery (a map, a list, a file, a census, the wall of a gallery, a card-index, a repertory); and you will find it" (ibid., 19).

96. Ibid., 16.

97. As Latour explains (ibid., 20, internal citations omitted):

The two-dimensional character of inscriptions allow them to merge with geometry. As we saw for perspective, space on paper can be made continuous with three-dimensional space. The result is that we can work on paper with rulers and numbers, but still manipulate three-dimensional objects "out there." Better still, because of this optical consistency, everything, no matter where it comes from, can be converted into diagrams and numbers, and combination of numbers and tables can be used that are still easier to handle than words or silhouettes. You cannot measure the sun, but you can measure a photograph of the sun with a ruler.

98. Ngai, *Ugly Feelings*, 8, citing Johnson, *The Feminist Difference: Literature, Psychoanalysis, Race, and Gender,* 13.

99. Ahmed writes, too, about the relationship between emotions and figures (though her figures are figures of speech: "I examine how different 'figures' get stuck together, and how sticking is dependent on past histories of association that often 'work' through concealment. The emotionality of texts is one way of describing how texts are 'moving,' or how they generate effects." Ahmed, *The Cultural Politics of Emotion*, 12–13.

100 Ngai, *Ugly Feelings*, 89.

101 Williams, *Hard Core: Power, Pleasure, and the "Frenzy of the Visible,"* 3.

Chapter 1

1. Harpham, "The Grotesque: First Principles," 461.

2. Ibid. The epigraph is from p. 463.

3. Goodwin, *Modern American Grotesque: Literature and Photography*, 7.

4. Aristotle, *On Poetry and Style*, 12.

5. Belfiore, *Tragic Pleasures: Aristotle on Plot and Emotion*, 300.

6. Aristotle, *On Poetry and Style*, 10.

7. Aristotle, *Nicomachean Ethics*, 26.

8. Montaigne called his essays "grotesque and monstrous bodies, pieced together for the most diverse members, without distinct form, in which order and proportion are left to chance." Cited in Kayser, *The Grotesque in Art and Literature*, 24.

9. Ruskin, *The Stones of Venice: Volume III*, 115.

10. "In the true grotesque, a man of naturally strong feeling is accidentally or resolutely apathetic; in the false grotesque, a man naturally apathetic is forcing himself into temporary excitement" (ibid., 142).

11. Ibid., 140.

12. Ibid. Emphasis in original.

13. Bakhtin, *Rabelais and His World*, 317–318.

14. Ibid., 339.

15. Ibid., 320.

16. Kayser, *The Grotesque in Art and Literature*, 184.

17. Ibid., 181–184 passim.

18. Ibid., 185.

19. Ibid., 187.

20. Ibid., 188.

21. Ibid.

22. Mark Fearnow, for instance, anchors his analysis in the Great Depression, arguing that the grotesque's embrace of contradiction was the only "critical idea" that could digest the era's "absurd contrasts" and produce from the "horrific materials of a world spinning towards conflagration . . . objects that may have been troubling but that nevertheless had been tamed." Fearnow, *The American Stage and the Great Depression: A Cultural History of the Grotesque*, 6.

23. Cassuto, *The Inhuman Race: The Racial Grotesque in American Literature and Culture*, 7.

24. Ibid., 16.

25. Russo, *The Female Grotesque: Risk, Excess and Modernity*, 8–9.

26. Ibid., 219.

27. Thomson, *The Grotesque*, 59.

28. Di Renzo, *American Gargoyles: Flannery O'Connor and the Medieval Grotesque*, 5.

29. Hönnighausen, *William Faulkner: The Art of Stylization in His Early Graphic and Literary Work*.

30. "During the college years West, according to his biographer, had a stronger interest in graphic art than in literature, and he devoted much time to pencil-and-ink drawings featuring facial caricatures, mythological creatures, and religious subjects, with an emphasis often on suffering and martyrdom." Goodwin, *Modern American Grotesque*, 76, citing Martin, *Nathanael West: The Art of His Life*, 64–65. *Miss Lonelyhearts* was almost subtitled "a novel in the form of a comic strip" (Goodwin, *Modern American Grotesque*, 76).

31. O'Connor, *Flannery O'Connor: The Cartoons*.

32. Hönnighausen, *William Faulkner*.

33 Krauss, "Grids," 50.

34. Kayser, *The Grotesque in Art and Literature*, 188.

35. "In the overall regularity of its organization, [the grid] is the result not of imitation, but of aesthetic decree." Krauss, "Grids," 50.

36. Bakhtin, *Rabelais and His World*, 373.

37. Cartwheels are even part of the novel's creation myth. Faulkner claimed to have written *As I Lay Dying* while working at the University of Mississippi's old power plant:

> I had invented a table out of a wheelbarrow in the coal bunker, just beyond a wall from where a dynamo ran. It made a deep, constant humming noise. There was no more work to do until about 4 A.M., when we would have to clean the fires and get up steam again. On these nights, between 12 and 4, I wrote *As I Lay Dying* in six weeks, without changing a word. (Faulkner, *Essays, Speeches & Public Letters*, 177–178)

38. Faulkner, *As I Lay Dying*, 108.

39. The abuse her body both sustains and metes out even seems to invoke the cart-wheel's association with the martyrdom of St. Catherine of Alexandria, who was reputedly tortured on a wheel that miraculously broke at her touch and so became her emblem.

The *OED Online* entry for "cart-wheel": "*to turn cart-wheels*: to execute a succession of lateral summersaults, as if the feet and hands were spokes of a wheel; also *Catherine-wheels*. (Street-boys did this by the side of a moving omnibus, etc., for chance coppers thrown to them.)" "Cart-Wheel, n."

40. Bakhtin explains (*Rabelais and His World*, 353):

> The entire logic of the grotesque movements of the body (still to be seen in shows and circus performances) is of a topographical nature. The system of these movements is oriented in relation to the upper and lower stratum; it is a system of flights and descents into the lower depths. Their simplest expression is the primeval phenomenon of popular humor, the cartwheel, which by the continual rotation of the upper and lower parts suggests the rotation of earth and sky. This is manifested in other movements of the clown: the buttocks persistently trying to take the place of the head and the head that of the buttocks.

41. Faulkner, *As I Lay Dying*, 88.

42. Ibid., 87:

> Cash is filling up the holes lie bored in the top of it. He is trimming out plugs for them, one at a time, the wood wet and hard to work He could cut up a tin can and hide the holes and nobody wouldn't know the difference. Wouldn't mind, anyway. I have seen him spend a hour trimming out a wedge like it was glass he was working, when, he could have reached around and picked tip a dozen sticks and drove them Into the joint and made it do.

. 43. "Jewel's eyes look like pale wood in his high-blooded face" (ibid.,17); "*He had that wooden look on his face again; that bold, surly high-colored rigid look like his face and eyes were two colors of wood, the wrong one pale and the wrong one dark*" (ibid., 181).

44. Faulkner, *As I Lay Dying*, 90, 96, 108, 144, 145, 165.

45. Zdebik, *Deleuze and the Diagram: Aesthetic Threads in Visual Organization*, 12.

46. Ibid., 1.

47. It is well known that anything William Faulkner wrote about himself or his writing must be taken with a grain of salt. His assertion that he never revised a word of *As I Lay Dying* after spending a mere six weeks writing it, for instance, strains credulity. What might ring truer, especially for this reading of the novel's geometric and diagrammatic proclivities, is this excerpt from his 1946 introduction to *The Sound and the Fury* (in Faulkner, *Essays, Speeches & Public Letters*, 297–298):

[T]his would be a deliberate book. I set out deliberately to write a tour-de-force. Before I ever put pen to paper and set down the first word, I knew what the last word would be and almost where the last period would fall. Before I began I said, I am going to write a book by which, at a pinch, I can stand or fall if I never touch ink again. So when I finished it the cold satisfaction was there, as I had expected, but as I had also expected that other quality which *The Sound and the Fury* had given me was absent: that emotion definite and physical and yet nebulous to describe: that ecstasy, that eager and joyous faith and anticipation of surprise which the yet unmarred sheet beneath my hand held inviolate and unfailing, waiting for release. It was not there in *As I Lay Dying*. I said, it is because I knew too much about this book before I began to write it. I said, More than likely I shall never again have to know this much about a book before I begin to write it, and next time it will return.

48. See Kaufmann, *Textual Bodies: Modernism, Postmodernism, and Print*; Matthews, "*As I Lay Dying* in the Machine Age"; Tucker, "William Faulkner's *As I Lay Dying*: Working Out the Cubistic Bugs."

49. Tucker, "William Faulkner's *As I Lay Dying*," 394.

50. Ibid.

51. Deleuze, *Foucault*, 34.

52. Tucker, "William Faulkner's *As I Lay Dying*," 396.

53. Bender and Marrinan, *The Culture of Diagram*, 10.

54. Faulkner, *As I Lay Dying*, 17.

55. Ibid.: "[E]yes like pale wood" (17), "wooden-faced" (94), "suffocated, furious, his lip lifted upon his teeth" (97), "eyes like marbles" (101), "kind of green, then it would go red and then green again" (126), "eyes . . . pale as two bleached chips in his face" (145), "*He had that wooden look on his face again; that bold, surly high-colored rigid look like his face and eyes were two colors of wood, the wrong one pale and the wrong one dark*" (181), "In the tall moonlight his eyes look like spots of white paper pasted on a high small football" (213).

56. Faulkner, *As I Lay Dying*, 209.

57. Ibid., 188.

58. Ibid., 173.

59 Cameron, *Impersonality: Seven Essays*, 12.

60. Ibid.

61. Ibid., ix.

62. Edwards, "Extremities of the Body: The Anoptic Corporeality of *As I Lay Dying*," 741, 743. Internal citations omitted.

63. Kayser, *The Grotesque in Art and Literature*, 188.

64. Serena Haygood Blount argues that the graphophone, despite its belated appearance and seemingly marginal position in the text, is the central image of the novel. See Blount, "Faulkner's Graphophone."

65. Faulkner, *As I Lay Dying*, 261.

66. Lethem, "The American Vicarious: An Introduction to *Miss Lonelyhearts & The Day of the Locust*," viii, ix.

67. West, "Some Notes on Miss L."

68. West, "Some Notes on Violence," 50.

69. Dewey, *Art as Experience*, 168.

70 Quoted in Goodwin, *Modern American Grotesque*, 81.

71. Ibid.

72. Ibid.

73. McCloud, *Understanding Comics: The Invisible Art*, 31.

74. Ibid., 63.

75. Ibid., 67.

76. Ibid., 65.

77. Ibid. Emphasis in original.

78. Ibid., 68.

79. Nieland, "West's Deadpan: Affect, Slapstick, and Publicity in *Miss Lonelyhearts*," 58.

80. Ibid.

81. Higgins, *The Grid Book*, 9.

82. Nieland, "West's Deadpan," 68.

83. West, *Miss Lonelyhearts & The Day of the Locust*, 5.

84. Ibid., 26.

85. Ibid., 27.

86. Ibid., 22.

87. Greenberg, "Nathanael West and the Mystery of Feeling," 606.

88. Hobby and DeBoer, "Carnival Virtues: Sex, Sacrilege, and the Grotesque in Nathanael West's *Miss Lonelyhearts*," 149.

89. West, *Miss Lonelyhearts & The Day of the Locust*, 6.

90. West also describes it "like the blade of a hatchet" (ibid., 7).

91. Nieland, "West's Deadpan," 76.

92. West, *Miss Lonelyhearts & The Day of the Locust*, 15.

93. Nieland, "West's Deadpan," 76.

94. West, *Miss Lonelyhearts & The Day of the Locust*, 45.

95. Ibid., 9.

96. "Lonelyhearts can't laugh at the letters because he can neither fully distance himself from their writers ('I'm glad I don't suffer as you do') nor adequately sympathize with them ('I suffer like you')." Nieland, "West's Deadpan," 69.

97. O'Connor, "Some Aspects of the Grotesque in Southern Literature," 44. See Gooch, *Flannery: A Life of Flannery O'Connor*, 181, for her appreciation of West and Faulkner: "Flannery recommended Nathanael West's defiantly original novel *Miss Lonelyhearts*, as well as Faulkner's *As I Lay Dying*, its central image of a mother's coffin a fixation in the novel she was writing [to her friend Robert Fitzgerald]."

98. O'Connor, "Some Aspects of the Grotesque in Southern Literature," 44.

99. Ibid., 43.

100. Ibid., 44.

101. See Box 31, Folders 1–2, Flannery O'Connor papers, Stuart A. Rose Manuscript, Archives, and Rare Book Library, Emory University.

102. Moser, "Working Backward: A Reflection on the Linoleum Cuts of Flannery O'Connor," vii.

103. Zdebik, *Deleuze and the Diagram*, 66.

104. Ciuba, "From Face Value to the Value in Faces: 'Wise Blood' and the Limits of Literalism," 72.

105. Gerald, "The Habit of Art," 124.

106. Ciuba, "From Face Value to the Value in Faces," 72.

107. O'Connor, *Wise Blood*, 72, 85, 82.

108. Ibid., 99.

109. Ibid., 84.

110 Di Renzo, *American Gargoyles*, 26.

111. Ibid., 25.

112. O'Connor, *Wise Blood*, 94.

113. Donald E. Hardy explores this and other syntactical phenomena across O'Connor's fiction at length in his study *The Body in Flannery O'Connor's Fiction*, arguing that "it is possible to illuminate the struggle with the divisions of spirit and matter by a close examination of the interactions of grammatical voice and the body at both the macrolevel and the microlevel of the narrative." His focus is on "when parts of the body act on their own and when characters act on parts of their own bodies as described in very particular sentences. That is, the body parts occur as semantic actors or goals, respectively, normally grammatical subjects or objects." Hardy, *The Body in Flannery O'Connor's Fiction: Computational Technique and Linguistic Voice*, 2.

114. O'Connor, *Wise Blood*, 94.

115. Ibid., 77.

116. Ibid., 92.

117. Ibid., 184–185.

118. Ibid., 187.

119. Here, as with "the eyes" looking at the thing in the case, we see the phenomenon Hardy computationally shows to be pervasive across O'Connor's fiction: "that body parts do sometimes seem to have a will of their own." Hardy, *The Body in Flannery O'Connor's Fiction*, 3.

120 O'Connor, *Wise Blood*, 187.

121. Ibid., 188.

122. Ibid., 176.

123. Check out Jones, *Looney Tunes (Wile E. Coyote and the Road Runner): Fast and Furry-ous*. https://www.youtube.com/watch?v=4iWvedIhWjM

Chapter 2

1 W. J. T. Mitchell, *What Do Pictures Want?*, 11, 34. Mitchell cites these terms directly from Fanon ("To us, the man who adores the Negro is as 'sick' as the man who abominates him" [Fanon, *Black Skin, White Masks*, 8]) and then connects to biblical warnings against idolatry.

2. Ibid., 58, 72.

3. Ibid., 85.

4. Lee Clark Mitchell, "Face, Race, and Disfiguration in Stephen Crane's 'The Monster,'" 86.

5. W. J. T. Mitchell, *What Do Pictures Want?*, 72.

6. Ibid., 85.

7. Ibid., 93.

8. Sedgwick, *Touching Feeling: Affect, Pedagogy, Performativity*, 14–15.

9. Lee, *Overwhelmed: Literature, Aesthetics, and the Nineteenth-Century Information Revolution*, 10.

10. "The formalism of identity in the liberal nation produces hierarchies of abstraction called identities: meanwhile, they deliver the bribe of a free and complex mentality to the citizen, who can develop any consciousness she wants so long as she declines to interfere with the pleasure and order her readable body creates for everyone else." Berlant, *The Female Complaint*, 258.

11. Entin, *Sensational Modernism: Experimental Fiction and Photography in Thirties America*, 51.

12. Morrison, *Playing in the Dark: Whiteness and the Literary Imagination*, 5.

13. Ibid., 43.

14. Schuller, *The Biopolitics of Feeling: Race, Sex, and Science in the Nineteenth Century*, 2.

15. Entin, *Sensational Modernism*, 51.

16. Hartman, "Venus in Two Acts," 2.

17. McKittrick, "Mathematics Black Life," 17.

18. Morrison, *Playing in the Dark: Whiteness and the Literary Imagination*, 32.

19. Ibid., 6.

20. Ibid., 7.

21. Ibid., 52.

22. Ibid., 57.

23. Weinstein, "When Is Now? Poe's Aesthetics of Temporality," 90–91.

24. See Tynan, "J. N. Reynolds' Voyage of the Potomac: Another Source for *The Narrative of Arthur Gordon Pym*."

25. Dayan, "Amorous Bondage: Poe, Ladies, and Slaves," 112.

26. See, for example, Weinstein, "When Is Now?"

27. Morrison, *Playing in the Dark*, 53.

28. Elliott, "Other Times: Herman Melville, Lewis Henry Morgan, and Ethnographic Writing in the Antebellum United States," 486.

29. Sekula, "The Body and the Archive," 30.

30. Ibid., 17.

31. Ibid., 58.

32. Gardner, *Master Plots: Race and the Founding of an American Literature 1787–1845*, 144.

33. Elliott, "Other Times," 485.

34. Poe, *The Narrative of Arthur Gordon Pym of Nantucket*, 85.

35. Johannes Fabian argues that, within the discipline of ethnography there is "a persistent and systematic tendency to place the referent(s) of anthropology in a Time other than the present of the producer of anthropological discourse." Fabian, *Time and the Other: How Anthropology Makes Its Object*, 31.

36. Rutherford, *Silhouette: The Art of the Shadow*, 36.

37. Drucker, *Graphesis: Visual Forms of Knowledge Production*, 26.

38. Rutherford, *Silhouette*, 188.

39. Ibid., 36.

40. Lukasik, *Discerning Characters: The Culture of Appearance in Early America*, 35.

41. Cowan, "The Ambivalence of Ornament: Silhouette Advertisements in Print and Film in Early Twentieth-Century Germany," 793.

42. According to Shaw (*Portraits of a People: Picturing African Americans in the Nineteenth Century*, 50):

> This tool for image-making was closely related to the polygraph machine that was owned by Thomas Jefferson, which was designed to make two copies of the same document at once. The polygraph was intended for making multiple documents, and the physiognotrace for making multiple images. . . . As a mechanically mediated visual presentation the portrait profiles made by the physiognotrace promised the early nineteenth-century viewer a certain indexical primacy that other forms of image making could not. . . . viewed by many to be a pure act of mechanical mimesis an image practically unmediated by human hands. . . . However, after the machine blind-embossed a line on the paper, hand-cutting was a necessary part of the hollow-cut silhouette's creation.

43. Williams used the profits from his silhouette cutting within the museum to, in the words of Peale's son Rembrandt, "buy a two story brick house, and actually married my father's white cook, who during his bondage would not permit him to eat at the same table with her." Ibid., 46.

44. Sacco, "Racial Theory, Museum Practice: The Coloured World of Charles Willson Peale," 26.

45. Ibid., 28.

46. Douglas, *Purity and Danger: An Analysis of Concepts of Pollution and Taboo*, 163.

47. Bhabha, "The Other Question . . . Homi K Bhabha Reconsiders the Stereotype and Colonial Discourse," 18.

48. Ibid.

49. Ibid., 12.

50. Ngai, *Ugly Feelings*, 12.

51. Ibid., 32.

52. Schuller, *The Biopolitics of Feeling*, 13.

53. "Grampus" as Jared Gardner notes, means "the killer whale—a name signifying, like *The Penguin* [the ship that rescues Augustus and Pym at the beginning of the novel], the joining of blackness and whiteness in one body, but here an image not of peace and 'reflection' but of violence and destruction" (Gardner, *Master Plots*, 142).

54. Poe, *The Narrative of Arthur Gordon Pym of Nantucket*, 122.

55. Ibid., 125.

56. Ibid., 85.

57. W. J. T. Mitchell, *What Do Pictures Want?*, 59.

58. Bhabha, "Of Mimicry and Man: The Ambivalence of Colonial Discourse," 132–133.

59. See Sollors, *Neither White Nor Black Yet Both: Thematic Explorations of Interracial Literature*, 62:

> Whereas [Joseph] Virey went for the biological approach of skull-measuring and anatomical contrasting, it is not without interest for an understanding of the emergence of "race" out of the denial of the "interracial" and "biracial" realms that one of Nott's first attempts at making the move toward race as species appeared in the *American Journal of Medical Sciences* in 1843 under the title "The Mulatto a Hybrid—probable extermination of the two races if the Whites and Blacks are allowed to intermarry." Defining the "Mulatto" as a "hybrid," Nott explicitly claimed that this meant "the offspring of two distinct species—as the mule from the horse and the ass." And he invoked evidence from Edward Long to a faulty reading of American census data in order to make his case for the "unnatural" character of interracial sexual relations and the "degeneracy" of their offspring.

60. Ibid., 127–128:

> The word "Mulatto," of sixteenth-century Spanish origin, documented in English since 1595, and designating a child of a black and a white parent, was long considered etymologically derived from "mule"; yet it may also come from the Arabic word *muvallad* (meaning "Mestizo" or mixed). The zoological analogy with mules may thus not have been the word's original, or exclusive, etymological source, but the term "Mulatto" certainly did become intertwined with the animal that was a cross between two species; and numerous texts have explicated, or alluded to, the etymology. (internal citations omitted)

61. Nott, "The Mulatto a Hybrid—Probably Extermination of the Two Races If the Whites and Blacks Are Allowed to Intermarry," 30.

62. Gardner notes that Peters is "clearly marked (by the 'bowed' legs and the crown of his head) in terms of the stereotypical descriptions of African Americans found in writings by Poe and others of the period. . . . [H]is resemblance to the simian culprit of 'Murders in the Rue Morgue' is striking" (Gardner, *Master Plots*, 144).

63. Poe, *The Narrative of Arthur Gordon Pym of Nantucket*, 131.

64. Ibid., 133.

65. Ibid., 132.

66. Ibid., 132–133.

67. Mastroianni, "Hospitality and the Thresholds of the Human in Poe's *The Narrative of Arthur Gordon Pym*," 191.

68. Cassuto, *The Inhuman Race: The Racial Grotesque in American Literature and Culture*, 128.

69. Ibid.

70. "Hermaphrodite, n. and adj." entry in *OED Online*.

71. Poe, *The Narrative of Arthur Gordon Pym of Nantucket*, 132, 85.

72. Ngai, *Ugly Feelings*, 98–99.

73. Compare to W. J. T. Mitchell's take on how images come to be animated via the projection of the viewers' desires (*What Do Pictures Want?*, 295):

> Images come alive, as we have seen, in two basic forms that vacillate between figurative and literal senses of vitality or animation. That is, they come alive because viewers believe they are alive, as in the case of weeping Madonnas and mute idols that demand human sacrifice or moral reformation. Or they come alive because a clever artist/technician has engineered them to appear alive, as when the puppeteer/ventriloquist animates his puppet with motion and voice, or the master painter seems to capture the life of the model with the flick of a brush. Thus the notion of images as life-forms always equivocates between questions of belief and knowledge, fantasy and technology, the golem and the clone.

74. Gross, *Puppet: An Essay on Uncanny Life*, 125.

75. W. J. T. Mitchell, *What Do Pictures Want?*, 295–296.

76. Gardner, *Master Plots*, 145.

77. Johnson, *Pym: A Novel*, 25.

78. Morrison, *Playing in the Dark*, 5.

79. Ibid.

80. "It is as though the meandering death ship has drawn out and drawn away Pym's waywardness and masochism, enabling him to be reborn as a rational, temperate leader of men." Sanborn, "A Confused Beginning: The Narrative of Arthur Gordon Pym, of Nantucket," 168.

81. Ibid.

82. "What he sees shining in Augustus's eyes is something beyond all the visions of suffering he had earlier entertained; if his own eyes are anything like Augustus's, he has forgotten, or almost forgotten, his humanity and his race" (ibid., 167).

83. Ibid.,169.

84. Ibid., 169–170.

85. Poe, *The Narrative of Arthur Gordon Pym of Nantucket*, 146.

86. Tompkins, *Racial Indigestion: Eating Bodies in the 19th Century*, 94.

87. Sanborn, "A Confused Beginning," 168.

88. Donegan, *Seasons of Misery: Catastrophe and Colonial Settlement in Early America*, 104. Citing Girard, *Violence and the Sacred*, 174.

89. Poe, *The Narrative of Arthur Gordon Pym of Nantucket*, 193.

90. Ibid., 189, 197.

91. Ibid., 238:

> He still obstinately lay in the bottom of the boat; and, upon reiterating the questions as to the motive, made use only of idiotic gesticulations, such as raising with his forefinger the upper lip, and displaying the teeth which lay beneath it. These were black. We had never before seen the teeth of an inhabitant of Tsalal.

See also Weinstein, "When Is Now?" 102:

> In what is perhaps the shortest sentence of the entire story, Pym remarks upon Nu-Nu's teeth, "These were black." We are finally back to the simple past. There is no need for more length. Racial clarity has replaced temporal uncertainty, which means that the vicissitudes of "now" are anchored in a space, made coherent by racial categories, that is conclusive.

92. Poe, *The Narrative of Arthur Gordon Pym of Nantucket*, 204.

93. "The blacks fulfill all of the whites' expectations: displaying cartoon-like gestures of delight and superstition, eager to please and easy to master" (Gardner, *Master Plots*, 147).

94. Poe, *The Narrative of Arthur Gordon Pym of Nantucket*, 190.

95. Ibid., 47: ". . . at last an Englishman, who had shipped as a raw hand, came up, weeping piteously, and entreating the mate, in the most humble manner, to spare his life. The only reply was a blow on the forehead from an axe. The poor fellow fell to the deck without a groan, and the black cook lifted him up in his arms as he would a child, and tossed him deliberately into the sea."

96. Ibid.,191.

97. Ibid.

98. Ibid., 113: "As I viewed myself in a fragment of looking-glass which hung up in the cabin, and by the dim light of a kind of battle-lantern, I was so impressed with a sense of vague awe at my appearance, and at the recollection of the terrific reality which I was thus representing, that I was seized with a violent tremour, and could scarcely summon resolution to go on with my part."

99. Ibid., 200.

100. Ibid., 212.

101. Rutherford, *Silhouette*, 196.

102. Ahmed, *The Cultural Politics of Emotion*, 10.

103. Named after Dutch experimental psychologist Edgar Rubin, who introduced the optical illusion in his 1915 thesis *Synsoplevede Figurer* (Visually experienced figures). Pind, "Figure and Ground at 100," 90.

104. Notably, a French translation by Baudelaire and a sequel written by Jules Verne called *Le Sphynx des glaces* (1897) (translated version of the title: *An Antarctic Mystery*). Verne, *An Antarctic Mystery*.

105. James, *Henry James, Literary Criticism: French Writers, Other European Writers, the Prefaces to the New York Edition*, 1259. Emphasis in original.

106. Ibid.

107. Sanborn, "A Confused Beginning," 173.

108. Ibid., 174.

109. Ibid.

110. Ibid., 175.

111. Poe, *The Narrative of Arthur Gordon Pym of Nantucket*, 238–239.

112. Morrison, *Playing in the Dark*, 33.

113. See Bhabha, "The Other Question," 27:

> The stereotype is not a simplification because it is a false representation of a given reality. It is a simplification because it is an arrested, fixated form of representation that, in denying the play of difference (that the negation through the Other permits), constitutes a problem for the *representation* of the subject in significations of psychic and social relations.

114. Morrison, *Playing in the Dark*, 46.

115 W. J. T. Mitchell, *What Do Pictures Want?*, 93.

116. Morrison, *Playing in the Dark*, 69.

117. Quoted in Saltz, "Kara Walker: Ill-Will and Desire," 82.

118. W. J. T. Mitchell speculates that "Turner's poem, 'The Origin of Vermilion, or the Loves of Painting and Music,' rewrites the ancient legend that the first drawing was a tracing of the silhouette of the beloved, using vermilion, the red ochre or cinnabar that 'chance' put in the artist's hand" (*What Do Pictures Want?*, 58).

119. Ibid., 66.

120. Rutherford, *Silhouette*, 36.

121. Shaw, *Seeing the Unspeakable: The Art of Kara Walker*, 20–21.

122. Raengo, *On the Sleeve of the Visual: Race as Face Value*, 148. Raengo's quotes in the epigraph are from pp. 151 and 148.

123. "It is the violent collision of the silhouettes' pristine and abstract forms with the carnality evoked by these bodies' behaviors and their compulsive penetrations that manifests the double legacy of Walker's figures—the use of the silhouette within the genre of portraiture and its use by institutions and disciplines for social control" (ibid., 147).

124. Sekula, "The Body and the Archive," 10.

125. As Darby English puts it, "The leveling action of the silhouette freezes all of her figures not in racial blackness but in a detour through the various forms of epidermalization (racializing or not) that abstract identities from bodies and individuals, as well as individuals from selves (the former being the social embodiment of the latter)." English, *How to See a Work of Art in Total Darkness*, 85.

126. Raengo, *On the Sleeve of the Visual*, 132.

127. Sedgwick, *Touching Feeling*, 8.

128. "Moving Pictures: Highlights—Kara Walker."

129. English, *How to See a Work of Art in Total Darkness*, 129.

130. Ibid., 95.

131. W. J. T. Mitchell, *Seeing Through Race*, 59.

132. Art21, Interview with Kara Walker.

133. Fried, *Realism, Writing, Disfiguration: On Thomas Eakins and Stephen Crane*, 73.

134. Ibid., 72.

135. Ibid., 73. Emphasis in original.

136. Glissant, *Poetics of Relation*, 189.

137. Ibid., 191.

138. Yao, *Disaffected: The Cultural Politics of Unfeeling in Nineteenth-Century America*, 22.

139. Glissant, *Poetics of Relation*, 193.

140. Sharpe, *In the Wake: On Blackness and Being*, 117. Internal citation omitted.

141. Harper, *Abstractionist Aesthetics: Artistic Form and Social Critique in African American Culture*, 33–34.

142. D. H. Lawrence snarkily described it as "Benjamin's barbed wire fence. He made himself a list of virtues, which he trotted inside like a grey nag in a paddock" (Lawrence, *Studies in Classic American Literature*, 16).

143. David Joselit notes that "One of the strongest accusations launched against Walker was that her work pandered to the largely white establishment of art critics, curators and collectors serving up racist messages in the guise of avant-garde experimentation." Joselit, "Notes on Surface: Toward a Genealogy of Flatness," 29.

144. Hartman, "Venus in Two Acts," 2.

145. Harper, *Abstractionist Aesthetics*, 42. Emphasis in original.

146. Art21, Interview with Kara Walker.

147 English, *How to See a Work of Art in Total Darkness*, 128.

148. Ibid.

149. Quoted in Shaw, *Seeing the Unspeakable*, 53.

150. See Tompkins, *Racial Indigestion*, 5: "[I]n the map of the nervous system that was promulgated by Sylvester Graham and William Alcott . . . and then reinterpreted by various of their cultural inheritors, including Louisa May Alcott . . . the mouth and the genitals function as coeval sites of erotic intensity in adults as well as in children. In Graham's writing both can be overstimulated, and indeed sensual indulgence at one of those sites inevitably drives the appetitive needs of the other."

151. Ibid.

152. English, *How to See a Work of Art in Total Darkness*, 86:

> Thus, a central strand of Walker's project involves the suggestion of an unfettered pursuit of a pleasure which, once stripped of the pretense of total success or mastery (as is possible only in fantasy) and proliferated, would remake the map of race relations that invocations of cultural landscapes compulsively posit as fixed. More important than the fact of pleasure, here, is that Walker figures its pursuit as integral to a history of exploitation.

153. Quoted in Shaw, *Seeing the Unspeakable*, 23.

154. Sedgwick, *Touching Feeling*, 8.

155. Ibid.

156. Raengo, *On the Sleeve of the Visual*, 147.

157. Levinas, *Difficult Freedom: Essays on Judaism*, 8.

158. Newton, *Narrative Ethics*, 193.

159. "For Walker the silhouette is also about 'indirection,' an 'avoidance of the subject'" (Sharpe, *Monstrous Intimacies: Making Post-Slavery Subjects*, 172).

160. Newton, *Narrative Ethics*, 192.

161. Berlant, "Poor Eliza," 655.

162. Ibid.

163. Johnson, *Pym: A Novel*, 7.

164. Ibid., 322.

165. Ibid., 16.

166. Ibid., 25.

167. Ibid., 52.

168. Ibid., 57.

169. Wilks, "'Black Matters': Race and Literary History in Mat Johnson's *Pym*," 6.

170. Johnson, *Pym*, 124.

171. Wilks, "'Black Matters,'" 12.

172. Johnson, *Pym*, 124.

173. Ibid., 125.

174. Ibid., 163–164.

175. Ibid., 178.

176. Ibid.

177. See Wilks, "Black Matters," 10: "As Chris assembles a crew for the appropriately named Creole Mining Company, so Johnson collects a range of archetypes through which to parse contemporary African American identity. . . . black nationalist . . . gay urbanites . . . upwardly mobile professionals."

178. Johnson, *Pym*, 192–193.

179. Ibid., 193.

180. Subtitled "*an Homage to the unpaid and overworked Artisans who have refined our Sweet tastes from the cane fields to the Kitchens of the New World on the Occasion*

of the demolition of the Domino Sugar Refining Plant," the installation, held in the old Domino Sugar Factory in Brooklyn prior to its demolition, featured a sphinx with the head of a caricatured "mammy" figure. The sphinx was approximately 75 feet long and 35 feet tall, constructed from 330 polystyrene blocks, and it was coated with 80 tons of sugar. Walker, *A Subtlety, or the Marvelous Sugar Baby.*

181. Chris also has an uncomfortable habit of objectifying and painting as consumable his own ex-wife, with a particular fixation on the darkness of her skin offset by white articles of clothing or accessories:

> She was standing in the lobby, the woman I used to call the Ashanti Doll, her skin a wealth of rich melanin above the white vinyl of her snowsuit. (Johnson, *Pym*, 83–84)

> [T]he darkness of her skin banished the thought of wrinkles, though. It still shone like the skin of an orca. Accented now by diamonds that covered most of her earlobes. (Ibid., 80)

182. Ibid., 193.

183. Christensen, "Little Debbie, or the Logic of Late Capitalism: Consumerism, Whiteness, and Addiction in Mat Johnson's *Pym*," 173.

184. Ibid., 175.

185. Johnson, *Pym*, 234.

186. Ibid., 184.

187. Christensen, "Little Debbie, or the Logic of Late Capitalism," 167.

188. Poe, *The Narrative of Arthur Gordon Pym of Nantucket*, 73:

> The white slip of paper could barely be discerned, and not even that when I looked at it directly; by turning the exterior portions of the retina toward it—that is to say, by surveying it slightly askance, I found that it became in some measure perceptible. . . . At last an idea occurred to me which seemed rational . . . I placed the slip of paper on the back of a book, and, collecting the fragments of the phosphorus matches which I had brought from the barrel, laid them together upon the paper. I then, with the palm of my hand, rubbed the whole over quickly, yet steadily. A clear light diffused itself immediately throughout the whole surface.

189. Ibid., 76.

190. Sekula, "The Body and the Archive," 58.

191. Sharpe, *In the Wake*, 76.

192. Ibid., 77, 80.

193 Sharpe, *In the Wake*, 80.

194. Johnson, *Pym*, 15.

195. Christensen, "Little Debbie, or the Logic of Late Capitalism," 191.

196. Johnson, *Pym*, 241.

197. Wilks, "'Black Matters,'" 13.

198. Johnson, *Pym*, 184.

199. Ibid., 248.

200. Sandler, "'Negras Aguas': The Poe Tradition and the Limits of American Africanism," 426.

201. Morrison, *Playing in the Dark*, 52.

Chapter 3

1. Homes, "A Real Doll," 169. Homes's chapter opening epigraph is on pp. 168–169.

2. Nina Freeman turns the question of how to make dolls have sex with each other into a video game. According to the game's website:

> "How do you Do It?'" puts players in the role of an 11-year-old girl whose mother has just stepped out for an errand. The girl immediately grabs her dolls and furtively attempts to figure out how sex works using these plastic surrogates. Using WASD keys to move your arms and J or K to rotate the dolls, players clack the pixelated plastic toys together attempting to beat the clock and make their crotches collide before the mother comes back from the store. At the end of the game, your "score" is something like this: "You might have done sex 97 times . . . ? Eep! Mom saw!"

3. Homes, "A Real Doll," 158–159.

4. Ibid., 166.

5. Ibid., 167–168:

> Between Barbie's legs Jennifer had drawn pubic hair in reverse. She'd drawn it upside down so it looked like a fountain spewing up and out in great wide arcs. I spit directly onto Barbie and with my thumb and first finger rubbed the ink lines, erasing them. Barbie moaned.
>
> "Why do you let her do this to you?"
>
> "Jennifer owns me," Barbie moaned.
>
> Jennifer owns me, she said, so easily and with pleasure. I was totally jealous. Jennifer owned Barbie and it made me crazy. Obviously it was one of those relationships that could only exist between women. Jennifer could own her because it didn't matter that Jennifer owned her. Jennifer didn't want Barbie, she had her.

6. See Bloch, *The Sexual Life of Our Time in Its Relations to Modern Civilization*. See also the entry "Pygmalionism, n." in *OED Online*.

7. No surviving examples of the original *dames de voyage* survive, but their existence is recounted in numerous stories. For example: "There is a story that the French philosopher Rene Descartes (1596–1650) carried with him on a mid–seventeenth century sea journey to Sweden a somewhat lifelike doll made of leather and metal which he referred to as his daughter. He even named her 'Francine'" (Ferguson, *The Sex Doll: A History*, 16).

8. Bloch, *The Sexual Life of Our Time*, 648–649.

9. Daša Drndić's recent novel *Trieste* includes a reverie on the history of the Nazi sex doll, in which she imagines one of its creators insisting emphatically (91):

> When a soldier makes love to Borghild (is the doll called Borghild because she is female cyborg Hilda?), when a soldier copulates with Borghild, this has nothing to do with love! Borghild will have a boyish haircut —she is part and parcel of our armed forces. She is a field whore, not the Mother of our Homeland.

10. Ferguson, *The Sex Doll: A History*, 24–25: ". . . in order to keep the troops away from potentially disease-riddled whores, the dolls would have to have realistic flesh, malleable limbs, and an enticingly realistic sex organ. It was also important that the doll reflect the Nordic/Aryan beauty ideal, with pale skin, blonde hair and blue eyes."

11. Ibid., 30.

12. Ibid., 5.

13. See Bernstein, *Racial Innocence*, 71:

> To say that the doll scripted behavior is to describe a set of prompts that the plaything issued. I understand a script as theater directors do: a script is a dynamic substance that deeply influences but does not entirely determine live performances, which vary according to agential individuals' visions, impulses, resistances, revisions, and management of unexpected disruptions. . . . [A] "scriptive thing," [is] an item of material culture that prompts meaningful bodily behaviors. The set of prompts that a thing issues is not the same as a performance because individuals commonly resist, revise, or ignore instructions.

14. Ferguson, *The Sex Doll*, 5.

15 See Ngai's *Our Aesthetic Categories: Zany, Cute, Interesting*, 91: "Roboticist Masohiro Mori's 'uncanny-valley' theory . . . argues that as stylistically simplified robots begin to look and behave more like actual humans, our affection toward them also grows up to a certain point, after which the resemblance produces a feeling of aversion."

16. Connor, "Guys and Dolls," 25. Connor's chapter opening epigraph is on p. 140.

17. Smith, *The Erotic Doll: A Modern Fetish*, 25.

18. Ngai, *Our Aesthetic Categories*, 64.

19. Ibid.

20. Ibid., 91.

21. Ibid., 65.

22 Williams, *Hard Core: Power, Pleasure, and the "Frenzy of the Visible,"* 3; Williams later quotes directly from Foucault, *The History of Sexuality*, 77:

> [F]or many years, we have all been living in the realm of Prince Mangogul: under the spell of an immense curiosity about sex, bent on questioning

it, with an insatiable desire to hear it speak and be spoken about, quick to invent all sorts of magical rings that might force it to abandon its discretion.

23. Hester, *Beyond Explicit: Pornography and the Displacement of Sex*, 184.

24. Ibid., 14.

25. Ibid., 188.

26. Ibid., 13: "Although there are various discourses surrounding photorealism that may effect the reception of specific pornographic artifacts, I can see no reason why the written word should be excluded from discussions of adult entertainment or the pornographic."

27. Williams, "Pornography, Porno, Porn: Thoughts on a Weedy Field," 36.

28. Hester, *Beyond Explicit*, 185. Internal citations omitted.

29. Nabokov, *Lolita*, 9.

30. Evocatively, but also somewhat extraneously, a "doll's head" is also a technical term for "a top-extension fitting into a mortice in the top of the standing-breech" of a rifle. "Doll, n." entry in *OED Online*.

31. Smith, *The Erotic Doll*, 26.

32. Translated in Monnet, "Anatomy of Permutational Desire: Perversion in Hans Bellmer and Oshii Mamoru," 290.

33. Nabokov, *Lolita*, 109.

34. Brinkema, "Violence and the Diagram; Or, 'The Human Centipede,'" 82.

35. Ibid., 87.

36. "Articulate, adj. and n." entry in *OED Online*.

37. Johnson, *Persons and Things*, 91.

38. Ibid. As James Tweedie asserts in "Lolita's Loose Ends: Nabokov and the Boundless Novel," 164:

> Humbert's solipsism and Lolita's ultimate absence put the lie to his claim that "this book is about Lolita"; or more accurately, his constant invocation of the name "Lolita," from his narrative's famous opening lines, belie the fact that the girl with a life of her own—the Dolores and Dolly Haze, and the Mrs. Richard F. Schiller who crop up in the speech of others—is only a bit player in his elaborate construction.

39. Ibid., 165.

40. Williams, *Hard Core*, 3.

41. Nabokov, *Lolita*, 134.

42. Williams, *Hard Core*, x.

43. Ibid., 32.

44. Ibid., 50.

45. Naiman, *Nabokov, Perversely*, 148: "Were Lolita to portray its heroine enjoying her sexual encounters with Humbert, the novel would risk toppling into the genre of at least soft-core pornography."

46. Williams, *Hard Core*, 49.

47. Nabokov, *Lolita*, 39.

48. Foucault, *Discipline and Punish: The Birth of the Prison*, 205.

49. Brinkema, "Violence and the Diagram," 82.

50. Nabokov, *Lolita*, 39.

51. Ibid., 107.

52. Ibid., 39.

53. Ibid., 62.

54. Ibid., 283.

55. Brinkema, "Violence and the Diagram," 87.

56. Ibid., 86.

57. Williams, *Hard Core*, 50.

58 Nabokov, *Lolita*, 32.

59. As "John Ray, Jr., Ph.D." writes in the Foreword, "While 'Haze' only rhymes with the heroine's real surname, her first name is too closely interwound with the inmost fiber of the book to allow one to alter it; nor (as the reader will perceive for himself) is there any practical necessity to do so" (Nabokov, *Lolita*, 4).

60. Tweedie, "Lolita's Loose Ends," 169.

61. Nabokov, *Lolita*, 52–53.

62. The only instance of the word "ejaculate" in the novel is in association, in fact, with another written name. As Humbert is tracking obscure (perhaps imaginary) traces of Quilty through motel ledgers, he exclaims at "What a shiver of triumph and loathing shook my frail frame when, among the plain innocent names in the hotel recorder, his fiendish conundrum would ejaculate in my face!" (ibid., 250).

63. Ibid., 24.

64. Ibid., 16–17:

> In fact, I would have the reader see "nine" and "fourteen" as the boundaries—the mirrory beaches and rosy rocks—of an enchanted island haunted by those nymphets of mine and surrounded by a vast, misty sea. Between those age limits, are all girl-children nymphets? Of course not. Otherwise, we who are in the know, we lone voyagers, we nympholepts, would have long gone insane. Neither are good looks any criterion; and vulgarity, or at least what a given community terms so, does not necessarily impair certain mysterious characteristics, the fey grace, the elusive, shifty, soul-shattering, insidious charm that separates the nymphet from such coevals of hers as are incomparably more dependent on the spatial world of synchronous phenomena than on that intangible island of entranced time where Lolita plays with her likes.

65. Ibid., 45–46.

66. Connor, "Guys and Dolls," 140.

67. Nabokov, *Lolita*, 124.

68. Ibid., 165.

69. Smith, *The Erotic Doll*, 74–75.

70. Ibid., 75.

71. Messbarger, "The Re-Birth of Venus in Florence's Royal Museum of Physics and Natural History," 1: "For a number of years . . . the most powerful magnet at the heart of the collection became the newly exhibited Anatomical Venus, capable of disassembly and recomposition."

72. Williams, *Hard Core*, 34. She goes on to directly quote Foucault, *The History of Sexuality*, 63:

> It is no longer a question of saying what was done—the sexual act—and how it was done; but of reconstructing, in and around the act, the thoughts that recapitulated it, the obsessions that accompanied it, the images, desires, modulations, and quality of the pleasure that animated it. For the first time. no doubt, a society has taken upon itself to solicit and hear the imparting of individual pleasures.

73. Messbarger, "The Re-Birth of Venus," 3: "The Florentine Venus, whose intricate anatomical systems and parts were designed for orderly, hands-on disassembly before a general public, epitomizes the ideal practical means and new accessibility to scientific knowledge of the late-eighteenth-century museum."

74. "Matrix, n." entry in *OED Online*.

75. Rosalind Krauss, herself well-known for theorizing the proliferation of grids in post-45 visual art, explicates Lyotard's slightly related use of "matrix," in his book *Discourse, Figure*, like this:

> [H]e argued that below the "seen" order of the image (that is, the object bounded by its contour) and below the visible but "unseen" order of the gestalt, which we could call the formal conditions of possibility of visualizing the object, there lies the order of the "invisible," to which Lyotard gives the name matrix. (Krauss, "The Im/Pulse to See," 64)

She continues her explication of Lyotard's "matrix":

> This form, which is that of on/off on/off on/off, is the alternating charge and discharge of pleasure, the oscillating presence and absence of contact, the rhythm "in whose regularity the subject's unconscious is, so to speak, 'caught,' the formal matrix of both dreams and symptoms." It is onto this form that the matrix figure's fantasized gesture of a spanking that is also a caress can be mapped; for it is this form that can represent the rhythmic oppositions between contact and rupture. But Lyotard cautions that, unlike a pulse which is understood in terms of a law of repetition, a principle of recurrence guaranteeing as it were that an "on" will always follow an "off," this pulse involves the constant threat of interruption. The anxiety that is

part of the affect of "A Child Is Being Beaten," combining with its erotic pleasure, arises precisely from the force of rupture that is recurrent in the rhythm of the figure, a rupture which is not experienced as the onset of yet another contact, but as an absolute break, that discontinuity without end that is death. Thus it is the death drive, operating below the pleasure principle, that transcodes this rhythm—as it beats with the alternation between pleasure and extinction—into a compulsion to repeat. The matrix is, then, the form that figures recurrence. (Ibid., 66–67)

76. Nabokov, *Lolita*, 43:

Gently I pressed my quivering sting along her rolling salty eyeball. "Goody-goody," she said nictating. "It is gone" "Now the other?" "You dope," she began, "there is noth—" but here she noticed the pucker of my approaching lips. "Okay," she said co-operatively, and bending toward her warm upturned russet face somber Humbert pressed his mouth to her fluttering eyelid. She laughed, and brushed past me out of the room. My heart seemed everywhere at once. Never in my life—not even when fondling my child-love in France—never—

77. Ibid., 156.
78. Baudrillard, "The Ecstasy of Communication," 130.
79. Nabokov, *Lolita*, 165.
80. Naiman, *Nabokov, Perversely*, 148.
81. Nabokov, *Lolita*, 14.
82. "Wherever there is repetition or complete similarity, we always suspect some mechanism at work behind the living." Bergson, *Laughter: An Essay on the Meaning of the Comic*, 34.
83. Johnson, *Persons and Things*, 58.
84. Nabokov, *Lolita*, 16: "their true nature which is not human, but nymphic (that is, demoniac)."
85. Ibid., 300.
86. Humbert's obsession with the downiness of Lolita's limbs is reminiscent, too, of Oskar Kokoschka's famously furry life-size doll modeled off of his erstwhile lover, Alma Mahler, who had an abortion, left him, and married Walter Gropius (see Figures 3.1 and 3.2). After receiving the finished doll, whose specifications he had meticulously, obsessively sent and resent to dressmaker Hermione Moos, Kokoschka wrote her, appalled, that "The outer shell is a polar-bear pelt, suitable for a shaggy imitation bedside rug rather than the soft and pliable skin of a woman" (Smith, *The Erotic Doll*, 127).
87. Nabokov, *Lolita*, 5.
88. Ibid., 102:

Suavely saying he had twins in my stepdaughter's class, my grotesque visitor unrolled a large diagram he had made of the accident. It was, as my stepdaughter would have put it, "a beaut," with all kinds of impressive arrows and dotted lines in varicolored inks. Mrs. H. H.'s trajectory was illustrated at several points by a series of those little outline figures—doll-like wee career girl or WAC—used in statistics as visual aids. Very clearly and conclusively, this route came into contact with a boldly traced sinuous line representing two consecutive swerves—one which the Beale car made to avoid the Junk dog (dog not shown), and the second, a kind of exaggerated continuation of the first, meant to avert the tragedy. A very black cross indicated the spot where the trim little outline figure had at last come to rest on the sidewalk. I looked for some similar mark to denote the place on the embankment where my visitor's huge wax father had reclined, but there was none. That gentleman, however, had signed the document as a witness underneath the name of Leslie Tomson, Miss Opposite and a few other people.

89. Ibid., 97–98.

90. Ibid., 226.

91. Ibid., 102.

92. Ibid., 108.

93. Ibid., 148.

94. Ibid., 193.

95. Ngai, *Our Aesthetic Categories*, 91:

It is worth noting here that while the cutest toys have faces and often overly large eyes perversely literalizing the gaze . . . associate[d] with the aura of autonomous art, other facial features—mouths in particular—tend to be simplified to the point of being barely there. Sanrio's Hello Kitty, for example, has no mouth at all: Thus while de Man equates the endowing of speech with "giving face," "giving face" in cuteness seems to amount to denying speech.

96. Nabokov, *Lolita*, 284.

97. Ibid.

98. Ibid., 39.

99. Ibid., 285.

100. Connor, "Guys and Dolls," 134.

101. Brinkema, "Violence and the Diagram," 89.

102. Ibid.

103. Sedgwick, *Touching Feeling: Affect, Pedagogy, Performativity*, 37. Emphasis in original.

104. Ibid., 38. Emphasis in original.

105. Nabokov, *Lolita*, 299.

106. Connor, "Guys and Dolls," 137.

107. Nabokov, *Lolita*, 283.

108. Video available on Narcissister's website: http://www.narcissister.com/#/upside-down/

109. As Ariel Osterweis explains ("Public Pubic: Narcissister's Performance of Race, Disavowal, and Aspiration," 102): "A merkin is a vagina wig—itself a kind of mask. Merkins emerged as a way for prostitutes and others to mask a pubic area affected by the hairlessness of venereal disease. Merkins have also been historically fetishized in pornography and burlesque performance, two of the various genres Narcissister straddles."

The fact that she begins the performance "naked," clothed only in artificial representations of hair, evokes Walter Benjamin's assertion about hair's status as frontier in fetishism:

> In fetishism, sex does away with the boundaries separating the organic world from the inorganic. Clothing and jewelry are its allies. It is as much at home with what is dead as it is with living flesh. The latter, moreover, shows it the way to establish itself in the former. Hair is a frontier region lying between the two kingdoms of sexus. (Benjamin, *The Arcades Project*, 42)

110. Narcissister, "Narcissister is You."

111 McCloud, *Understanding Comics: The Invisible Art*, 42.

112 Harper, *Abstractionist Aesthetics*, 62.

113. McMillan, *Embodied Avatars: Genealogies of Black Feminist Art and Performance*, 220.

114. According to Ferguson (*The Sex Doll*, 28): "[L]egend has it that she was initially offered for sale to gentlemen who frequented the bars and tobacco shops of Hamburg's Reiperbahn, a notorious German red light district. . . . While the Lilli doll was not a penetration toy, she was created as a type of pornographic caricature."

115. Johnson, *Persons and Things*, 165.

116. For more on the fraught history of attempts to create racially diverse Barbies, see Ducille, "Black Barbie and the Deep Play of Difference":

> Made from essentially the same mold as what Mattel considers its signature doll—the traditional, blonde, blue-eyed Barbie—tawny-tinted ethnic reproductions are both signs and symptoms of an easy pluralism that simply melts down and adds on a reconstituted other without transforming the established social order without changing the mold. (338)

117. Bernstein, *Racial Innocence*, 20.

118. Ngai, *Our Aesthetic Categories*, 72. This inextricability of cuteness and vulgarity is a trait of Humbert's Lolita:

> What drives me insane is the twofold nature of this nymphet—of every nymphet, perhaps; this mixture in my Lolita of tender dreamy childishness and a kind of eerie vulgarity, stemming from the snub-nosed cuteness of

> ads and magazine pictures, from the blurry pinkness of adolescent maidser-
> vants in the Old Country (smelling of crushed daisies and sweat); and from
> very young harlots disguised as children in provincial brothels. (44–45)

119. Ngai, *Our Aesthetic Categories*, 60. See Merish, "Cuteness and Commodity
Aesthetics: Shirley Temple and Tom Thumb."

120. Ngai, *Our Aesthetic Categories*, 263–264:

> [T]he cute comic American child seems to have been consistently racial-
> ized. Indeed, cuteness arguably evolved in close association with minstrelsy
> and other aesthetic practices explicitly negotiating the experience of race
> as indelibly shaped by American slavery, a system sustained precisely by
> the ideological conflation of kinship and ownership that the cute similarly
> activates. Cuteness is thus in many ways, as Merish suggests, a distinctively
> American phenomenon.

121. Sánchez-Eppler, *Touching Liberty: Abolition, Feminism, and the Politics of the
Body*, 133.

122. Bernstein, *Racial Innocence*, 20.

123. Ibid., 81.

124. Ibid., 20.

125. Ibid., 81.

126. Schopenhauer, *The World as Will and Idea*; Bergson, *Laughter*, 37.

127. Osterweis, "Public Pubic," 109.

128. Ibid., 107.

129. See, for instance, Stratton, *The Desirable Body: Cultural Fetishism and the
Erotics of Consumption*.

130. Benjamin, *The Arcades Project*, 8: "Fashion stands in opposition to the organic.
It couples the living body to the inorganic world. To the living, it defends the rights of
the corpse. The fetishism that succumbs to the sex appeal of the inorganic is its vital
nerve. The cult of the commodity presses such fetishism into its service."

131. Worringer, *Abstraction and Empathy: A Contribution to the Psychology of
Style*, 4.

132. Ibid., 5.

133. Ross, *Oreo*, 5, 4.

134. Ibid., 7.

135. Ibid., 22.

136 Ibid.

137. Ibid.

138. Mullen, "'Apple Pie with Oreo Crust': Fran Ross's Recipe for an Idiosyncratic
American Novel," 118.

139. Ross, *Oreo*, 39:

> People had been calling the child various things as she toddled down the
> street after Louise, cursing them under her breath. They called her Brown

Sugar and Chocolate Drop and Honeybun. But when they looked at Christine's rich brown color and her wide smile full of sugar-white baby teeth, they said to themselves, "Why, that child does put me in mind of an Oreo cookie—side view." And that is how Oreo got her name. Nobody knew that Louise was saying "Oriole." When, through a fluke, Louise found out what everyone thought she was saying, it was all right with her. "I never did like flyin' birds, jus' eatin' ones," she said. "But I jus' loves dem Oreos." And this time she meant what everyone else meant.

140. Cook and Tatum, *African American Writers and Classical Tradition*, 296.

141. Schopenhauer, *The World as Will and Idea*, Book I, sec. 13.

142. Carpio, *Laughing Fit to Kill: Black Humor in the Fictions of Slavery*, 7.

143 Ross, *Oreo*, 45. As Cook and Tatum comment (*African American Writers and Classical Tradition*, 293): "Readers of Oreo need to like dictionaries."

144. Ross, *Oreo*, 45–46.

145. Ibid., 46.

146. Cook and Tatum, *African American Writers and Classical Tradition*, 295.

147. Sontag, "The Pornographic Imagination," 208.

148. Limon, *Stand-up Comedy in Theory, or, Abjection in America*, 9.

149. According to an interview with her lover Ann Grifalconi, Ross not only worked in the 1960s as a ghostwriter for an older male Jewish comic, but also aspired to be a stand-up comedian herself. She was so good at ventriloquizing a particularly Yiddish style of humor, at puppeteering the sort of figure who has been the American default in the realm of stand-up, that the comedian accosted her on the street years later and bemoaned, "Why aren't you writing for me anymore?" She was a stand-up Cyrano (though offstage, she got the girl). For much more on Ross's biography and her involvement with feminist organizing, see Saul, "The Great Deflector."

150. Linda Williams quotes Stephen Ziplow's *The Film Maker's Guide to Pornography* as the epigraph to her chapter on "Fetishism and Hard Core: Marx, Freud, and the 'Money Shot'" in *Hard Core*:

> There are those who believe that the come shot, or, as some refer to it, "the money shot," is the most important element in the movie and that everything else (if necessary) should be sacrificed at its expense. Of course, this depends on the outlook of the producer, but one thing is for sure: if you don't have the come shots, you don't have a porno picture. Plan on at least ten separate come shots.

151. Limon, *Stand-up Comedy in Theory*, 6.

152. Limon glosses Kristeva's theory of abjection as "a psychic worrying of those aspects of oneself that one cannot be rid of, that seem, but are not quite, alienable—for example, blood, urine, feces, nails, and the corpse . . . what cannot be subject or object to you" (ibid., 4).

153. Limon, *Stand-up Comedy in Theory, or, Abjection in America*, 4.

154 Ibid., 31.

155. Ibid., 6.

156. Ibid.

157. Bergson, *Laughter*, 77. Emphasis in original.

158. Ibid., 130.

159. Ibid., 69.

160. Cook and Tatum, *African American Writers and Classical Tradition*, 303.

161. Ross, *Oreo*, 56.

162. Ibid., 57.

163. Ibid., 58–59.

164. Hume references Barthes and Gardner in her discussion of *Oreo* ("Narrative Speed in Contemporary Fiction," 111):

> One way for a writer to achieve speed, therefore, is to cut out the Barthesian effects of the real—the narrative material a traditional reader expects to provide what John Gardner's Grendel calls "a gluey whine of connectedness." When the details that stabilize fictional "reality" are absent, those trained in conventional literature feel that absence as an artifact of speeding along too fast. Ross ostentatiously calls attention to cutting such detail. (internal citations omitted)

165. Zdebik, *Deleuze and the Diagram: Aesthetic Threads in Visual Organization*, 1.

166. Sedgwick, "Jane Austen and the Masturbating Girl," 819, 821.

167. Ross, *Oreo*, 59.

168. Ibid., 59–60.

169. Ibid., 60.

170. Bergson, *Laughter*, 37.

171. Ibid., 10.

172. Carpio, "'Am I Dead?': Slapstick Antics and Dark Humor in Contemporary Immigrant Fiction," 345. As Carpio describes it:

> Falls and blows are at the core of what makes physical comedy slapstick, which is generally based on absurd and silly circumstances that nonetheless include extreme forms of violence against the body. (Slapstick derives its name from the two thin slats of wood used by actors of commedia dell'arte in sixteenth-century Italy to slap one another for comedic effect.)

173 Ross, *Oreo*, 60–61.

174. Crafton, "Pie and Chase: Gag, Spectacle and Narrative in Slapstick Comedy," 356.

175. Ibid.

176. See, for instance. Desens, *The Bed-Trick in English Renaissance Drama: Explorations in Gender, Sexuality, and Power*.

177. Crafton, "Pie and Chase," 355.

178. Ross, *Oreo*, 60–61.

179. Leverette, "Traveling Identities: Mixed Race Quests and Fran Ross's 'Oreo,'" 86.

180. Ross, *Oreo*, 146.

181. Ibid., 156–157.

182. Mary Ann Doane argues that "There is always a certain excessiveness, a difficulty associated with women who appropriate the gaze, who insist upon looking." Doane, "Film and the Masquerade: Theorizing the Female Spectator," 187.

183. Ross, *Oreo*, 158.

184. Ibid., 160.

185. Ibid.

186. Hume, "Narrative Speed in Contemporary Fiction," 111.

187. Ross, *Oreo*, 160–161.

188. Limon, *Stand-up Comedy in Theory*, 5.

189. Johnson, *Persons and Things*, 75.

190. Sharon Marcus, a few decades after *Oreo*, famously defines rape via the notion of scripts, arguing that understanding it this way rather than as a presupposed given for women opens up strategies for prevention ("Fighting Bodies, Fighting Words: A Theory and Politics of Rape Prevention," 392):

> By defining rape as a scripted performance, we enable a gap between script and actress which can allow us to rewrite the script, perhaps by refusing to take it seriously and treating it as a farce, perhaps by resisting the physical passivity which it directs us to adopt.

191. Senna, "Foreword," xv–xvi.

192. Spillers, "Mama's Baby, Papa's Maybe: An American Grammar Book," 67.

193. Weheliye, *Habeas Viscus: Racializing Assemblages, Biopolitics, and Black Feminist Theories of the Human*, 90.

194. Brooks, *Bodies in Dissent: Spectacular Performances of Race and Freedom, 1850–1910*, 5.

195. Kim Lee, "Staying In: Mitski, Ocean Vuong, and Asian American Asociality," 29.

196. Crafton, "Pie and Chase," 363.

197. Ibid., 359.

198. Ngai, *Our Aesthetic Categories*, 9.

199. Williams, "Film Bodies: Gender, Genre, and Excess," 4.

200. Ngai, *Our Aesthetic Categories*, 8.

201. This slapstick pornographic frenzy of *Oreo*'s stylistic and formal excess perhaps does not preclude it from still being arousing, a possibility given added credence by the eagerness of our Amazon reviewer to point out, pooh-pooh, and summarily distance his NPR-listening self from the narratively extraneous "chapter of explicit pornography."

202. Crafton, "Pie and Chase," 356.

203. Ross, *Oreo*, 146.

204. Cook and Tatum, *African American Writers and Classical Tradition*, 302.

205. Carpio, *Laughing Fit to Kill*, 229.

206. Rogin, *Blackface, White Noise: Jewish Immigrants in the Hollywood Melting Pot*, 52–53.

207. Bernstein, *Racial Innocence*, 168. She expands this argument in a discussion of the Raggedy Ann doll's whitewashed minstrelsy (181):

> Raggedy Ann's ancestors marked her not with a mixture of "blackness" and "whiteness," but rather with the "black-and-whiteness" of the blacked-up minstrel performer or the topsy-turvy doll—bodies that do not merely mingle blackness and whiteness, but that instead keep blackness and whiteness simultaneously in tense distinction and in intimate contact. Raggedy Ann does not represent a black, white, or racially amalgamated body, just as the topsy-turvy doll does not refer simply or directly to a mixed-race child.

208. Ross, *Oreo*, 6: "He purposely cultivated a strictly Jewish clientele, whom he overcharged outrageously. He researched his market carefully; he studied Torah and Talmud, collected *midrashim*, quoted Rabbi Akiba—root and herb of all the jive-ass copy he wrote for the *chrain*-storm of flyers he left in Jewish neighborhoods."

209. Bernstein, *Racial Innocence*, 71.

210. Ibid.

211. Kim Lee, "Staying In," 29.

212. Sedgwick, "Jane Austen and the Masturbating Girl," 829.

213. Ross, *Oreo*, 55. After repulsing Kirk, Oreo puts her highly developed brand of self-defense, "the Way of the Interstitial Thrust, or WIT" to work on Parnell:

> WIT was based on an Oriental dedication to attacking the body's soft, vulnerable spaces or, au fond, to making such spaces, or interstices, where previously none had existed; where, for example, a second before there had been an expanse of smooth, nonabraded skin and sturdy, unbroken bone.

. 214. For more on this Jerry Lewis coinage, see Dale, *Comedy Is a Man in Trouble: Slapstick in American Movies*, 18.

215. Sedgwick, *Touching Feeling*, 14.

Chapter 4

1. Manovich, "Database as a Symbolic Form," 81. The chapter opening epigraph by Manovich is from p. 86.

2. "Nosepicking Contests," 110.

3. Rose, "At Home with Oedipa Maas," 39.

4. Manovich, "Database as a Symbolic Form," 87.

5. Pynchon, *The Crying of Lot 49*, 24.

6. McKenna, "'A Kiss of Cosmic Pool Balls': Technological Paradigms and Narrative Expectations Collide in 'The Crying of Lot 49,'" 33.

7. Ibid., 32.

8. Shmoop, "The Crying of Lot 49—Analysis: Steaminess Rating." Accessed in 2018. The "Steaminess Rating" section has subsequently disappeared entirely from the Shmoop study guides.

9. Pynchon, *The Crying of Lot 49*, 25.

10. Ibid., 28.

11. Serpell, *Seven Modes of Uncertainty*, 67. "This image of the broken mirror hanging in the air, like the metaphor as 'projectile frozen in midflight,' accentuates a dilation of time."

12. Pynchon, *The Crying of Lot 49*, 25.

13. Ahmed, *The Cultural Politics of Emotion*, 87.

14. Ibid., 91.

15. Pynchon, *The Crying of Lot 49*, 29.

16. Brinkema, *The Forms of the Affects*, 288.

17. Ngai, *Our Aesthetic Categories: Zany, Cute, Interesting*, 5.

18. Liu, *The Laws of Cool: Knowledge Work and the Culture of Information*, 3. Italics added.

19. Ibid., 175.

20. Ibid., 177.

21. Brinkema explains:

> In other words, disgust is the expression of an ugliness that fails to represent, that cannot therefore be reinscribed into an aesthetic or—in a different sense of its failure to represent—political economy; it is a representation that, in Derrida's words, "annuls itself," that fails in relation to the representable, that "forces one to consume, but without allowing any chance for idealization."

Brinkema, *The Forms of the Affects*, 128, citing Derrida, "Economimesis," 22.

22. Ahmed, *The Cultural Politics of Emotion*. 93: "To name something as disgusting—typically, in the speech act, 'That's disgusting!'—is performative. It relies on previous norms and conventions of speech, and it generates the object that it names (the disgusting object/event)."

23. Liu, *The Laws of Cool*, 179.

24. *Jacobellis v. Ohio* (1964), declared by Supreme Court Justice Potter Stewart: "I shall not today attempt further to define the kinds of material I understand to be embraced within that shorthand description [hard-core pornography], and perhaps I could never succeed in intelligibly doing so. But I know it when I see it, and the motion picture involved in this case is not that."

25. See, for example, Petillon, "A Re-Cognition of Her Errand into the Wilderness," and Palmeri, "Neither Literally nor as Metaphor: Pynchon's the *Crying of Lot 49* and the Structure of Scientific Revolutions."

26. Pynchon, *The Crying of Lot 49*, 14.

27. Manovich, "Data Visualization as New Abstraction and Anti-Sublime," 7.

28. Pynchon, *The Crying of Lot 49*, 14.

29. Lee, *Overwhelmed: Literature, Aesthetics, and the Nineteenth-Century Information Revolution*, 15–16.

30. Gitelman and Jackson, *Raw Data Is an Oxymoron*, 12.

31. Krauss, "Grids," 50.

32. Ibid., 54.

33. Ibid.

34. Israel, *Spirals: The Whirled Image in Twentieth-Century Literature and Art*, 190.

35. Krauss, "Grids," 50.

36. Ngai, *Our Aesthetic Categories*, 6.

37. Brinkema, *The Forms of the Affects*, 178.

38. See Miller, *The Anatomy of Disgust*, 43: "According to Mary Douglas's well-known structural theory of pollution and purity, the polluting, and by extension the disgusting (she does not talk about disgust), is utterly contingent on the conceptual grid that structures the particular domain."

39. Ibid., 130: "Disgust is a beyond of any singular or objectal thing. It is the promise of worsening, this possibility of something more disgusting than the disgusting. Giving disgust its contents, then, filling in its gut with objectal specificities, avows that the excluded can be known, perceived, bounded, and therefore limited."

40. Krauss, "Grids," 60–61.

41. The novel's ending is itself an infamously centrifugal grid-like gesture outward towards the never-to-be-heard (or perhaps already just read) "crying of lot 49": "The auctioneer cleared his throat. Oedipa settled back, to await the crying of lot 49" (Pynchon, *The Crying of Lot 49*, 152).

42. Liu, *Local Transcendence: Essays on Postmodern Historicism and the Database*, 294. Emphasis in original.

43. Pynchon, *The Crying of Lot 49*, 95.

44. Ibid.

45. Krauss, "Grids," 50.

46. See Stephens, *The Poetics of Information Overload: From Gertrude Stein to Conceptual Writing*, 8: "Among the most consistently articulated concerns of those who have written on the subject [of information overload] has been the sense that workers, readers, and computer users experience fatigue."

47. Latour, "Visualisation and Cognition: Drawing Things Together," 27.

48. Ibid., 7.

49. Ibid., 10.

50. Ibid., 19.

51. Ibid., 6.

52. Drucker, *Graphesis: Visual Forms of Knowledge Production*, 89. The chapter opening epigraph by Drucker is from p. 8. Emphasis in original.

53. Ibid., 128: "*Data are capta*, taken not given, constructed as an interpretation of the phenomenal world, not inherent in it."

54. Halpern, *Beautiful Data: A History of Vision and Reason Since 1945*, 94.

55. Two-dimensional inscriptions that are "*mobile* but also *immutable, presentable, readable* and *combinable* with one another" (Latour, "Visualisation and Cognition," 7). Emphasis in original.

56. McCloud, *Understanding Comics: The Invisible Art*, 28.

57. Ibid., 41.

58. Thence the magic of calculus can arrest and quantify the curve's progress at that single point by determining the derivative, aka the slope, aka the change over time of the line that radiates from it.

59. de Certeau, *The Practice of Everyday Life*, 126.

60. Ibid., 127.

61. Pynchon, *The Crying of Lot 49*, 129.

62. Interesting resonance here with Heidegger from "The Age of the World Picture," 60:

> Mathematical research into nature is not, however, exact because it calculates precisely; rather, it must calculate precisely because the way it is bounded to it domain of objects has the character of exactness. The human sciences, by contrast, indeed all the sciences that deal with living things, precisely in order to remain disciplined and rigorous, are necessarily inexact. One can, indeed, view living things, too, as magnitudes of spatiotemporal motion, but what one apprehends is then no longer living.

63. Does the novel itself, though, take the "high magic to low puns" as deadly seriously as does its protagonist? Is Oedipa's DT/dt pun a model for the type of detective work she is or ought to be doing, or is it Pynchon's way of mocking it? Namwali Serpell argues that "the novel's self-aware mockery of linguistic interpretation—here reduced to the level of aligning acronyms—casts continual doubt on all of the signs we read" (*Seven Modes of Uncertainty*, 64). Pynchon seems to be pointing an accusing finger at us for wanting to make, like Oedipa, tangents out of tremors.

64. Serpell, *Seven Modes of Uncertainty*, 70.

65. Pynchon, *The Crying of Lot 49*, 102:

> She was overcome all at once by a need to touch him, as if she could not believe in him, or would not remember him, without it. Exhausted, hardly knowing what she was doing, she came the last three steps and sat, took the man in her arms, actually held him, gazing out of her smudged eyes down the stairs, back into the morning. She felt wetness against her breast and saw that he was crying again. He hardly breathed but tears came as if being pumped. "I can't help," she whispered, rocking him, "I can't help." It was already too many miles to Fresno.

66. Ibid., 105.

67. For more on theory and the twenty-first century American novel, see Konstantinou, *Cool Characters: Irony and American Fiction*; Kelly, "The New Sincerity"; and Ryan, *The Novel After Theory*.

68 Dames, "The Theory Generation."

69. Ibid.

70. Pieter Vermeulen, "Flights of Memory: Teju Cole's *Open City* and the Limits of Aesthetic Cosmopolitanism," 42.

71. Wood, "The Arrival of Enigmas," 70.

72. Ibid., 68: "Cole has made his novel as close to a diary as a novel can get, with room for reflection, autobiography, stasis, and repetition."

73. Michiko Kakutani, "Roaming the Streets, Taking Surreal Turns."

74. Dames, "The Theory Generation." Emphasis in original.

75. Lee, *Overwhelmed*, 4: "[C]haracterized by instrumentalism, objectivity, transparency, bureaucratic impersonality, calculation, and reconfigurable data."

76. de Certeau, *The Practice of Everyday Life*, 92.

77. Cole, *Open City: A Novel*, 3.

78. Ibid., 259.

79. Vermeulen, "Reading Alongside the Market: Affect and Mobility in Contemporary American Migrant Fiction," 280.

80. de Certeau, *The Practice of Everyday Life*, 92–93.

81. Cole, *Open City*, 58.

82. Ibid.

83. Krishnan, "Postcoloniality, Spatiality and Cosmopolitanism in the *Open City*," 693.

84. Latour, "Visualisation and Cognition," 30.

85. Wood, "The Arrival of Enigmas," 70.

86. de Certeau, *The Practice of Everyday Life*, 92.

87. Booth, "M. H. Abrams: Historian as Critic, Critic as Pluralist," 439.

88. Miller, "The Critic as Host," 442.

89. Ibid.

90. Ibid., 441.

91. Ibid.

92. Ibid., 446.

93. Ibid. The irony—or maybe the poetry—of Miller's article is that, since he did all the etymological legwork, 444 or so other scholars (according to a cursory Google Scholar search) have saved themselves the grief by just (para)-citing him (it's usually the same choice morsel of a paragraph that gets consumed, too).

94. Serres, *The Parasite*, 5. The epigraph that begins this section is from p. 16.

95. Ibid., 8.

96. Ibid., 111.

97. Ibid., 71.

98. Ibid., 79.

99. Ibid.

100. Ibid., 190.

101. Gullestad, "Literature and the Parasite," 308.

102. Ibid., 103.

103. Serres, *The Parasite*, 193.

104. Ibid., 6.

105. Ibid., 202.

106. Dames, "The Theory Generation."

107. Miller, "The Critic as Host," 441.

108. Wood, "The Arrival of Enigmas," 68.

109. Cole, *Open City*, 7.

110. de Certeau, *The Practice of Everyday Life*, 127.

111. Serres, *The Parasite*, 196.

112. Cole, *Open City*, 59.

113. Barnes, *States of Sympathy: Seduction and Democracy in the American Novel*, 4.

114. Cole, *Open City*, 168.

115. Ibid., 171.

116. Ibid., 173.

117. Ibid., 171.

118. Ibid.

119. Ibid., 174.

120. Yes, I googled this, as Cole is almost begging his readers to do. This report exists. Does this change anything in the reading of it? http://www.whale.to/a/campbell.html

121. Cole, *Open City*, 175.

122. Ibid., 173.

123. Ibid., 168.

124. Ibid., 173.

125. Liu, *The Laws of Cool*, 177.

126. Cole, *Open City*, 201.

127. Manovich, "Database as a Symbolic Form," 84.

128. Latour, "Visualisation and Cognition," 19.

129. See Inda, "Foreign Bodies: Migrants, Parasites, and the Pathological Body Politic," 47: "So just as nineteenth-century scientists attributed illness to the pathogenic incursions of foreign bodies, late-twentieth-century nativists ascribed the sicknesses of the nation to the influx of foreign populations."

130. Cole, *Open City*, 139.

131. Ibid., 140.

132. Ngai, *Our Aesthetic Categories*, 5.

133. Ibid.

134. Ibid.

135. Vermeulen, "Reading Alongside the Market," 282.

136. Ibid., 280.

137. Ahmed, *The Cultural Politics of Emotion*, 94.

138. See Foster, "Postmodernism in Parallax," 17–18, on "correct distance":

> In Benjamin the withering of aura, the loss of distance, impacts on the body as well as on the image: the two cannot be separated. At one point he makes an analogy between a painter and a magician on the one hand, and a cameraman and a surgeon on the other: whereas the first two maintain a "natural distance" from the motif to paint or the body to heal, the second two "penetrate deeply into its web." The new visual technologies are thus "surgical": they reveal the world in new representations, shock the observer into new perceptions. For Benjamin this "optical unconscious" renders us both more critical and more distracted (such is his great hope for cinema), and he insists on this paradox as a dialectic.

139. Vermeulen, "Flights of Memory," 45.

140. Ibid., 48. Internal citations omitted.

141. Dames writes something intriguingly similar in "The Theory Generation," in synesthetic mixed metaphor, of the cacophony of Theory, using the example of Tassie in Lorrie Moore's *A Gate at the Stairs*:

> [I]t's all just a conversation overheard—which encapsulates the constant state of Theory in the American classroom, where debates with concealed or unnamed interlocutors (Derrida with Marx; Foucault with Hegel) become a cacophony of crossed lines. What is audible to her is intonation, the grain of those theoretical voices.

. 142. Vermeulen, "Reading Alongside the Market," 282.

143. Cole, *Open City*, 9.

144. Isabella Rossellini might be as good a guide as any. See Rossellini, "Bedbug."

145. Stutt and Siva-Jothy, "Traumatic Insemination and Sexual Conflict in the Bed Bug *Cimex lectularius*," 2683.

146. Dalley, "The Idea of 'Third Generation Nigerian Literature': Conceptualizing Historical Change and Territorial Affiliation in the Contemporary Nigerian Novel," 244.

147. Cole, *Open City*, 244.

148. Ibid., 246.

149. Ngai, *Our Aesthetic Categories*, 132.

150. Ibid., 18.

151. Latour, "Visualisation and Cognition," 14.

152. In his very definition of "cool," too, Liu dips a toe simultaneously in both ends of the graphic pool, analogizing the chilly "proscriptive ellipsis" to the incest prohibition.

The proscriptive ellipsis, I suggest, tells as much upon the elementary structures of cool as the incest prohibition—another universal nix—upon what Claude Levi-

Strauss called the elementary structures of kinship. "Thou shalt not commit incest" and "thou shalt be cool" are strangely correlative laws, even though in some senses cool is precisely the incest of information (information fed back into its own signal). Liu, *The Laws of Cool*, 179.

153. Karen Jacobs sees Julius's emotional and narrative turning away from Moji as one of a series of "aporias" in the novel. These moments of "narrative suspension and deflection" reveal "the ways in which the (always delimited) knowledge of the other is further complicated and mitigated by the subject's traumatically limited self-knowledge" (Jacobs, "Teju Cole's Photographic Afterimages," 101). The novel, Jacobs argues, constitutes a "challenge to what can be securely known and represented of the African diaspora" (ibid., 87). Katherine Hallemeier, too, sees Moji's rape as emblematic of "a narrative pattern" that primarily illuminates the limits of Julius's "self-knowledge," and, with it, the mode of Western literary aesthetic cosmopolitanism he strives to embody. Hallemeier, "Literary Cosmopolitanisms in Teju *Cole's Every Day Is for the Thief* and *Open City*," 246.

154. Krishnan, "Postcoloniality, Spatiality and Cosmopolitanism in the *Open City*," 699.

155. Wood, "The Arrival of Enigmas," 70.

156. Ibid, 72.

157. Brinkema, *The Forms of the Affects*, 131.

158. Drucker, *Graphesis*, 54.

Conclusion

1. Baudrillard, "The Ecstasy of Communication," 130.

2. Serpell, "The Banality of Empathy."

3. Seigworth and Gregg, "An Inventory of Shimmers," 3.

4. Widmer, "R. Crumb, The Art of Comics No. 1."

5. Nordyke, "Review: Prairie State Blues by Bill Bergeron," 37.

6. Quoted in Widmer, "R. Crumb, The Art of Comics No. 1."

7. Gardner, *Projections: Comics and the History of Twenty-First-Century Storytelling*, 126.

8. Brinkema, *The Forms of the Affects*, 140.

9. Chute, *Graphic Women: Life Narrative and Contemporary Comics*, 10.

10. Baetens, "Revealing Traces: A New Theory of Graphic Enunciation," 147:

> Every drawing bears the traces of "graphiation," or the specific enunciative act uttered by the author or agent when he or she makes the drawings and does the lettering of the panels. Graphiation cannot be observed directly since, logically speaking, what we see is the result of the enunciative act, not the enunciation itself. . . . The closer a drawing is to a sketch, the more the reader has the impression that he or she can discover something of the initial graphiation.

11. Ibid.

12. Szép, *Comics and the Body: Drawing, Reading, and Vulnerability*, 5.

13. For more on the tactile and other sensory experiences of comics, see Hague, *Comics and the Senses: A Multisensory Approach to Comics and Graphic Novels*; and Orbán, "A Language of Scratches and Stitches: The Graphic Novel Between Hyperreading and Print."

14. McCloud, *Understanding Comics: The Invisible Art*, 63.

15. Ibid., 65–68.

16. Polak, *Ethics in the Gutter: Empathy and Historical Fiction in Comics*, 15.

17. Kristeva, *Powers of Horror*, 4.

18. Brinkema, *The Forms of the Affects*, 130.

19. Ware, *Building Stories*.

20. Ware, "Interviews: On Cartooning."

21. Ball and Kuhlman, *The Comics of Chris Ware: Drawing Is a Way of Thinking*, x.

22. Ibid.

23. McCloud, *Understanding Comics*, 31.

24. Ibid., 41, 30.

25. Ibid., 31.

26. Cates, "Comics and the Grammar of Diagrams," 97.

27. Ngai, *Our Aesthetic Categories: Zany, Cute, Interesting*, 5.

28. Chute, *Graphic Women*, 61.

29. Gloeckner, *A Child's Life and Other Stories*, 6.

30. Chute, *Graphic Women*, 64.

31. Gloeckner, *A Child's Life and Other Stories*, 7.

32. Ibid., 4.

33. Quoted in ibid., 5. Emphasis in original.

34. Many thanks to one of this book's anonymous readers for enthusiastically contributing much of this list of rapidly proliferating -graphics.

35. Yao, *Disaffected: The Cultural Politics of Unfeeling in Nineteenth-Century America*, 27.

36. See Bloom, *Against Empathy: The Case for Rational Compassion*; Serpell, "The Banality of Empathy"; Nakamura, "Feeling Good About Feeling Bad: Virtuous Virtual Reality and the Automation of Racial Empathy"; Zeavin, "A New AI Lexicon: EMPATHY."

37. See, for instance, Saidiya Hartman's reminder that empathy "fails to expand the space of the other but merely places the self in its stead." Hartman, *Scenes of Subjection: Terror, Slavery, and Self-Making in Nineteenth-Century America*, 20. And, more recently, Alisha Gaines's *Black for a Day: White Fantasies of Race and Empathy*.

38. Nakamura, "Feeling Good About Feeling Bad," 48.

39. Ibid., 53, 51.

Bibliography

Ahmed, Sara. *The Cultural Politics of Emotion*. New York: Routledge, 2004.

Aristotle. *Nicomachean Ethics*. Translated by Roger Crisp. Cambridge: Cambridge University Press, 2004.

———. *On Poetry and Style*. Translated by G. M. A. Grube. Indianapolis and Cambridge: Hackett, 1989.

Art21. Interview with Kara Walker. "Projecting Fictions: 'Insurrection! Our Tools Were Rudimentary, Yet We Pressed On'" (November 2011). https://art21.org/read/kara-walker-projecting-fictions-insurrection-our-tools-were-rudimentary-yet-we-pressed-on/

"Articulate, adj. and n." *OED Online*. Oxford University Press, March 2017.

Baetens, Jan. "Revealing Traces: A New Theory of Graphic Enunciation." In *The Language of Comics: Word and Image*. Edited by Robin Varnum and Christina T. Gibbons, pp. 145–155. Jackson: University Press of Mississippi, 2001.

Bakhtin, Mikhail Mikhaïlovich. *Rabelais and His World*. Bloomington: Indiana University Press, 1984.

Ball, David M., and Martha B. Kuhlman, eds. *The Comics of Chris Ware: Drawing Is a Way of Thinking*. Jackson: University Press of Mississippi, 2010.

Barnes, Elizabeth. *States of Sympathy: Seduction and Democracy in the American Novel*. New York: Columbia University Press, 1997.

Baudrillard, Jean. "The Ecstasy of Communication." In *The Anti-Aesthetic: Essays on Postmodern Culture*. Edited by Hal Foster, translated by John Johnson, pp. 126–133. New York: New Press, 1983.

Belfiore, Elizabeth S. *Tragic Pleasures: Aristotle on Plot and Emotion*. Princeton: Princeton University Press, 2014.

Bender, John, and Michael Marrinan. *The Culture of Diagram*. Stanford: Stanford University Press, 2010.

Benjamin, Walter. *The Arcades Project*. Translated by Howard Eiland and Kevin McLaughlin. Cambridge, MA: Belknap Press, 1999.

Bergson, Henri. *Laughter: An Essay on the Meaning of the Comic*. Translated by Cloudesley Brereton and Fred Rothwell. New York: Macmillan, 1914.

Berlant, Lauren. *The Female Complaint*. Durham: Duke University Press, 2008.

———. "Poor Eliza." *American Literature* 70, no. 3 (September 1998): 635–668.

———. "Structures of Unfeeling: 'Mysterious Skin.'" *International Journal of Politics, Culture, and Society* 28, no. 3 (2015): 191–213. https://doi.org/10.1007/s10767-014-9190-y

Bernstein, Robin. *Racial Innocence*. New York: NYU Press, 2011.

Bertin, Jacques. *Semiology of Graphics: Diagrams, Networks, Maps*. Translated by William J. Berg. Madison, WI: ESRI Press, 2011.

Bertram, John, and Yuri Leving, eds. *Lolita: The Story of a Cover Girl: Vladimir Nabokov's Novel in Art and Design*. Blue Ash, Ohio: Print Books, 2013.

Bhabha, Homi K. "Of Mimicry and Man: The Ambivalence of Colonial Discourse." *October* 28, Discipleship: A Special Issue on Psychoanalysis (Spring 1984): 125–133.

———. "The Other Question . . . Homi K. Bhabha Reconsiders the Stereotype and Colonial Discourse." *Screen* 24, no. 6 (1983): 18–36.

Bloch, Iwan. *The Sexual Life of Our Time in Its Relations to Modern Civilization*. New York: Allied Books, 1928.

Bloom, Paul. *Against Empathy: The Case for Rational Compassion*. New York: Random House, 2017.

Blount, Serena Haygood. "Faulkner's Graphophone." PhD dissertation. University of Alabama, 2008.

Booth, Wayne. "M. H. Abrams: Historian as Critic, Critic as Pluralist." *Critical Inquiry* 2, no. 3 (Spring 1976): 411–445.

Bora, Renu. "Outing Texture." In *Novel Gazing*. Edited by Eve Kosofsky Sedgwick, pp. 94–127. Durham: Duke University Press, 1997.

Brinkema, Eugenie. *The Forms of the Affects*. Durham: Duke University Press, 2014.

———. "Violence and the Diagram; Or, 'The Human Centipede.'" *Qui Parle* 24, no. 2 (Spring–Summer 2016): 75–108.

Brooks, Daphne. *Bodies in Dissent: Spectacular Performances of Race and Freedom, 1850–1910*. Durham: Duke University Press, 2006.

Cameron, Sharon. *Impersonality: Seven Essays*. Chicago: University of Chicago Press, 2007.

Carpio, Glenda R. "'Am I Dead?': Slapstick Antics and Dark Humor in Contemporary Immigrant Fiction." *Critical Inquiry* 43, no. 2 (Winter 2017): 341–360.

———. *Laughing Fit to Kill: Black Humor in the Fictions of Slavery*. Oxford: Oxford University Press, 2008.

"Cart-Wheel, n." *OED Online*. Oxford University Press, January 2018.

Cassuto, Leonard. *The Inhuman Race: The Racial Grotesque in American Literature and Culture*. New York: Columbia University Press, 1997.

Cates, Isaac. "Comics and the Grammar of Diagrams." In *The Comics of Chris Ware: Drawing Is a Way of Thinking*, pp. 90–104. Jackson: University Press of Mississippi, 2010.

Chaouli, Michel. "Van Gogh's Ear: Toward a Theory of Disgust." In *Modern Art and the Grotesque*. Edited by Frances S. Connelly, pp. 47–62. Cambridge: Cambridge University Press, 2003.

Christensen, Tim. "Little Debbie, or the Logic of Late Capitalism: Consumerism, Whiteness, and Addiction in Mat Johnson's *Pym*." *College Literature* 44, no. 2 (Spring 2017): 166–199.

Chute, Hillary L. *Graphic Women: Life Narrative and Contemporary Comics*. New York: Columbia University Press, 2010.

Ciuba, Gary M. "From Face Value to the Value in Faces: 'Wise Blood' and the Limits of Literalism." *Modern Language Studies* 19, no. 3 (Summer 1989): 72–80.

Cole, Teju. *Open City: A Novel*. New York: Random House, 2012.

Connor, Steven. "Guys and Dolls." *Women: A Cultural Review* 26, no. 1–2 (2015): 129–142.

Cook, William W., and James Tatum. *African American Writers and Classical Tradition*. Chicago: University of Chicago Press, 2010.

Cowan, Michael. "The Ambivalence of Ornament: Silhouette Advertisements in Print and Film in Early Twentieth-Century Germany." *Art History* 36, no. 4 (September 2013): 784–809.

Crafton, Donald. "Pie and Chase: Gag, Spectacle and Narrative in Slapstick Comedy." In *The Cinema of Attractions Reloaded*. Edited by Wanda Strauven, pp. 355–364. Amsterdam: Amsterdam University Press, 2006.

Crumb, Robert. *My Troubles with Women*. San Francisco: Last Gasp, 2003.

———. *R. Crumb's Sex Obsessions*. New York: Taschen, 2015.

Cvetkovich, Ann. "Affect." In *Keywords for American Cultural Studies*, 3rd ed. Edited by Bruce Burgett and Glenn Hendler, vol. 11, pp. 11–13. New York: NYU Press, 2020.

Dale, Alan. *Comedy Is a Man in Trouble: Slapstick in American Movies*. Minneapolis: University of Minnesota Press, 2002.

Dalley, Hamish. "The Idea of 'Third Generation Nigerian Literature': Conceptualizing Historical Change and Territorial Affiliation in the Contemporary Nigerian Novel." *Research in African Literatures* 44, no. 4 (Winter 2013): 15–34.

Dames, Nicholas. "The Theory Generation." *n+1,* no. 14 (October 24, 2012). https://www.nplusonemag.com/issue-14/reviews/the-theory-generation/

Da Silva, Denise Ferreira. *Toward a Global Idea of Race*. Minneapolis: University of Minnesota Press, 2007.

Dayan, Joan. "Amorous Bondage: Poe, Ladies, and Slaves." *American Literature* 66, no. 2 (June 1994): 239–273.

de Certeau, Michel. *The Practice of Everyday Life*. Translated by Steven Rendall. Berkeley: University of California Press, 1984.

Deleuze, Gilles. *Foucault*. Translated by Seán Hand. Minneapolis: University of Minnesota Press, 1986.

Derrida, Jacques, and R. Klein. "Economimesis." *Diacritics* 11, no. 2 (1981): 3–25.

Desens, Marliss C. *The Bed-Trick in English Renaissance Drama: Explorations in Gender, Sexuality, and Power*. Newark: University of Delaware Press, 1994.

Dewey, John. *Art as Experience.* New York: Pedigree, 1934.

Di Renzo, Anthony. *American Gargoyles: Flannery O'Connor and the Medieval Grotesque.* Carbondale and Edwardsville: Southern Illinois University Press, 1993.

Doane, Mary Ann. "Film and the Masquerade: Theorizing the Female Spectator." In *Writing on the Body: Female Embodiment and Feminist Theory.* Edited by Katie Conboy, Nadia Medina, and Sarah Stanbury, pp. 176–194. New York: Columbia University Press, 1997.

"Doll, n." *OED Online.* Oxford University Press, March 2018.

Donegan, Kathleen. *Seasons of Misery: Catastrophe and Colonial Settlement in Early America.* Philadelphia: University of Pennsylvania Press, 2013.

Douglas, Mary. *Purity and Danger: An Analysis of Concepts of Pollution and Taboo.* London and New York: Routledge, 2003.

Drndić, Daša. *Trieste.* Translated by Ellen Elias-Bursać. Boston: Houghton Mifflin Harcourt, 2014.

Drucker, Johanna. *Graphesis: Visual Forms of Knowledge Production.* Cambridge, MA: Harvard University Press, 2014.

Ducille, Ann. "Black Barbie and the Deep Play of Difference." In *The Feminism and Visual Culture Reader.* Edited by Amelia Jones, pp. 337–348. New York: Routledge, 2003.

Edwards, Erin E. "Extremities of the Body: The Anoptic Corporeality of *As I Lay Dying.*" *MFS Modern Fiction Studies* 55, no. 4 (Winter 2009): 739–764.

Elliott, Michael A. "Other Times: Herman Melville, Lewis Henry Morgan, and Ethnographic Writing in the Antebellum United States." *Criticism* 49, no. 4 (Fall 2007): 481–503.

English, Darby. *How to See a Work of Art in Total Darkness.* Cambridge, MA: MIT Press, 2007.

Entin, Joseph B. *Sensational Modernism: Experimental Fiction and Photography in Thirties America.* Chapel Hill: University of North Carolina Press, 2007.

Faulkner, William. *As I Lay Dying* [1930]. New York: Knopf Doubleday, 2011.

———. *Essays, Speeches & Public Letters.* Edited by James B. Meriwether. New York: Modern Library, 2004.

Fearnow, Mark. *The American Stage and the Great Depression: A Cultural History of the Grotesque.* Cambridge: Cambridge University Press, 1997.

Ferguson, Anthony. *The Sex Doll: A History.* Jefferson, NC: McFarland, 2010.

Foster, Hal. "Postmodernism in Parallax." *October* 63 (January 1, 1993): 3–20.

———. *The Return of the Real: The Avant-Garde at the End of the Century.* Cambridge, MA: MIT Press, 1996.

Foucault, Michel. *Discipline and Punish: The Birth of the Prison.* Translated by Alan Sheridan. New York: Vintage, 1977.

———. *The History of Sexuality.* Translated by Robert Hurley. New York: Vintage, 1990.

Franklin, Benjamin. *The Autobiography of Benjamin Franklin.* New York: P. F. Collier & Son, 1909.

Freeman, Nina. *How Do You Do It?* 2014. Videogame. ninasays.so/howdoyoudoit/

Fried, Michael. *Realism, Writing, Disfiguration: On Thomas Eakins and Stephen Crane.* Chicago: University of Chicago Press, 1988.

Gaines, Alisha. *Black for a Day: White Fantasies of Race and Empathy.* Chapel Hill: University of North Carolina Press, 2017.

Garcia-Rojas, Claudia. "(Un)Disciplined Futures: Women of Color Feminism as a Disruptive to White Affect Studies." *Journal of Lesbian Studies* 21, no. 3 (2017): 254–271.

Gardner, Jared. *Master Plots: Race and the Founding of an American Literature 1787–1845.* Baltimore: Johns Hopkins University Press, 1998.

———. *Projections: Comics and the History of Twenty-First-Century Storytelling.* Stanford: Stanford University Press, 2012.

Gerald, Kelly. "The Habit of Art." In *Flannery O'Connor: The Cartoons,* by Flannery O'Connor. Edited by Kelly Gerald, pp. 101–131. Seattle: Fantagraphics, 2012.

Girard, Rene. *Violence and the Sacred.* Baltimore: Johns Hopkins University Press, 1977.

Gitelman, Lisa and Virginia Jackson. "Introduction." In *Raw Data Is an Oxymoron.* Edited by Lisa Gitelman, pp. 1–14. Cambridge, MA: MIT Press, 2013.

Glissant, Édouard. *Poetics of Relation.* Translated by Betsy Wing. Ann Arbor: University of Michigan Press, 1997.

Gloeckner, Phoebe. *A Child's Life and Other Stories.* Berkeley: Frog Books, 2000.

Gooch, Brad. *Flannery: A Life of Flannery O'Connor.* New York: Little, Brown, 2009.

Goodwin, James. *Modern American Grotesque: Literature and Photography,* 2nd ed. Columbus: Ohio State University Press, 2009.

"Graphic." *Merriam-Webster.* https://www.merriam-webster.com/dictionary/graphic (accessed February 4, 2022)

Greenberg, Jonathan Daniel. "Nathanael West and the Mystery of Feeling." *MFS Modern Fiction Studies* 52, no. 3 (Fall 2006): 588–612.

Gross, Kenneth. *Puppet: An Essay on Uncanny Life.* Chicago: University of Chicago Press, 2011.

Gullestad, Anders M. "Literature and the Parasite." *Deleuze Studies* 5, no. 3 (2011): 301–323.

Hague, Ian. *Comics and the Senses: A Multisensory Approach to Comics and Graphic Novels.* New York: Routledge, 2014.

Hallemeier, Katherine. "Literary Cosmopolitanisms in Teju Cole's *Every Day Is for the Thief* and *Open City.*" *Ariel: A Review of English Literature* 44, no. 203 (July 2013): 239–250.

Halpern, Orit. *Beautiful Data: A History of Vision and Reason Since 1945.* Durham: Duke University Press, 2014.

Hardy, Donald E. *The Body in Flannery O'Connor's Fiction: Computational Technique and Linguistic Voice.* Columbia: University of South Carolina Press, 2007.

Harper, Phillip Brian. *Abstractionist Aesthetics: Artistic Form and Social Critique in African American Culture.* New York: NYU Press, 2015.

Harpham, Geoffrey. "The Grotesque: First Principles." *Journal of Aesthetics and Art Criticism* 34, no. 4 (Summer 1976): 461–468.

Hartman, Saidiya. "Venus in Two Acts." *Small Axe* 12, no. 2 (June 2008): 1–14.

Hartman, Saidiya V. *Scenes of Subjection: Terror, Slavery, and Self-Making in Nineteenth-Century America*. New York: Oxford University Press, 1997.

Heidegger, Martin. "The Age of the World Picture (1938)." In *Off the Beaten Track*. Translated by Julian Young and Kenneth Haynes, pp. 57–85. Cambridge: Cambridge Scholars Publishing, 2002.

Hemmings, Clare. "Invoking Affect: Cultural Theory and the Ontological Turn." *Cultural Studies* 19, no. 5 (2005): 548–567.

"Hermaphrodite, n. and adj." *OED Online*. Oxford University Press, March 2018.

Hester, Helen. *Beyond Explicit: Pornography and the Displacement of Sex*. Albany: SUNY Press, 2014.

Higgins, Hannah B. *The Grid Book*. Cambridge, MA: MIT Press, 2009.

Hobby, Blake G., and Zachary DeBoer. "Carnival Virtues: Sex, Sacrilege, and the Grotesque in Nathanael West's *Miss Lonelyhearts*." In *The Grotesque*. Edited by Harold Bloom and Blake G. Hobby, pp. 145–153. New York: Bloom's Literary Criticism, 2009.

Homes, A. M. "A Real Doll." In *The Safety of Objects*, pp. 147–172. New York: Norton, 1990.

Hönnighausen, Lothar. *William Faulkner: The Art of Stylization in His Early Graphic and Literary Work*. Cambridge: Cambridge University Press, 1987.

Houser, Heather. *Infowhelm: Environmental Art and Literature in an Age of Data*. New York: Columbia University Press, 2020.

Hume, Kathryn. "Narrative Speed in Contemporary Fiction." *Narrative* 13, no. 2 (May 2005): 105–124.

"Identity, n." *OED Online*. Oxford University Press, March 2018.

Inda, Jonathan Xavier. "Foreign Bodies: Migrants, Parasites, and the Pathological Body Politic." *Discourse* 22, no. 3 (Fall 2000): 46–62.

Israel, Nico. *Spirals: The Whirled Image in Twentieth-Century Literature and Art*. New York: Columbia University Press, 2015.

Jacobellis v. Ohio, no. 378 U.S. 184 (1964).

Jacobs, Karen. "Teju Cole's Photographic Afterimages." *Image (&) Narrative* 15, no. 2 (2014): 87–105.

James, Henry. *Henry James, Literary Criticism: French Writers, Other European Writers, the Prefaces to the New York Edition*. Edited by Leon Edel and Mark Wilson. New York: Library of America, 1984.

Johnson, Barbara. *Persons and Things*. Cambridge, MA: Harvard University Press, 2008.

Johnson, Mat. *Pym: A Novel*. New York: Spiegel & Grau, 2011.

Jones, Charles M. *Looney Tunes (Wile E. Coyote and the Road Runner): Fast and Furryous*. Warner Brothers, 1949. https://www.youtube.com/watch?v=4iWvedIhWjM

Joselit, David. "Notes on Surface: Toward a Genealogy of Flatness." *Art History* 23, no. 1 (March 2000): 19–34.

Kakutani, Michiko. "Roaming the Streets, Taking Surreal Turns." *New York Times* (May

18, 2011). https://www.nytimes.com/2011/05/19/books/open-city-by-teju-cole-book-review.html

Kaufmann, Michael. *Textual Bodies: Modernism, Postmodernism, and Print*. Lewisburg, PA: Bucknell University Press, 1994.

Kayser, Wolfgang. *The Grotesque in Art and Literature*. Translated by Ulrich Weisstein. New York: Columbia University Press, 1957.

Kelly, Adam. "The New Sincerity." In *Postmodern/Postwar and After: Rethinking American Literature*. Edited by Jason Gladstone, Andrew Hoberek, and Daniel Worden, pp. 197–208. Iowa City: University of Iowa Press, 2016.

Kim Lee, Summer. "Staying In: Mitski, Ocean Vuong, and Asian American Asociality." *Social Text* 37, no. 1 (March 2019): 27–50.

Kolnai, Aurel. *On Disgust*. Edited by Barry Smith and Carolyn Korsmeyer. Peru, IL: Open Court, 2004.

Konstantinou, Lee. *Cool Characters: Irony and American Fiction*. Cambridge, MA: Harvard University Press, 2016.

Krauss, Rosalind. "Grids." *October* 9 (Summer 1979): 50–64.

———. "The Im/Pulse to See." In *Vision and Visuality*. Edited by Hal Foster, pp. 51–79. Seattle: Bay Press, 1988.

Krishnan, Madhu. "Postcoloniality, Spatiality and Cosmopolitanism in the *Open City*." *Textual Practice* 29, no. 4 (2015): 678–696.

Kristeva, Julia. *Powers of Horror: An Essay on Abjection*. Translated by Leon S. Roudiez. New York: Columbia University Press, 1982.

Lancaster, Lex Morgan. "Feeling the Grid: Lorna Simpson's Concrete Abstraction." *ASAP/Journal* 2, no. 1 (January 2017): 131–155.

Latour, Bruno. "Visualisation and Cognition: Drawing Things Together." In *Representation in Scientific Practice*. Edited by Michael E. Lynch and Steve Woolgar, pp. 19–68. Cambridge, MA: MIT Press, 1990.

Lavater, Johann Kaspar. *Essays on Physiognomy: For the Promotion of the Knowledge and the Love of Mankind*. Translated by Thomas Holcroft. Boston: Printed for William Spotswood, & David West, 1794.

Lawrence, D. H. *Studies in Classic American Literature*. New York: T. Seltzer, 1923.

Lee, Maurice S. *Overwhelmed: Literature, Aesthetics, and the Nineteenth-Century Information Revolution*. Princeton: Princeton University Press, 2019.

Lethem, Jonathan. "The American Vicarious: An Introduction to *Miss Lonelyhearts & The Day of the Locust*." In *Miss Lonelyhearts & The Day of the Locust*, pp. vii–xi. New York: New Directions, 2009.

Leverette, Tru. "Traveling Identities: Mixed Race Quests and Fran Ross's 'Oreo.'" *African American Review* 40, no. 1 (Spring 2006): 79–91.

Levinas, Emmanuel. *Difficult Freedom: Essays on Judaism*. Translated by Seán Hand. Baltimore: Johns Hopkins University Press, 1990.

Limon, John. *Stand-up Comedy in Theory, or, Abjection in America*. Durham and London: Duke University Press Books, 2000.

Liu, Alan. *The Laws of Cool: Knowledge Work and the Culture of Information.* Chicago and London: University of Chicago Press, 2004.

———. *Local Transcendence: Essays on Postmodern Historicism and the Database.* Chicago: University of Chicago Press, 2009.

Lukasik, Christopher J. *Discerning Characters: The Culture of Appearance in Early America.* Philadelphia: University of Pennsylvania Press, 2011.

Manovich, Lev. "Database as a Symbolic Form." *Convergence* 5, no. 2 (June 1999): 80–99.

———. "Data Visualization as New Abstraction and Anti-Sublime." *Small Tech: The Culture of Digital Tools* 3, no. 9 (2002): 3–9.

Marcus, Sharon. "Fighting Bodies, Fighting Words: A Theory and Politics of Rape Prevention." In *Feminists Theorize the Political.* Edited by Judith Butler and Joan W. Scott, pp. 385–403. New York: Routledge, 1992.

Martin, Jay. *Nathanael West: The Art of His Life.* New York: Hayden, 1970.

Massumi, Brian. "The Autonomy of Affect." *Cultural Critique*, no. 31 (Autumn 1995): 83–109. https://doi.org/10.2307/1354446

Mastroianni, Dominic. "Hospitality and the Thresholds of the Human in Poe's *The Narrative of Arthur Gordon Pym.*" *Studies in American Fiction* 40, no. 2 (2013): 185–202.

"Matrix, n." *OED Online.* Oxford University Press, March 2017.

Matthews, John T. "*As I Lay Dying* in the Machine Age." *Boundary* 2 19, no. 1 (Spring 1992): 69–94.

McCloud, Scott. *Understanding Comics: The Invisible Art.* New York: Harper Perennial, 1994.

McKenna, Christopher J. "'A Kiss of Cosmic Pool Balls': Technological Paradigms and Narrative Expectations Collide in 'The Crying of Lot 49.'" *Cultural Critique*, no. 44 (Winter 2000): 29–42.

McKittrick, Katherine. "Mathematics Black Life." *The Black Scholar* 44, no. 2 (Summer 2014): 16–28.

McMillan, Uri. *Embodied Avatars: Genealogies of Black Feminist Art and Performance.* New York: NYU Press, 2015.

Menninghaus, Winfried. *Disgust.* Albany: SUNY Press, 2003.

Merish, Lori. "Cuteness and Commodity Aesthetics: Shirley Temple and Tom Thumb." In *Freakery: Cultural Spectacles of the Extraordinary.* Edited by Rosémarie Thomson, pp. 185–203. New York: NYU Press, 1996.

Messbarger, Rebecca. "The Re-Birth of Venus in Florence's Royal Museum of Physics and Natural History." *Journal of the History of Collections* (2012): 1–21.

Miller, J. Hillis. "The Critic as Host." *Critical Inquiry* 3, no. 3 (Spring 1977): 438–447.

Miller, William Ian. *The Anatomy of Disgust.* Cambridge, MA: Harvard University Press, 2009.

Mitchell, Lee Clark. "Face, Race, and Disfiguration in Stephen Crane's 'The Monster.'" *Critical Inquiry* 17, no. 1 (October 1, 1990): 174–192.

Mitchell, W. J. T. *Seeing Through Race*. Cambridge, MA: Harvard University Press, 2012.

———. *What Do Pictures Want?* Chicago: University of Chicago Press, 2004.

Monnet, Livia. "Anatomy of Permutational Desire: Perversion in Hans Bellmer and Oshii Mamoru." *Mechamedia* 5, no. 1 (2010): 285–309.

Morrison, Toni. *Playing in the Dark: Whiteness and the Literary Imagination*. New York: Vintage, 1992.

Moser, Barry. "Working Backward: A Reflection on the Linoleum Cuts of Flannery O'Connor." In *Flannery O'Connor: The Cartoons*, by Flannery O'Connor. Edited by Kelly Gerald, pp. vii–ix. Seattle: Fantagraphics, 2012.

"Moving Pictures: Highlights—Kara Walker." *Guggenheim*. http://pastexhibitions .guggenheim.org/moving_pictures/highlights_10b.html

Mullen, Harryette. "'Apple Pie with Oreo Crust': Fran Ross's Recipe for an Idiosyncratic American Novel." *MELUS* 27, no. 1 (Spring 2002): 107–129.

Nabokov, Vladimir. *Lolita*. New York: Vintage, 1955.

Naiman, Eric. *Nabokov, Perversely*. Ithaca: Cornell University Press, 2010.

Nakamura, Lisa. "Feeling Good About Feeling Bad: Virtuous Virtual Reality and the Automation of Racial Empathy." *Journal of Visual Culture* 19, no. 1 (2020): 47–64.

Narcissister. "Narcissister is You." *Narcissister* (2014). http://www.narcissister.com/ narcissister-is-youu/

———. *Upside Down*. New York: America's Got Talent, 2011. http://www.narcissister .com/#/upside-down/

Newton, Adam Z. *Narrative Ethics*. Cambridge, MA: Harvard University Press, 1995.

Ngai, Sianne. *Our Aesthetic Categories: Zany, Cute, Interesting*. Cambridge, MA: Harvard University Press, 2012.

———. *Ugly Feelings*. Cambridge, MA: Harvard University Press, 2005.

Nieland, Justus. "West's Deadpan: Affect, Slapstick, and Publicity in *Miss Lonelyhearts*." *NOVEL: A Forum on Fiction* 38, no. 1 (Fall 2004): 57–83.

Nordyke, Jim. "Review: Prairie State Blues by Bill Bergeron." *Chicago Review* 25, no. 3 (1973): 37–38.

"Nosepicking Contests." *Time* (May 6, 1966). http://content.time.com/time/subscriber /article/0,33009,901889,00.html

Nott, Josiah Clark. "The Mulatto a Hybrid—Probably Extermination of the Two Races If the Whites and Blacks Are Allowed to Intermarry." *Boston Medical and Surgical Journal* 29, no. 2 (1843): 29–32.

O'Connor, Flannery. *Flannery O'Connor: The Cartoons*. Edited by Kelly Gerald. Seattle: Fantagraphics, 2012.

———. "Some Aspects of the Grotesque in Southern Literature." In *Mysteries and Manners: Occasional Prose*, pp. 36–50. New York: Farrar, Straus and Giroux, 1969.

———. *Wise Blood*. New York: Farrar, Straus and Giroux, 1952.

Orbán, Katalin. "A Language of Scratches and Stitches: The Graphic Novel Between Hyperreading and Print." *Critical Inquiry* 40, no. 3 (2014): 169–181.

Osterweis, Ariel. "Public Pubic: Narcissister's Performance of Race, Disavowal, and Aspiration." *TDR* 59, no. 4 (Winter 2015): 101–116.

Palmer, Tyrone S. "'What Feels More Than Feeling?': Theorizing the Unthinkability of Black Affect." *Critical Ethnic Studies* 3, no. 2 (2017): 31–56.

Palmeri, Frank. "Neither Literally nor as Metaphor: Pynchon's *The Crying of Lot 49* and the Structure of Scientific Revolutions." *ELH* 54, no. 4 (Winter 1987): 979–999.

Petillon, Pierre-Yves. "A Re-Cognition of Her Errand into the Wilderness." In *New Essays on The Crying of Lot 49*. Edited by Patrick O'Donnell, pp. 127–162. Cambridge and New York: Cambridge University Press, 1991.

Pind, Jörgen L. "Figure and Ground at 100." *The Psychologist* 25, no. 1 (January 2012): 90–91.

Poe, Edgar Allan. *The Narrative of Arthur Gordon Pym of Nantucket* [1838]. Edited by Harold Beaver. New York: Penguin Classics, 1975.

Polak, Kate. *Ethics in the Gutter: Empathy and Historical Fiction in Comics*. Columbus: Ohio State University Press, 2017.

"Pygmalionism, n." *OED Online*. Oxford University Press, March 2017.

Pynchon, Thomas. *The Crying of Lot 49*. New York: Harper Perennial, 1966.

Raengo, Alessandra. *On the Sleeve of the Visual: Race as Face Value*. Hanover, NH: Dartmouth College Press, 2013.

Rogin, Michael. *Blackface, White Noise: Jewish Immigrants in the Hollywood Melting Pot*. Berkeley: University of California Press, 1996.

Rose, Remington. "At Home with Oedipa Maas." *The New Republic* (May 14, 1966): 39–40.

Ross, Fran. *Oreo*. New York: New Directions, 2015.

Rossellini, Isabella. "Bedbug." *SundanceTV* on YouTube (May 29, 2014). https://www.youtube.com/watch?v=1LLGe1xh87c

Ruskin, John. *The Stones of Venice: Volume III*. Edited by J. G. Links. New York: Peter Fenelon Collier & Son, 1900.

Russo, Mary. *The Female Grotesque: Risk, Excess and Modernity*. New York: Routledge, 2012.

Rutherford, Emma. *Silhouette: The Art of the Shadow*. New York: Rizzoli, 2009.

Ryan, Judith. *The Novel After Theory*. New York: Columbia University Press, 2012.

Sacco, Ellen Fernandez. "Racial Theory, Museum Practice: The Coloured World of Charles Willson Peale." *Museum Anthropology* 20, no. 2 (1996): 25–32.

Sack, Warren. "Aesthetics of Information Visualization." In *Context Providers: Conditions of Meaning in Media Arts*. Edited by Margot Lovejoy, Christiane Paul, and Victoria Vesna, pp. 123–150. Chicago: University of Chicago Press, 2011.

Saltz, Jerry. "An Explosion of Color, in Black and White." *New York Magazine* (November 1, 2007). http://nymag.com/arts/art/reviews/40277/

———. "Kara Walker: Ill-Will and Desire." *Flash Art* 29, no. 191 (November–December 1996): 82–86.

Sanborn, Geoffrey. "A Confused Beginning: *The Narrative of Arthur Gordon Pym, of*

Nantucket." In *The Cambridge Companion to Edgar Allan Poe.* Edited by Kevin J. Hayes, pp. 163–177. Cambridge: Cambridge University Press, 2002.

Sánchez-Eppler, Karen. *Touching Liberty: Abolition, Feminism, and the Politics of the Body.* Berkeley: University of California Press, 1993.

Sandler, Matt. "'Negras Aguas': The Poe Tradition and the Limits of American Africanism." *Comparative Literature* 67, no. 4 (2015): 415–428.

Saul, Scott, "The Great Deflector." *Los Angeles Review of Books* (July 22, 2019). https://lareviewofbooks.org/article/the-great-deflector/

Schopenhauer, Arthur. *The World as Will and Idea.* Translated by R. B. Haldane and J. Kemp. London: Routledge, 1907.

Schuller, Kyla. *The Biopolitics of Feeling: Race, Sex, and Science in the Nineteenth Century.* Durham: Duke University Press, 2018.

Sedgwick, Eve Kosofsky. "Jane Austen and the Masturbating Girl." *Critical Inquiry* 17, no. 4 (Summer 1991): 818–837.

———. *Touching Feeling: Affect, Pedagogy, Performativity.* Durham: Duke University Press, 2003.

Seigworth, Gregory J., and Melissa Gregg. "An Inventory of Shimmers." In *The Affect Theory Reader.* Edited by Melissa Gregg and Gregory J. Seigworth, pp. 1–25. Durham: Duke University Press, 2010.

Sekula, Allan. "The Body and the Archive." *October* 39 (1986): 3–64.

Senna, Danzy. "Foreword." In *Oreo,* by Fran Ross. New York: New Directions, 2015.

Serpell, C. Namwali. *Seven Modes of Uncertainty.* Cambridge, MA: Harvard University Press, 2014.

Serpell, Namwali. "The Banality of Empathy." *New York Review of Books* (March 2, 2019). https://www.nybooks.com/daily/2019/03/02/the-banality-of-empathy/

Serres, Michel. *The Parasite.* Minneapolis: University of Minnesota Press, 2007.

Sharpe, Christina. *In the Wake: On Blackness and Being.* Durham: Duke University Press, 2016.

———. *Monstrous Intimacies: Making Post-Slavery Subjects.* Durham: Duke University Press, 2010.

Shaw, Gwendolyn DuBois. *Portraits of a People: Picturing African Americans in the Nineteenth Century.* Andover, MA, and Seattle: Addison Gallery of American Art/University of Washington Press, 2006.

———. *Seeing the Unspeakable: The Art of Kara Walker.* Durham and London: Duke University Press, 2004.

Shmoop. "The Crying of Lot 49—Analysis: Steaminess Rating." http://www.shmoop.com/crying-of-lot-49/sex-rating.html (accessed April 26, 2018)

Smith, Marquard. *The Erotic Doll: A Modern Fetish.* New Haven: Yale University Press, 2014.

Sollors, Werner. *Neither White nor Black Yet Both: Thematic Explorations of Interracial Literature.* New York: Oxford University Press, 1997.

Sontag, Susan. "The Pornographic Imagination." In *Susan Sontag: Essays of the 1960s & 1970s*. Edited by David Rieff, pp. 205–233. New York: Library of America, 2013.

Spillers, Hortense J. "Mama's Baby, Papa's Maybe: An American Grammar Book." *Diacritics* 17, no. 2 (Summer 1987): 64–81.

Stephens, Paul. *The Poetics of Information Overload: From Gertrude Stein to Conceptual Writing*. Minneapolis: University of Minnesota Press, 2015.

Stratton, Jon. *The Desirable Body: Cultural Fetishism and the Erotics of Consumption*. Manchester: Manchester University Press, 1996.

Stutt, Alastair D., and Michael T. Siva-Jothy. "Traumatic Insemination and Sexual Conflict in the Bed Bug Cimex Lectularius." *Proceedings of the National Academy of Sciences* 98, no. 10 (May 8, 2001): 5683–5687.

Szép, Eszter. *Comics and the Body: Drawing, Reading, and Vulnerability*. Columbus: Ohio State University Press, 2020.

Thomson, Philip. *The Grotesque*. London: Methuen, 1972.

Tompkins, Kyla Wazana. *Racial Indigestion: Eating Bodies in the 19th Century*. New York: NYU Press, 2012.

Tucker, John. "William Faulkner's *As I Lay Dying*: Working Out the Cubistic Bugs." *Texas Studies in Literature and Language* 26, no. 4 (Winter 1984): 388–404.

Tweedie, James. "Lolita's Loose Ends: Nabokov and the Boundless Novel." *Twentieth Century Literature* 46, no. 2 (2000): 150–170.

Tynan, Daniel J. "J. N. Reynolds' Voyage of the Potomac: Another Source for *The Narrative of Arthur Gordon Pym*." *Poe Studies* 4, no. 2 (December 1971): 35–37.

Vermeulen, Pieter. "Reading Alongside the Market: Affect and Mobility in Contemporary American Migrant Fiction." *Textual Practice* 29, no. 2 (2015): 273–293.

———. "Flights of Memory: Teju Cole's *Open City* and the Limits of Aesthetic Cosmopolitanism." *Journal of Modern Literature* 37, no. 1 (Fall 2013): 40–57.

Verne, Jules. *An Antarctic Mystery*. Translated by Mrs. Cashel Hoey. Philadelphia: J. B. Lippincott, 1899. http://www.gutenberg.org/files/10339/10339-h/10339-h.htm

Vesna, Victoria, ed. *Database Aesthetics: Art in the Age of Information Overflow*. Minneapolis and London: University of Minnesota Press, 2007.

Walker, Kara. *A Subtlety, or the Marvelous Sugar Baby*. Installation (May 10, 2014). http://creativetime.org/projects/karawalker/

Ware, Chris. *Building Stories*. New York: Pantheon Books, 2012.

———. "Interviews: On Cartooning." *POV: Tintin and I* (July 2006). http://archive.pov .org/tintinandi/interview-on-cartooning/7

Weheliye, Alexander G. *Habeas Viscus: Racializing Assemblages, Biopolitics, and Black Feminist Theories of the Human*. Durham: Duke University Press, 2014.

Weinstein, Cindy. "When Is Now? Poe's Aesthetics of Temporality." *Poe Studies* 41, no. 1 (October 2008): 81–107.

West, Nathanael. *Miss Lonelyhearts & The Day of the Locust*. New York: New Directions, 2009.

———. "Some Notes on Miss L." In *Nathanael West: A Collection of Critical Essays*. Edited by Jay Martin, pp. 66–67. Englewood Cliffs: Prentice-Hall, 1971.

———. "Some Notes on Violence." In *Nathanael West: A Collection of Critical Essays*. Edited by Jay Martin, pp. 50–51. Englewood Cliffs: Prentice-Hall, 1971.

Widmer, Ted. "R. Crumb, The Art of Comics No. 1." *Paris Review*, no. 193 (Summer 2010). http://www.theparisreview.org/interviews/6017/the-art-of-comics-no-1-r-crumb

Wilks, Jennifer M. "'Black Matters': Race and Literary History in Mat Johnson's *Pym*." *European Journal of American Studies* 11, no. 1 (2016): 1–20.

Williams, Linda. "Film Bodies: Gender, Genre, and Excess." *Film Quarterly* 44, no. 4 (1991): 2–13.

———. *Hard Core: Power, Pleasure, and the "Frenzy of the Visible."* Berkeley: University of California Press, 1989.

———. "Pornography, Porno, Porn: Thoughts on a Weedy Field." In *Porn Archives*. Edited by Tim Dean, Steven Ruszczycky, and David Squires, pp. 29–43. Durham: Duke University Press, 2014.

Wood, James. "The Arrival of Enigmas." *New Yorker* (February 20, 2011): 68–72. https://www.newyorker.com/magazine/2011/02/28/the-arrival-of-enigmas

Worringer, Wilhelm. *Abstraction and Empathy: A Contribution to the Psychology of Style*. Translated by Michael Bullock. Chicago: Ivan R. Dee, 1953.

Yao, Xine. *Disaffected: The Cultural Politics of Unfeeling in Nineteenth-Century America*. Durham: Duke University Press, 2021.

Zdebik, Jakub. *Deleuze and the Diagram: Aesthetic Threads in Visual Organization*. New York: Continuum, 2012.

Zeavin, Hannah. "A New AI Lexicon: EMPATHY." *A New AI Lexicon* (blog) (September 16, 2021). https://medium.com/a-new-ai-lexicon/a-new-ai-lexicon-empathy-4da12b82e280

Index

See also slapstick (comedy); stand-up comedy

comic (aesthetic), 144–45, 153, 168, 258n120

comics, 38–40, 172–73, 182, 188, 215–28, 270n13

comics studies, 220

computer age. *See* information age

Connor, Steven, 111, 115, 137, 139

consumerism, 106

contact, 189–92, 198–208, 222–23, 255n75, 262n207

contact zones, 189

cool (aesthetic), 171–83, 203–12, 226, 268n152–269n152

The Cook, the Thief, His Wife, and Her Lover (Greenway), 183

cosmopolitanism, 184, 192–94, 202, 208–10

countersentimental texts, 8. *See also* Berlant, Lauren; postsentimentality

"The Critic as Host" (Miller), 195. *See also* host; parasite; theory

criticism. *See* theory

Crumb, Robert, 20, 215–28

The Crying of Lot 49 (Pynchon), 20, 172, 264n41

The Cultural Politics of Emotion (Ahmed), 231n8, 233n51, 235n99

cuteness, 115–17, 136, 144, 256n95, 257n118, 258n120. *See also* Ngai, Sianne

Dames, Nicholas, 192–93, 198, 268n141. *See also* Theory Generation

Darwin, Charles, 177

data, 3, 10–21, 28, 146, 171–73, 179–95, 200–208, 212–29

database, 10, 171, 173, 187, 200, 204, 208, 213

datafication, 214, 228

data points, 18, 21, 171–72, 187, 191, 212, 215, 222. *See also* points

data visualization, 172, 180, 186–87

The Day of the Locust (West), 41

death drive, 255n75

de Certeau, Michel, 189–90, 193–94, 199. *see also touche* model

Deleuze, Gilles, 16, 35, 156

Derrida, Jacques, 263n21

Descartes, René, 250n7

Dewey, John, 38

the diagrammatic, 16–20, 32–36, 71, 122–27, 135, 156, 168, 176–86, 208–22, 237n47

diagrams, 156, 235n97

dimensionality, 19, 44–60, 71, 150, 156, 168–90, 205–16, 228, 234n97–235n97

Discourse, Figure (Lyotard), 254n75–255n75

disgust, 3, 12–18, 41, 54, 96, 118, 176–83, 206–26, 263n21–263n22, 264n38–264n39

disinterest, 3, 8, 58, 88, 109, 115, 176

distance, 206–7, 211–12, 216–18, 268n138

dolls: Ashanti, 249n181; Black Barbie, 164, 257n116; black gutta-percha, 167; erotic, 115, 120, 130; furry, 255n86; head of, 252n30; hollow, 212; lifelike, 250n7, 251n10, 255n86; medical, 135; Nazi, 251n9; rag, 139, 262n207; Raggedy Ann, 262n207; Sambo, 70–72; as scripts, 251n13; sex, 18–21, 111–23, 128–29, 136–39, 145–46, 153–69, 177, 215, 250n2, 251n9; topsy-turvy, 144–45, 166–69, 262n207; wax, 130–35. *See also* "Alma Doll" (Kokoschka); Barbie; Black Barbie; *La Poupée (The Doll)* (Bellmer); "A Real Doll" (Homes)

Dome of Light (Karvel), 106–9. *See also Pym* (Johnson)

Donegan, Kathleen, 74. *See also* cannibalism

Douglas, Mary, 65, 183

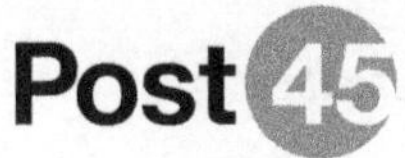

Palmer Rampell, *Genres of Privacy in Postwar America*

Joseph Darda, *The Strange Career of Racial Liberalism*

Jordan Carroll, *Reading the Obscene: Transgressive Editors and the Class Politics of US Literature*

Michael Dango, *Crisis Style: The Aesthetics of Repair*

Mary Esteve, *Incremental Realism: Postwar American Fiction, Happiness, and Welfare-State Liberalism*

Dorothy J. Hale, *The Novel and the New Ethics*

Christine Hong, *A Violent Peace: Race, U.S. Militarism, and Cultures of Democratization in Cold War Asia and the Pacific*

Sarah Brouillette, *UNESCO and the Fate of the Literary*

Sophie Seita, *Provisional Avant-Gardes: Little Magazine Communities from Dada to Digital*

Guy Davidson, *Categorically Famous: Literary Celebrity and Sexual Liberation in 1960s America*

Joseph Jonghyun Jeon, *Vicious Circuits: Korea's IMF Cinema and the End of the American Century*

Lytle Shaw, *Narrowcast: Poetry and Audio Research*

Stephen Schryer, *Maximum Feasible Participation: American Literature and the War on Poverty*